# THE AMERICAN MEDICAL ASSOCIATION

# WOMEN: HOW TO UNDERSTAND YOUR SYMPTOMS

Editors-in-chief  **Charles B. Clayman, MD**
**Jeffrey R. M. Kunz, MD**

**RANDOM HOUSE
NEW YORK**

Library of Congress Cataloging-in-Publication Data

Main entry under title:

Women, how to understand your symptoms.

    Includes index.
    1. Women – Diseases – Diagnosis – Popular works.
    2. Symptomatology – Popular works.
    3. Self-care, Health.
    I. American Medical Association.

RG107.A475    1986      616.07′2     85-25768
ISBN 0-394-74045-9

Manufactured in the United States of America

2 4 6 8 9 7 5 3

First American Edition

# Preface

For most people, most of the time, that miraculous machine we call the human body functions with remarkable reliability. It does, however, require maintenance and occasional repair, and we as a people have demonstrated an increasing willingness to devote a growing share of our national resources to health. Americans spent 4 percent of the U.S. gross national product on health in 1940; today we spend over 10 percent.

At the same time, we have grown more self-reliant, recognizing that the health decisions we make on everything from watching weight to seeking medical care can affect our well-being as well as our pocketbook. The purpose of this book is to *extend* individual competence in making medical decisions about personal health.

When symptoms appear, when the body sends out signals that something is wrong, the trouble may be only a common, simple illness. It can be a minor cold or some other self-limiting ailment from which we will recover with or without medical intervention.

But minor symptoms, sometimes even a headache or a cough, may also be the first warning of something serious. The decision charts in this book enable you to interpret body signals more accurately, allowing you to distinguish between what may be a minor problem and what may not be so minor. The charts will also help you with the question that everyone has to ask from time to time: How long does a worried but sensible person wait before seeking medical help?

This book is not intended to teach you medical diagnosis; no book can do that. But it will give you a more *informed* understanding of your ailments; it will provide scientifically valid answers to everyday questions; and it will allay many of the needless anxieties that arise when signs of illness first appear. In addition, it includes illustrated sections on first aid and emergency treatment.

These self-help medical charts have been developed under medical supervision, tested on patients under real conditions and reviewed by American medical authorities. We are pleased to add this book to the American Medical Association Home Health Library, a series of books aimed at widening the health education of the American public.

**James H. Sammons, M.D.**
**Executive Vice President**
**American Medical Association**

## American Medical Association

*Executive Vice President*  James H. Sammons, M.D.

*Vice President, Publishing*  John T. Baker

*Director, Consumer Book Program*  Frank D. Campion

*Former Director, Consumer Book Program*  Charles C. Renshaw, Jr.

## Editorial Staff

*Editors-in-Chief*  Charles B. Clayman, M.D.
Jeffrey R.M. Kunz, M.D.

*Managing Editor*  Heidi Hough

*Associate Editor*  Robin Fitzpatrick Husayko

*Administrative Assistant*  Jacquelyn Price Martin

## Consultants

Byron J. Bailey, M.D., Galveston, Tex.
Bruce M. Berkson, M.D., Chicago, Ill.
Frederick C. Blodi, M.D., Iowa City, Iowa
Philip D. Darney, M.D., San Francisco, Calif.
Richard N. Foltz, M.D., Rhinelander, Wis.
Norman Fost, M.D., Madison, Wis.
Ian D. Hay, M.D., Ph.D., Rochester, Minn.
Nicholas C. Hightower, Jr., M.D., Temple, Tex.
Linda Hughey Holt, M.D., Chicago, Ill.
Burton J. Kushner, M.D., Madison, Wis.

Dennis Maki, M.D., Madison, Wis.
Sylvia Peterson, Park Ridge, Ill.
Domeena C. Renshaw, M.D., Chicago, Ill.
Carlotta M. Rinke, M.D., Chicago, Ill.
Philip D. Shenefelt, M.D., Madison, Wis.
Alfred Soffer, M.D., Chicago, Ill.
Thomas N. Thies, D.D.S., Stoughton, Wis.
David T. Uehling, M.D., Madison, Wis.
Maurice W. Van Allen, M.D., Iowa City, Iowa
American Dental Association, Chicago, Ill.

## The American Medical Association Home Health Library

The AMA Family Medical Guide

The AMA Handbook of First Aid and Emergency Care

The AMA Guide to BackCare – Revised and Updated Edition

The AMA Guide to HeartCare – Revised and Updated Edition

The AMA Guide to WomanCare – Revised and Updated Edition

The AMA Guide to Health and Well-Being After Fifty

The AMA Guide to Better Sleep

Children: How to Understand Their Symptoms

Men: How to Understand Your Symptoms.

# Contents

## Introduction

## The symptoms

### 1 General medical
page 21

### 2 Sex and fertility
page 125

### 3 Pregnancy and childbirth
page 133

# The female body

A woman is female from the moment she is conceived. Gender is determined by the pattern of chromosomes (thread-like structures within each living cell that contain genetic information) in the fertilized egg. Every woman has 23 pairs of chromosomes; 22 are the same as for men, but the 23rd pair is different. It consists of two X chromosomes (men have one X and one Y chromosome), which are responsible for the development of the genitals. Hormones secreted by the ovaries and other glands during fetal growth are thought to affect the development of the brain and its sense of being female.

The mature feminine body shape is largely the result of the action of the sex hormones estrogen and progesterone. These develop the body features known as secondary sexual characteristics – full, mature breasts; rounded hips and buttocks; thighs well padded with fat; and absence of hair on the torso and face. Other distinctly female characteristics include a relatively high-pitched voice and a higher proportion of body fat. The rising and falling levels of the same two hormones secreted by the ovaries are also responsible for *the menstrual cycle* (see p.117).

Because of the differences in a woman's physical and hormonal makeup, there are small but important variations in her susceptibility to certain disorders. The monthly periods experienced by women mean they more often suffer from anemia (lack of sufficient red blood cells). Also, the 5 to 10 percent less water in a woman's body than in a man's means that any alcohol she drinks is more concentrated in her body and that liver damage can occur more easily. On the positive side, the female sex hormones are thought to provide protection against coronary disease up until the menopause. Women generally live longer than men; the average life expectancy of women in the U.S. is 76, for men it is 70. Some of these additional years can be attributed to the fact that few women smoked during the period from 1900 to 1914. However, this gap is narrowing as a result of the changes in women's life-styles over the past few decades.

### The changing body

Most of the body systems lose some of their efficiency with age, partly because specialist cells die and are not replaced and partly because the tissues become less elastic and more fibrous. Loss of elasticity due to age is most obvious in the skin, and this process may be accelerated by excessive exposure to sunlight and by smoking. Life-style once maturation has occurred plays an important role in maintaining good health. Good hygiene, proper diet and regular exercise promote normal function of our organs and musculoskeletal system. Attention to how much you eat or drink, whether or not you smoke, and how much you exercise, all contribute to the body's well-being. The most significant event of the middle years is the menopause, when a woman ceases to be fertile and menstruation no longer occurs. Menopause, like puberty, is a natural transitional state.

Following the menopause, the aging process continues. There is an acceleration in the loss of calcium, sometimes leading to thinning of the bones (osteoporosis), which may become brittle and easily broken by minor falls. Regular weight-bearing exercise (e.g., walking) and drinking milk or using calcium salts (e.g., calcium carbonate) and vitamin D may prevent the onset of osteoporosis. The older body has fewer resources with which to withstand periods of ill health and the healing process of minor injuries becomes noticeably slower with age. However, if a woman is psychologically healthy, has exercised vigorously and regularly during her life and has maintained a moderate weight, she is likely to have much the same vitality at 60 as she had at 30.

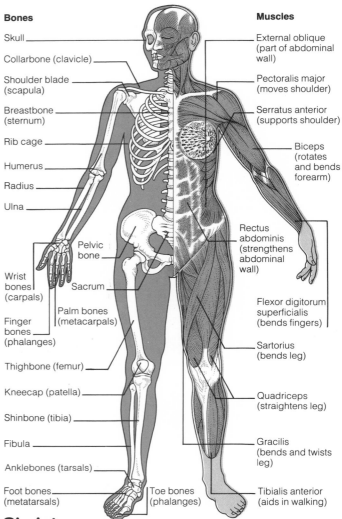

**Bones**
- Skull
- Collarbone (clavicle)
- Shoulder blade (scapula)
- Breastbone (sternum)
- Rib cage
- Humerus
- Radius
- Ulna
- Pelvic bone
- Wrist bones (carpals)
- Sacrum
- Palm bones (metacarpals)
- Finger bones (phalanges)
- Thighbone (femur)
- Kneecap (patella)
- Shinbone (tibia)
- Fibula
- Anklebones (tarsals)
- Foot bones (metatarsals)
- Toe bones (phalanges)

**Muscles**
- External oblique (part of abdominal wall)
- Pectoralis major (moves shoulder)
- Serratus anterior (supports shoulder)
- Biceps (rotates and bends forearm)
- Rectus abdominis (strengthens abdominal wall)
- Flexor digitorum superficialis (bends fingers)
- Sartorius (bends leg)
- Quadriceps (straightens leg)
- Gracilis (bends and twists leg)
- Tibialis anterior (aids in walking)

## Skeleton

The bony skeleton provides the rigid structure that supports the muscles and provides a protective framework for the organs. Female bones are generally slightly lighter than the male's, and the female pelvis is wider in order to allow a baby's head and body to pass during childbirth. Bone itself is made up of protein hardened with calcium salts. It is a living material with cells that are constantly replacing old bone with new material. To maintain healthy bones, you need adequate amounts of protein, calcium and vitamins.

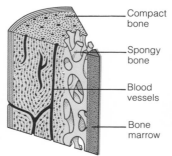

- Compact bone
- Spongy bone
- Blood vessels
- Bone marrow

**Bone marrow**
The marrow inside the bones is a fatty material with a plentiful blood supply. Certain bones – particularly those of the breastbone, vertebrae, ribs and pelvis – also contain blood-forming tissues that produce the red and white blood cells.

### Symptoms

The most common problems affecting the skeleton in women of all ages include breakage (fractures) of the bones as a result of injury, damage to the joints between bones as a result of injury or wear and tear, and a tendency toward thinning. Bone infections and tumors are rare. Symptoms of skeletal disorders include pain, swelling, and redness and heat (inflammation) around the affected part.

See also the following diagnostic charts: **56** Back pain **57** Painful or stiff neck **58** Painful arm **59** Painful knee **60** Painful leg **61** Painful or swollen joints **62** Foot problems

## Muscles

Muscles are composed of a soft tissue arranged in fibers that contract and relax to produce movement of the body and its internal organs. There are two distinct types of muscles: the voluntary muscles, which are attached to the skeleton and subject to our conscious control; and the involuntary muscles, which are responsible for movement such as the rhythmical contraction of the uterus during labor.

Muscles thrive on work and will remain in good condition if used regularly. Vigorous exercise increases the size of muscles and improves the circulation of blood to them, thereby increasing their capacity for still more strenuous activity. Inactivity can soon lead to weakness. Muscle disorders are rare, but can be caused by inherited chemical abnormalities or hormonal imbalances.

### How muscles work

Most voluntary muscles are fixed to two or more adjacent bones, often by means of a fibrous tendon. When a muscle contracts, the bones to which it is attached move. Muscles usually work in groups where the contraction of one muscle is accompanied by the relaxation of another.

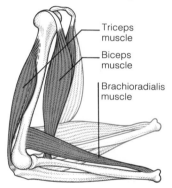

Triceps muscle
Biceps muscle
Brachioradialis muscle

### Symptoms

Damage to muscles from injury normally produces pain, stiffness and sometimes swelling and inflammation. Muscles may also become weak or painful as a result of virus infection.

See also the following diagnostic charts: **56** Back pain **57** Painful or stiff neck **58** Painful arm **59** Painful knee **60** Painful leg **61** Painful or swollen joints

## Respiratory system

Respiration, inhaling (breathing in) and exhaling (breathing out), allows the blood to absorb oxygen that enables the body's cells to form energy.

The respiratory system consists of the rib cage, the diaphragm, the lungs, and the tubes through which air passes on its way to and from the lungs. Air is breathed in through the nose and mouth, passes down the trachea (windpipe), and enters the lungs through a branching tree of tubes – the bronchi and bronchioles. The lungs are sponge-like organs composed of millions of air sacs (alveoli).

The respiratory system is vulnerable to repeated infection and exposure to pollutants including tobacco smoke and dust from industrial or agricultural processes.

### Symptoms

The most common disorders of the respiratory tract are caused by infection, leading to inflammation of the lining of the tract or of the lung tissues themselves. This may result in coughing and the production of excessive amounts of mucus. If the breathing mechanism is severely damaged, there may be shortness of breath. Chest pain is a common symptom of respiratory infections.

See also the following diagnostic charts: **32** Runny nose **33** Sore throat **34** Hoarseness or loss of voice **35** Wheezing **36** Coughing **37** Difficulty breathing **55** Chest pain

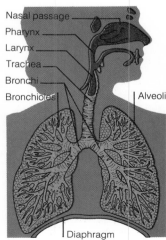

Nasal passage
Pharynx
Larynx
Trachea
Bronchi
Bronchioles
Alveoli
Diaphragm

## Fat distribution

Fat is deposited in a layer under the skin and within the tissues in other parts of the body including the buttocks, breasts and inside the chest and abdominal cavities. Fat comprises up to about 20 to 25 percent of a woman's weight (compared with 15 percent of a man's) and is distributed in such a way as to give a woman's body its contours. Fat is laid down when food intake is greater than is needed to fuel the body's energy requirements. It is burned when food intake fails to equal the body's energy output. Fat also acts as insulation against cold.

Both too much and too little fat can be unhealthy. Being too fat can lead to heart and circulation problems. Being too thin is less of a health risk, but may be a sign of undernourishment and can reduce your resistance to a variety of diseases. Fluctuations in the level of fat deposits are almost always the result of an imbalance between food intake and energy output.

### Skin-fold test

You may be too fat if a fold of skin pinched from the abdomen is thicker than 1 in. (25 mm).

### Symptoms

The weight chart on p.26 shows the healthy weight for someone of your height. Weight gain or loss usually indicates a change in your level of fat deposits.

See also the following diagnostic charts: **3** Loss of weight **4** Overweight

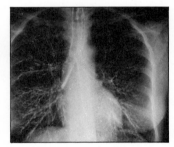

Breathing in          Breathing out

### How you breathe

As you breathe in, the diaphragm (the sheet of muscle between the chest and abdomen) contracts and flattens and the rib cage expands. This causes the lungs to expand as air is sucked in. When you breathe out, the diaphragm relaxes into a dome shape. The rib cage contracts and the lungs contract, expelling the air.

### Bronchogram of the lungs

A small amount of liquid visible on X rays is trickled down the throat into the lungs; it outlines the breathing pattern of the trachea and bronchi.

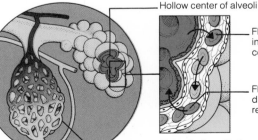

Hollow center of alveoli
Flow of oxygen into red blood cells
Flow of carbon dioxide from red blood cells
Network of capillaries

### The alveoli

The lungs are sponge-like organs made up of millions of air sacs known as alveoli. Each alveolar lining is surrounded by blood capillaries – tiny vessels that connect arteries with veins. Blood enters the lungs (via the pulmonary artery), going through the capillaries surrounding the alveoli, where oxygen is picked up from breathed-in air and carbon dioxide and some water vapor is given up to be breathed out.

# Heart and circulation

The heart is a muscular pump with four chambers into which enter the major blood vessels carrying blood to and from the body. Blood flows as the heart rhythmically squeezes the chambers, making them expand and contract.

Blood circulates via the arteries and veins, carrying oxygen and nutrients (see *Blood analysis,* p.22) to the body and carrying away waste products. The muscular arteries and their smaller branches (arterioles) dilate or contract to regulate body temperature. Good blood circulation depends on the efficient functioning of the heart muscle and partly on the ease of blood flow through the arteries.

A healthy circulatory system depends on the blood vessels remaining free from obstructions such as fatty deposits or blood clots. It is also important that the pressure of the circulating blood not exceed certain levels. For advice on reducing the risks of diseases of the heart and circulation, see *Coronary heart disease,* p.101.

Women under the age of 50 who are neither diabetic nor hypertensive are relatively free from coronary heart disease. This is thought to be partly due to large amounts of the hormones progesterone and estrogen present in the body.

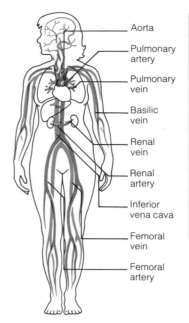

Aorta
Pulmonary artery
Pulmonary vein
Basilic vein
Renal vein
Renal artery
Inferior vena cava
Femoral vein
Femoral artery

## Symptoms

The symptoms of impaired circulation depend on the organs or region affected. Heart disease may cause chest pain, palpitations or breathlessness; poor circulation to the brain may cause fainting, dizzy spells or confusion; circulation problems in the limbs may cause pain or swelling.

See also the following diagnostic charts: **10** Faintness and fainting **12** Dizziness **13** Numbness or tingling **16** Forgetfulness and confusion **37** Difficulty breathing **54** Palpitations **55** Chest pain **58** Painful arm **60** Painful leg

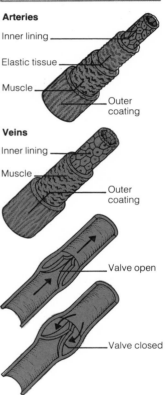

**Arteries**

Inner lining
Elastic tissue
Muscle
Outer coating

**Veins**

Inner lining
Muscle
Outer coating

Valve open

Valve closed

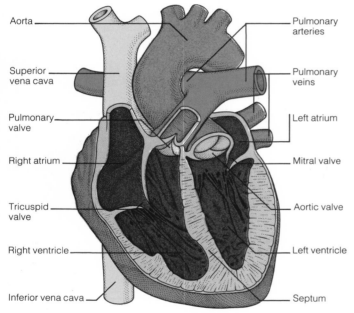

Aorta
Superior vena cava
Pulmonary valve
Right atrium
Tricuspid valve
Right ventricle
Inferior vena cava

Pulmonary arteries
Pulmonary veins
Left atrium
Mitral valve
Aortic valve
Left ventricle
Septum

### The circulatory system

The circulatory system carries blood to and from every part of the body. Arteries carry oxygenated blood away from the heart; veins return "used" blood to the heart.

### Arteries and veins

The walls of arteries are made up of four layers. They need to be strong because blood is forced along them under high pressure. Veins have less elastic, less muscular walls. Valves in the veins stop blood from flowing in the wrong direction.

### Heart vessels

The heart is divided in two by the septum. Each side has two chambers, an atrium and a ventricle, linked by a one-way valve. The left atrium and ventricle control oxygenated blood, and those on the right control deoxygenated ("used") blood. The septum prevents the two types of blood from mixing.

# Blood circulation through the heart and lungs

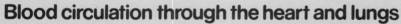
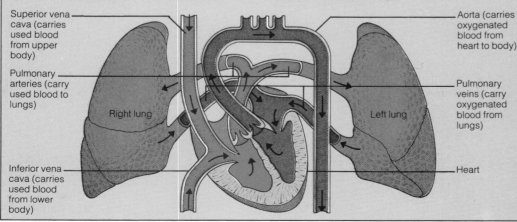

Superior vena cava (carries used blood from upper body)
Pulmonary arteries (carry used blood to lungs)
Inferior vena cava (carries used blood from lower body)

Right lung
Left lung

Aorta (carries oxygenated blood from heart to body)
Pulmonary veins (carry oxygenated blood from lungs)
Heart

Deoxygenated ("used") blood is carried back to the heart via the superior and inferior branches of the vena cava, which enters the right atrium. The blood then passes into the right ventricle, from where it is pumped along the pulmonary artery to the lungs. As blood passes through the network of small blood vessels surrounding the lungs, it absorbs oxygen from the breathed-in air and discharges carbon dioxide to be breathed out. The newly oxygenated blood then returns to the heart via the pulmonary veins, enters the left atrium and passes into the left ventricle. The oxygenated blood is then pumped from the left ventricle through the aorta to all parts of the body.

# Brain and nervous system

The brain and nervous system together provide the control mechanism for conscious activities such as thought and movement, and unconscious body functions such as breathing and digestion. Nerves also provide the means by which we register pain, touch and temperature.

The brain and nervous system require a constant supply of oxygenated blood. Disruption of the blood flow to the system is one of the most common causes of malfunctioning of the brain and nervous system. Therefore, the prevention of circulatory trouble (see *Heart and circulation,* opposite) is important. Injury, infection, degeneration, tumors and diseases of unknown cause may also affect the brain and nervous system. Certain disorders may arise out of abnormal electrical activity or chemical imbalances in the brain.

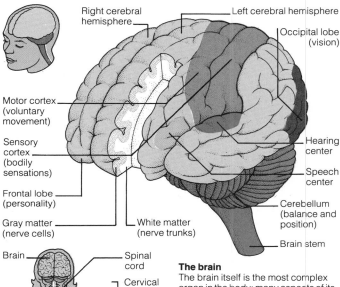

Right cerebral hemisphere
Left cerebral hemisphere
Occipital lobe (vision)
Motor cortex (voluntary movement)
Sensory cortex (bodily sensations)
Frontal lobe (personality)
Gray matter (nerve cells)
White matter (nerve trunks)
Hearing center
Speech center
Cerebellum (balance and position)
Brain stem

Brain
Spinal cord
Cervical nerves
Thoracic nerves
Lumbar nerves
Sacral nerves

### The brain
The brain itself is the most complex organ in the body; many aspects of its structure and function are not yet fully understood. Different parts of the brain control different activities. The two cerebral hemispheres control conscious thought and movement and interpret signals from the sensory organs. The cerebellum regulates some subconscious activities such as coordination of movement and balance. The brain stem governs vital body functions such as heartbeat and breathing.

### The nervous system
The brain and the nerve tracts of the spinal cord constitute the central nervous system. A network of peripheral nerves, named after the four regions of the spine, links the central system with other parts of the body.

## Symptoms
The symptoms of brain and nervous system disorders depend on the part of the system affected. Symptoms may include pain, loss of sensation, and weakness. Brain disorders may cause a variety of psychological symptoms as well as physical symptoms such as headache, drowsiness, confusion and hallucinations.

See also the following diagnostic charts: **10** Faintness and fainting **11** Headache **12** Dizziness **13** Numbness or tingling **14** Twitching and trembling **15** Pain in the face **16** Forgetfulness and confusion **17** Difficulty speaking **19** Depression **56** Back pain

# The senses

The senses are the means by which we monitor the different aspects of our environment. Five separate systems respond to different types of physical stimuli: the eyes enable us to interpret visual information; the ears monitor sound and control balance; the nose and tongue respond to different smells and tastes, respectively; and the sensory nerves in the skin allow us to feel physical contact (touch), changes in temperature, and pain.

**Hearing and balance**
The ear is described on p.65.

**Sight**
The eye is described on p.63.

**Smell**
Smells are detected by the olfactory nerves. These hair-like organs project into the top of the nasal cavity and absorb and analyze molecules from the breathed-in air. The sense of smell may be damaged by smoking and may be temporarily impaired by a common cold or hayfever. Permanent loss of the sense of smell may occur after nerve damage, as a result of a skull injury, or because of a disorder affecting the part of the brain responsible for interpreting smell sensations.

**Taste**
The primary taste organs are the taste buds, located in hair-like papillae that project from the upper surface of the tongue. The taste buds for each of the four basic tastes (sweet, sour, salty and bitter) are located in a different area of the tongue. The sense of taste is closely allied to the sense of smell, which helps us to differentiate a greater range of flavors. Loss of the sense of smell is the usual cause of any impairment in the sense of taste, but certain drugs and, occasionally, a zinc deficiency may also influence our sense of taste.

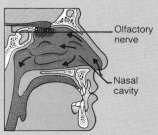

Olfactory nerve
Nasal cavity

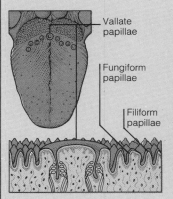

Vallate papillae
Fungiform papillae
Filiform papillae

## Symptoms
The main symptom of any disorder of the senses is partial or total loss of sensitivity. There may also be pain or other symptoms affecting the sensory organ concerned.

See also the following diagnostic charts: **12** Dizziness **13** Numbness or tingling **27** Painful or irritated eye **28** Disturbed or impaired vision **29** Earache **30** Noises in the ear **31** Deafness

**Touch**
The sense of touch is conveyed through the nerves from the sensory receptors that lie under the surface of the skin. A different type of receptor is responsible for monitoring each of the main sensations. The number of sense receptors varies from one part of the body to another: the fingertips and the area around the mouth have a large number of receptors, whereas the skin of the middle of the back has very few. The sense of touch may be impaired by damage to the skin or to the nerve endings or fibers, after an injury or any of the diseases that damage nerve fibers, or from a more generalized condition affecting the brain and/or nervous system.

Skin surface
Free nerve endings
Nerves bundled together and leading to the spinal cord

# The digestive system

The series of organs extending from the mouth to the anus is known as the digestive tract. The digestive tract is made up of a tube in which food is broken down so that minerals, vitamins, carbohydrates, fats and proteins can be absorbed into the body and the waste products can be excreted.

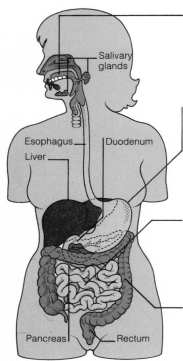

**Mouth**
Digestion begins in the mouth when, as you chew food, enzymes in the saliva break down certain carbohydrates. The tongue and the muscles of the pharynx then propel the mixture of food and saliva, known as the bolus, into the esophagus and down into the stomach.

**Stomach**
Food may spend several hours in the stomach being churned and partially digested by acid and more enzymes until the food becomes a semiliquid consistency called chyme. The chyme passes into the duodenum, where it is further broken down by digestive juices from the liver (via the gall-bladder) and pancreas.

**Small intestine**
The final stage of digestion is completed in the small intestine, where the nutrients are split into chemical units small enough to pass through the wall of the intestine into the network of blood vessels and lymphatics.

**Large intestine**
Undigested material is passed into the large intestine (the colon), where water is absorbed, and then into the rectum, from which the undigested matter is expelled from the body.

## Symptoms

The lining of the intestines is renewed every 24 hours so it can cope with the wide range of substances that are passed through it every day. The digestive system also reacts quickly against contaminated food, viruses or bacteria.

See also the following diagnostic charts: **3** Loss of weight **41** Vomiting **42** Recurrent vomiting **43** Abdominal pain **44** Recurrent abdominal pain **45** Swollen abdomen **46** Excess gas **47** Diarrhea **48** Constipation **49** Abnormal-looking bowel movements

# The lymphatic system

This system consists of the lymph glands (found mainly in the neck, armpits and groin) and the small vessels that connect them (the lymphatics). The lymph glands produce a type of white blood cell called lymphocytes, and antibodies that defend the body against infection. The glands and the spleen act as barriers to the spread of infection by trapping any infection-carrying microbes that travel along the lymphatic vessels, preventing them from reaching vital organs.

## Symptoms

In the majority of cases, any lump or swelling beneath the surface of the skin indicates that the lymphatic system is working normally; that is, it is protecting your body against infection. In some cases, however, it may indicate a more serious underlying disorder.

See also the following diagnostic chart: **9** Lumps and swellings

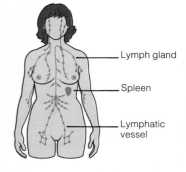

Lymph gland

Spleen

Lymphatic vessel

# The endocrine system

Endocrine glands manufacture hormones and distribute them to all parts of the body via the bloodstream. These hormones help regulate the body's internal chemistry, its responses to hunger, stress, infection and disease, and its preparation for physical activity.

**Pituitary gland**
This is a peanut-sized organ situated in the base of the brain. The pituitary gland's most important role is to stimulate and coordinate the functions of the other endocrine glands so that they produce their own hormones. It also manufactures the growth hormone, and hormones to control the thyroid, the volume of urine, the contraction of the uterus during labor, the milk-producing activity of the breasts, the function of the ovaries, and the activity of pigment-forming glands in the skin.

**Thyroid gland**
This gland, located just below the Adam's apple, is responsible for producing thyroglobulin, the hormone that controls the body's metabolism. It also helps regulate the body's internal thermostat.

**Parathyroid glands**
These four glands are embedded into the back surface of the thyroid. The hormone they produce controls the levels of calcium and phosphorous (essential for healthy bones and for functional efficiency of nerves and muscles).

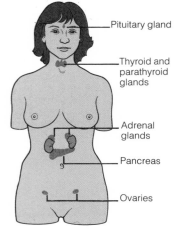

Pituitary gland

Thyroid and parathyroid glands

Adrenal glands

Pancreas

Ovaries

## Symptoms

Disorders usually occur when the level of a particular hormone increases or decreases, upsetting the body's chemical balance. Any disorder and the symptoms involved depend on which hormone is affected. For instance, if production of the hormone insulin is disrupted, diabetes mellitus (the most common endocrine gland disorder) may result. Changes in hormonal levels are also responsible for the natural physical changes in your body during puberty, menstruation and the menopause.

See also the following diagnostic charts: **2** Tiredness **3** Loss of weight **4** Overweight **7** Excessive sweating

**Adrenal glands**
The adrenal glands lie immediately above the kidneys. Each adrenal consists of two parts: the cortex and the medulla. The adrenal cortex produces steroid hormones, which help to regulate the amounts of sugar, salt and water in the body, and it influences the shape and distribution of body hair. The adrenal medulla produces adrenaline and noradrenaline, the hormones that increase the flow of blood to the muscles, heart and lungs so that they are prepared to deal with excitement or physical and mental threats.

**Pancreas**
The pancreas lies at the back of the abdomen behind the stomach. It produces enzymes that help digest food in the duodenum. It also produces the hormones insulin and glucagon, which play a vital part in regulating the glucose level in blood.

**Ovaries**
The ovaries are situated in the abdomen below the navel. They produce eggs ready for fertilization and secrete the hormones estrogen and progesterone, which determine female characteristics and the pattern of menstruation.

# The urinary system

All of the body's blood passes through the kidneys many times each day. The kidneys filter and purify the blood; the waste material is dealt with by a series of organs that make up the urinary tract (see *Structure of the urinary tract,* p. 95).

## Symptoms

Infection of the urethra or bladder, causing pain when you pass urine, is the most common disorder of the urinary system. In rare cases, the infection may spread to the kidneys, sometimes causing a pain in the middle to lower part of the back. Change in the frequency of urination, or in the color of your urine, may indicate an underlying disorder.

See also the following diagnostic charts: **51** Abnormally frequent urination **52** Painful urination **53** Poor bladder control **56** Back pain

# The reproductive system

The organs of the reproductive system consist of two ovaries, each one connected to the uterus by a fallopian tube; and the vagina, the passage that leads from the uterus to the external genitals. Every month, between puberty and menopause, one of the ovaries releases an egg into a fallopian tube, a process known as ovulation. If, as it travels slowly down the tube, the egg is fertilized by a sperm and becomes embedded in the lining of the uterus, you have become pregnant. If the egg is not fertilized, it is lost. Two weeks later the lining of the uterus sheds during menstruation.

# Pregnancy

If you are generally healthy you should have little difficulty during pregnancy, although most women have some symptoms (such as nausea). As soon as you think you might be pregnant, see your physician for confirmation and arrange to have regular, prenatal checkups. By doing this, any problems can be detected early and prompt medical help or advice can be given.

## Symptoms

The most common problems of the reproductive system are difficulties with menstrual periods, most often premenstrual tension and pain, irregular and heavy bleeding, or a change in the pattern of menstruation. Any change in the color or consistency of vaginal discharge is often a symptom of an infection in the vagina, uterus or fallopian tubes. Additional problems can occur after the menopause if the vaginal walls become dry and sore.

See also the following diagnostic charts: **64** Absent periods **65** Heavy periods **66** Painful periods **67** Irregular vaginal bleeding **68** Abnormal vaginal discharge **69** Genital irritation **70** Painful intercourse **73** Failure to conceive

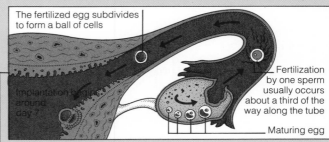

The fertilized egg subdivides to form a ball of cells

Implantation begins around day 7

Fertilization by one sperm usually occurs about a third of the way along the tube

Maturing egg

## Symptoms

Most women go through pregnancy without major difficulties. Sometimes, however, there are minor problems. For instance, sudden high levels of hormones may cause nausea and vomiting; softening and stretching of the ligaments can contribute to backache; and pressure from the growing fetus on the diaphragm may cause shortness of breath.

See also the following diagnostic charts: **74** Nausea and vomiting in pregnancy **75** Skin changes in pregnancy **76** Back pain in pregnancy **77** Heartburn in pregnancy **78** Vaginal bleeding in pregnancy **79** Shortness of breath in pregnancy **80** Ankle-swelling in pregnancy **81** Am I in labor? **82** Breast-feeding problems **83** Depression after childbirth

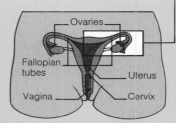

Ovaries

Fallopian tubes

Uterus

Vagina

Cervix

### Fertilization

If an egg is penetrated by a sperm in one of the fallopian tubes shortly after ovulation, it becomes fertilized. It takes only one of the millions of sperm ejaculated during intercourse to fertilize an egg. When the sperm's nucleus joins with the egg's nucleus, cell division begins. The cells, which contain chromosomal information from the father and mother, divide every few hours as the fertilized egg travels along the fallopian tube toward the uterus. The ball of cells embeds itself in the wall of the uterus about a week after fertilization.

### The growing embryo

The developing baby is called an embryo until about the 12th week of pregnancy. From then until delivery, the baby is called a fetus. Between weeks 5 and 7 the embryo, though small, has begun to develop rapidly.

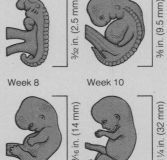

Week 5

3/32 in. (2.5 mm)

Week 7

3/8 in. (9.5 mm)

Week 8

9/16 in. (14 mm)

Week 10

1¼ in. (32 mm)

By week 7, the limbs are beginning to develop as buds, and the intestines are almost completely formed. All the internal organs are in place by week 8. By week 10 the embryo looks recognizably human.

### Placenta

The fetus is attached to the placenta by the umbilical cord – three intertwined blood vessels. Blood flows from the fetus to the placenta, where it absorbs oxygen, nutrients and protective antibodies from the mother's blood. The placenta itself is firmly rooted to the wall of the uterus throughout pregnancy. After delivery of the baby, it becomes separated and is then expelled.

Blood vessels in umbilical cord

Pockets of mother's blood

Maternal blood vessels

Uterine wall

The close entwining of the blood vessels of mother and baby allows the passage of oxygen and nutrients from mother to baby and the diffusion of waste products such as carbon dioxide from the baby to the mother. This takes place without the blood mixing.

## Your changing body

**Early signs:** Several changes take place in your body during pregnancy. The most obvious is the absence of periods. Early in pregnancy, this may be accompanied by nausea or vomiting (see p.134), commonly called "morning sickness" (although it may occur at other times of the day or night).

**Breasts:** You may notice a tingling sensation in your nipples, and your breasts will probably become enlarged. The skin around your nipples may darken and the small lubricating glands in this area may become more prominent, creating small bumps.

**Skin:** Skin also changes during pregnancy. The skin around the nipples may darken and so may the skin around the upper part of your cheeks and forehead. Some women notice a dark line extending from the navel down to the pubic hair. This coloring should fade, but may not disappear altogether after delivery. "Stretch marks," tiny scars under the skin, may appear on the stomach, breasts, buttocks and thighs, but they usually fade after delivery until they become barely noticeable.

**Uterus:** The uterus is normally about the size and shape of a pear. In early pregnancy, as your uterus begins to grow, it presses on the bladder. This makes the bladder want to expel urine, even in small amounts, so you will feel the need to pass urine more frequently than usual. For the first three months of pregnancy, the size of the uterus does not change very much, but the enlargement becomes more noticeable in the fourth month. By the end of the fifth month, when the fetus is about eight inches long, the increase in size becomes more rapid.

By the end of the pregnancy, the total weight of the uterus, fetus and amniotic fluid is about 16 pounds.

### Hormonal changes and your emotions

During pregnancy, hormones are produced first by the ovaries and the placenta (afterbirth) to suppress ovulation and help the early growth of the uterus and the fetus. Later in pregnancy, hormones promote the development of the breasts and the softening of the ligaments of the back and pelvis in preparation for labor. They also contribute to the emotional changes that you feel during pregnancy. Later in the pregnancy, and sometimes after childbirth, depression may set in (see *Depression after childbirth*, p.141). It may help you cope with the upsets if you realize that your hormones are the culprits.

# Safeguarding your health

Good health and susceptibility to disease are, to a great extent, determined by inheritance. However, whatever your family history of disease, you can improve your chances of remaining in good health by paying attention to the avoidable risk factors in your life-style – by improving your diet, reducing your alcohol intake, giving up smoking and exercising regularly. You can improve your physical well-being at any age by adopting a healthier life-style following the guidelines described here.

### Diet

Diet plays a fundamental part in determining general health. To function efficiently, your body requires adequate amounts of each nutrient in the table below. The main risk of eating a typical western diet is overnutrition. Eating too many refined carbohydrates leads to obesity and eating large amounts of foods containing fats leads to heart disease. Be sure to include plenty of fruits and vegetables in your diet.

| Proteins | Carbohydrates |
|---|---|
| Proteins are needed for growth, repair and replacement of body tissues. Animal products such as meat, fish, eggs and cheese (and other milk products) are high in protein, as are legumes (e.g., peas, beans, lentils). **Diet advice:** Many protein-rich animal products are also high in fat, so make a point of eating nonanimal sources of protein such as peas, beans and unrefined grains as an alternative. | Carbohydrates are a major source of energy but, eaten in excess, they are stored in the body as fat. Carbohydrates are present as natural sugars and starches in cereals, grains and root vegetables. **Diet advice:** Eat unrefined products (such as whole-grain bread and brown rice, which also contain fiber and other nutrients), green and yellow vegetables and potatoes. Avoid eating white bread and refined cereals. |

| Fats | Fiber |
|---|---|
| Fats are a concentrated source of energy that provide more calories than any other food. Saturated fats are found mainly in animal products, dairy produce and eggs. Monounsaturated fats are most commonly found in poultry, margarine and olive oil. Polyunsaturated fats are found in fish, corn oil and safflower oil. **Diet advice:** Intake of saturated fats should be kept to a minimum, so use vegetable fats when cooking. | Fiber is the indigestible residue of plant products that passes through the digestive system. **Diet advice:** While it contains no energy value or nutrients, fiber is important for healthy bowel action and may prevent colon cancer. |

| Minerals | Vitamins |
|---|---|
| Minerals and certain salts are needed in minute quantities. These include iron, potassium, calcium and sodium (found in salt). **Diet advice:** Too much salt (sodium) in the diet may be harmful. | Vitamins are complex chemical compounds needed by the body in tiny quantities to regulate metabolism and to help convert carbohydrates and fats into energy. **Diet advice:** Vitamins can be destroyed by lengthy cooking, so keep cooking time to a minimum and eat raw vegetables and fruit regularly. |

### Weight

Being overweight (according to the weight chart on p.26) is dangerous to your health. It increases the risk of serious disorders such as diabetes, high blood pressure, heart disease and stroke, and exaggerates the symptoms of many other disorders. Obesity makes childbirth and surgery more complicated and, in pregnancy, can lead to low back pain (p.135) and varicose veins (p.109).

Most women can achieve and maintain an ideal weight if they follow a sensible weight-reducing diet (see *How to lose weight,* p.27) and exercise regularly (see *Exercise and weight loss,* p.25). However, do not wait until you are on the verge of obesity before doing something to control your weight. It is far easier to prevent yourself from becoming overweight by eating a balanced diet than to lose weight.

### Exercise

To be fit, you must exercise regularly. Exercise helps the body maintain mobility and body strength and conditions the heart and lungs. Physical activity makes your muscles need more oxygen – so you breathe more deeply to get oxygen into your lungs and your heart beats faster to pump blood to the muscles. There are many health benefits to be gained from exercise. The more muscles and joints you include in your exercise program and the more activities you undertake that involve a high degree of physical exertion to make you feel breathless and sweaty, the greater the benefits. Exercise is essential if you need to lose weight (see *Exercise and weight loss,* p.25) when it is combined with a sensible weight-reducing diet (see *How to lose weight,* p.27). Team sports and solitary exercise such as jogging are among the most popular forms of exercise, but walking and bicycling, if you do them energetically, are also good exercise. There are also psychological benefits to regular exercise.

### Smoking

If you smoke, give it up. Smoking is beyond doubt the main cause of many serious illnesses (see *The dangers of smoking,* p.72), including lung cancer, emphysema and diseases of the heart and circulation. If you smoke regularly, you are probably losing about 5 minutes of life for each cigarette smoked. By giving up smoking, your chances of suffering from tobacco-related diseases lessen with each successive year.

### Alcohol

Alcohol is a drug that can damage your health if consumed in large quantities. You may be putting your health at serious risk if you regularly exceed the safe limits outlined in *The effects of alcohol,* p.22, and/or if drinking ever becomes a necessity. The action of alcohol on the body and mind depends on the concentration of alcohol in the blood, so it varies from person to person according to individual weight. Women, who tend to weigh less than men, usually feel the effects of the same amount of alcohol slightly earlier. Factors such as the type of alcohol you drink and the speed at which you drink also affect the action of alcohol. During pregnancy any amount of alcohol can put the healthy development of the unborn baby at risk. If you want to reduce your alcohol intake but find you cannot, accept that alcohol is a serious problem for you. Seek help from your physician.

## Over-the-counter medications

There are many over-the-counter medications at the pharmacy, available in almost every imaginable form. Some of them may have no direct effect on the cause of a condition but they may relieve painful or uncomfortable symptoms. For instance, some of the remedies for coughs and colds are soothing, and mild analgesics such as aspirin and aspirin substitutes relieve pain.

However, in most cases, the speed of your recovery depends more on your age and general health than on any such treatment. Nevertheless, if such "cures" make you feel better, they are unlikely to be harmful if you follow the instructions. In some cases your physician may actually recommend a particular over-the-counter preparation. If you are unsure about how to use the medication or how to receive its maximum benefit (for instance, whether you can drink alcohol or drive after taking the medication), ask your physician for advice.

# Medical checkups

Many women feel that they need only visit their physicians when they are sick. However, certain disorders such as high blood pressure and cervical cancer may be present in early stages without symptoms until the disease has reached a fairly advanced stage. It is then more difficult to treat. Periodic examinations are particularly important for women taking the birth-control pill. It is important to check weight, blood pressure, blood sugar and liver function once a year to monitor some of the potential adverse effects of the birth-control pill.

Talk to your physician about having regular medical checkups. The record from your first medical checkup will serve as a guideline against which the significance of any further changes in your health can be measured. Your physician may use the checkup to assess your general life-style, to listen to your heart and breathing and to examine your eyes and ears. You should also confirm with him or her that you have been immunized against infectious diseases, especially tetanus and polio.

## Testing blood pressure

Blood pressure is measured as systolic over diastolic pressure. Systolic pressure is the peak pressure at the moment when your heart contracts in the process of pumping out blood. Diastolic pressure is the pressure at a moment when your heart relaxes to permit the inflow of blood. A healthy young adult has a reading of about 110/75, which rises by age 60 to about 130/90.

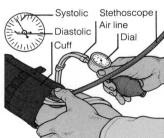

Your physician will place a soft cuff around your upper arm and inflate it until it is tight enough to stop the blood flow. The cuff is slowly deflated until the physician can hear (through a stethoscope) the blood forcing its way along the main artery. Your physician can then measure systolic pressure. Next the physician will deflate the cuff and listen for blood flowing steadily through the now-open artery; this will be the diastolic pressure.

| NAME OF TEST AND PURPOSE | WHEN RECOMMENDED | WHEN TO BEGIN IF HEALTHY | FREQUENCY OF FOLLOW-UPS |
|---|---|---|---|
| **Complete physical examination** | | | |
| To check on the general health of your heart, lungs, brain and major internal organs | If you have a family history of disorders of any of these organs and as a preventive measure | Every 3 to 5 years up to age 50 | Annually |
| **Blood pressure** (see above right) | | | |
| To check the condition of your heart and arteries. If there is any rise in blood pressure, this may cause serious medical problems | If you have a family history of high blood pressure, heart or kidney disease, stroke or diabetes, or if you are overweight or taking the birth-control pill | From the age of 20 onward | Every 3 to 5 years. Every year if you are taking the birth-control pill or are in a high-risk group |
| **Rectal examination** | | | |
| To detect rectal cancer | If you have a family history of colon or rectal cancer | Annual digital rectal exam after age 20 | After age 50 stools should be tested annually; general exam every 3 to 5 years |
| **Vaginal examination** (see also p.122) | | | |
| To examine the pelvic floor, perineum and pelvic organs | Before you start any new contraceptive, if you are pregnant or if you have a pelvic inflammation | Regular checkups are not needed, unless stated otherwise | Not needed |
| **Cervical (Pap) smear** (see also p.121) | | | |
| To detect any premalignant or malignant changes in the cervix at an early stage | If you bleed between periods or have irregular periods | From the age of 25 onward, or as soon as you are sexually active | After 2 annual negative tests, every 3 years until menopause; thereafter, every 3 to 5 years |
| **Mammography** (breast X ray) | | | |
| To detect signs of breast cancer before it becomes noticeable through physical examination | If you have a family history of breast cancer | Once between the ages of 35 and 40 | Every 1 to 2 years between the ages of 40 and 50; annually between ages 50 and 60. |
| **Eye tests** (see also p.62) | | | |
| Even if you can see well you should have regular vision tests | If you have difficulty seeing | From the age of 40 onward | Annually |
| **Dental checkups** | | | |
| Regular inspections are vital so that your dentist can examine your teeth, mouth and gums for signs of decay, infection or other problems | If you have not had regular check-ups, start now rather than waiting until you have a toothache or painful gums | From childhood | Every 6 months before the age of 21, then every 1 to 2 years |

# When you are sick

Recovery from most illnesses is more speedy if you stop work, stay at home and take things easy. There is no need to stay in bed as long as you stay in a warm environment. For the period that you feel sick, stop smoking and do not drink alcohol. Drink plenty of fluids, especially if you have a fever or diarrhea. Also, eat small, frequent meals.

If your illness persists for more than 48 hours despite your taking self-help measures or you are worried about your symptoms, see your physician. If you have been taking your temperature, record it and the time it was taken. Keep specimens of stools, vomit or urine if they have an unusual color (especially if black or bloodstained), as this will help your physician to make a firm diagnosis. Also, try to remember when various symptoms started.

# Medication guide

New drugs are constantly being discovered. Many of the drugs in common use twenty years ago have been superseded by newer, safer compounds with broader applications. This guide is an index of major groups of drugs; it gives their uses and possible side effects and, in many cases, warnings about when they should *not* be taken.

When taking any medicine, a few precautionary measures can ensure the drug's effectiveness and safe use. Never exceed the stated dosage. Always check with your physician or pharmacist if you are unsure exactly when or how frequently the medicine should be taken (for example, some drugs work most efficiently when taken with a meal). As a general rule, avoid drinking alcohol when taking medicine, as its effects are aggravated by certain drugs. Also, even if you think it unnecessary and you *seem* to have no more symptoms, complete the prescribed course of medicine. Failure to do so may prevent complete recovery.

In general, the fewer drugs you take, the better. Except for minor symptoms (such as an occasional cough or headache), let your physician prescribe all the medicines you need. He or she will balance the potential benefits of the medication against its side effects. Below is a guide to the more common drugs.

## Drugs and pregnancy

During pregnancy it is important to avoid any substances that could put the development of the fetus at risk. Most drugs pass from the mother's circulation to the fetus. While some are known to be harmless, there are others that can, in.certain instances and at certain times during pregnancy, threaten the health of the fetus. Therefore, if you are pregnant or are contemplating pregnancy, you will need to ask your physician for advice before taking any drugs, including those available over-the-counter. If you suffer from a chronic condition for which you are receiving medication, your physician will advise you on the best treatment while you are pregnant. Both alcohol and smoking are known to have harmful effects on the developing fetus.

It is common practice during pregnancy to be prescribed iron tablets (to prevent anemia) and vitamin supplements. In severe cases, a physician may prescribe safe antinausea tablets.

## Drugs and breast-feeding

If possible, try to avoid taking drugs of any sort while breast-feeding. However, if you need drug treatment, there is usually no reason why you should not continue to breast-feed your baby; most drugs pass into the milk in insignificant quantities (your physician will advise you). If you do have to take a drug that is potentially harmful to your baby or to your breast milk (some laxatives and tranquilizers are harmful), you can express your milk to maintain your baby's supply before taking the drug. You can then resume normal breast-feeding after you finish treatment.

## Home medical supplies

Below is a list of items to keep at home to deal with common problems such as indigestion and muscle strain and a list to deal with accidents and emergencies.

**Home medicine cabinet**
The best place to keep prescribed medications and common, over-the-counter remedies is in a section of a medicine cabinet that can be locked. This will keep the items dry and away from children. Many over-the-counter preparations have a shelf life of 1 year and should be replaced regularly. You are likely to need:

Clinical thermometer
Antiseptic cream (cuts and scrapes)
Insect-sting reliever
Antacid liquid or tablets (indigestion)
Milk of magnesia (constipation and heartburn)
Kaolin (diarrhea)
Oil of cloves (toothache)
Motion-sickness tablets
Protective sunscreen
Calamine lotion
Petroleum jelly (chafing)
Elastic bandages
Eye wash
Aspirin or aspirin substitute

**Home first-aid kit**
In cases of emergency, you are likely to need additional supplies. These should be stored in a well-sealed metal or plastic box that is clearly labeled and easy for you to open. It should be kept in a dry place, out of reach of children and should include:

Packet of sterile cotton
Sterile prepared bandages (2 large, 2 medium, 2 small)
Sterile gauze squares in several sizes
Sterile triangular bandages (2)
Gauze bandages (2) and at least 1 crepe bandage
Finger-size gauze with applicator
Rubbing alcohol
Waterproof plasters in assorted sizes
Surgical tape in wide and narrow widths
Safety pins
Small mirror
Tweezers
Scissors

**Safety note:** Remember that it is important to keep all medicines safely out of the reach of children. A locked wall cabinet is usually the best place.

## Medications

**ANALGESICS** Drugs that relieve pain. Many also reduce inflammation and fever (see ANTI-INFLAMMATORIES). There are 3 main types: simple analgesics – usually containing aspirin or acetaminophen – for mild pain; antiinflammatories, often given for muscular aches and pains and arthritis; and narcotic analgesics – usually chemically related to morphine – for severe pain.
*Possible side effects:* Nausea, constipation, dizziness, dependence and development of tolerance to the drug.

**ANTACIDS** Drugs that neutralize stomach acid (relieving heartburn and similar conditions). They contain simple chemicals such as sodium bicarbonate, calcium carbonate, aluminum hydroxide and/or magnesium trisilicate.
*Possible side effects:* Belching (sodium bicarbonate preparations), constipation (aluminum or calcium preparations) and diarrhea (magnesium preparations).
*Warning:* Seek medical advice if you

are taking other drugs. Antacids should be taken by anyone with a kidney disorder only on medical advice.

**ANTIANXIETY DRUGS** (sometimes called anxiolytics, sedatives or minor tranquilizers). Drugs that reduce feelings of anxiety and relax muscles. May also be used as sleeping drugs to relieve premenstrual tension.
*Possible side effects:* Drowsiness, dizziness, confusion, unsteadiness and lack of coordination.
*Warning:* Not to be taken if you intend to drive or operate potentially dangerous machinery. Antianxiety drugs may increase the effects of alcohol. They can be habit-forming and should not be used for more than a few weeks. After prolonged use, withdrawal symptoms may occur if treatment is halted abruptly.

**ANTIBIOTICS** Substances (that are often derived from living organisms such as molds or bacteria) that kill or inhibit the growth of bacteria in the

body. Some of the newer antibiotics are synthetic versions of naturally occurring substances. Any one type of antibiotic is effective only against certain strains of bacteria; some, known as broad-spectrum antibiotics, combat a wide range of bacteria.
*Possible side effects:* Nausea, vomiting and diarrhea. Some people may be allergic to certain antibiotics and may experience symptoms such as rashes, fever, joint pain, swelling and wheezing. Following treatment with broad-spectrum antibiotics, secondary fungal infection (thrush) – for example, of the mouth or vagina – may sometimes occur.
*Warning:* Always complete a prescribed course of antibiotics. Failure to do so, even when symptoms have cleared, may lead to a recurrence of infection that is more difficult to treat (due to resistance of the bacteria to the antibiotic).

**ANTICOAGULANTS** (including thrombolytics). Drugs that prevent and/or

disperse blood clots.
*Possible side effects:* Increased tendency to bleed from the nose or gums or under the skin (bruising). Blood may also appear in the urine or stool.
*Warning:* Anticoagulants may react more intensely with other drugs, including aspirin. Consult your physician before taking any other medicines so that the effectiveness of the anticoagulant is not altered. If you are on regular anticoagulant treatment, you will be advised to carry a warning card or ID tag.

**ANTICONVULSANTS** Drugs used in the prevention and treatment of epilepsy.
*Possible side effects:* Drowsiness, rashes, dizziness, headache, nausea and thickening of the gums.
*Warning:* Alcohol may increase the likelihood and severity of side effects and is best avoided, as are ANTI-HISTAMINES. Consult your physician before driving and/or operating potentially dangerous machinery.

14

**ANTIDEPRESSANTS** Drugs that counter depression. These fall into two main groups: tricyclics and their derivatives, and monoamine oxidase (MAO) inhibitors. Because their side effects are likely to be more serious, MAO inhibitors are usually only prescribed for those types of severe depression that are less likely to respond to treatment with tricyclics.
*Possible side effects:* Drowsiness, dry mouth, blurred vision, constipation, difficulty urinating, faintness, sweating, trembling, rashes, palpitations and headaches.
*Warning:* MAO inhibitors react adversely with a number of foods and drugs, possibly leading to a serious rise in blood pressure. Your physician will advise you and may recommend that you carry a warning card or ID tag. During both types of antidepressant treatment, alcohol intake should be limited; ask you physician whether it is advisable to drive or operate machinery.

**ANTIDIARRHEALS** Drugs used to control and treat diarrhea. There are two main types: those that absorb excess water and toxins in the bowel (for example, those containing kaolin, bismuth compounds, chalk or charcoal) and those that reduce the contractions of the bowel, thus decreasing the frequency with which stools are passed (including codeine, morphine and opium mixtures).
*Possible side effects:* Constipation.
*Warning:* Antidiarrheals relieve symptoms but do not treat the underlying cause of diarrhea and may prolong the course of toxic or infectious diarrhea. They should not be taken for more than a day or so before seeking medical advice. When treating diarrhea, always drink plenty of fluids. See also REHYDRATION TREATMENTS.

**ANTIEMETICS** Drugs used to suppress nausea and vomiting. Most also suppress vertigo (dizziness). The main groups of drugs in this category include certain ANTIHISTAMINES (especially for nausea caused by motion sickness or by ear disorders), ANTISPASMODICS, and certain tranquilizers. Because antiemetic treatment may hinder diagnosis, such drugs are not usually prescribed when the cause of vomiting is unknown or when vomiting is unlikely to persist for longer than a day or so, as in gastroenteritis. Antiemetics are prescribed early in pregnancy only when symptoms are severe.
*Possible side effects:* These vary according to the drug group prescribed. Prolonged treatment with certain tranquilizers may cause involuntary movement of the facial muscles. These drugs should never be taken for more than a few days at a time.
*Warning:* Because most antiemetics may cause drowsiness, do not drink alcohol and seek your physician's advice before driving or operating potentially dangerous machinery.

**ANTIFUNGALS** Drugs used to treat fungal infections such as ringworm, athlete's foot or thrush.
*Possible side effects:* Oral antifungals may cause nausea, vomiting, diarrhea and/or headaches; locally applied (topical) preparations may cause irritation.
*Warning:* Always finish a course of antifungal treatment as prescribed; otherwise the infection may recur. Some infections, especially of the nails, may require treatment with oral antifungals for many months.

**ANTIHISTAMINES** Drugs mostly used to counteract the effects of histamine, one of the chemicals involved in allergic reactions. They are most often used to relieve the symptoms of seasonal hay fever, and may also clear a stuffy or runny nose, nausea or dizziness. Another class of antihistamine interferes with gastric acid secretion and is used to treat peptic ulcers.
*Possible side effects:* Drowsiness, dry mouth and blurred vision.
*Warning:* Driving or drinking alcohol should be avoided after taking an antihistamine.

**ANTIHYPERTENSIVES** Drugs that lower blood pressure. BETA-BLOCKERS and DIURETICS and, more recently, enzyme inhibitors or receptor blockers (which affect the action of hormones controlling blood pressure), and calcium blockers (which affect the internal chemistry of the heart and arteries) are those most commonly used.
*Possible side effects:* Dizziness, rashes, impotence, nightmares and lethargy.

**ANTI-INFLAMMATORIES** Drugs used to reduce inflammation. This is the redness, heat, swelling, pain and increased blood flow that is found in infections and in many chronic noninfective diseases such as rheumatoid arthritis and gout. Three main types of drugs are used as anti-inflammatories: ANALGESICS such as aspirin, CORTICOSTEROIDS and nonsteroidal anti-inflammatory drugs such as indomethacin which is used especially in the treatment of arthritis and muscle disorders. CORTICOSTEROIDS may be applied locally as cream or eyedrops for inflammation of the skin or eyes, but they are not generally prescribed for chronic rheumatic conditions except in unusual circumstances.
*Possible side effects:* Rashes and stomach irritation and occasionally bleeding, disturbances in hearing and wheezing.

**ANTIPYRETICS** Drugs that reduce fever. The most commonly used are aspirin and acetaminophen, which are both also ANALGESICS. This double action makes them particularly effective for relieving the symptoms of an illness such as flu.
*Possible side effects:* Rashes and stomach irritation and occasionally bleeding, disturbances in hearing and wheezing.

**ANTISPASMODICS** Drugs for reducing spasm of the bowel to relieve the pain of conditions such as irritable colon or diverticular disease.
*Possible side effects:* Dry mouth, palpitations, difficulty urinating, constipation and blurred vision.

**ANTIVIRALS** Drugs used to treat viral infections or to provide temporary protection against infections such as the flu. Few viral disorders respond to drugs, and those that do respond, such as cold sores and shingles, will do so only if treatment is started early.
*Possible side effects:* Antivirals used to treat cold sores, herpes genitalis and shingles may cause a stinging sensation, rashes and occasionally loss of sensation in the skin.

**BETA- BLOCKERS** Drugs that reduce the oxygen requirements of the heart by reducing heart rate. They are used as ANTIHYPERTENSIVES to treat angina due to exertion and to ease symptoms such as palpitations and tremors.
*Possible side effects:* Nausea, insomnia, tiredness and diarrhea.
*Warning:* Overdose can cause dizziness and fainting spells. Withdrawal from these drugs should be gradual, never abrupt. Beta-blockers are not prescribed for people who suffer from asthma or heart failure.

**BRONCHODILATORS** Drugs that open up the bronchial tubes within the lungs when the tubes have become narrowed by muscle spasm. Bronchodilators, taken by aerosol spray, ease breathing in diseases such as asthma. Effects usually last for 3 to 5 hours.
*Possible side effects:* Rapid heartbeat, palpitations, tremor, headache and dizziness.

**CORTICOSTEROIDS** These preparations are made from synthetic HORMONES and are used mainly as ANTI-INFLAMMATORIES (in the treatment of arthritis and other disorders), as BRONCHODILATORS (in the treatment of asthma), or as IMMUNOSUPPRESSIVES, though they may be useful for treating certain malignant neoplasms or in compensating for a deficiency of natural hormones.
*Possible side effects:* Weight gain, redness of the face, stomach irritation, mental disturbances and increase in body hair.

**DIURETICS** Drugs that increase the quantity of urine produced by the kidneys and passed out of the body, thus ridding the body of excess fluid. Diuretics reduce excess fluid that has collected in the tissues as a result of any disorder of the heart, kidneys and liver. They are useful in treating mildly raised blood pressure.
*Possible side effects:* Rashes, dizziness, weakness, numbness, tingling in the hands and feet and excessive loss of potassium.

**HORMONES** Chemicals produced naturally by the endocrine (pituitary, thyroid, adrenal, ovary/testis, pancreas or parathyroid) glands. When they are not produced naturally (because of some disorder), they can be replaced by natural or synthetic hormones (hormone replacement therapy). See SEX HORMONES.
*Possible side effects:* There may be an exaggeration of the secondary sexual characteristics, so estrogens given to a man may increase the size of his breasts, and androgens given to a woman may cause increased body hair and deepening of the voice. Estrogens also affect blood clotting and so may cause heart attack, stroke or thrombosis in the legs.

**HYPOGLYCEMICS** Drugs that lower the level of glucose in the blood. Oral hypoglycemic drugs are used in the treatment of diabetes mellitus if it cannot be controlled by diet alone, and does not require treatment with injections of insulin.
*Possible side effects:* Loss of appetite, nausea, indigestion, numbness or tingling in the skin, fever and rashes.
*Warning:* If the glucose level falls too low, weakness, dizziness, pallor, sweating, increased saliva flow, palpitations, irritability and trembling may result. If such symptoms occur several hours after eating, this may indicate that the dose is too high. Report symptoms to your physician.

**IMMUNOSUPPRESSIVES** Drugs that prevent or reduce the body's normal reaction to invasion by disease or by foreign tissues. Immunosuppressives are used to treat autoimmune diseases (in which the body's defenses work abnormally and attack the body's own tissues) and to help prevent rejection of organ transplants.
*Possible side effects:* Susceptibility to infection (especially chest infections, fungal infections of the mouth and skin and virus infections) is increased. Some immunosuppressives may damage the bone marrow, causing anemia, and may cause nausea and vomiting.

**LAXATIVES** Drugs that increase the frequency and ease of bowel movements. They work by stimulating the bowel wall, by increasing the bulk of bowel contents, or by increasing the fluid content of the stool.
*Warning:* Laxatives are not to be taken regularly; the bowel may become unable to work properly without them.

**REHYDRATION TREATMENTS** Powders or solution used to prevent and treat dehydration caused by loss of water and salts from the body as a result of diarrhea (with or without persistent vomiting). The powders and solution contain sodium chloride, glucose and other mineral salts.
*Possible side effects:* Fluid accumulation may occur as a result of sodium retention.

**SEX HORMONES (FEMALE)** The hormones responsible for the development of secondary sexual characteristics and regulation of the menstrual cycle. There are two main types of hormone drugs: estrogens and progestogens. They are used in the treatment of menstrual and menopausal disorders and as birth-control pills.
*Possible side effects:* Nausea, weight gain, headache and depression.

**VASODILATORS** Drugs that dilate blood vessels. Most widely used in prevention and treatment of angina, but also for treating heart failure and circulatory disorders.
*Possible side effects:* Headache, palpitations, flushing, faintness, nausea, vomiting, diarrhea and stuffy nose.

# How to use the charts

The 83 diagnostic charts in this book have been compiled to help you find probable reasons for your symptoms. Each chart shows in detail a single symptom – for instance, vomiting, headache or a rash – and explores the possible causes of the symptom by means of a logically organized sequence of questions, each answerable by a simple YES or NO. Your responses will lead you toward a clearly worded end point, which suggests what may be wrong and offers advice on whether your disorder requires professional attention. To see how the charts work, examine the accompanying sample chart and study the explanatory notes. In particular, make sure you understand the exact meanings of the systematized action codes that indicate the relative urgency of the need to consult a physician (see *What the instructions mean,* opposite).

Note that every chart is numbered and bears a label defining or describing the key symptom. An introductory paragraph provides further description and explanation of the purpose of the chart. Read this paragraph carefully to make sure you have chosen the most appropriate pathway toward an analysis of your problem; then proceed as indicated in the chart itself. Always begin with the first question and follow through to the end point that fits your special situation. In many cases, extensive boxed information accompanying the chart will enhance your understanding of specific diagnoses as well as likely treatment for underlying disorders. Always read through such information texts (except, of course, in emergencies, when swift action is essential).

It is important to consult the *correct* chart at the *correct* time. For instructions on how to recognize and define your symptom and how to choose the precise chart you need, turn to p. 18.

**Chart group**
The charts are divided into sections according to whether they cover a general medical problem or a specific area, such as *Sex and fertility.*

**Chart number**
Each chart has a number so that it can be easily found and cross-referenced. Occasionally, you will be advised to turn to a more appropriate chart.

Go to chart

Chart title

**Chart title**
A short, descriptive term for the symptom heads each chart.

**Definition**
Each symptom is defined in simple, nontechnical terms and an indication of when a symptom is severe enough to cause concern is given.

**The questions**
These are structured so that you follow either a YES or a NO pathway from each question. Follow the series of questions, answering as appropriate in your case. In almost all cases you will then arrive at a possible reason for your symptoms.

**The diagnosis**
Each series of questions usually leads to a possible diagnosis and the treatment you are likely to need. The diagnoses take various forms according to the potential seriousness of a complaint. For example, it takes the form of a warning in cases where you may need urgent medical attention (see *What the instructions mean,* opposite). You are usually referred to other sections of the book for further information.

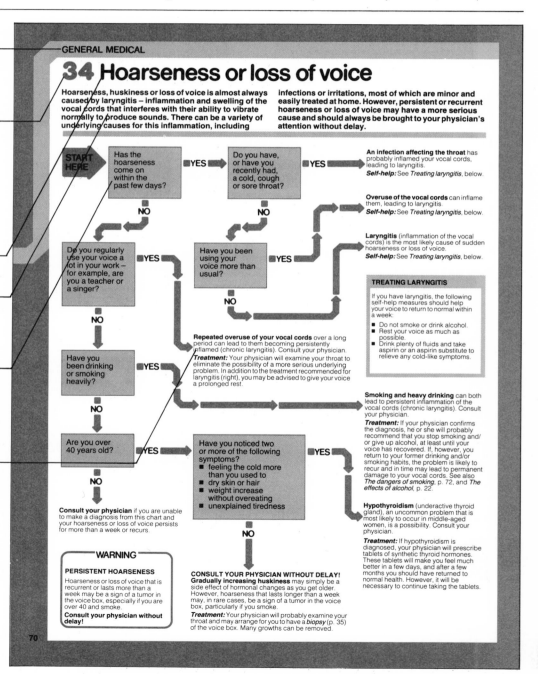

GENERAL MEDICAL

# 34 Hoarseness or loss of voice

Hoarseness, huskiness or loss of voice is almost always caused by laryngitis – inflammation and swelling of the vocal cords that interferes with their ability to vibrate normally to produce sounds. There can be a variety of underlying causes for this inflammation, including infections or irritations, most of which are minor and easily treated at home. However, persistent or recurrent hoarseness or loss of voice may have a more serious cause and should always be brought to your physician's attention without delay.

START HERE

Has the hoarseness come on within the past few days? — **YES** → Do you have, or have you recently had, a cold, cough or sore throat? — **YES** → **An infection affecting the throat** has probably inflamed your vocal cords, leading to laryngitis.
*Self-help:* See *Treating laryngitis,* below.

**NO** / **NO**

Do you regularly use your voice a lot in your work – for example, are you a teacher or a singer? — **YES** → Have you been using your voice more than usual? — **YES** → **Overuse of the vocal cords** can inflame them, leading to laryngitis.
*Self-help:* See *Treating laryngitis,* below.

**NO** / **NO**

**Laryngitis** (inflammation of the vocal cords) is the most likely cause of sudden hoarseness or loss of voice.
*Self-help:* See *Treating laryngitis,* below.

Have you been drinking or smoking heavily? — **YES** → **Repeated overuse of your vocal cords** over a long period can lead to them becoming persistently inflamed (chronic laryngitis). Consult your physician.
*Treatment:* Your physician will examine your throat to eliminate the possibility of a more serious underlying problem. In addition to the treatment recommended for laryngitis (right), you may be advised to give your voice a prolonged rest.

**NO**

Are you over 40 years old? — **YES** → Have you noticed two or more of the following symptoms?
■ feeling the cold more than you used to
■ dry skin or hair
■ weight increase without overeating
■ unexplained tiredness — **YES** →

**NO**

**Consult your physician** if you are unable to make a diagnosis from this chart and your hoarseness or loss of voice persists for more than a week or recurs.

**NO**

### TREATING LARYNGITIS

If you have laryngitis, the following self-help measures should help your voice to return to normal within a week:

■ Do not smoke or drink alcohol.
■ Rest your voice as much as possible.
■ Drink plenty of fluids and take aspirin or an aspirin substitute to relieve any cold-like symptoms.

**Smoking and heavy drinking** can both lead to persistent inflammation of the vocal cords (chronic laryngitis). Consult your physician.

*Treatment:* If your physician confirms the diagnosis, he or she will probably recommend that you stop smoking and/or give up alcohol, at least until your voice has recovered. If, however, you return to your former drinking and/or smoking habits, the problem is likely to recur and in time may lead to permanent damage to your vocal cords. See also *The dangers of smoking,* p. 72, and *The effects of alcohol,* p. 22.

**Hypothyroidism** (underactive thyroid gland), an uncommon problem that is most likely to occur in middle-aged women, is a possibility. Consult your physician.

*Treatment:* If hypothyroidism is diagnosed, your physician will prescribe tablets of synthetic thyroid hormones. These tablets will make you feel much better in a few days, and after a few months you should have returned to normal health. However, it will be necessary to continue taking the tablets.

#### WARNING

**PERSISTENT HOARSENESS**

Hoarseness or loss of voice that is recurrent or lasts more than a week may be a sign of a tumor in the voice box, especially if you are over 40 and smoke.
**Consult your physician without delay!**

**CONSULT YOUR PHYSICIAN WITHOUT DELAY!**
**Gradually increasing huskiness** may simply be a side effect of hormonal changes as you get older. However, hoarseness that lasts longer than a week may, in rare cases, be a sign of a tumor in the voice box, particularly if you smoke.

*Treatment:* Your physician will probably examine your throat and may arrange for you to have a *biopsy* (p. 35) of the voice box. Many growths can be removed.

70

**WARNING:** Though self-treatment is recommended for many minor disorders, remember that the charts provide only *likely* diagnoses. If you have any doubt about the diagnosis or treatment of any symptom, *always consult your physician.*

## What the instructions mean

**EMERGENCY**
**GET MEDICAL HELP NOW!**

The condition may threaten life or lead to permanent disability if not given immediate medical attention. Get medical help by the fastest

means possible, usually by calling an ambulance. In some cases it may be better to call your own physician or take the patient to the hospital yourself.

**CALL YOUR PHYSICIAN NOW!**
There is a possibility of a serious condition that may warrant

immediate treatment and perhaps hospital admission. Seek medical advice immediately – day or night – usually by telephoning your physician, who will then decide on further action. If you are unable to make contact with your physician within an hour or so, emergency action (left) may be justified.

**CONSULT YOUR PHYSICIAN WITHOUT DELAY!**
The condition is serious and needs urgent medical assessment, but a few hours' delay in seeking treatment is unlikely to be damaging. Seek your physician's advice within 24 hours. This will usually mean telephoning for an appointment the same day.

**Consult your physician.**
A condition for which medical treatment is advisable, but for which reasonable delay is unlikely to lead to problems. Seek medical advice as soon as practical.

**Discuss with your physician.**
The condition is nonurgent and specific treatment is unlikely. However, your physician's advice may be helpful. Seek medical advice as soon as practical.

## Boxed information
On most charts there are boxes containing important additional information to expand on either a diagnosis or a form of treatment. See the information and self-help boxes below.

---

**GENERAL MEDICAL**

# 35 Wheezing

Wheezing sometimes occurs when breathing out if you have a chest cold, and this is no cause for concern as long as breathing is otherwise normal. Such wheezing can usually be heard only through a stethoscope, but it may become more apparent to you when you exhale

violently (during exercise, for example). Loud wheezing, especially if you also feel breathless or if breathing is painful, may be a sign of a number of more serious conditions, including congestive heart failure, asthma and bronchitis, which require medical attention.

**START HERE** → **Has the wheezing started within the past few hours?** — YES → **Have you coughed up frothy pink or white phlegm?** — YES →

**CALL YOUR PHYSICIAN NOW!**
**A dangerous buildup of fluid in the lungs,** perhaps as a result of heart disease, is a possibility. Sit upright in a chair and try to keep calm; this will make breathing easier for you until help arrives.
*Treatment:* Keep a sample of the phlegm if possible in a glass or paper cup; this will help your physician to make a quick diagnosis of the problem. You will probably be admitted to the hospital where you will be given oxygen and drugs to assist breathing. These may include a *diuretic*, to drain fluid from the lungs, or a *bronchodilator*, to open up blocked airways in the lungs. When the lungs have cleared, treatment will depend on the underlying problem.

(Has the wheezing – NO) ↓   (coughed up phlegm – NO) ↓

**EMERGENCY**
**GET MEDICAL HELP NOW!**
**A severe attack of asthma** is a possibility.
*Treatment:* While waiting for help to arrive, carry out the first-aid measures described below. A severe attack usually requires hospital admission. Drugs will be given and, if necessary, the physician may use a mechanical respirator to assist breathing.

**Is breathing so difficult that you feel you are suffocating?** — YES →

**A mild attack of asthma** is probably making you wheeze.
*Self-help:* Since asthma is most often due to an allergy, try to find which substances you are allergic to, and avoid contact with them as much as possible. Consult your physician, who will be able to prescribe drugs to prevent further attacks, and to help you when attacks occur. In addition, he or she may arrange for you to undergo special allergy tests to help identify the cause of your asthma.

(Is breathing – NO) ↓

**Is your temperature 100°F (38°C) or above?**

| 102 | — 39 |
| 101 | |
| 100 | 38 |

— YES →

**Acute bronchitis** (infection of the airways in the lungs) is a possibility.
*Self-help:* Take aspirin or an aspirin substitute, drink fluids and stay in a warm, humidified environment. Call your physician if you have difficulty breathing, or if you are no better in 48 hours.

(Is your temperature – NO) ↓

**Do you wheeze a little most days?** — YES →

**Do you cough up gray or greenish-yellow phlegm most days?** — YES →

**Chronic bronchitis** (persistent inflammation of the airways in the lungs) may be the cause of the wheezing, especially if you smoke and have had similar periods of wheezing in the past. Consult your physician.
*Treatment:* Your physician will advise you to give up smoking, if you are a smoker, as this is likely to make the problem worse. After tests have been done, such as a *chest X ray* (p. 73), he or she may prescribe *antibiotics* in the form of tablets or capsules. An aerosol inhaler may help you if you suffer from breathlessness.

(Do you wheeze – NO) ↓   (Do you cough up – NO) ↓

**Consult your physician** if you are unable to make a diagnosis from this chart.

---

**FIRST AID FOR ASTHMA**
A severe attack of asthma, in which the person is fighting for breath and/or becomes pale and clammy with a blue tinge to the tongue or lips, is an emergency and admission to the hospital is essential. Call an ambulance or go to the emergency room of your local hospital immediately. Most people with asthma already have drugs or an inhaling apparatus, both of which should be administered. If one dose of inhalant does not quickly relieve the wheezing, it should be repeated only once.

In all cases, help the asthmatic to find the most comfortable position while you are waiting for medical help. The best position is sitting up, leaning forward on the back of a chair, and taking some of the weight on the arms (right). Plenty of fresh air will also help. A sudden severe attack of asthma can be very frightening for the family as well as the asthmatic. However, anxiety can make the attack worse, so only one other person should remain with the asthmatic and this person should be calm until help is provided.

71

---

## WARNING

Symptoms that indicate an immediate danger to life are highlighted in these boxes. Where appropriate, steps that can be taken while waiting for medical help to arrive are explained.

## FIRST AID

Where symptoms may require either simple first-aid or lifesaving measures, you will find boxed information on what action you should take.

## INFORMATION

These boxes expand on the possible diagnoses and likely forms of treatment for specific symptoms. For example, several of them contain an explanation of a particular medical procedure. Where applicable, self-help treatment is included.

## SELF-HELP

Where self-help measures may be effective in dealing with a symptom, advice is given on ways in which you may alleviate the problem.

# How to find the correct chart

There are three ways to find the appropriate diagnostic chart for your symptom. You can use the *Pain-site map*, the *System-by-system chartfinder* or the *Chart index*, depending on the nature of the symptom, where it is located, and how easily you are able to define it. Whatever method you choose to find your chart, you will be given the title of the appropriate chart and its number.

**2 System-by-system chartfinder**
If you know the body area or the body system affected, but are unsure how to define your symptom, consult the system-by-system chartfinder (opposite).

**3 Chart index**
For other symptoms (when you have no difficulty naming your symptom), consult the chart index (p. 20). If you are suffering from more than one symptom at the same time, concentrate on finding the chart for the symptom that causes you the most distress or that is the most prominent.

**1 Pain-site map**
If you are in pain, the quickest way to find your chart is by reference to the pain-site map (below).

## 1 Pain-site map

Consult this section to find the correct diagnostic chart for your symptom if you are suffering from pain in any part of the body. The illustrations below indicate possible areas of pain and are keyed in to the titles and numbers of the charts that deal with pain in that part of the body.

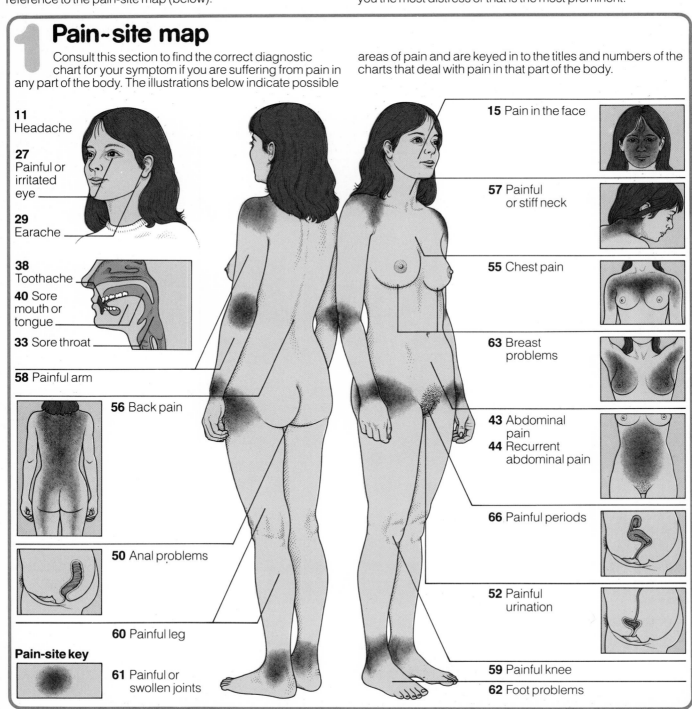

**11** Headache

**27** Painful or irritated eye

**29** Earache

**38** Toothache

**40** Sore mouth or tongue

**33** Sore throat

**58** Painful arm

**56** Back pain

**50** Anal problems

**60** Painful leg

**Pain-site key**

**61** Painful or swollen joints

**15** Pain in the face

**57** Painful or stiff neck

**55** Chest pain

**63** Breast problems

**43** Abdominal pain
**44** Recurrent abdominal pain

**66** Painful periods

**52** Painful urination

**59** Painful knee

**62** Foot problems

# 2 System-by-system chartfinder

Consult this section if you know what body system your symptom originates in. A list of the diagnostic charts is given under each main heading. Select the chart that most closely fits your symptom.

## General symptoms

1 Feeling under the weather
2 Tiredness
3 Loss of weight
4 Overweight
5 Difficulty sleeping
6 Fever

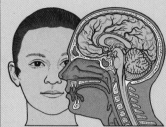

## Head, brain and psychological symptoms

10 Faintness and fainting
11 Headache
12 Dizziness
13 Numbness or tingling
14 Twitching and trembling
15 Pain in the face
16 Forgetfulness and confusion
17 Difficulty speaking
18 Disturbing thoughts and feelings
19 Depression
20 Anxiety
83 Depression after childbirth

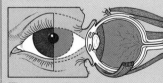

## Eye and sight symptoms

27 Painful or irritated eye
28 Disturbed or impaired vision

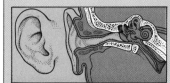

## Ear and hearing symptoms

29 Earache
30 Noises in the ear
31 Deafness

## Mouth, tongue and throat symptoms

33 Sore throat
38 Toothache
39 Difficulty swallowing
40 Sore mouth or tongue

## Skin, hair and nail symptoms

7 Excessive sweating
8 Itching
9 Lumps and swellings
21 Hair and scalp problems
22 Nail problems
23 General skin problems
24 Spots and rashes
25 Raised spots or lumps on the skin
26 Rash with fever
75 Skin changes in pregnancy

## Muscle, bone and joint symptoms

56 Back pain
57 Painful or stiff neck
58 Painful arm
59 Painful knee
60 Painful leg
61 Painful or swollen joints
62 Foot problems
80 Ankle-swelling in pregnancy

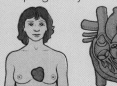

## Heart symptoms

54 Palpitations
55 Chest pain

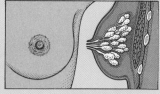
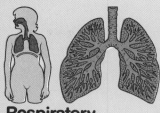

## Respiratory symptoms

32 Runny nose
33 Sore throat
34 Hoarseness or loss of voice
35 Wheezing
36 Coughing
37 Difficulty breathing
55 Chest pain

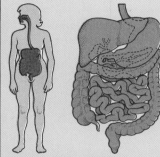

## Abdominal and digestive symptoms

41 Vomiting
42 Recurrent vomiting
43 Abdominal pain
44 Recurrent abdominal pain
45 Swollen abdomen
46 Excess gas
47 Diarrhea
48 Constipation
49 Abnormal-looking bowel movements
50 Anal problems
74 Nausea and vomiting in pregnancy
77 Heartburn in pregnancy

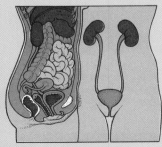

## Urinary symptoms

51 Abnormally frequent urination
52 Painful urination
53 Poor bladder control

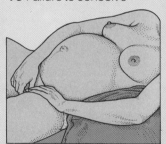

## Breast symptoms

63 Breast problems
82 Breast-feeding problems

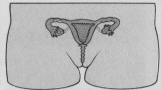

## Gynecologic symptoms

64 Absent periods
65 Heavy periods
66 Painful periods
67 Irregular vaginal bleeding
68 Abnormal vaginal discharge
69 Genital irritation

## Sexual symptoms

70 Painful intercourse
71 Loss of interest in sex
72 Choosing a contraceptive method
73 Failure to conceive

## Pregnancy symptoms

74 Nausea and vomiting in pregnancy
75 Skin changes in pregnancy
76 Back pain in pregnancy
77 Heartburn in pregnancy
78 Vaginal bleeding in pregnancy
79 Shortness of breath in pregnancy
80 Ankle-swelling in pregnancy
81 Am I in labor?
82 Breast-feeding problems
83 Depression after childbirth

# 3 Chart index

Consult this index if you think that you know the correct name for your symptom. The chart titles and their numbers are listed alphabetically together with possible alternative names for symptoms (for example, *Raised temperature* for *Fever*). In this section you will also find the titles of information boxes within the diagnostic charts.

## A

Abdomen, swollen **45**
Abdominal pain **43, 44;**
  recurrent **44**
Abnormal-looking bowel
  movements **49**
Abnormal-looking urine **51**
Abnormally frequent urination
  **51**
Abnormal vaginal
  discharge **68**
Absent periods **64**
Acne **23**
Am I in labor? **81**
Anal problems **50**
Ankle-swelling in pregnancy
  **80**
Anxiety **20**
Arm, painful **58**

## B

Back pain **56, 76**
Back pain in pregnancy **76**
Bad breath **40**
Balance, loss of **12**
Bladder control, lack of **53**
Bleeding, irregular vaginal
  **67, 78**
Blood, coughing up **36**
Blood in bowel
  movements **49**
Blood in vomit **41**
Body odor **7**
Bowel, irritable **44**
Bowel movements,
  abnormal-looking **49;**
  blood in **49;** hard **48;** soft **47**
Breast-feeding problems **82**
Breast problems **63**
Breathing, difficulty **35, 37, 79**
Breathlessness in
  pregnancy **79**
Bruising **24**

## C

Chest pain **55**
Choosing a contraceptive
  method **72**
Conceive, failure to **73**
Confusion **16**
Constipation **48**
Contraception **72**
Coughing **36**
Coughing up blood **36**

## D

Deafness **31**
Depression **19, 83;**
  postpartum **83**
Depression after childbirth **83**

Diarrhea **47**
Difficulty breathing **37**
Difficulty sleeping **5**
Difficulty speaking **17**
Difficulty swallowing **39**
Discharge, abnormal
  vaginal **68**
Disturbed vision **28**
Disturbing feelings **18**
Disturbing thoughts **18**
Dizziness **12**
Drowsiness **2**

## E

Ear, noises in the **30**
Earache **29**
Eczema **23, 24**
Elbow, painful **58**
Excess gas **46**
Excessive sweating **7**
Eye, painful or irritated **27**
Eye problems **27, 28**
Eyestrain **27**

## F

Face, pain in the **15**
Failure to conceive **73**
Fainting **10**
Faintness **10**
Feelings, disturbing **18**
Feeling under the weather **1**
Fertility problems **73**
Fever **6, 26**
Fever, rash with **26**
Foot problems **62**
Forgetfulness **16**

## G

Gas, excess **46**
General skin problems **23**
Genital irritation **69**

## H

Hemorrhoids **50**
Hair problems **21**
Headache **11**
Heartburn in pregnancy **77**
Heart flutterings **54**
Heavy periods **65**
High temperature **6**
Hoarseness **34**

## I

Impaired vision **28**
Intercourse, painful **70**
Irregular vaginal bleeding **67**
Irritable bowel **44**
Irritated eye **27**
Irritation, genital **69**
Itching **8**

## J

Joints, painful or swollen **61**

## K

Knee, painful **59**

## L

Labor **81**
Lack of bladder control **53**
Leg, painful **60**
Loss of interest in sex **71**
Loss of voice **34**
Loss of weight **3**
Lumps **9, 25, 63**

## M

Memory, impaired **16**
Mouth, sore **40**

## N

Nail problems **22**
Nausea **41, 74**
Nausea in pregnancy **74**
Neck, painful or stiff **57**
Noises in the ear **30**
Nose, runny **32**
Nosebleeds **32**
Numbness **13**

## O

Overweight **4**

## P

Painful arm **58**
Painful elbow **58**
Painful eye **27**
Painful intercourse **70**
Painful joints **61**
Painful knee **59**
Painful leg **60**
Painful neck **57**
Painful periods **66**
Painful shoulder **58**
Painful urination **52**
Pain in the face **15**
Palpitations **54**
Panic attacks **20**
Periods absent **64;** heavy **65;**
  painful **66**
Postpartum depression **83**
Pregnancy, ankle-swelling in
  **80;** back pain in **76;** heart-
  burn in **77;** nausea in **74;**
  shortness of breath in **79;**
  skin changes in **75;** vaginal
  bleeding in **78;** vomiting
  in **74**

## R

Raised lumps on the skin **25**
Raised spots on the skin **25**
Raised temperature **6**
Rashes **23, 24, 26**
Rash with fever **26**
Recurrent abdominal pain **44**
Recurrent vomiting **42**
Run down, feeling **1, 2**
Runny nose **32**

## S

Scalp problems **21**
Sex, loss of interest in **71;**
  painful **70**
Shortness of breath in
  pregnancy **79**
Shoulder, painful **58**
Sickness **41, 42**
Skin changes in
  pregnancy **75**
Skin problems **8, 9, 23, 24, 25,
  26, 69, 75**
Sleeping, difficulty **5**
Sore mouth **40**
Sore throat **33**
Sore tongue **40**
Speaking, difficulty **17**
Spots **23, 24, 25**
Stomachache **43, 44**
Stiff neck **57**
Stress **2, 19, 20**
Swallowing, difficulty **39**
Sweating, excessive **7**
Swellings **9, 63**
Swollen abdomen **45**
Swollen joints **61**

## T

Temperature, high **6**
Tension **20**
Thoughts, disturbing **18**
Throat, sore **33**
Tingling **13**
Tiredness **2**
Tiredness in early
  pregnancy **2**
Tongue, sore **40**
Toothache **38**
Trembling **14**
Twitching **14**

## U

Urinary problems **51, 52, 53**
Urination, abnormally
  frequent **51;** painful **52;**
  uncontrolled **53**

## V

Vaginal bleeding **67, 78**
Vaginal bleeding in
  pregnancy **78**
Vaginal discharge,
  abnormal **68**
Vaginal irritation **69**
Varicose veins **60**
Vision, disturbed or
  impaired **28**
Voice, loss of **34**
Vomiting **41, 42, 74;** recurrent
  **42;** in pregnancy **74**

## W

Weight, excess **4;** loss of **3**
Wheezing **35**
Worrying **20**

# 1 General medical symptoms

1 Feeling under the weather  2 Tiredness  3 Loss of weight
4 Overweight  5 Difficulty sleeping  6 Fever  7 Excessive
sweating  8 Itching  9 Lumps and swellings  10 Faintness and
fainting  11 Headache  12 Dizziness  13 Numbness or
tingling  14 Twitching and trembling  15 Pain in the face
16 Forgetfulness and confusion  17 Difficulty speaking
18 Disturbing thoughts and feelings  19 Depression
20 Anxiety  21 Hair and scalp problems  22 Nail problems
23 General skin problems  24 Spots and rashes  25 Raised
spots or lumps on the skin  26 Rash with fever  27 Painful or
irritated eye  28 Disturbed or impaired vision  29 Earache
30 Noises in the ear  31 Deafness  32 Runny nose  33 Sore
throat  34 Hoarseness or loss of voice  35 Wheezing
36 Coughing  37 Difficulty breathing  38 Toothache
39 Difficulty swallowing  40 Sore mouth or tongue  41 Vomiting
42 Recurrent vomiting  43 Abdominal pain  44 Recurrent
abdominal pain  45 Swollen abdomen  46 Excess gas
47 Diarrhea  48 Constipation  49 Abnormal-looking bowel
movements  50 Anal problems  51 Abnormally frequent
urination  52 Painful urination  53 Poor bladder control
54 Palpitations  55 Chest pain  56 Back pain  57 Painful or stiff
neck  58 Painful arm  59 Painful knee  60 Painful leg
61 Painful or swollen joints  62 Foot problems  63 Breast
problems  64 Absent periods  65 Heavy periods  66 Painful
periods  67 Irregular vaginal bleeding  68 Abnormal vaginal
discharge  69 Genital irritation

# 1 Feeling under the weather

Sometimes you may have a vague, generalized feeling of being sick without being able to locate a specific symptom such as pain. This may be the result of a minor infection or unhealthy life-style, but occasionally it may be a sign of a more serious underlying problem that requires medical treatment.

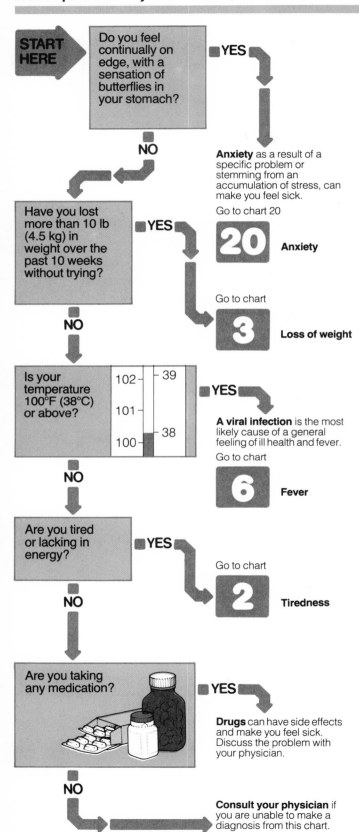

**START HERE**

Do you feel continually on edge, with a sensation of butterflies in your stomach?

**YES** →

**Anxiety** as a result of a specific problem or stemming from an accumulation of stress, can make you feel sick.

Go to chart 20

**20** Anxiety

**NO** ↓

Have you lost more than 10 lb (4.5 kg) in weight over the past 10 weeks without trying?

**YES** →

Go to chart

**3** Loss of weight

**NO** ↓

Is your temperature 100°F (38°C) or above?

| 102 | 39 |
| 101 | 38 |
| 100 | |

**YES** →

**A viral infection** is the most likely cause of a general feeling of ill health and fever.

Go to chart

**6** Fever

**NO** ↓

Are you tired or lacking in energy?

**YES** →

Go to chart

**2** Tiredness

**NO** ↓

Are you taking any medication?

**YES** →

**Drugs** can have side effects and make you feel sick. Discuss the problem with your physician.

**NO** ↓

**Consult your physician** if you are unable to make a diagnosis from this chart.

---

## THE EFFECTS OF ALCOHOL

The main immediate effect of alcohol is to dull the reactions of the brain. In small quantities, this can produce a pleasantly relaxed feeling but in larger amounts can lead to gross impairment of memory, judgment, coordination and emotional reactions.

Alcohol also widens the blood vessels, making you feel temporarily warm. However, body heat is rapidly lost from the dilated blood vessels and this can lead to severe chilling (hypothermia).

After a heavy drinking session, you are likely to feel tired and nauseated, and may have a headache, as a result of dehydration and the damaging effect of alcohol on the stomach and intestines.

### Long-term effects

Regular consumption of large amounts of alcohol can lead to the following serious health problems:

- **Obesity** is likely as a result of the high-energy value of most alcoholic drinks.
- **Liver damage** (cirrhosis, when the liver can no longer process nutrients or drugs) is almost inevitable.
- **Brain shrinkage** has been observed in many heavy drinkers.
- **Addiction** with accompanying social problems is a real risk for even moderate regular drinkers.

### Women and alcohol

Excessive alcohol consumption has special dangers for women. It is now known that women are more susceptible than men to the harmful effects of alcohol on the liver. This is because of differences in the way their livers process alcohol. Apart from endangering their own health, women who drink during pregnancy risk damaging the unborn baby. Even small amounts of alcohol may increase the chance of a baby being born underweight and mentally retarded.

### Maximum safe alcohol intake

Anyone who regularly drinks more than 3 alcoholic drinks or goes on drinking binges is risking serious health problems. For safety, keep your drinking at a much lower level.

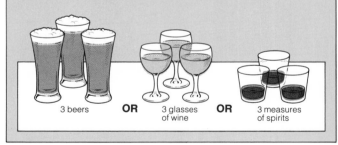

3 beers **OR** 3 glasses of wine **OR** 3 measures of spirits

---

## BLOOD ANALYSIS

Blood is the principal transport medium of the body. It carries oxygen, nutrients and other vital substances to the body tissues and carries waste products away. The blood is composed of three principal parts: red cells containing the red pigment (hemoglobin), which carries oxygen; the white cells (which fight infection) and platelets (which fight infection and seal damaged blood vessels); and the plasma, a yellowish fluid in which the blood cells, nutrients, chemicals and waste products are suspended.

Modern techniques for counting the numbers of different types of blood cells contained in a blood sample – a procedure known as a blood count – can help in the diagnosis of blood disorders. And examination of the chemicals in the plasma can give clues to diseases of many other parts of the body.

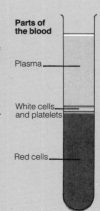

**Parts of the blood**

Plasma

White cells and platelets

Red cells

# 2 Tiredness

Consult this chart if you feel tired or lacking in energy during the day or if you spend more time asleep than you normally do. Lethargy is a common symptom of many disorders, some that require medical treatment. Sudden severe drowsiness is a serious symptom and requires prompt medical attention.

continued from previous column

**START HERE** → **Could you be suffering from sleeplessness?**

**YES** → **Insufficient or disturbed sleep** for more than a few days, for instance, as a result of jet lag, is almost certain to make you feel tired during the day. A night or two of sound, uninterrupted sleep will probably make you feel much better. If you have difficulty getting to sleep or if you regularly wake during the night, Go to chart

 **5** **Difficulty sleeping**.

**NO** ↓

**Do you have two or more of the following symptoms?**
- feeling the cold more than you used to
- thinning or brittle hair
- unexplained weight gain
- dry skin

**YES** → **Hypothyroidism** (underactive thyroid gland), a problem that is most likely to occur in middle-aged women, is a possibility. Consult your physician.

**Treatment:** If hypothyroidism is diagnosed, your physician will probably prescribe tablets of synthetic thyroid hormones. These tablets will make you feel much better in a few days, and after a few months you should have returned to normal health. However, it will probably be necessary to keep taking the tablets.

**NO** ↓

**Do you have two or more of the following symptoms?**
- paleness
- faintness
- breathlessness
- palpitations

**YES** → **Anemia** is a possibility, especially if you have heavy periods, eat a restricted diet or have had blood loss. Consult your physician.

**Treatment:** Your physician will probably take a sample of blood for analysis (see *Blood analysis*, opposite). If you are found to have anemia due to iron deficiency, your physician may give you iron in the form of tablets or injections. In addition, he or she will probably advise you to make sure that you eat plenty of iron-rich foods such as meat, whole-grain bread, dried fruits and green leafy vegetables. Other forms of anemia require laboratory investigation before treatment can be given.

**NO** ↓

**Do you drink more than 3 small glasses of wine, 3 small beers or 3 shots of whiskey (or the equivalent) most days?**

**YES** → **Regular consumption of alcohol**, even in seemingly moderate quantities, can have a depressant effect, making you feel tired (see also the box on *The effects of alcohol*, opposite).

**Self-help:** Cutting out alcohol for a week or so and making sure that you get enough sleep should make you feel better. If you find it hard to cut down or if you have difficulty getting to sleep without the help of alcohol, consult your physician.

**NO** ↓ *Go to next column*

---

**Do you have one or more of the following symptoms?**
- inability to concentrate or make decisions
- lack of interest in sex
- recurrent headaches
- feeling low or "blue"

**YES** → **Depression** can make you feel tired and run down.

Go to chart

 **19** **Depression**.

**NO** ↓

### TIREDNESS IN EARLY PREGNANCY

Tiredness is an almost universal symptom of early pregnancy. Some women notice it even before the pregnancy has been confirmed. So, if you are feeling tired for no apparent reason, and you have missed a period, consider the possibility that you may be pregnant.

Tiredness in pregnancy is a normal reaction to the major changes in your body, and does not indicate any special problem. The best way of coping with it is to take more rest. Try taking an afternoon nap or go to bed an hour or so earlier. Most women start to feel more energetic by the fourth month of pregnancy, although tiredness is likely to return in the final 6 weeks before delivery.

**Have you been working hard without a break for several weeks?**

**YES** → **Overworking** for an extended period has probably caused your tiredness. Women who work and who have demanding children or relatives to care for often become run down without realizing it.

**Self-help:** Try to take some time off, if possible, or rearrange your routine to allow yourself more time for relaxation. If you find it difficult to arrange for help at home, discuss the problem with your physician who may be able to organize some help for you.

**NO** ↓

**Have you recently recovered from an infectious illness, for example, the flu or infectious mononucleosis?**

**YES** → **Recovery** from many such illnesses can take several weeks. During this period you are likely to feel tired and depressed.

**Self-help:** Do not expect too much of yourself at first. Make sure that you eat a nourishing diet and take things easy until you feel better. If symptoms persist for more than a month, consult your physician.

**NO** ↓

**Consult your physician** if you are unable to make a diagnosis from this chart.

# 3 Loss of weight

Minor fluctuations in weight of only a few pounds, as a result of temporary changes in the amount of exercise you take or the amount of food you eat, are normal. However, more severe unintentional weight loss, especially when combined with loss of appetite or other symptoms, usually requires medical attention. Consult this chart if you have lost more than 10 lb (4.5 kg) in a period of 10 weeks or less, or if you have any of the signs of weight loss described in the box on the facing page.

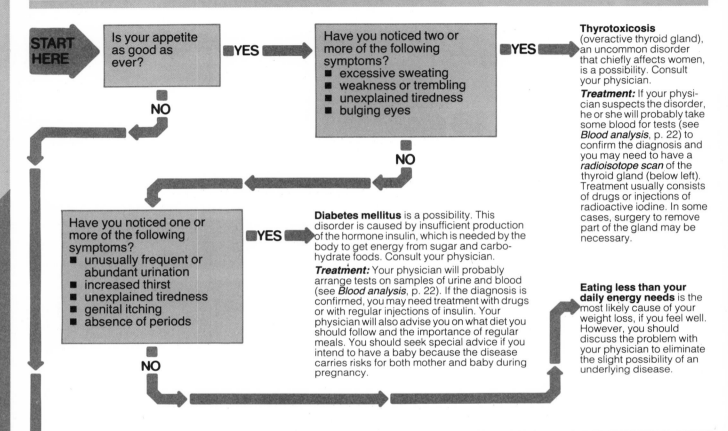

**START HERE**

**Is your appetite as good as ever?**

YES → **Have you noticed two or more of the following symptoms?**
- excessive sweating
- weakness or trembling
- unexplained tiredness
- bulging eyes

YES → **Thyrotoxicosis** (overactive thyroid gland), an uncommon disorder that chiefly affects women, is a possibility. Consult your physician.
*Treatment:* If your physician suspects the disorder, he or she will probably take some blood for tests (see *Blood analysis*, p. 22) to confirm the diagnosis and you may need to have a *radioisotope scan* of the thyroid gland (below left). Treatment usually consists of drugs or injections of radioactive iodine. In some cases, surgery to remove part of the gland may be necessary.

NO (from appetite question)

NO (from symptoms question)

**Have you noticed one or more of the following symptoms?**
- unusually frequent or abundant urination
- increased thirst
- unexplained tiredness
- genital itching
- absence of periods

YES → **Diabetes mellitus** is a possibility. This disorder is caused by insufficient production of the hormone insulin, which is needed by the body to get energy from sugar and carbohydrate foods. Consult your physician.
*Treatment:* Your physician will probably arrange tests on samples of urine and blood (see *Blood analysis*, p. 22). If the diagnosis is confirmed, you may need treatment with drugs or with regular injections of insulin. Your physician will also advise you on what diet you should follow and the importance of regular meals. You should seek special advice if you intend to have a baby because the disease carries risks for both mother and baby during pregnancy.

**Eating less than your daily energy needs** is the most likely cause of your weight loss, if you feel well. However, you should discuss the problem with your physician to eliminate the slight possibility of an underlying disease.

NO

---

### RADIOISOTOPE SCAN

Physicians sometimes use this type of scan to find out whether and how a gland or organ is malfunctioning. A radioactive chemical is injected into the bloodstream and is absorbed by the organ being examined. This organ is then scanned with specialized equipment to determine whether or not the chemical is being absorbed evenly and normally. The result of the scan is shown either on photographs or on a television screen.

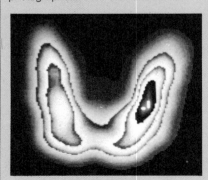

The dark area in this scan of a thyroid gland shows a possible thyroid nodule.

---

### WEIGHT LOSS IN PREGNANCY

Most women lose some weight in the first 3 months of pregnancy, as a result mainly of loss of appetite, nausea and vomiting. This usually is not considered a problem unless you lose more than 8 lb (about 4 kg) or are extremely thin. In this case it is advisable to consult your physician, because it may mean that persistent vomiting is preventing you from obtaining adequate nourishment. Nausea and vomiting normally subside by the 12th week of pregnancy and by the 14th to 16th week you should begin to gain about 1 lb (about 0.5 kg) a week, until about the 38th week.

### Abnormal weight loss

If you fail to gain weight at a satisfactory rate or if you lose weight after the first 3 months, you should consult your physician. He or she will ensure that you are eating properly and may arrange for tests, including urine and *blood analysis* (p.22) and possibly an *ultrasound scan* (p. 136) to make sure that the placenta is functioning properly and that the baby is developing normally. It is extremely important for you to get prenatal checkups throughout pregnancy so that a close watch may be kept on your weight gain and action taken when necessary.

**Pattern of weight gain and loss in pregnancy**

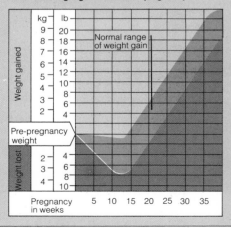

Go to next page

*Continued from previous page*

Have you noticed one or more of these symptoms?
- recurrent bouts of diarrhea
- recurrent constipation
- recurrent abdominal pain
- blood in the stools
- recurrent nausea or vomiting

**■YES■**

**NO**

**CONSULT YOUR PHYSICIAN WITHOUT DELAY!**
**A digestive tract disorder** may be causing your weight loss. Your intestines may be inflamed or you may have an ulcer, but there is also a possibility of a tumor, especially if you are over 40.

**Treatment:** Your physician will probably arrange for a variety of diagnostic tests. These may include analysis of samples of blood (p. 22) and bowel movements, *barium X rays* (p. 83) and possibly *sigmoidoscopy* (p. 92).

Have you noticed two or more of the following symptoms?
- profuse sweating at night
- recurrent raised temperature
- general feeling of ill health
- persistent cough
- blood in phlegm

**■YES■**

**NO**

**CONSULT YOUR PHYSICIAN WITHOUT DELAY!**
**A chronic lung infection,** such as tuberculosis or brucellosis, or another chronic infection, is possible.

**Treatment:** Your physician will probably take samples of blood and phlegm for analysis. You may also be given a *chest X ray* (p. 73) and a special skin test for tuberculosis. If you are found to have tuberculosis, you will be given a long course of special medications. With prompt treatment, complete recovery in a few months is probable.

Do you have one or more of the following symptoms?
- feeling low or "blue"
- difficulty sleeping
- lack of interest in sex
- inability to concentrate or make decisions

**■YES■**

**NO**

**Depression** can sometimes cause a marked loss of appetite, leading to weight loss.

Go to chart

**19** **Depression**.

**Consult your physician** if you are unable to make a diagnosis from this chart.

---

### EXERCISE AND WEIGHT LOSS
For those who are overweight (see p. 27) exercise is a useful accompaniment to a planned reducing diet. While exercise alone will not solve a serious weight problem, it will boost the amount of energy (calories) you burn and will help tone up slack muscles. But if you are already thin, further weight loss may be unhealthy. It is therefore important for those involved in strenuous physical activity—for example, dancers and athletes—to ensure that they eat an adequate diet that takes account of their increased energy requirements.

If you increase your energy output without a corresponding increase in your intake of food, the body burns up fat reserves and the result is weight loss.

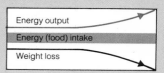

Energy output
Energy (food) intake
Weight loss

---

### ANOREXIA NERVOSA
Anorexia is a psychological disturbance in which a person (most commonly a teenage girl or young woman) refuses food because of an irrational fear of putting on weight. An anorectic convinces herself that she is too fat, that she has not lost weight even though she has, and that there is nothing wrong with her even when she has lost an excessive amount of weight. Many young women go through a temporary phase of excessive dieting, but only a minority develop anorexia nervosa, which can lead to a dangerous loss of weight, hormonal disturbances and even death.

**The signs of anorexia**
The illness usually starts with normal dieting, but the anorectic eats less each day. She does this because she thinks that her arms or legs are still too fat. The less she eats, the less she wants to eat and, even if her figure becomes skeletal, she still sees herself as fat and is terrified of putting on weight. She may be reluctant to undress in front of others in order to conceal weight loss. To avoid family pressure to eat sensibly she may hide food and throw it away. Or she may eat a great deal of food and then make herself vomit after meals, a variation of anorexia known as bulimia. Anorectics often take large quantities of laxatives to keep their weight down.

As weight loss progresses, most anorectics cease to have periods. Skin may become sallow and a fine down may appear on the body. Without treatment, many anorectics become severely depressed and in some cases suicidal.

**How you can help**
If you know someone who has an unrealistic image of herself as being too fat and who seems to be dieting excessively, although already painfully thin, try to persuade her to consult a physician. While she may be unwilling to act on your advice, you should persevere until she does, because this can be a life-threatening condition.

An anorectic sees herself as overweight, even though in reality she is extremely thin.

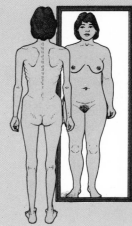

---

### SIGNS OF WEIGHT LOSS
If you lose weight without deliberately attempting to slim down, you should always take the matter seriously, especially if other symptoms suggest the possibility of illness. If you do not weigh yourself regularly, the following signs may indicate that you have lost weight:
- People remark on your changed appearance.
- Your cheeks become sunken.
- Your skirts or pants become loose around the waist.
- Your shirt collars become loose.
- You need a smaller bra size.

# 4 Overweight

Normally, fat accounts for no more than 25 percent of the weight of an adult woman. Any more than this is both unnecessary and unhealthy, increasing the risk of diseases such as diabetes, high blood pressure and arthritis. Most people reach their ideal weight in their teens and gradually gain a little weight as they get older, reaching their heaviest at about 50. Consult this chart if you weigh more than the healthy weight for your height shown in the chart below, or if you can pinch a fold of flesh that is more than an inch thick on your abdomen. In most cases, weight gain is due simply to eating more than you need and can be remedied by a balanced reducing diet, but occasionally there may be a medical reason for putting on weight.

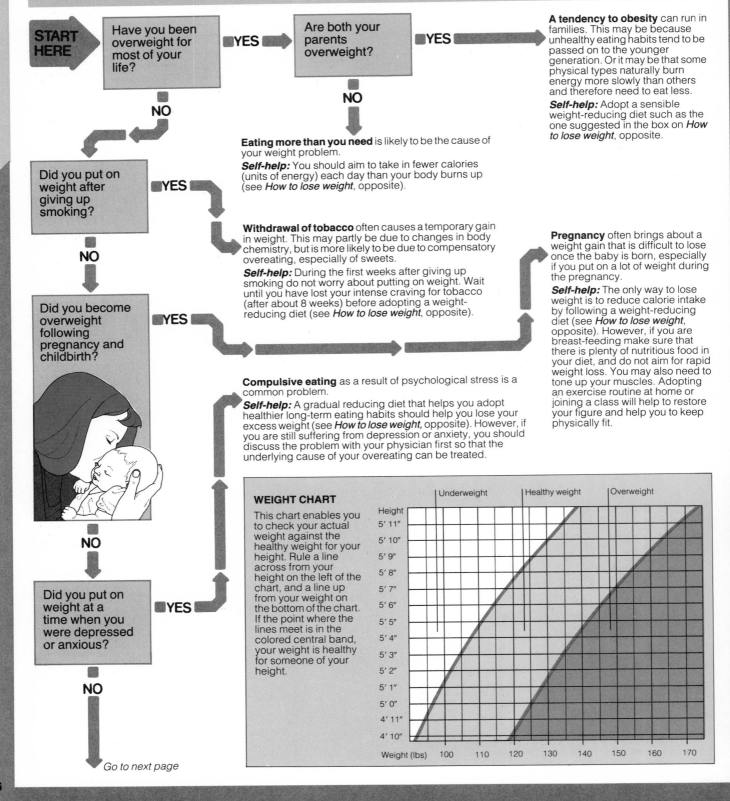

**START HERE**

Have you been overweight for most of your life?

**YES** →

Are both your parents overweight?

**YES** →

**A tendency to obesity** can run in families. This may be because unhealthy eating habits tend to be passed on to the younger generation. Or it may be that some physical types naturally burn energy more slowly than others and therefore need to eat less.

*Self-help:* Adopt a sensible weight-reducing diet such as the one suggested in the box on *How to lose weight*, opposite.

**NO**

**NO**

**Eating more than you need** is likely to be the cause of your weight problem.

*Self-help:* You should aim to take in fewer calories (units of energy) each day than your body burns up (see *How to lose weight*, opposite).

Did you put on weight after giving up smoking?

**YES**

**Withdrawal of tobacco** often causes a temporary gain in weight. This may partly be due to changes in body chemistry, but is more likely to be due to compensatory overeating, especially of sweets.

*Self-help:* During the first weeks after giving up smoking do not worry about putting on weight. Wait until you have lost your intense craving for tobacco (after about 8 weeks) before adopting a weight-reducing diet (see *How to lose weight*, opposite).

**Pregnancy** often brings about a weight gain that is difficult to lose once the baby is born, especially if you put on a lot of weight during the pregnancy.

*Self-help:* The only way to lose weight is to reduce calorie intake by following a weight-reducing diet (see *How to lose weight*, opposite). However, if you are breast-feeding make sure that there is plenty of nutritious food in your diet, and do not aim for rapid weight loss. You may also need to tone up your muscles. Adopting an exercise routine at home or joining a class will help to restore your figure and help you to keep physically fit.

**NO**

Did you become overweight following pregnancy and childbirth?

**YES**

**Compulsive eating** as a result of psychological stress is a common problem.

*Self-help:* A gradual reducing diet that helps you adopt healthier long-term eating habits should help you lose your excess weight (see *How to lose weight,* opposite). However, if you are still suffering from depression or anxiety, you should discuss the problem with your physician first so that the underlying cause of your overeating can be treated.

**NO**

Did you put on weight at a time when you were depressed or anxious?

**YES**

**WEIGHT CHART**

This chart enables you to check your actual weight against the healthy weight for your height. Rule a line across from your height on the left of the chart, and a line up from your weight on the bottom of the chart. If the point where the lines meet is in the colored central band, your weight is healthy for someone of your height.

| Height | Underweight | Healthy weight | Overweight |
|---|---|---|---|
| 5' 11" | | | |
| 5' 10" | | | |
| 5' 9" | | | |
| 5' 8" | | | |
| 5' 7" | | | |
| 5' 6" | | | |
| 5' 5" | | | |
| 5' 4" | | | |
| 5' 3" | | | |
| 5' 2" | | | |
| 5' 1" | | | |
| 5' 0" | | | |
| 4' 11" | | | |
| 4' 10" | | | |

Weight (lbs)   100   110   120   130   140   150   160   170

**NO**

*Go to next page*

*Continued from previous page*

Did the weight gain follow a change from a physically active life or strenuous job to a more sedentary life-style or work?

**YES**

**Energy requirements** of the body vary according to the amount of exercise your daily routine involves. For instance, if you have a desk job, your average daily calorie requirement may be only 2,000 calories, but if you have a more active job you may require 2,500 calories.

*Self-help:* Adjusting your food intake to take account of your reduced energy requirements should help you to lose the weight you have put on. This may mean changing eating habits you have developed over many years and it may take a little while for you to become accustomed to your new diet. See *How to lose weight*, right, for some advice on a healthy reducing diet. You should also try to incorporate some physical exercise into your new routine to help keep your muscles firm and to assist weight loss.

**NO**

Have you noticed two or more of the following symptoms since you began to put on weight?
- feeling the cold more than you used to
- thinning or brittle hair
- dry skin
- unexplained tiredness

**YES**

**Hypothyroidism** (underactive thyroid gland), a disorder that is most common in middle-aged women, is a possibility. Consult your physician.

*Treatment:* If hypothyroidism is diagnosed, your physician will probably prescribe tablets of synthetic thyroid hormones. These tablets will help your body to burn up excess fat and after a few months you should have returned to your normal weight. However, it will probably be necessary to keep on taking the tablets indefinitely.

**NO**

Are you taking any medications?

**YES**

**Certain drugs**, particularly steroids prescribed for problems such as asthma or rheumatoid arthritis, can cause weight gain as a side effect. Discuss the problem with your physician.

**NO**

Are you over 40 years old?

**YES**

**Growing older** is often accompanied by a gradual gain in weight. This is more than likely because you begin to exercise less at a time in your life when your body is beginning to take longer to burn up food.

*Self-help:* Reduce your food intake to correspond with your lower energy consumption (see *How to lose weight*, above).

**NO**

**Overeating** is the likely cause of your excess weight.

*Self-help:* Follow the recommended reducing diet (see *How to lose weight,* above). If after a month you fail to lose weight, consult your physician, who will find out if the problem is due to any underlying disorder.

---

## HOW TO LOSE WEIGHT

If you are fat, it is because your body is not using all the energy you feed it. To lose weight you must expend more energy than you take in, first by changing your diet, second by exercising more. It is best to avoid crash diets, which have no lasting effect because they do not encourage you to adopt healthy new habits. You will find it more helpful to follow this step-by-step diet, which is designed to help you change your eating habits over time.

**1** Try to cut out, or at least cut down on, all foods in group 1, the sweet or rich foods. Reduce your daily alcohol intake to no more than two 12-oz cans of beer, two 6-oz glasses of wine or 2 shots (1.5 oz) of whiskey (or the equivalent). If you drink hard liquor, use low calorie mixers or unsweetened fruit juices. Eat normal portions of food from groups 2 and 3.

**2** If you have not lost any weight after 2 weeks, stop having any group 1 foods, halve your helpings of group 2 foods and eat as much as you want from group 3. Cut down further on (or eliminate) your consumption of alcohol.

**3** If you fail to lose weight after 2 more weeks, halve your helpings of group 3 foods and eat as little as possible from group 2. Consult your physician if you fail to lose weight after 4 more weeks.

| Meat | Vegetables | Dairy foods | Fish | Other |
|---|---|---|---|---|
| **Group 1 foods** | | | | |
| Visible fat on any meat<br>Bacon<br>Duck, goose<br>Sausages, salami<br>Pâtés | | Butter<br>Cream<br>Ice cream | | Thick gravies or sauces<br>Fried food<br>Sugar, candies<br>Cakes, pies, cookies<br>Puddings<br>Canned fruits in syrup<br>Dried fruits<br>Nuts<br>Jams, syrups<br>Carbonated drinks<br>Sherbets |
| **Group 2 foods** | | | | |
| Lean beef<br>Lamb<br>Pork | Beans<br>Lentils | Eggs<br>Cheeses (other than cottage cheese)<br>Whole milk | Oily fish (e.g., herring, mackerel, sardines, tuna packed in oil) | Pasta or rice<br>Soups<br>Breads, crackers<br>Unsweetened cereals<br>Margarine<br>Polyunsaturated vegetable oils |
| **Group 3 foods** | | | | |
| Poultry other than duck or goose (not including the skin) | Potatoes<br>Vegetables (raw or lightly cooked)<br>Clear or vegetable-only soups | Skim milk<br>Yogurt<br>Cottage cheese | Nonoily fish (e.g., haddock, perch, cod)<br>Shellfish (e.g., crab, shrimp)<br>Tuna packed in water | Bran<br>Fresh fruit<br>Unsweetened fruit juice |

# 5 Difficulty sleeping

It is quite common to have an occasional night when you find it difficult to get to sleep and this need not be a cause for concern. Consult this chart if you regularly have difficulty falling asleep at night or if you wake during the night or early in the morning (a problem sometimes known as insomnia).

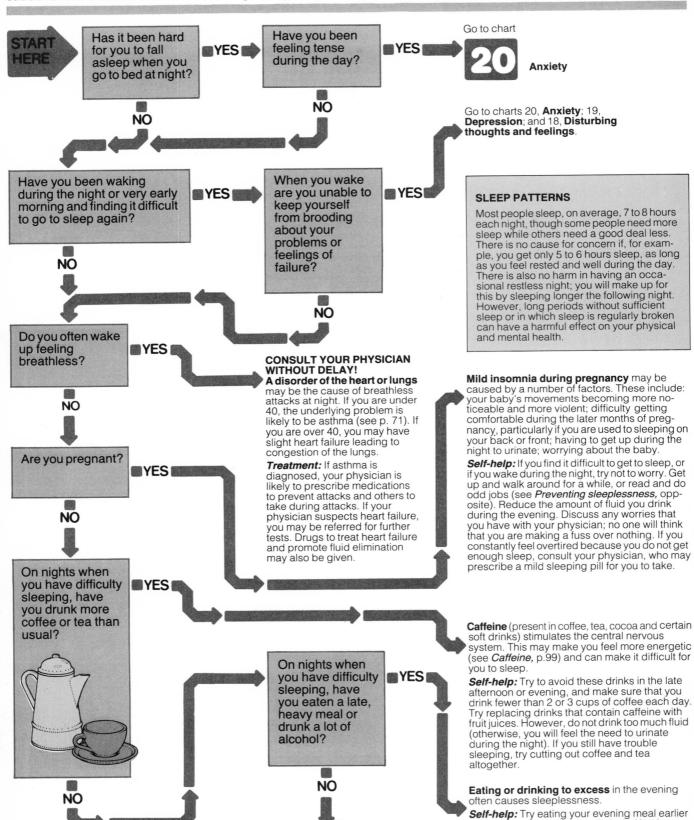

**START HERE**

**Has it been hard for you to fall asleep when you go to bed at night?** — YES → **Have you been feeling tense during the day?** — YES → Go to chart **20** Anxiety

NO (from feeling tense) and NO (from hard to fall asleep)

Go to charts 20, **Anxiety**; 19, **Depression**; and 18, **Disturbing thoughts and feelings**.

**Have you been waking during the night or very early morning and finding it difficult to go to sleep again?** — YES → **When you wake are you unable to keep yourself from brooding about your problems or feelings of failure?** — YES →

NO

NO

**Do you often wake up feeling breathless?** — YES →

NO

**Are you pregnant?** — YES →

NO

**On nights when you have difficulty sleeping, have you drunk more coffee or tea than usual?** — YES →

NO

**On nights when you have difficulty sleeping, have you eaten a late, heavy meal or drunk a lot of alcohol?** — YES →

NO

*Go to next page*

## SLEEP PATTERNS

Most people sleep, on average, 7 to 8 hours each night, though some people need more sleep while others need a good deal less. There is no cause for concern if, for example, you get only 5 to 6 hours sleep, as long as you feel rested and well during the day. There is also no harm in having an occasional restless night; you will make up for this by sleeping longer the following night. However, long periods without sufficient sleep or in which sleep is regularly broken can have a harmful effect on your physical and mental health.

**CONSULT YOUR PHYSICIAN WITHOUT DELAY!**
**A disorder of the heart or lungs** may be the cause of breathless attacks at night. If you are under 40, the underlying problem is likely to be asthma (see p. 71). If you are over 40, you may have slight heart failure leading to congestion of the lungs.

***Treatment:*** If asthma is diagnosed, your physician is likely to prescribe medications to prevent attacks and others to take during attacks. If your physician suspects heart failure, you may be referred for further tests. Drugs to treat heart failure and promote fluid elimination may also be given.

**Mild insomnia during pregnancy** may be caused by a number of factors. These include: your baby's movements becoming more noticeable and more violent; difficulty getting comfortable during the later months of pregnancy, particularly if you are used to sleeping on your back or front; having to get up during the night to urinate; worrying about the baby.

***Self-help:*** If you find it difficult to get to sleep, or if you wake during the night, try not to worry. Get up and walk around for a while, or read and do odd jobs (see *Preventing sleeplessness,* opposite). Reduce the amount of fluid you drink during the evening. Discuss any worries that you have with your physician; no one will think that you are making a fuss over nothing. If you constantly feel overtired because you do not get enough sleep, consult your physician, who may prescribe a mild sleeping pill for you to take.

**Caffeine** (present in coffee, tea, cocoa and certain soft drinks) stimulates the central nervous system. This may make you feel more energetic (see *Caffeine,* p.99) and can make it difficult for you to sleep.

***Self-help:*** Try to avoid these drinks in the late afternoon or evening, and make sure that you drink fewer than 2 or 3 cups of coffee each day. Try replacing drinks that contain caffeine with fruit juices. However, do not drink too much fluid (otherwise, you will feel the need to urinate during the night). If you still have trouble sleeping, try cutting out coffee and tea altogether.

**Eating or drinking to excess** in the evening often causes sleeplessness.

***Self-help:*** Try eating your evening meal earlier and reducing your food and alcohol intake.

*Continued from previous page*

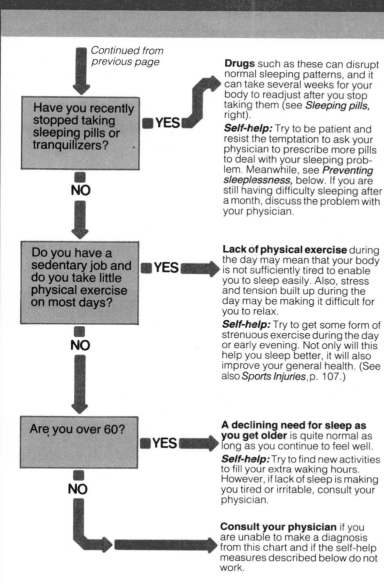

**Have you recently stopped taking sleeping pills or tranquilizers?** ▸ **YES** ▸

**NO**

**Do you have a sedentary job and do you take little physical exercise on most days?** ▸ **YES** ▸

**NO**

**Are you over 60?** ▸ **YES** ▸

**NO**

**Drugs** such as these can disrupt normal sleeping patterns, and it can take several weeks for your body to readjust after you stop taking them (see *Sleeping pills,* right).

**Self-help:** Try to be patient and resist the temptation to ask your physician to prescribe more pills to deal with your sleeping problem. Meanwhile, see *Preventing sleeplessness,* below. If you are still having difficulty sleeping after a month, discuss the problem with your physician.

**Lack of physical exercise** during the day may mean that your body is not sufficiently tired to enable you to sleep easily. Also, stress and tension built up during the day may be making it difficult for you to relax.

**Self-help:** Try to get some form of strenuous exercise during the day or early evening. Not only will this help you sleep better, it will also improve your general health. (See also *Sports Injuries,*p. 107.)

**A declining need for sleep as you get older** is quite normal as long as you continue to feel well.

**Self-help:** Try to find new activities to fill your extra waking hours. However, if lack of sleep is making you tired or irritable, consult your physician.

**Consult your physician** if you are unable to make a diagnosis from this chart and if the self-help measures described below do not work.

---

### SLEEPING PILLS

If you have difficulty sleeping at night, your physician may prescribe sleeping pills. These may be useful if you cannot sleep because of pain after an injury or during an illness, or at times of emotional stress – for example, following a bereavement.

**What drugs are used?**
There are two main types of drug used to treat sleeplessness: antianxiety drugs and barbiturates. Both act in a similar way, but physicians usually prefer to prescribe an antianxiety drug because of the greater danger of overdose with barbiturates.

**How do sleeping drugs work?**
All sleeping drugs work by suppressing brain function in some way. This means that the sleep you get when taking a sleeping drug is not normal and may leave you less rested than after a natural night's sleep. This also means that if you suddenly stop taking sleeping pills after having used them regularly, you may sleep restlessly and have vivid dreams while your brain readjusts to normal *sleep patterns* (opposite).

**Are sleeping pills dangerous?**
Sleeping pills that are taken on your physician's advice and according to the dosage prescribed are unlikely to do you any harm, even if taken for many years. However, you may become dependent on these drugs if you take them regularly. If you wish to stop taking them, discuss this with your physician. In addition, you should consult your physician if you have difficulty waking up in the morning or if you find that your sleeping pills no longer work as effectively as before; you may need a change of drug.
People who take sleeping pills should always remember the following safety rules:

- Never take a larger dose than prescribed.
- Never drive or operate machinery before the effects of the sleeping drugs have worn off.
- Never take alcohol with these drugs; stop drinking at least 2 hours before taking a sleeping pill and do not start to drink until at least 8 hours afterward.
- Never give your sleeping pills to others, especially children.
- Never keep your tablets on your bedside table; there is a danger that you may accidentally take an additional dose when half asleep.

---

### PREVENTING SLEEPLESSNESS

If you find that you cannot get to sleep as soon as you go to bed, try not to worry about it; this will only make matters worse. Even if you just relax or doze for a few hours you will probably be getting enough rest. The following self-help suggestions may help you get a good night's sleep:

- Try to do some form of physical exercise during the day so that your body needs rest because it is tired. A short, gentle stroll in the open air an hour or so before going to bed may also help.
- A full stomach generally is not conducive to sleep, but a warm, milky drink or even a *small* whiskey (1 ounce or less) at bedtime may help you to feel sleepy.

- Avoid heavy drinking.
- A warm bath is often relaxing. A shower may not be a good idea if it is too invigorating.
- Recreational reading, which is not associated with work or study, often makes people sleepy.
- Make sure that you are neither too hot nor too cold. Most people sleep best in a room temperature of 60 to 65°F.
- Make your environment as conducive to sleep as possible. Make sure that there are no irritating, dripping faucets or knocking radiators. A comfortable bed will help (see *Preventing backache,* p.103).
- Sex may help you relax and fall asleep.

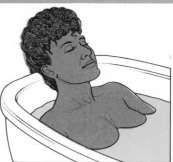

# 6 Fever

A fever (an abnormally high body temperature) can be a symptom of many diseases, but usually is a sign that your body is fighting infection. You may suspect that you have a fever if you feel hot or alternately hot, shivery and sweaty, and if you feel sick. To confirm that you have a fever, take your temperature as described below. Consult this chart if your temperature is 100°F (38°C) or above. Call your physician at once if your temperature rises above 104°F (40°C) or remains elevated for longer than 48 hours – whatever the suspected cause.

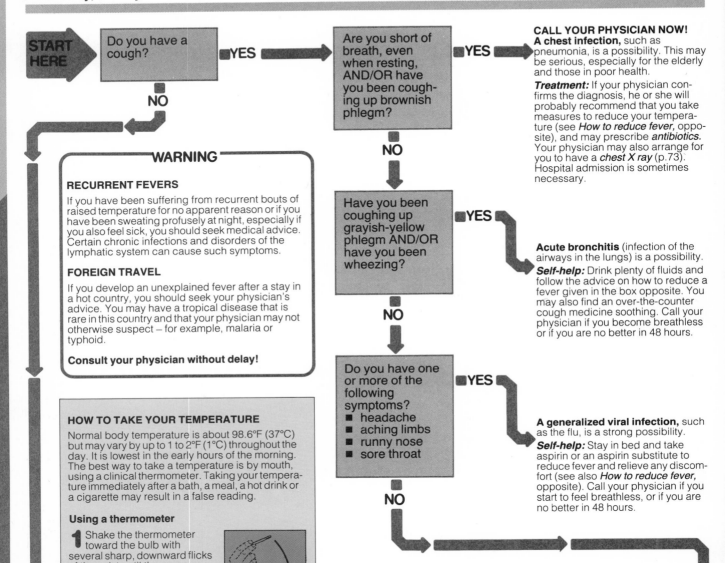

**START HERE**

**Do you have a cough?**

**YES** →

**NO** ↓

**Are you short of breath, even when resting, AND/OR have you been coughing up brownish phlegm?**

**YES** →

**NO** ↓

**CALL YOUR PHYSICIAN NOW!**
**A chest infection,** such as pneumonia, is a possibility. This may be serious, especially for the elderly and those in poor health.

***Treatment:*** If your physician confirms the diagnosis, he or she will probably recommend that you take measures to reduce your temperature (see *How to reduce fever,* opposite), and may prescribe *antibiotics.* Your physician may also arrange for you to have a *chest X ray* (p.73). Hospital admission is sometimes necessary.

**Have you been coughing up grayish-yellow phlegm AND/OR have you been wheezing?**

**YES** →

**NO** ↓

**Acute bronchitis** (infection of the airways in the lungs) is a possibility.
***Self-help:*** Drink plenty of fluids and follow the advice on how to reduce a fever given in the box opposite. You may also find an over-the-counter cough medicine soothing. Call your physician if you become breathless or if you are no better in 48 hours.

**Do you have one or more of the following symptoms?**
- headache
- aching limbs
- runny nose
- sore throat

**YES** →

**NO** ↓

**A generalized viral infection,** such as the flu, is a strong possibility.
***Self-help:*** Stay in bed and take aspirin or an aspirin substitute to reduce fever and relieve any discomfort (see also *How to reduce fever,* opposite). Call your physician if you start to feel breathless, or if you are no better in 48 hours.

## WARNING

### RECURRENT FEVERS
If you have been suffering from recurrent bouts of raised temperature for no apparent reason or if you have been sweating profusely at night, especially if you also feel sick, you should seek medical advice. Certain chronic infections and disorders of the lymphatic system can cause such symptoms.

### FOREIGN TRAVEL
If you develop an unexplained fever after a stay in a hot country, you should seek your physician's advice. You may have a tropical disease that is rare in this country and that your physician may not otherwise suspect – for example, malaria or typhoid.

**Consult your physician without delay!**

### HOW TO TAKE YOUR TEMPERATURE
Normal body temperature is about 98.6°F (37°C) but may vary by up to 1 to 2°F (1°C) throughout the day. It is lowest in the early hours of the morning. The best way to take a temperature is by mouth, using a clinical thermometer. Taking your temperature immediately after a bath, a meal, a hot drink or a cigarette may result in a false reading.

#### Using a thermometer

**1** Shake the thermometer toward the bulb with several sharp, downward flicks of the wrist until the mercury level is well below the normal mark.

**2** Place the thermometer under your tongue and make sure that your mouth is closed. Do not bite the thermometer.

**3** Remove the thermometer after 3 minutes and hold it up to the light. The top of the mercury column shows the temperature against the scale.

| 36 | 37 | 38 | 39 | 40 |
|---|---|---|---|---|
| Normal | | | Fever | |
| 97 | 98 | 99 | 100 | 101 | 102 | 103 | 104 |

**4** Finally, wash the thermometer in cool water, to which antiseptic has been added, and dry it so that it is ready to use the next time.

### LUMBAR PUNCTURE
Lumbar puncture is a test that is used to diagnose disorders of the brain and nervous system, in particular infections such as meningitis. A sample of the fluid that surrounds the brain and spinal cord is taken from the base of the spine for analysis. The area may be first numbed by local anesthetic. Then a needle is inserted between the bones of the lower spine and a small amount of fluid is drained off.

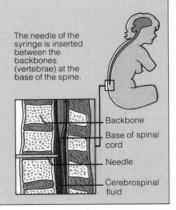

The needle of the syringe is inserted between the backbones (vertebrae) at the base of the spine.

- Backbone
- Base of spinal cord
- Needle
- Cerebrospinal fluid

*Continued from previous page column 1*

*Continued from previous page column 2*

**Do you have a severe headache?**

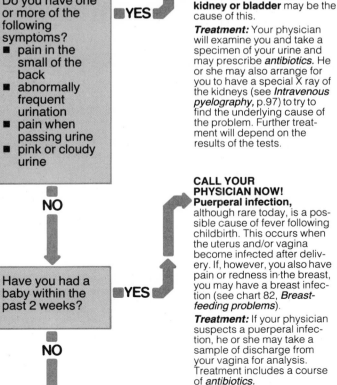

■ **YES**

**Do you have one or more of the following symptoms?**
■ pain when you bend your head forward
■ nausea or vomiting
■ dislike of bright light
■ drowsiness or confusion

■ **YES**

**CALL YOUR PHYSICIAN NOW!**
**Meningitis,** inflammation (due to infection) of the membranes surrounding the brain or spinal cord, may be the cause of such symptoms.

***Treatment:*** You will probably require a *lumbar puncture* (opposite). If the infection is found to be bacterial, you will be given *antibiotics,* possibly by intravenous drip. If the infection is viral, no specific treatment is necessary, but you will be given painkillers and intravenous fluids. Recovery normally takes 2 to 3 weeks.

**NO**

**Do you have one or more of the following symptoms?**
■ aching limbs
■ runny nose
■ sore throat

■ **YES**

**A generalized viral infection,** such as the flu, is a strong possibility.

***Self-help:*** Stay in bed and take aspirin or an aspirin substitute to reduce fever and relieve any discomfort (see also *How to reduce fever,* below). Call your physician if you start to feel breathless or if you are no better in 48 hours.

**NO**                **NO**

**Do you have a sore throat?**

■ **YES**

A **throat infection** is likely.

Go to chart

## 33   Sore throat

**NO**

**HOW TO REDUCE FEVER**

If you have a fever, whatever the suspected cause, the following self-help measures should help to lower your temperature and make you feel more comfortable.

■ Take the recommended dose of aspirin or aspirin substitute.
■ Drink plenty of cold, nonalcoholic fluids.
■ Remove excess clothing and rest in a cool room.
■ For a high fever, sponge your body with tepid water.

Consult your physician if your temperature continues to rise in spite of these measures.

**Do you have one or more of the following symptoms?**
■ pain in the small of the back
■ abnormally frequent urination
■ pain when passing urine
■ pink or cloudy urine

■ **YES**

**CONSULT YOUR PHYSICIAN WITHOUT DELAY!**
**An acute infection of the kidney or bladder** may be the cause of this.

***Treatment:*** Your physician will examine you and take a specimen of your urine and may prescribe *antibiotics.* He or she may also arrange for you to have a special X ray of the kidneys (see *Intravenous pyelography,* p.97) to try to find the underlying cause of the problem. Further treatment will depend on the results of the tests.

**Do you have pain in the lower abdomen AND/OR have you had an unusually heavy or unpleasant-smelling vaginal discharge?**

■ **YES**

**An infection of the fallopian tubes** (sometimes known as salpingitis) is a possible cause of such symptoms. Consult your physician.

***Treatment:*** Your physician will probably do a vaginal examination (p.122) and will take a sample of vaginal discharge for analysis. If tests confirm the diagnosis, you will probably be given a course of *antibiotics.*

**NO**

**CALL YOUR PHYSICIAN NOW!**
**Puerperal infection,** although rare today, is a possible cause of fever following childbirth. This occurs when the uterus and/or vagina become infected after delivery. If, however, you also have pain or redness in the breast, you may have a breast infection (see chart 82, *Breast-feeding problems*).

***Treatment:*** If your physician suspects a puerperal infection, he or she may take a sample of discharge from your vagina for analysis. Treatment includes a course of *antibiotics.*

**NO**

**Have you had a baby within the past 2 weeks?**

■ **YES**

**Have you spent most of the day in strong sunlight or in very hot conditions?**

■ **YES**

**Exposure to heat** may cause your temperature to rise. In most cases this is not serious and your temperature will return to normal if you rest for an hour in a cool room. Call your physician at once if the fever continues to rise despite attempts to lower it.

**NO**

**NO**

**Consult your physician** if you are unable to make a diagnosis from this chart and your temperature has not returned to normal within 48 hours or if it rises again.

# 7 Excessive sweating

Sweating is a natural mechanism for regulating body temperature and is the normal response to hot conditions or strenuous exercise. Some people naturally sweat more than others, so, if you have always sweated profusely, there is unlikely to be anything wrong. However, sweating that is not brought on by heat or exercise or that is more profuse than you are used to may be a sign of a number of medical conditions.

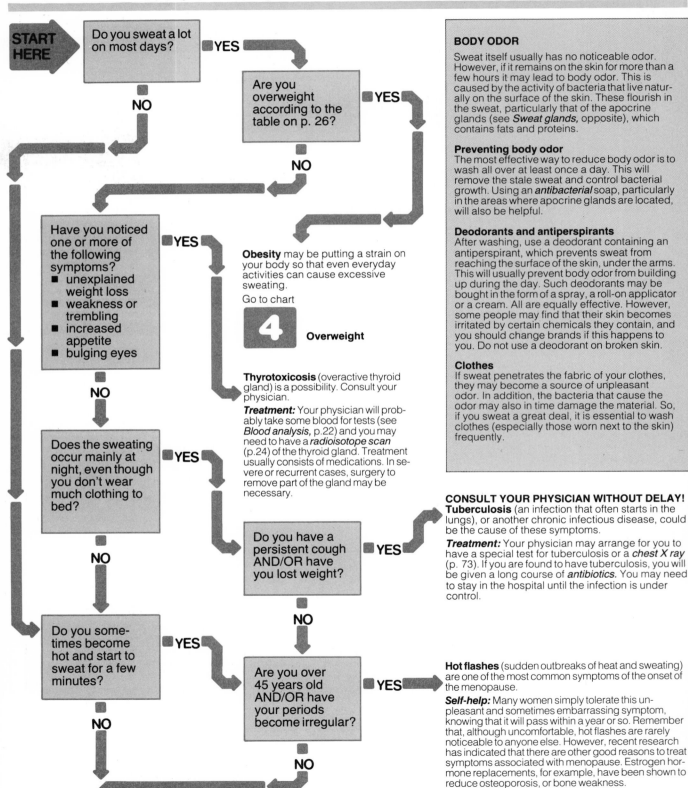

**START HERE**

**Do you sweat a lot on most days?** — **YES** →

**Are you overweight according to the table on p. 26?** — **YES** →

NO ↓ (from "Do you sweat a lot")

NO ↓ (from "Are you overweight")

**Obesity** may be putting a strain on your body so that even everyday activities can cause excessive sweating.

Go to chart

**4** Overweight

**Have you noticed one or more of the following symptoms?**
- unexplained weight loss
- weakness or trembling
- increased appetite
- bulging eyes

**YES** →

**Thyrotoxicosis** (overactive thyroid gland) is a possibility. Consult your physician.

**Treatment:** Your physician will probably take some blood for tests (see *Blood analysis*, p.22) and you may need to have a *radioisotope scan* (p.24) of the thyroid gland. Treatment usually consists of medications. In severe or recurrent cases, surgery to remove part of the gland may be necessary.

NO ↓

**Does the sweating occur mainly at night, even though you don't wear much clothing to bed?** — **YES** →

**Do you have a persistent cough AND/OR have you lost weight?** — **YES** →

**CONSULT YOUR PHYSICIAN WITHOUT DELAY!**
**Tuberculosis** (an infection that often starts in the lungs), or another chronic infectious disease, could be the cause of these symptoms.

**Treatment:** Your physician may arrange for you to have a special test for tuberculosis or a *chest X ray* (p. 73). If you are found to have tuberculosis, you will be given a long course of *antibiotics*. You may need to stay in the hospital until the infection is under control.

NO ↓

**Do you sometimes become hot and start to sweat for a few minutes?** — **YES** →

NO ↓ (from cough question)

**Are you over 45 years old AND/OR have your periods become irregular?** — **YES** →

**Hot flashes** (sudden outbreaks of heat and sweating) are one of the most common symptoms of the onset of the menopause.

**Self-help:** Many women simply tolerate this unpleasant and sometimes embarrassing symptom, knowing that it will pass within a year or so. Remember that, although uncomfortable, hot flashes are rarely noticeable to anyone else. However, recent research has indicated that there are other good reasons to treat symptoms associated with menopause. Estrogen hormone replacements, for example, have been shown to reduce osteoporosis, or bone weakness.

NO ↓

NO ↓

*Go to next page*

## BODY ODOR

Sweat itself usually has no noticeable odor. However, if it remains on the skin for more than a few hours it may lead to body odor. This is caused by the activity of bacteria that live naturally on the surface of the skin. These flourish in the sweat, particularly that of the apocrine glands (see *Sweat glands,* opposite), which contains fats and proteins.

### Preventing body odor
The most effective way to reduce body odor is to wash all over at least once a day. This will remove the stale sweat and control bacterial growth. Using an *antibacterial* soap, particularly in the areas where apocrine glands are located, will also be helpful.

### Deodorants and antiperspirants
After washing, use a deodorant containing an antiperspirant, which prevents sweat from reaching the surface of the skin, under the arms. This will usually prevent body odor from building up during the day. Such deodorants may be bought in the form of a spray, a roll-on applicator or a cream. All are equally effective. However, some people may find that their skin becomes irritated by certain chemicals they contain, and you should change brands if this happens to you. Do not use a deodorant on broken skin.

### Clothes
If sweat penetrates the fabric of your clothes, they may become a source of unpleasant odor. In addition, the bacteria that cause the odor may also in time damage the material. So, if you sweat a great deal, it is essential to wash clothes (especially those worn next to the skin) frequently.

*Continued from previous page*

**Is your temperature 100°F (38°C) or above?**

**YES** →

Sweating is the normal response to fever.

Go to chart

**6** **Fever**

**NO** ↓

**Does the excessive sweating occur only during your periods?**

**YES** →

**Changes in the hormone balance** cause increased sweating during menstruation in some women. This is no cause for concern.

**NO** ↓

---

**Did you notice the sweating after you had been drinking alcohol or taking large doses of aspirin?**

**YES** →

**Alcohol or aspirin** can cause increased sweating.

*Self-help:* If alcohol seems to be causing the problem, cut down on your drinking (see *The effects of alcohol,* p. 22). If aspirin taken for some other problem seems to be the cause of your sweating, ask your physician for advice.

**NO** ↓

**Are you wearing clothes (or are your sleep clothes) made of nylon or other man-made materials?**

**YES** →

**Synthetic materials** often cause a noticeable increase in sweating. This is because they do not absorb moisture or allow your skin to breathe.

*Self-help:* Try wearing natural fibers, such as cotton or wool, as often as possible. In addition, make sure that your clothing is loose; this will increase the circulation of air and allow the sweat to evaporate more quickly.

**NO** ↓

**Is the excessive sweating confined to your feet or hands?**

**YES** →

**A high concentration of sweat glands** on the hands and feet (see *Sweat glands,* left) makes these parts of the body react most noticeably to increases in temperature. This is no cause for concern.

*Self-help:* If your hands are sweaty, wash them frequently. The problem is likely to become worse if you worry, so try to relax. Make sure that you wash and dry your feet carefully at least once a day. It is best to avoid wearing shoes, hose and socks made of synthetic materials. If the problem is severe or causes embarrassment, consult your physician.

**NO** ↓

**Do you notice the sweating only when you are anxious or excited?**

**YES** →

**Emotional stress** can easily cause an increase in sweating. This in itself is not a cause for concern, but, if it happens regularly or causes embarrassment, consult your physician.

*Treatment:* Your physician will advise you on the best methods of controlling the sweating. He or she will also discuss with you the possible causes of any underlying anxiety and may recommend medication. (See also chart 20, *Anxiety.*)

**NO** ↓

**Are you in your teens?**

**YES** →

**The development of additional (apocrine) sweat glands during puberty** (see *Sweat glands,* left) usually causes an increase in sweating that is particularly noticeable under the arms. This is quite normal.

*Self-help:* There is no need to be embarrassed about any increased sweating. However, you will need to wash regularly and you may want to use an antiperspirant deodorant to reduce wetness and to prevent unpleasant body odor (see *Body odor,* opposite).

**NO** ↓

**Consult your physician** if you are unable to make a diagnosis from this chart and your excessive sweating continues to worry you. There is, however, not likely to be a serious cause for this symptom.

---

### SWEAT GLANDS

Sweat glands are found under the skin all over the body and release moisture (sweat) through pores in the surface of the skin. There are two types of sweat glands – eccrine and apocrine glands – and these produce different kinds of sweat.

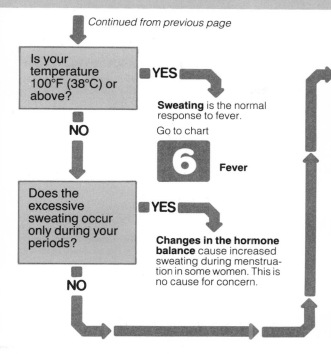

Skin surface
Hair
Pore
Sweat gland

**Eccrine glands**
Eccrine glands are found all over the body and are active from birth onward. The sweat from these glands is a clear, salty fluid containing various waste chemicals. It evaporates on the surface of the skin to reduce body temperature as necessary. The eccrine glands may also produce sweat in response to anxiety or fear. Eccrine glands are most concentrated on the forehead, palms and soles of the feet (see below), and profuse sweating is likely to become apparent first in these areas.

**Apocrine glands**
Apocrine glands become active during adolescence. They are mainly concentrated in the armpits, the groin and around the nipples (see below). These glands produce a sticky, milky fluid that contains fats and proteins. The scent from this type of gland is thought to play a role in attracting the opposite sex. However, if it is allowed to remain on the skin for long, it may interact with bacteria to produce a particularly pungent type of body odor (see *Body odor,* opposite).

**Distribution of sweat glands**

☐ Eccrine glands    ■ High concentration of eccrine glands    ▨ Apocrine glands

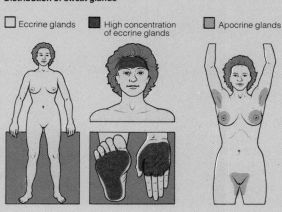

# 8 Itching

Itching (skin irritation that makes you want to scratch) is usually produced by contact with certain types of fabric or with a substance to which you are sensitive. Many skin disorders that produce a rash also cause itching.

Occasionally, itching is a sign of an underlying disease or of psychological stress. Irritation is likely to be most severe if you are hot or if your skin is dry, and is likely to be made worse by rubbing or scratching.

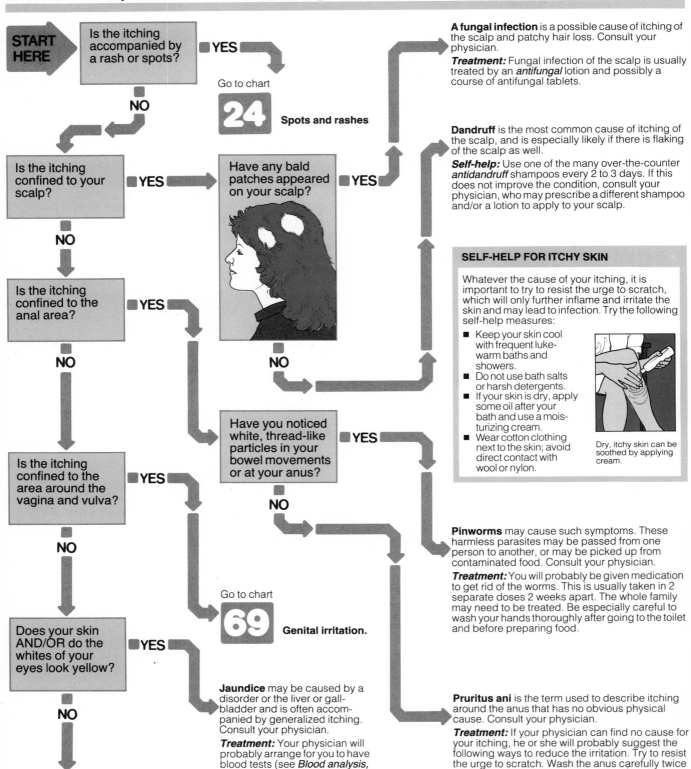

**START HERE**

Is the itching accompanied by a rash or spots? — **YES** → Go to chart **24** **Spots and rashes**

**NO**

Is the itching confined to your scalp? — **YES** → Have any bald patches appeared on your scalp? — **YES** →

**A fungal infection** is a possible cause of itching of the scalp and patchy hair loss. Consult your physician.

*Treatment:* Fungal infection of the scalp is usually treated by an *antifungal* lotion and possibly a course of antifungal tablets.

**NO** (from bald patches)

**Dandruff** is the most common cause of itching of the scalp, and is especially likely if there is flaking of the scalp as well.

*Self-help:* Use one of the many over-the-counter *antidandruff* shampoos every 2 to 3 days. If this does not improve the condition, consult your physician, who may prescribe a different shampoo and/or a lotion to apply to your scalp.

**NO** (scalp)

Is the itching confined to the anal area? — **YES** →

Have you noticed white, thread-like particles in your bowel movements or at your anus? — **YES** →

**NO** (anal area)

Is the itching confined to the area around the vagina and vulva? — **YES** → Go to chart **69** **Genital irritation.**

**NO**

Does your skin AND/OR do the whites of your eyes look yellow? — **YES** →

**Jaundice** may be caused by a disorder or the liver or gall-bladder and is often accompanied by generalized itching. Consult your physician.

*Treatment:* Your physician will probably arrange for you to have blood tests (see *Blood analysis,* p.22) and possibly an *ultrasound scan* (p.136) to find the cause of the trouble. Treatment will depend on the nature of the underlying disorder.

**NO**

**Consult your physician** if you are unable to make a diagnosis from this chart and your itching persists for longer than 3 days.

## SELF-HELP FOR ITCHY SKIN

Whatever the cause of your itching, it is important to try to resist the urge to scratch, which will only further inflame and irritate the skin and may lead to infection. Try the following self-help measures:

- Keep your skin cool with frequent luke-warm baths and showers.
- Do not use bath salts or harsh detergents.
- If your skin is dry, apply some oil after your bath and use a moisturizing cream.
- Wear cotton clothing next to the skin; avoid direct contact with wool or nylon.

Dry, itchy skin can be soothed by applying cream.

**Pinworms** may cause such symptoms. These harmless parasites may be passed from one person to another, or may be picked up from contaminated food. Consult your physician.

*Treatment:* You will probably be given medication to get rid of the worms. This is usually taken in 2 separate doses 2 weeks apart. The whole family may need to be treated. Be especially careful to wash your hands thoroughly after going to the toilet and before preparing food.

**Pruritus ani** is the term used to describe itching around the anus that has no obvious physical cause. Consult your physician.

*Treatment:* If your physician can find no cause for your itching, he or she will probably suggest the following ways to reduce the irritation. Try to resist the urge to scratch. Wash the anus carefully twice a day, using mild, unscented soap. Use only soft toilet paper and wipe gently. Avoid tight underpants made of artificial fibers; cotton is best. Your physician may also prescribe a soothing ointment.

# 9 Lumps and swellings

Consult this chart if you notice one or more swollen areas or lumps beneath the surface of the skin. In most cases, such swellings are the result of enlargement of the lymph glands, which is a natural response to the presence of infection. You should always consult your physician about a painful or persistent swelling.

**For lumps and swellings in the breast, see chart 63, Breast problems**

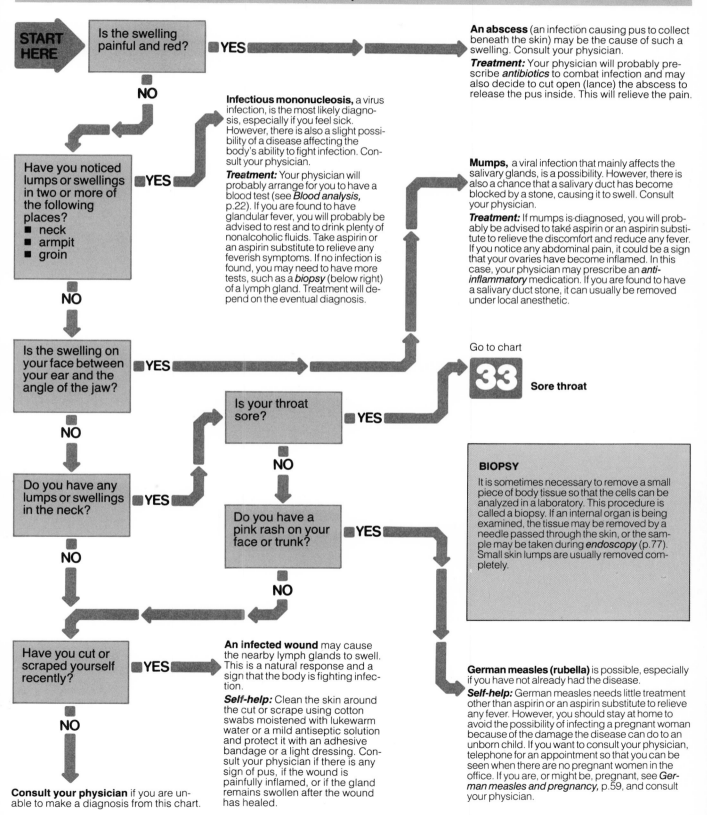

# 10 Faintness and fainting

Fainting – a brief loss of consciousness – is usually preceded by a sensation of lightheadedness or dizziness, and you may be pale and suddenly feel cold or clammy. Such feelings of faintness may sometimes occur on their own without loss of consciousness. Faintness is usually the result of a sudden drop in blood pressure – as a result, for example, of an emotional shock – or it may be caused by an abnormally low level of sugar in the blood. Isolated episodes of fainting with no other symptoms are hardly ever a cause for concern but, if you suffer repeated fainting attacks or have additional symptoms, you should seek medical advice.

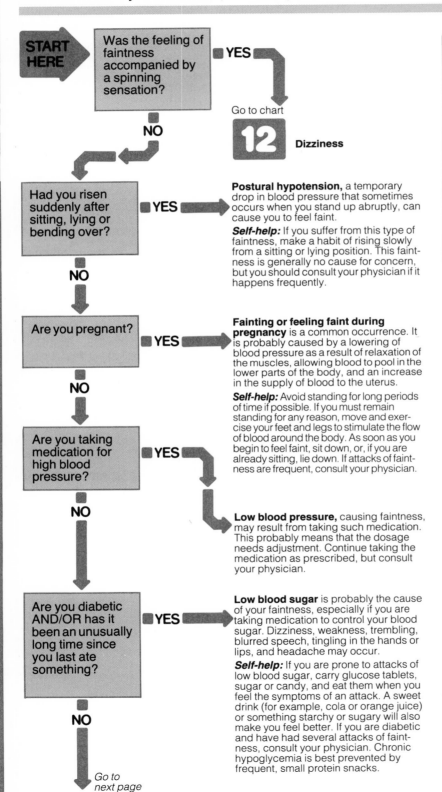

**START HERE**

Was the feeling of faintness accompanied by a spinning sensation?

**YES** → Go to chart **12** Dizziness

**NO** ↓

Had you risen suddenly after sitting, lying or bending over?

**YES** → **Postural hypotension,** a temporary drop in blood pressure that sometimes occurs when you stand up abruptly, can cause you to feel faint.
*Self-help:* If you suffer from this type of faintness, make a habit of rising slowly from a sitting or lying position. This faintness is generally no cause for concern, but you should consult your physician if it happens frequently.

**NO** ↓

Are you pregnant?

**YES** → **Fainting or feeling faint during pregnancy** is a common occurrence. It is probably caused by a lowering of blood pressure as a result of relaxation of the muscles, allowing blood to pool in the lower parts of the body, and an increase in the supply of blood to the uterus.
*Self-help:* Avoid standing for long periods of time if possible. If you must remain standing for any reason, move and exercise your feet and legs to stimulate the flow of blood around the body. As soon as you begin to feel faint, sit down, or, if you are already sitting, lie down. If attacks of faintness are frequent, consult your physician.

**NO** ↓

Are you taking medication for high blood pressure?

**YES** → **Low blood pressure,** causing faintness, may result from taking such medication. This probably means that the dosage needs adjustment. Continue taking the medication as prescribed, but consult your physician.

**NO** ↓

Are you diabetic AND/OR has it been an unusually long time since you last ate something?

**YES** → **Low blood sugar** is probably the cause of your faintness, especially if you are taking medication to control your blood sugar. Dizziness, weakness, trembling, blurred speech, tingling in the hands or lips, and headache may occur.
*Self-help:* If you are prone to attacks of low blood sugar, carry glucose tablets, sugar or candy, and eat them when you feel the symptoms of an attack. A sweet drink (for example, cola or orange juice) or something starchy or sugary will also make you feel better. If you are diabetic and have had several attacks of faintness, consult your physician. Chronic hypoglycemia is best prevented by frequent, small protein snacks.

**NO** ↓

*Go to next page*

## WARNING

### PROLONGED LOSS OF CONSCIOUSNESS

Momentary loss of consciousness – fainting – is not usually a cause for concern if the person is breathing normally and regains consciousness within a minute or two. If someone in your presence remains unconscious for longer, or if breathing slows or becomes irregular or noisy, get medical help at once. While waiting for medical help to arrive, place the person on her stomach as shown.

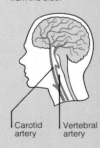

### HOW BLOOD FLOWS TO THE BRAIN

The brain is more dependent on a constant supply of oxygenated blood that any other organ in the body. Temporary interruption in this supply is likely to cause the brain to malfunction, and more serious disruption to the blood flow may cause lasting damage to brain cells.

View of the brain from beneath.

View of the brain from the side.

Carotid artery    Vertebral artery

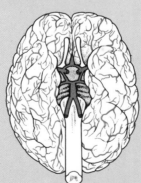

Anterior cerebral arteries

Middle cerebral arteries

Carotid arteries

Posterior cerebral arteries

Vertebral arteries

**The main arteries of the brain**
The brain is supplied with blood by 2 pairs of arteries in the neck: the vertebral arteries and the carotid arteries. At the bottom of the brain they join to form a circular junction from which other arteries – the anterior cerebral, the middle cerebral, and the posterior cerebral – run to all parts of the brain.

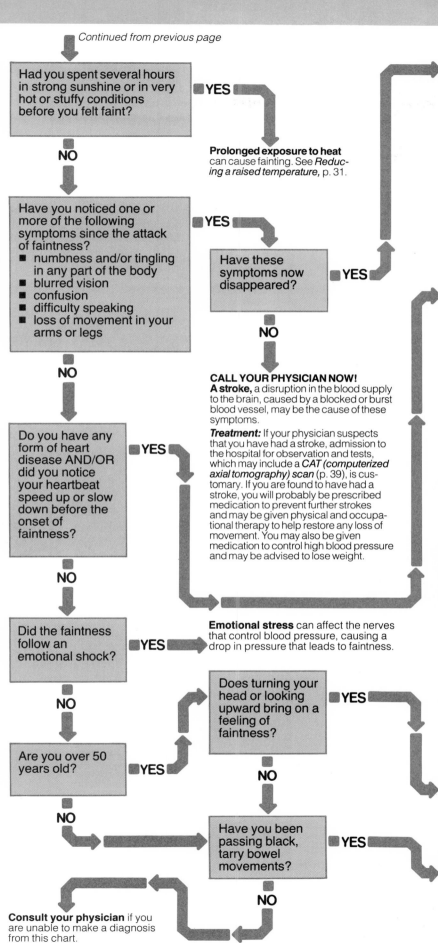

*Continued from previous page*

**Had you spent several hours in strong sunshine or in very hot or stuffy conditions before you felt faint?**

**YES** → **Prolonged exposure to heat** can cause fainting. See *Reducing a raised temperature,* p. 31.

**NO** ↓

**Have you noticed one or more of the following symptoms since the attack of faintness?**
- numbness and/or tingling in any part of the body
- blurred vision
- confusion
- difficulty speaking
- loss of movement in your arms or legs

**YES** → **Have these symptoms now disappeared?**

**YES** →

**CONSULT YOUR PHYSICIAN WITHOUT DELAY!**
**A transient ischemic attack –** a temporary interruption in the blood supply to the brain, sometimes linked to a narrowing of the arteries (see *How blood flows to the brain,* opposite) – may have caused your symptoms.

***Treatment:*** If your physician suspects that this is the problem, you will probably be referred to a specialist for tests, including *electrocardiography* (p.99). At a later stage, you may need to undergo *angiography* (p.109) of the arteries. Treatment consists of taking steps to reduce factors that may contribute to narrowing of the arteries. These are discussed in the box on *Coronary heart disease* (p.101). You may also be prescribed medication to control high blood pressure, if you have it, and further medication to prevent the formation of blood clots. Surgery may be necessary in some cases.

**NO** ↓

**CALL YOUR PHYSICIAN NOW!**
**A stroke,** a disruption in the blood supply to the brain, caused by a blocked or burst blood vessel, may be the cause of these symptoms.

***Treatment:*** If your physician suspects that you have had a stroke, admission to the hospital for observation and tests, which may include a *CAT (computerized axial tomography) scan* (p. 39), is customary. If you are found to have had a stroke, you will probably be prescribed medication to prevent further strokes and may be given physical and occupational therapy to help restore any loss of movement. You may also be given medication to control high blood pressure and may be advised to lose weight.

**CONSULT YOUR PHYSICIAN WITHOUT DELAY!**
**An Adams-Stokes attack** (sudden alteration of the heart rhythm) could have caused the fainting. Such attacks may be a sign of an underlying disorder of heart rate or rhythm.

***Treatment:*** If your physician suspects the possibility of such a disorder, he or she will arrange for you to undergo *electrocardiography* (p.99). If this shows abnormal heart rhythms, you will probably be prescribed medication to regulate the heart's activity.

**NO** ↓

**Do you have any form of heart disease AND/OR did you notice your heartbeat speed up or slow down before the onset of faintness?**

**YES** →

**NO** ↓

**Did the faintness follow an emotional shock?**

**YES** → **Emotional stress** can affect the nerves that control blood pressure, causing a drop in pressure that leads to faintness.

**NO** ↓

**Are you over 50 years old?**

**YES** →

**Does turning your head or looking upward bring on a feeling of faintness?**

**YES** → **Cervical osteoarthritis,** a disorder of the bones and joints in the neck, can cause feelings of faintness. Consult your physician.

***Treatment:*** See *Cervical osteoarthritis,* p. 104.

**NO** ↓

**NO** →

**Have you been passing black, tarry bowel movements?**

**YES** → **CALL YOUR PHYSICIAN NOW!**
**Bleeding in the digestive tract,** perhaps from a stomach ulcer, is a possibility.

***Treatment:*** Your physician will probably arrange for you to have tests, such as *endoscopy* (p.77), a *biopsy* (p. 35) of the stomach lining and a *barium X ray* (p. 83). These tests should reveal the underlying cause of your symptoms.

**NO** ↓

**Consult your physician** if you are unable to make a diagnosis from this chart.

---

**FIRST AID**

**Dealing with faintness**
If you feel faint, lie down with your legs raised or, if this is not possible, sit with your head between your knees until you feel better.

**Dealing with fainting**
To help someone who has fainted, check that breathing is normal. Lay the person on her back with legs raised as high as possible above the level of the head. Hold the legs up, or rest them on a chair. Loosen any tight clothing (e.g., collar or waistband) and make sure that the person gets plenty of fresh air. If you are indoors, open the windows to allow air to circulate. If you are outdoors, make sure that the person is in the shade. When she regains consciousness, it is important that she remain lying down for a few minutes before attempting to get up.

# 11 Headache

From time to time nearly everyone suffers from headaches that develop gradually and clear up after a few hours, leaving no aftereffects. Headaches like this are unlikely to be a sign of any disorder and are usually caused by factors such as tension, tiredness, excessive consumption of alcohol or staying in an overheated or smoke-filled atmosphere. However, a headache that is severe, lasts for more than 24 hours, or recurs several times during one week should be brought to your physician's attention.

**START HERE** →

**Is your temperature 100°F (38°C) or above?**

**YES** →

**NO** ↓

**Many illnesses with fever** may cause a headache.

Go to chart

**6** **Fever**

**Have you injured your head within the past few days?**

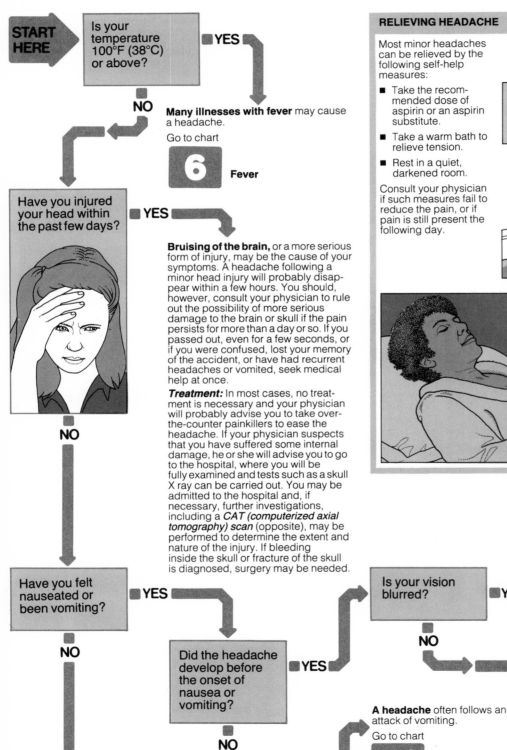

**YES** →

**Bruising of the brain,** or a more serious form of injury, may be the cause of your symptoms. A headache following a minor head injury will probably disappear within a few hours. You should, however, consult your physician to rule out the possibility of more serious damage to the brain or skull if the pain persists for more than a day or so. If you passed out, even for a few seconds, or if you were confused, lost your memory of the accident, or have had recurrent headaches or vomited, seek medical help at once.

***Treatment:*** In most cases, no treatment is necessary and your physician will probably advise you to take over-the-counter painkillers to ease the headache. If your physician suspects that you have suffered some internal damage, he or she will advise you to go to the hospital, where you will be fully examined and tests such as a skull X ray can be carried out. You may be admitted to the hospital and, if necessary, further investigations, including a *CAT (computerized axial tomography) scan* (opposite), may be performed to determine the extent and nature of the injury. If bleeding inside the skull or fracture of the skull is diagnosed, surgery may be needed.

**NO** ↓

**Have you felt nauseated or been vomiting?**

**YES** →

**NO** ↓

**Did the headache develop before the onset of nausea or vomiting?**

**YES** →

**NO** ↓

**A headache** often follows an attack of vomiting.

Go to chart

**41** **Vomiting**

**Is your vision blurred?**

**YES** →

**NO** ↓

**CALL YOUR PHYSICIAN NOW!**
**Acute glaucoma,** a serious disorder associated with increased pressure in the eye, is a possibility, especially if you are over 40.

***Treatment:*** If your physician confirms the diagnosis, you will probably be given eye drops to allow fluid to drain from the eye. In addition you may be given a *diuretic* to prevent fluid retention. Once the pressure has been relieved, an operation to prevent a recurrence of the problem is sometimes performed.

**RELIEVING HEADACHE**

Most minor headaches can be relieved by the following self-help measures:

- Take the recommended dose of aspirin or an aspirin substitute.
- Take a warm bath to relieve tension.
- Rest in a quiet, darkened room.

Consult your physician if such measures fail to reduce the pain, or if pain is still present the following day.

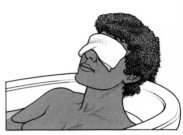

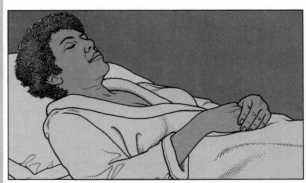

1 *Go to next page column 1*

2 *Go to next page column 2*

① *Continued from previous page column 1*

② *Continued from previous page column 2*

## Do you have a stuffy nose?

**YES**

**Sinusitis** (inflammation of the membranes lining the air spaces in the skull) may be the cause of this problem, although it is possible that you have a common cold.

***Self-help:*** Stay inside in a warm and humid atmosphere and take aspirin or an aspirin substitute to relieve the discomfort. If you are no better in 48 hours, consult your physician, who may prescribe *antibiotics* and *decongestants.*.

**NO**

## Did the headache occur after you had been reading or doing other close work?

**YES**

**Muscle strain** in your neck as a result of poor posture or tension from concentration is the likely cause of your headache (see *Eyestrain,* p.60).

***Self-help:*** In order to prevent the problem from recurring, make sure that when you read you are not sitting in an awkward position or in poor light. Periodic rest from whatever you are doing for a few minutes of relaxation will also help. If headaches recur, consult your physician, who may recommend that you have an *eye test* (p.62).

**NO**

## Are you sleeping poorly AND/OR are you feeling tense or under stress?

**YES**

**Tension headaches** are often caused by psychological stress.

Go to chart

 **20** **Anxiety**

**NO**

## Are you currently taking any medication AND/OR are you taking a birth-control pill?

**YES**

**Certain medications** can cause headaches as a side effect. Discuss the problem with your physician. If you are taking the pill and have recurrent headaches, your physician may suggest that you use an alternative form of contraception.

See also chart

 **72** **Choosing a contraceptive method**

**NO**

 **Consult your physician** if you are unable to make a diagnosis from this chart and if the headache persists overnight or if you develop other symptoms.

## Have you suddenly begun to have a severe, throbbing pain in one or both temples?

**YES**

**CONSULT YOUR PHYSICIAN WITHOUT DELAY!**
**Temporal arteritis,** inflammation of the arteries of the head, is a possibility, especially if you are over 50. Urgent treatment may be needed to prevent this condition from affecting your eyesight.

***Treatment:*** Your physician will probably prescribe medication to reduce the inflammation and it may be necessary for you to have regular blood tests to confirm that the treatment is effective.

**NO**

## Was your vision disturbed in any way before the onset of pain?

**YES**

**Migraine,** a recurrent, severe headache that usually occurs on one side of the head, but may occasionally be on both sides, may be the explanation for your symptoms. Migraines often occur before or during menstruation. They may also be brought on by different "trigger" factors such as stress, eating cheese or chocolate, or drinking red wine. Consult your physician.

***Treatment:*** You may find that the pain can be eased by self-help measures (see *Relieving headache,* opposite). It will also help if you can discover what causes your migraines. Your physician may offer medication if self-help measures are not effective or if the attacks recur.

**NO**

**CONSULT YOUR PHYSICIAN WITHOUT DELAY!**
**Unexplained headaches,** especially if severe and accompanied by additional symptoms such as nausea and vomiting, should always be brought to your physician's attention.

---

### CAT SCAN

A CAT (computerized axial tomography) scan is a safe and painless procedure that helps in the diagnosis of certain conditions. It involves hundreds of tiny X-ray pictures being taken as a camera revolves around the body. The readings are fed into a computer, which assembles them into an accurate picture of the area. CAT scans can be taken of most parts of the body, but they are especially used to diagnose brain disorders.

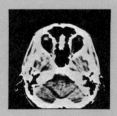

**CAT scan at eyelid level**
This scan shows a cross section of a normal brain at eyelid level. The front of the head is at the top, where the dark areas indicate the eye sockets and air spaces in the skull. The white areas indicate bone.

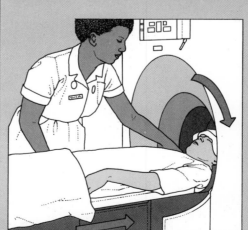

**CAT scan of the head**
For a CAT scan of the head (above) you will lie on a movable table with your head resting inside the machine. You will be told not to make any movement so that the pictures are not blurred.

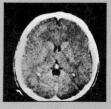

**CAT scan at mid-forehead level**
This scan shows a cross section of the same brain as shown above taken at mid-forehead level.

# 12 Dizziness

Dizziness is a feeling of unsteadiness or that everything around you is spinning. This usually occurs when you have been spinning around – for example, on a merry-go-round. If you feel dizzy for no reason, it may be a symptom of an underlying disorder and should be brought to your physician's attention.

**START HERE**

**Have you noticed one or more of the following symptoms since you felt dizzy?**
- difficulty speaking
- temporary total or partial loss of vision in one or both eyes
- weakness in your arms or legs
- numbness and/or tingling in any part or your body

**YES** →

**Have all your symptoms now disappeared?**

**YES** →

### CONSULT YOUR PHYSICIAN WITHOUT DELAY!
**A transient ischemic attack** – a temporary interruption in the blood supply to the brain, sometimes linked to a narrowing of the arteries (see *How blood flows to the brain,* p.36) – may have caused your symptoms.

***Treatment:*** If your physician suspects that this is the problem, you will probably need to have tests, including *electrocardiography* (p. 99). At a later stage, you may need to undergo *angiography* (p. 109) or *ultrasound scanning* (p. 136) of the arteries. Treatment consists of taking steps to reduce factors that may contribute to narrowing of the arteries. These are discussed in the box on *Coronary heart disease* (p. 100). You may also be prescribed medication to control high blood pressure, if you have it, and further medication to prevent the formation of blood clots. Surgery may be necessary in some cases.

**NO**

### CALL YOUR PHYSICIAN NOW!
**A stroke,** a disruption in the blood supply to the brain caused by a blocked or burst blood vessel, may be the cause of these symptoms.

***Treatment:*** If your physician suspects that you have had a stroke, admission to the hospital for observation and tests, which may include a *CAT (computerized axial tomography) scan* (p. 39) is customary. If you are found to have had a stroke, you will probably be prescribed medication to prevent further strokes and may be given therapy to help restore any loss of movement. You may also be given medication to help control high blood pressure and may be advised to lose weight.

**NO**

**Have you been vomiting AND/OR finding it difficult to keep your balance?**

**YES** →

**NO**

**Labyrinthitis,** inflammation of the part of the inner ear that is responsible for maintaining balance (see *How you keep your balance,* right) due to viral infection, may cause these symptoms. Consult your physician.

***Treatment:*** Your physician will examine your ears. If labyrinthitis is diagnosed, you will probably be prescribed tranquilizers to alleviate your symptoms and you will be advised to rest quietly in bed for a week or so. Most cases clear up within 3 weeks.

**Have you noticed some loss of hearing AND/OR noises in the ear?**

**YES** →

**NO**

**Ménière's disease** may be the problem. This is a relatively uncommon disorder that occurs when there is an increase in the amount of fluid in the labyrinth (see *How you keep your balance,* right). Ménière's disease is most common in middle age. Consult your physician.

***Treatment:*** Your physician will probably arrange for you to undergo tests in the hospital to confirm the diagnosis. If you are found to have Ménière's disease, you will probably be given medication to reduce the amount of fluid in the labyrinth. You may be advised to cut down on your intake of salt to reduce the frequency of further attacks. Rarely, an operation is recommended.

**Does turning your head or looking upwards bring on dizziness?**

**YES** →

**NO**

**Cervical osteoarthritis,** a disorder of the bones and joints in the neck that may cause pressure on nearby nerves and blood vessels, may be the cause of this, especially if you are over 50. Consult your physician.

***Treatment:*** Your physician may arrange for you to have an X ray of your neck. If he or she thinks that your dizziness is due to this disorder, you may be given a collar to wear for about 3 months to reduce the mobility of your neck and to relieve pressure on the nerves and blood vessels. Aspirin or an aspirin substitute can be taken to relieve any discomfort.

**Consult your physician** if you are unable to make a diagnosis from this chart.

---

### HOW YOU KEEP YOUR BALANCE

The brain relies on information from the labyrinth, a structure in the inner ear, to help you to keep your balance. The labyrinth sends messages about your movements to the brain, where they are coordinated with other information from your eyes, limbs and muscles, to assess your exact position so that your body can make adjustments to keep balanced.

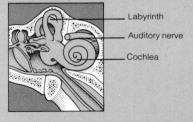

Labyrinth

Auditory nerve

Cochlea

**The semicircular canals**
Each of the three fluid-filled semicircular canals that make up the labyrinth lies at a right angle to the other two (above), so that whichever way you move your head – whether you shake it, nod it or tilt it – one of the canals will detect this movement and relay the information to the brain.

# 13 Numbness or tingling

It is normal to experience numbness or tingling if you are cold, sitting in an awkward position or sleeping on an arm. The feeling disappears as soon as you move around and is rarely a circulation problem. Numbness or tingling that occurs without apparent cause may need medical treatment.

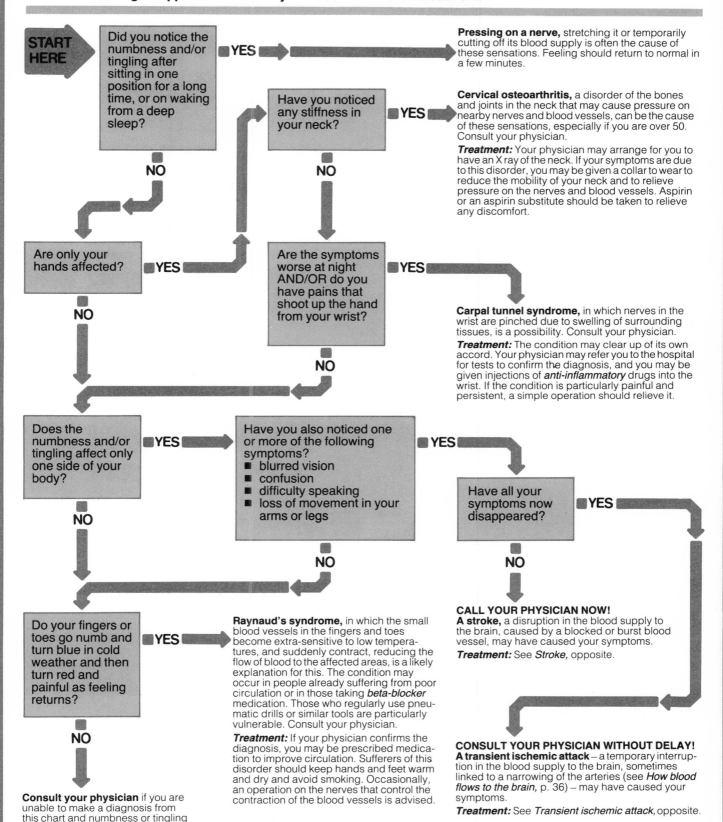

**START HERE**

**Did you notice the numbness and/or tingling after sitting in one position for a long time, or on waking from a deep sleep?**

YES ➡

**Pressing on a nerve,** stretching it or temporarily cutting off its blood supply is often the cause of these sensations. Feeling should return to normal in a few minutes.

NO

**Have you noticed any stiffness in your neck?**

YES

**Cervical osteoarthritis,** a disorder of the bones and joints in the neck that may cause pressure on nearby nerves and blood vessels, can be the cause of these sensations, especially if you are over 50. Consult your physician.

***Treatment:*** Your physician may arrange for you to have an X ray of the neck. If your symptoms are due to this disorder, you may be given a collar to wear to reduce the mobility of your neck and to relieve pressure on the nerves and blood vessels. Aspirin or an aspirin substitute should be taken to relieve any discomfort.

NO

**Are only your hands affected?**

YES

**Are the symptoms worse at night AND/OR do you have pains that shoot up the hand from your wrist?**

YES

NO

**Carpal tunnel syndrome,** in which nerves in the wrist are pinched due to swelling of surrounding tissues, is a possibility. Consult your physician.

***Treatment:*** The condition may clear up of its own accord. Your physician may refer you to the hospital for tests to confirm the diagnosis, and you may be given injections of ***anti-inflammatory*** drugs into the wrist. If the condition is particularly painful and persistent, a simple operation should relieve it.

NO

**Does the numbness and/or tingling affect only one side of your body?**

YES

**Have you also noticed one or more of the following symptoms?**
- blurred vision
- confusion
- difficulty speaking
- loss of movement in your arms or legs

YES

**Have all your symptoms now disappeared?**

YES

NO

NO

NO

**Do your fingers or toes go numb and turn blue in cold weather and then turn red and painful as feeling returns?**

YES

**Raynaud's syndrome,** in which the small blood vessels in the fingers and toes become extra-sensitive to low temperatures, and suddenly contract, reducing the flow of blood to the affected areas, is a likely explanation for this. The condition may occur in people already suffering from poor circulation or in those taking ***beta-blocker*** medication. Those who regularly use pneumatic drills or similar tools are particularly vulnerable. Consult your physician.

***Treatment:*** If your physician confirms the diagnosis, you may be prescribed medication to improve circulation. Sufferers of this disorder should keep hands and feet warm and dry and avoid smoking. Occasionally, an operation on the nerves that control the contraction of the blood vessels is advised.

**CALL YOUR PHYSICIAN NOW!**
**A stroke,** a disruption in the blood supply to the brain, caused by a blocked or burst blood vessel, may have caused your symptoms.
***Treatment:*** See *Stroke,* opposite.

**CONSULT YOUR PHYSICIAN WITHOUT DELAY!**
**A transient ischemic attack** — a temporary interruption in the blood supply to the brain, sometimes linked to a narrowing of the arteries (see *How blood flows to the brain,* p. 36) — may have caused your symptoms.
***Treatment:*** See *Transient ischemic attack,* opposite.

NO

**Consult your physician** if you are unable to make a diagnosis from this chart and numbness or tingling persists.

# 14 Twitching and trembling

Consult this chart if you experience any involuntary or uncontrolled movements of any part of your body. Such movements may range from slight twitching to persistent trembling or shaking – for example, of the eyelid, hands, arms or head. In many cases, such movements are no cause for concern, being simply the result of tiredness, stress or an inherited tendency. Occasion-ally, however, twitching and trembling may be caused by problems that require medical treatment, such as excessive consumption of alcohol, a disorder of the thyroid gland or parkinsonism. Involuntary movements that are accompanied by weakness or stiffness of the affected part of the body should be brought to your physician's attention.

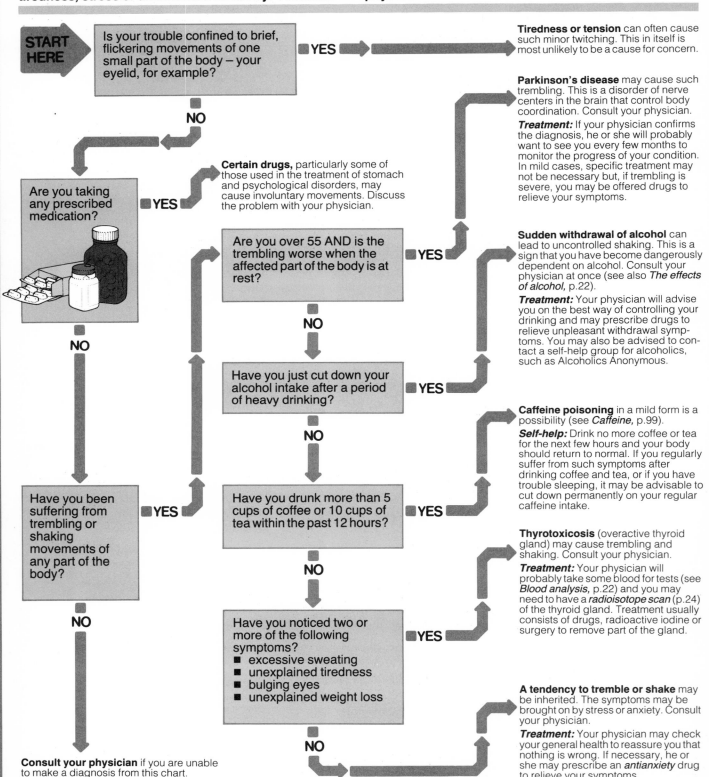

**START HERE**

Is your trouble confined to brief, flickering movements of one small part of the body – your eyelid, for example?

**YES** ➡ **Tiredness or tension** can often cause such minor twitching. This in itself is most unlikely to be a cause for concern.

**NO**

Are you taking any prescribed medication?

**YES** ➡ **Certain drugs,** particularly some of those used in the treatment of stomach and psychological disorders, may cause involuntary movements. Discuss the problem with your physician.

**NO**

Are you over 55 AND is the trembling worse when the affected part of the body is at rest?

**YES** ➡ **Parkinson's disease** may cause such trembling. This is a disorder of nerve centers in the brain that control body coordination. Consult your physician.

*Treatment:* If your physician confirms the diagnosis, he or she will probably want to see you every few months to monitor the progress of your condition. In mild cases, specific treatment may not be necessary but, if trembling is severe, you may be offered drugs to relieve your symptoms.

**NO**

Have you just cut down your alcohol intake after a period of heavy drinking?

**YES** ➡ **Sudden withdrawal of alcohol** can lead to uncontrolled shaking. This is a sign that you have become dangerously dependent on alcohol. Consult your physician at once (see also *The effects of alcohol,* p.22).

*Treatment:* Your physician will advise you on the best way of controlling your drinking and may prescribe drugs to relieve unpleasant withdrawal symptoms. You may also be advised to contact a self-help group for alcoholics, such as Alcoholics Anonymous.

**NO**

Have you been suffering from trembling or shaking movements of any part of the body?

**YES**

Have you drunk more than 5 cups of coffee or 10 cups of tea within the past 12 hours?

**YES** ➡ **Caffeine poisoning** in a mild form is a possibility (see *Caffeine,* p.99).

*Self-help:* Drink no more coffee or tea for the next few hours and your body should return to normal. If you regularly suffer from such symptoms after drinking coffee and tea, or if you have trouble sleeping, it may be advisable to cut down permanently on your regular caffeine intake.

**NO**

Have you noticed two or more of the following symptoms?
- excessive sweating
- unexplained tiredness
- bulging eyes
- unexplained weight loss

**YES** ➡ **Thyrotoxicosis** (overactive thyroid gland) may cause trembling and shaking. Consult your physician.

*Treatment:* Your physician will probably take some blood for tests (see *Blood analysis,* p.22) and you may need to have a *radioisotope scan* (p.24) of the thyroid gland. Treatment usually consists of drugs, radioactive iodine or surgery to remove part of the gland.

**NO**

**A tendency to tremble or shake** may be inherited. The symptoms may be brought on by stress or anxiety. Consult your physician.

*Treatment:* Your physician may check your general health to reassure you that nothing is wrong. If necessary, he or she may prescribe an *antianxiety* drug to relieve your symptoms.

**NO**

**Consult your physician** if you are unable to make a diagnosis from this chart.

# 15 Pain in the face

Consult this chart if you have pain or discomfort that is limited to the area of the face and/or forehead. Facial pain may be dull and throbbing or sharp and stabbing. It is usually caused by infection or inflammation of the underlying tissues. Although it may be distressing, it is not often a sign of a serious disorder.

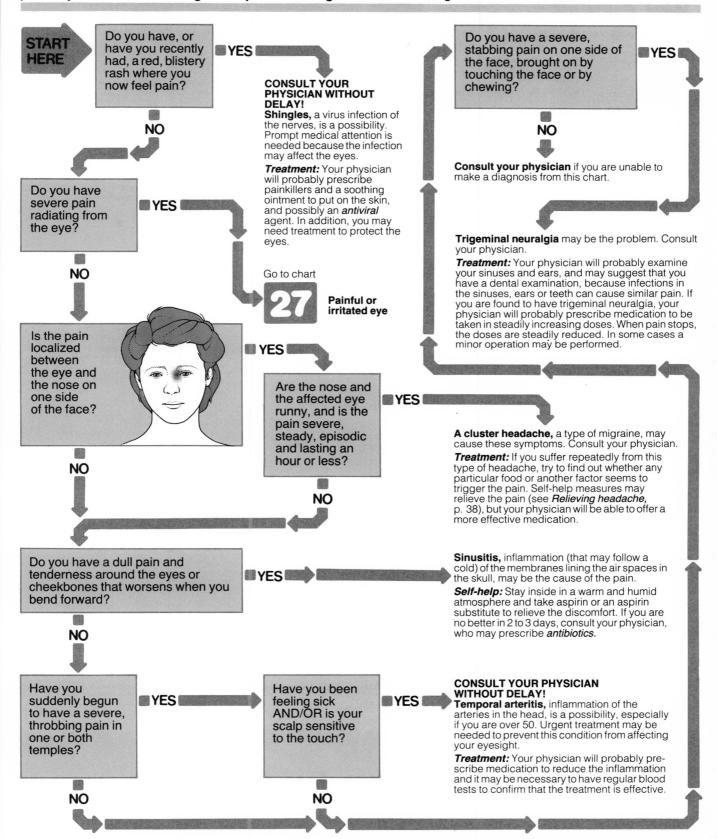

**START HERE**

Do you have, or have you recently had, a red, blistery rash where you now feel pain?

**YES**

**NO**

Do you have severe pain radiating from the eye?

**YES**

**NO**

Is the pain localized between the eye and the nose on one side of the face?

**NO**

**CONSULT YOUR PHYSICIAN WITHOUT DELAY!**
**Shingles,** a virus infection of the nerves, is a possibility. Prompt medical attention is needed because the infection may affect the eyes.
**Treatment:** Your physician will probably prescribe painkillers and a soothing ointment to put on the skin, and possibly an *antiviral* agent. In addition, you may need treatment to protect the eyes.

Go to chart

**27** **Painful or irritated eye**

**YES**

Are the nose and the affected eye runny, and is the pain severe, steady, episodic and lasting an hour or less?

**YES**

**NO**

Do you have a severe, stabbing pain on one side of the face, brought on by touching the face or by chewing?

**YES**

**NO**

**Consult your physician** if you are unable to make a diagnosis from this chart.

**Trigeminal neuralgia** may be the problem. Consult your physician.
**Treatment:** Your physician will probably examine your sinuses and ears, and may suggest that you have a dental examination, because infections in the sinuses, ears or teeth can cause similar pain. If you are found to have trigeminal neuralgia, your physician will probably prescribe medication to be taken in steadily increasing doses. When pain stops, the doses are steadily reduced. In some cases a minor operation may be performed.

**A cluster headache,** a type of migraine, may cause these symptoms. Consult your physician.
**Treatment:** If you suffer repeatedly from this type of headache, try to find out whether any particular food or another factor seems to trigger the pain. Self-help measures may relieve the pain (see *Relieving headache,* p. 38), but your physician will be able to offer a more effective medication.

Do you have a dull pain and tenderness around the eyes or cheekbones that worsens when you bend forward?

**YES**

**NO**

**Sinusitis,** inflammation (that may follow a cold) of the membranes lining the air spaces in the skull, may be the cause of the pain.
**Self-help:** Stay inside in a warm and humid atmosphere and take aspirin or an aspirin substitute to relieve the discomfort. If you are no better in 2 to 3 days, consult your physician, who may prescribe *antibiotics.*

Have you suddenly begun to have a severe, throbbing pain in one or both temples?

**YES**

**NO**

Have you been feeling sick AND/OR is your scalp sensitive to the touch?

**YES**

**NO**

**CONSULT YOUR PHYSICIAN WITHOUT DELAY!**
**Temporal arteritis,** inflammation of the arteries in the head, is a possibility, especially if you are over 50. Urgent treatment may be needed to prevent this condition from affecting your eyesight.
**Treatment:** Your physician will probably prescribe medication to reduce the inflammation and it may be necessary to have regular blood tests to confirm that the treatment is effective.

# 16 Forgetfulness and confusion

We all suffer from mild forgetfulness and, to a lesser extent, confusion from time to time. Often such "absent-mindedness" happens because we are tense or preoccupied. This is no cause for concern. However, if confusion comes on suddenly or if forgetfulness and confusion are so severe that they disrupt everyday life, there may be an underlying medical disorder. This chart deals with sudden or severe confusion or forgetfulness that you are aware of in yourself or in a relative or friend who may not be aware of the problem. Remember that loss of memory for recent events is a natural aging phenomenon. Its onset occurs at different ages.

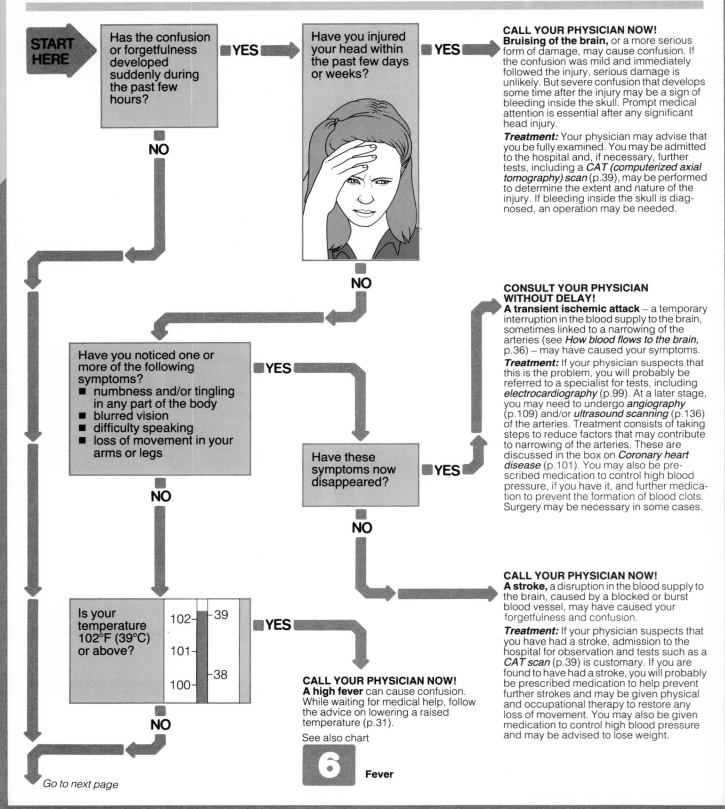

**START HERE**

**Has the confusion or forgetfulness developed suddenly during the past few hours?**

YES → **Have you injured your head within the past few days or weeks?**

YES →

**CALL YOUR PHYSICIAN NOW!**
**Bruising of the brain,** or a more serious form of damage, may cause confusion. If the confusion was mild and immediately followed the injury, serious damage is unlikely. But severe confusion that develops some time after the injury may be a sign of bleeding inside the skull. Prompt medical attention is essential after any significant head injury.

*Treatment:* Your physician may advise that you be fully examined. You may be admitted to the hospital and, if necessary, further tests, including a *CAT (computerized axial tomography) scan* (p.39), may be performed to determine the extent and nature of the injury. If bleeding inside the skull is diagnosed, an operation may be needed.

NO (from first box)

NO (from head injury box)

**Have you noticed one or more of the following symptoms?**
- numbness and/or tingling in any part of the body
- blurred vision
- difficulty speaking
- loss of movement in your arms or legs

YES → **Have these symptoms now disappeared?**

YES →

**CONSULT YOUR PHYSICIAN WITHOUT DELAY!**
**A transient ischemic attack** — a temporary interruption in the blood supply to the brain, sometimes linked to a narrowing of the arteries (see *How blood flows to the brain,* p.36) — may have caused your symptoms.

*Treatment:* If your physician suspects that this is the problem, you will probably be referred to a specialist for tests, including *electrocardiography* (p.99). At a later stage, you may need to undergo *angiography* (p.109) and/or *ultrasound scanning* (p.136) of the arteries. Treatment consists of taking steps to reduce factors that may contribute to narrowing of the arteries. These are discussed in the box on *Coronary heart disease* (p.101). You may also be prescribed medication to control high blood pressure, if you have it, and further medication to prevent the formation of blood clots. Surgery may be necessary in some cases.

NO (from symptoms box)

NO (from disappeared box)

**CALL YOUR PHYSICIAN NOW!**
**A stroke,** a disruption in the blood supply to the brain, caused by a blocked or burst blood vessel, may have caused your forgetfulness and confusion.

*Treatment:* If your physician suspects that you have had a stroke, admission to the hospital for observation and tests such as a *CAT scan* (p.39) is customary. If you are found to have had a stroke, you will probably be prescribed medication to help prevent further strokes and may be given physical and occupational therapy to restore any loss of movement. You may also be given medication to control high blood pressure and may be advised to lose weight.

**Is your temperature 102°F (39°C) or above?**

102 — 39
101 — 
100 — 38

YES →

**CALL YOUR PHYSICIAN NOW!**
**A high fever** can cause confusion. While waiting for medical help, follow the advice on lowering a raised temperature (p.31).

See also chart

**6** Fever

NO

*Go to next page*

*Continued from previous page*

**Are you suffering from a heart or lung disease, or from diabetes?**

**YES** →

**CALL YOUR PHYSICIAN NOW!**
**Sudden worsening** of any of these disorders can cause confusion. If you suspect that diabetes is the cause of the problem, eating or drinking something sweet may help to relieve the confusion.

**NO** ↓

**Are you taking any medication?**

**YES** →

**Certain medications,** especially certain *sedatives,* can cause forgetfulness and confusion. Discuss the problem with your physician.

**NO** ↓

**Have you recently been drinking alcohol?**

**YES** →

**Excessive consumption of alcohol** is a frequent cause of loss of memory and confusion as well as many other adverse effects on the body (see *The effects of alcohol,* p.22).

*Self-help:* Your confusion should clear as the effect of the alcohol wears off. However, if you regularly drink enough alcohol to make you confused, you should try to cut down on your drinking because of the danger of alcoholism. If you find it hard to reduce your alcohol intake, have difficulty sleeping without the help of alcohol, or if you have suffered from total loss of memory (blackouts) on several occasions, consult your physician.

**NO** ↓

**Has memory loss and/or confusion developed gradually over the past few months or years?**

**YES** →

**Have you noticed two or more of the following symptoms?**
- inability to cope with everyday matters
- change in personality
- decline in standards of hygiene
- difficulty following complex conversations and instructions

**YES** →

**Dementia,** when the brain ceases to function normally, is most common in people over 65 but may occur in younger people. Sometimes there may be an underlying cause of the problem, such as an infection, diabetes, stroke, heart trouble or hypothermia. Other times the cause may be a disorder known as Alzheimer's disease. Seek medical advice.

*Treatment:* Your physician will carry out a physical examination to find out if there is an underlying disease. If such a disease is found, treatment of that disorder should relieve the confusion. If no other disorder is found, your physician will be able to suggest ways of coping with the problem and will provide information about community services.

---

**WARNING**

**SERIOUSLY DISTURBED BEHAVIOR**

If a friend or relative becomes severely confused, agitated, or disoriented, or is seeing or hearing nonexistent things, medical attention is required immediately.

**Call your physician now!**

---

**NO** ↓

**Absentmindedness** that occurs only occasionally is unlikely to be a cause for medical concern. Consult your physician, however, if you are worried, or if forgetfulness and confusion are disrupting your everyday life.

**NO** ↓

**Is the loss of memory total?**

**YES** →

**Hysteria,** a form of overreaction to an experience or situation, may be the cause. It may be triggered by an event that the sufferer wants to forget. Seek medical advice.

*Treatment:* Hysteria is extremely difficult to diagnose. Tests will probably be needed to make sure that the problem is not physical. If no physical disorder is found, tests to uncover any underlying emotional cause of the hysteria will be needed. This may involve *psychotherapy* (p.49). *Tranquilizers* may be prescribed. In older persons, memory may suddenly be lost for several hours, followed by recovery. This is called "transient global amnesia."

**NO** ↓

**Consult your physician** if you are unable to make a diagnosis from this chart.

# 17 Difficulty speaking

Consult this chart if you have difficulty finding, using or defining words, or if your speech becomes slurred or unclear. Such speech difficulties may be related to disorders or medication affecting the speech centers in the brain or they may be due to a disorder affecting the movement of the mouth or tongue.

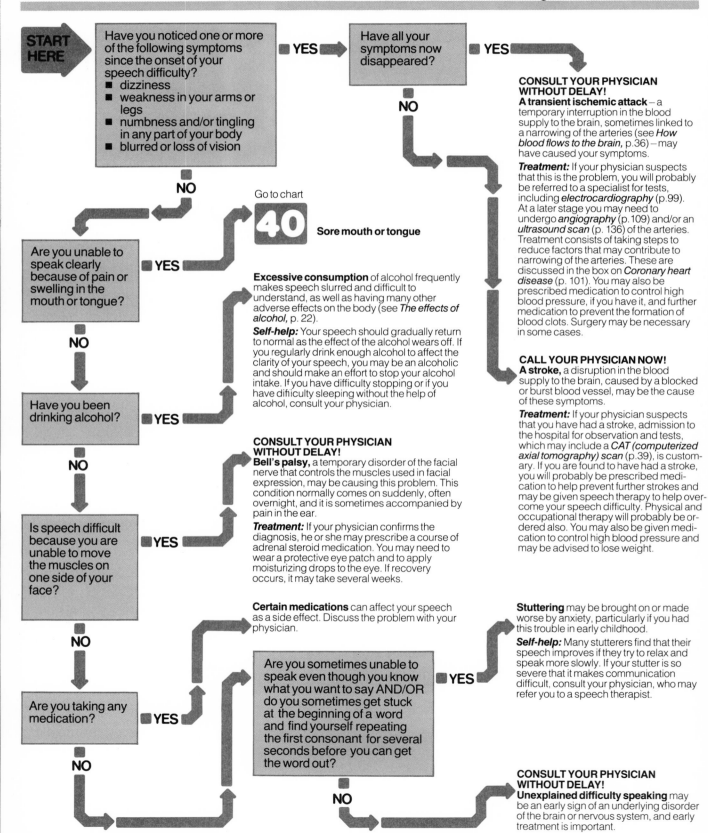

**START HERE**

**Have you noticed one or more of the following symptoms since the onset of your speech difficulty?**
- dizziness
- weakness in your arms or legs
- numbness and/or tingling in any part of your body
- blurred or loss of vision

**YES** → **Have all your symptoms now disappeared?**

**YES** →

**CONSULT YOUR PHYSICIAN WITHOUT DELAY!**
**A transient ischemic attack** – a temporary interruption in the blood supply to the brain, sometimes linked to a narrowing of the arteries (see *How blood flows to the brain,* p.36) – may have caused your symptoms.

**Treatment:** If your physician suspects that this is the problem, you will probably be referred to a specialist for tests, including *electrocardiography* (p.99). At a later stage you may need to undergo *angiography* (p.109) and/or an *ultrasound scan* (p. 136) of the arteries. Treatment consists of taking steps to reduce factors that may contribute to narrowing of the arteries. These are discussed in the box on *Coronary heart disease* (p. 101). You may also be prescribed medication to control high blood pressure, if you have it, and further medication to prevent the formation of blood clots. Surgery may be necessary in some cases.

**NO**

**CALL YOUR PHYSICIAN NOW!**
**A stroke,** a disruption in the blood supply to the brain, caused by a blocked or burst blood vessel, may be the cause of these symptoms.

**Treatment:** If your physician suspects that you have had a stroke, admission to the hospital for observation and tests, which may include a *CAT (computerized axial tomography) scan* (p.39), is customary. If you are found to have had a stroke, you will probably be prescribed medication to help prevent further strokes and may be given speech therapy to help overcome your speech difficulty. Physical and occupational therapy will probably be ordered also. You may also be given medication to control high blood pressure and may be advised to lose weight.

**NO**

Go to chart
**40**
**Sore mouth or tongue**

**Are you unable to speak clearly because of pain or swelling in the mouth or tongue?** — **YES** →

**Excessive consumption** of alcohol frequently makes speech slurred and difficult to understand, as well as having many other adverse effects on the body (see *The effects of alcohol,* p. 22).
**Self-help:** Your speech should gradually return to normal as the effect of the alcohol wears off. If you regularly drink enough alcohol to affect the clarity of your speech, you may be an alcoholic and should make an effort to stop your alcohol intake. If you have difficulty stopping or if you have difficulty sleeping without the help of alcohol, consult your physician.

**NO**

**Have you been drinking alcohol?** — **YES** →

**NO**

**CONSULT YOUR PHYSICIAN WITHOUT DELAY!**
**Bell's palsy,** a temporary disorder of the facial nerve that controls the muscles used in facial expression, may be causing this problem. This condition normally comes on suddenly, often overnight, and it is sometimes accompanied by pain in the ear.
**Treatment:** If your physician confirms the diagnosis, he or she may prescribe a course of adrenal steroid medication. You may need to wear a protective eye patch and to apply moisturizing drops to the eye. If recovery occurs, it may take several weeks.

**Is speech difficult because you are unable to move the muscles on one side of your face?** — **YES** →

**NO**

**Certain medications** can affect your speech as a side effect. Discuss the problem with your physician.

**Stuttering** may be brought on or made worse by anxiety, particularly if you had this trouble in early childhood.
**Self-help:** Many stutterers find that their speech improves if they try to relax and speak more slowly. If your stutter is so severe that it makes communication difficult, consult your physician, who may refer you to a speech therapist.

**Are you taking any medication?** — **YES** →

**Are you sometimes unable to speak even though you know what you want to say AND/OR do you sometimes get stuck at the beginning of a word and find yourself repeating the first consonant for several seconds before you can get the word out?** — **YES** →

**NO**

**NO**

**CONSULT YOUR PHYSICIAN WITHOUT DELAY!**
**Unexplained difficulty speaking** may be an early sign of an underlying disorder of the brain or nervous system, and early treatment is important.

# 18 Disturbing thoughts and feelings

Consult this chart if you begin to have thoughts and feelings that worry you or that seem to you or to others to be abnormal or unhealthy. Such feelings may include aggressive or sexual thoughts and unfamiliar or uncontrolled emotions. If your thoughts and feelings continue to worry you, whatever your particular problem, talk to your physician, who may be able to help you put your feelings into proper context and offer treatment where appropriate. Simply talking about your problem may make you feel better.

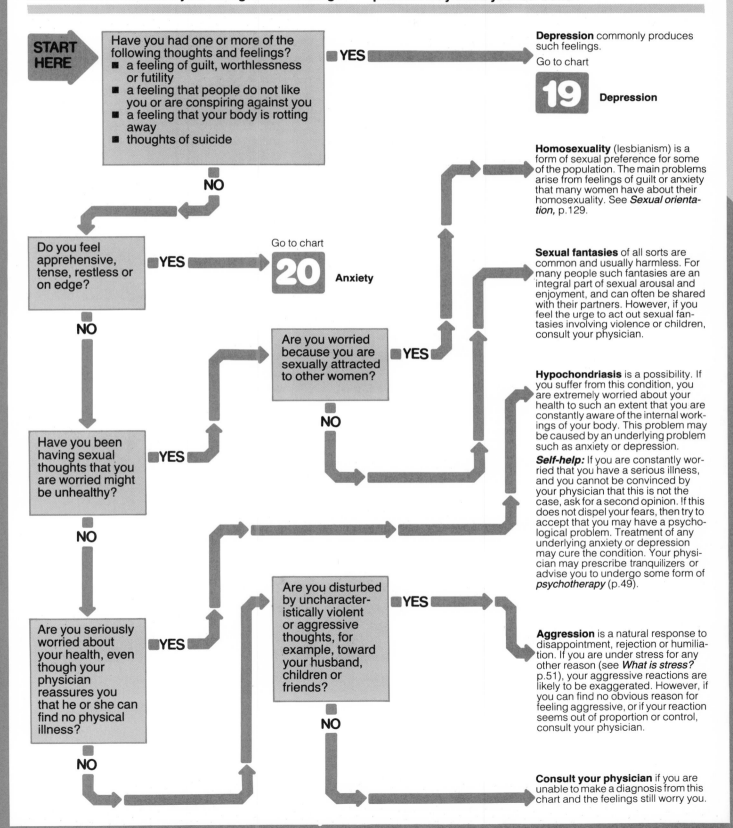

**START HERE**

Have you had one or more of the following thoughts and feelings?
- a feeling of guilt, worthlessness or futility
- a feeling that people do not like you or are conspiring against you
- a feeling that your body is rotting away
- thoughts of suicide

**YES** → **Depression** commonly produces such feelings.

Go to chart

**19** Depression

**NO**

Do you feel apprehensive, tense, restless or on edge?

**YES** → Go to chart **20** Anxiety

**NO**

Have you been having sexual thoughts that you are worried might be unhealthy?

**YES** →

Are you worried because you are sexually attracted to other women?

**YES** → **Homosexuality** (lesbianism) is a form of sexual preference for some of the population. The main problems arise from feelings of guilt or anxiety that many women have about their homosexuality. See *Sexual orientation,* p.129.

**NO** →

**Sexual fantasies** of all sorts are common and usually harmless. For many people such fantasies are an integral part of sexual arousal and enjoyment, and can often be shared with their partners. However, if you feel the urge to act out sexual fantasies involving violence or children, consult your physician.

**NO**

Are you seriously worried about your health, even though your physician reassures you that he or she can find no physical illness?

**YES** →

Are you disturbed by uncharacteristically violent or aggressive thoughts, for example, toward your husband, children or friends?

**YES** → **Hypochondriasis** is a possibility. If you suffer from this condition, you are extremely worried about your health to such an extent that you are constantly aware of the internal workings of your body. This problem may be caused by an underlying problem such as anxiety or depression.

*Self-help:* If you are constantly worried that you have a serious illness, and you cannot be convinced by your physician that this is not the case, ask for a second opinion. If this does not dispel your fears, then try to accept that you may have a psychological problem. Treatment of any underlying anxiety or depression may cure the condition. Your physician may prescribe tranquilizers or advise you to undergo some form of *psychotherapy* (p.49).

**NO** →

**Aggression** is a natural response to disappointment, rejection or humiliation. If you are under stress for any other reason (see *What is stress?* p.51), your aggressive reactions are likely to be exaggerated. However, if you can find no obvious reason for feeling aggressive, or if your reaction seems out of proportion or control, consult your physician.

**NO**

**Consult your physician** if you are unable to make a diagnosis from this chart and the feelings still worry you.

# 19 Depression

Most people have minor ups and downs in mood, feeling particularly good one day but low the next. This is often due to an identifiable cause, and quickly passes. More severe depression, characterized by feelings of futility and guilt and often with physical symptoms such as headache, insomnia, lack of appetite, loss of weight, constipation and delusion, is sometimes brought on by some major event, such as bereavement, divorce or becoming unemployed. Some people, however, are prone to repeated attacks of depression that have no apparent cause. Also, there are certain times when we are more susceptible to depression – for instance, during adolescence, after having a baby, at middle age and at retirement.

**START HERE**

**As well as feeling low or "blue," do you have two or more of the following symptoms?**
- difficulty sleeping
- loss of appetite
- loss of energy
- loss of interest in sex
- recurrent headaches

**YES**

**A depressive illness** is a possibility. This often develops with no apparent cause and, in the most severe cases, it may be accompanied by severe psychological symptoms such as feelings of persecution, guilt and worthlessness. Some sufferers lose all energy and enthusiasm, sleep poorly and wake early. A severely depressed person may contemplate suicide. Consult your physician if you are experiencing these feelings. A threat of suicide should always be taken seriously, even if such threats have been made before (see *Suicide,* below).

**Treatment:** This depends on the type and severity of your symptoms. Your physician may refer you to a specialist for treatment that is likely to consist of a combination of drugs and *psychotherapy* (opposite). *Antidepressants,* if prescribed, usually begin to relieve mild depression in 2 or 3 weeks. If you are severely depressed, the specialist may recommend that you spend some time in the hospital.

**NO**

**Did the onset of depression follow a bereavement?**

**YES**

**Grief** over the death of someone you have loved may naturally lead to a period of depression. This time of mourning is an essential part of the process of adjustment to the loss and should not be unnaturally hurried by well-meaning family and friends. During this period many people think they see or hear the dead person and this is perfectly normal.

**Self-help:** Do not expect to return to normal within a few days or weeks. Many people take months to accept their loss. Do not, however, believe that you must not give in or that admitting to unhappiness is a sign of weakness. If depression is preventing you from coping with everyday life, or if you have difficulty sleeping, consult your physician. Sometimes *antidepressants* or *tranquilizers* are helpful.

**NO**

**Did your depression follow a distressing event, such as a divorce or losing your job?**

**YES**

**Distressing events** are often followed by a period of depression. This is known as "reactive depression." Some people react more severely than others. If your depression makes life unbearable, prevents you from coping with everyday life, begins to get worse or if your friends are clearly worried about you, consult your physician.

**Treatment:** This depends on the type and the severity of your symptoms. Your physician may prescribe *antidepressants,* which will usually relieve a mild depression in 2 to 3 weeks. If you are severely depressed, you may be referred to a specialist for treatment, which is likely to consist of a combination of drugs and *psychotherapy* (opposite). In some cases, it may be necessary to spend some time in the hospital, where treatment can be supervised.

**NO**

---

**WARNING**

**SUICIDE**

Medical help should be sought at once if you (or someone you know) feel so depressed that you think that life is no longer worthwhile, or if you have contemplated suicide or discussed it with relatives or friends. The Samaritans, a voluntary organization specializing in helping people who are contemplating suicide, are available on the telephone 24 hours a day to offer support. Or look in the telephone book under "Suicide Prevention Service."

**Seek medical help without delay!**

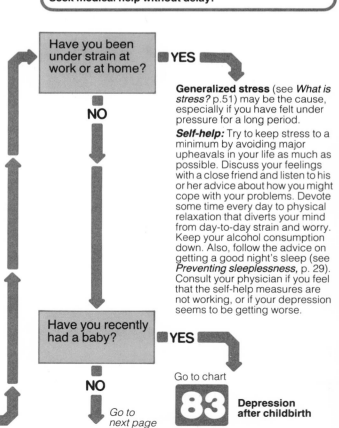

**Have you been under strain at work or at home?**

**YES**

**Generalized stress** (see *What is stress?* p.51) may be the cause, especially if you have felt under pressure for a long period.

**Self-help:** Try to keep stress to a minimum by avoiding major upheavals in your life as much as possible. Discuss your feelings with a close friend and listen to his or her advice about how you might cope with your problems. Devote some time every day to physical relaxation that diverts your mind from day-to-day strain and worry. Keep your alcohol consumption down. Also, follow the advice on getting a good night's sleep (see *Preventing sleeplessness,* p. 29). Consult your physician if you feel that the self-help measures are not working, or if your depression seems to be getting worse.

**NO**

**Have you recently had a baby?**

**YES**

Go to chart

**83**

**Depression after childbirth**

**NO**

Go to next page

*Continued from previous page*

**Do you feel depressed or irritable in the days before your period?**

**YES** → **Premenstrual syndrome (PMS)** is a common occurrence. It can vary from anything as mild as a feeling of moderate unhappiness to a depression so severe that it affects all bodily functions. It is often accompanied by increased irritability, aggression and physical symptoms such as a slight increase in weight, lower abdominal pain, bloated stomach and swollen ankles, which make matters worse (see *The menstrual cycle,* p.117). If your symptoms are severe enough to interfere with your day-to-day routine, consult your physician.

*Treatment:* Your physician will reassure you and advise you to keep premenstrual days as nonstressful as possible. He or she may also prescribe drugs to counteract the physical symptoms (see *Treatment of menstrual problems,* p.119).

**NO** ↓

**Have you recently recovered from an infectious illness, such as the flu or glandular fever?**

**YES** → **Infectious illnesses** are often followed by a period of depression.

*Self-help:* Do not try to return to your normal routine too quickly after you have had such an illness. Make sure that you eat well and get plenty of sleep to allow your strength to build up. If your depression lasts longer than 2 weeks, consult your physician, who may prescribe an *antidepressant.*

**NO** ↓

**Have you been drinking alcohol every day for a prolonged period?**

**YES** → **Regular consumption of alcohol,** even in seemingly moderate amounts over a period of time, has a depressive effect on the body and mind, and this may persist on days when you have had no alcohol (see *The effects of alcohol,* p.22).

*Self-help:* Your depression should clear if you stop drinking alcohol. If you find it difficult to cut down on the amount of alcohol you drink, or your depression persists or begins to get worse, consult your physician.

**NO** ↓

**Emotional instability** in the years surrounding the menopause may be the cause of your depression. Social and psychological factors such as fear of approaching old age and curtailment of opportunities for advancement in your job may contribute to depression. A further complication is the hormonal upheaval that takes place at this age, sometimes with unpleasant symptoms such as hot flashes and dryness or itching of the vagina (see *Menopause,* p.116).

*Self-help:* Try to accept that the menopause is a natural fact of life. Discuss your feelings with your partner or with friends in a similar position. You may find it helpful to find new interests – for example, starting a job, if you have not been working, or taking up a new hobby. Maintain your physical health by ensuring that you do not become overweight (see *How to lose weight,* p.27) and exercise regularly (see *Sports injuries,* p.107). If these measures do not work, or if your depression is so severe that you cannot cope, consult your physician, who will examine you to make sure that there is no underlying condition. He or she may recommend hormone replacement therapy (see *Menopause,* p.116) and, possibly, an *antidepressant.*

**Are you between 40 and 55 years old?**

**YES** ↑

**NO** ↓

**Are you currently taking any medication?**

**YES** → **Certain drugs,** especially sedatives, can cause depression. Discuss the problem with your physician.

**NO** ↓

**Consult your physician** if you are unable to find a cause for your depression from this chart.

## PSYCHOTHERAPY

Psychotherapy is the treatment of psychological problems by a therapist who encourages you to talk about your feelings and fears, and who can provide expert help and advice. This process may range from talking about your troubles with your own physician, to an extended course of psychoanalysis with a psychiatrist. The more common forms of psychotherapy are described here.

### Group therapy

This involves a number of sessions during which the therapist guides a discussion among a group of people with a problem in common. The advantage of group psychotherapy is that the members of the group gain strength from knowing that other people have the same problem and that they can learn from each other's experiences. There is also a certain amount of group pressure to develop a healthier attitude to personal problems and group support for this attitude to continue.

### Behavior therapy

This is usually used in the treatment of specific phobias, such as fear of flying, or fear of dogs or spiders. In one form of behavior therapy known as desensitization, the sufferer is gradually helped by the therapist to overcome the fear. For example, in the case of fear of flying, the therapist encourages you to imagine the events associated with the flight – taking a bus to the airport, waiting in the terminal, dealing with the ticket agent, boarding, and finally sitting on the plane while it taxis on the runway, takes off and lands. Later, when you actually come to fly, you will feel as though you have been through it before and it will hold no fear for you.

Another method, called flooding, involves a confrontation, under the supervision of your therapist, with the object of your fears in an extreme form – for example, a confrontation with a dog as treatment for fear of dogs. Experiencing the worst imaginable degree of exposure helps you to realize that all along there has been no real danger involved and that your fear has been exaggerated. Both methods should be attempted only under the guidance of a trained therapist.

### Psychoanalysis

This form of psychotherapy, based on the belief that much human behavior is determined by early childhood conflicts, was developed in the late 19th and early 20th centuries. Psychoanalysis involves a series of meetings with a psychoanalyst during which he or she will encourage you to talk at will. He or she may ask occasional questions to guide the direction of your thoughts. By listening to your recollections, thoughts and feelings, he or she may be able to pinpoint the root of your problem and, through discussion, enable you to reach a better understanding of yourself and help you reconcile any internal conflicts.

# 20 Anxiety

If you are suffering from anxiety, you will feel tense and unable to concentrate, think clearly or sleep well. Some people have headaches, chest pains, palpitations, backache, abdominal distress and a general feeling of tired- ness. This is often a natural reaction to a stressful situa- tion and is only temporary. Other people, however, suf- fer from anxiety that comes on without apparent cause and persists for long periods.

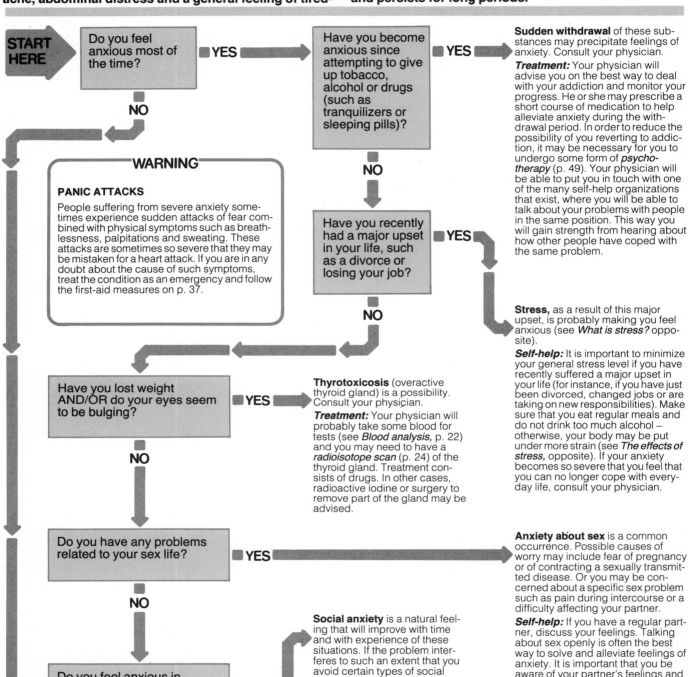

**START HERE**

**Do you feel anxious most of the time?** — **YES** →

**NO** ↓

**Have you become anxious since attempting to give up tobacco, alcohol or drugs (such as tranquilizers or sleeping pills)?** — **YES** →

**NO** ↓

**Have you recently had a major upset in your life, such as a divorce or losing your job?** — **YES** →

**NO** ↓

### WARNING

**PANIC ATTACKS**

People suffering from severe anxiety some- times experience sudden attacks of fear com- bined with physical symptoms such as breath- lessness, palpitations and sweating. These attacks are sometimes so severe that they may be mistaken for a heart attack. If you are in any doubt about the cause of such symptoms, treat the condition as an emergency and follow the first-aid measures on p. 37.

**Have you lost weight AND/OR do your eyes seem to be bulging?** — **YES** →

**NO** ↓

**Thyrotoxicosis** (overactive thyroid gland) is a possibility. Consult your physician.

**Treatment:** Your physician will probably take some blood for tests (see *Blood analysis,* p. 22) and you may need to have a *radioisotope scan* (p. 24) of the thyroid gland. Treatment con- sists of drugs. In other cases, radioactive iodine or surgery to remove part of the gland may be advised.

**Do you have any problems related to your sex life?** — **YES** →

**NO** ↓

**Do you feel anxious in certain social situations – for instance, meeting people, going to parties or during interviews?** — **YES** →

**NO** ↓

*Go to next page*

**Social anxiety** is a natural feel- ing that will improve with time and with experience of these situations. If the problem inter- feres to such an extent that you avoid certain types of social contact because of anxiety, consult your physician.

**Treatment:** He or she may pre- scribe a mild *tranquilizer* to be taken just before you enter any social situation where you will feel anxious (until you gain enough confidence to do with- out). If your physician feels that your anxiety is severe, he or she may suggest that you undergo *psychotherapy* (p. 49) to help you overcome the problem.

**Sudden withdrawal** of these sub- stances may precipitate feelings of anxiety. Consult your physician.

**Treatment:** Your physician will advise you on the best way to deal with your addiction and monitor your progress. He or she may prescribe a short course of medication to help alleviate anxiety during the with- drawal period. In order to reduce the possibility of you reverting to addic- tion, it may be necessary for you to undergo some form of *psycho- therapy* (p. 49). Your physician will be able to put you in touch with one of the many self-help organizations that exist, where you will be able to talk about your problems with people in the same position. This way you will gain strength from hearing about how other people have coped with the same problem.

**Stress,** as a result of this major upset, is probably making you feel anxious (see *What is stress?* oppo- site).

**Self-help:** It is important to minimize your general stress level if you have recently suffered a major upset in your life (for instance, if you have just been divorced, changed jobs or are taking on new responsibilities). Make sure that you eat regular meals and do not drink too much alcohol – otherwise, your body may be put under more strain (see *The effects of stress,* opposite). If your anxiety becomes so severe that you feel that you can no longer cope with every- day life, consult your physician.

**Anxiety about sex** is a common occurrence. Possible causes of worry may include fear of pregnancy or of contracting a sexually transmit- ted disease. Or you may be con- cerned about a specific sex problem such as pain during intercourse or a difficulty affecting your partner.

**Self-help:** If you have a regular part- ner, discuss your feelings. Talking about sex openly is often the best way to solve and alleviate feelings of anxiety. It is important that you be aware of your partner's feelings and vice versa. If this does not help because you are unable to communi- cate satisfactorily with each other, or you do not have a regular partner with whom you can talk, consult your physician, who will be able to offer helpful advice or possibly refer you for *sex counseling* (p. 128). For diag- nosis of specific sex problems, see the *Sex and fertility charts,* pp. 125- 132.

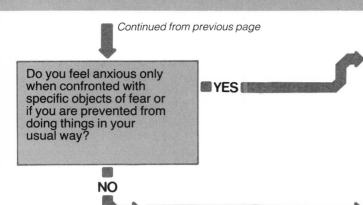

*Continued from previous page*

Do you feel anxious only when confronted with specific objects of fear or if you are prevented from doing things in your usual way?

**YES**

**A phobia or compulsive disorder** may cause your anxiety. A phobia is an irrational fear of a specific object or situation. For instance, you may have a fear of enclosed spaces (claustrophobia). If you have a compulsive disorder, you feel an irresistible need to behave in a certain fashion, even though you may know that it is unreasonable. For example, you may feel that you have to walk to work on the same side of the street and, if prevented from doing so, you worry about it. Consult your physician.

*Treatment:* Your physician will try to discover the underlying cause of the problem and may be able to reassure you that your worries and fears are understandable but that it is possible to come to terms with them. He or she may decide that *antidepressants* or *tranquilizers* will help. If your symptoms are severe, he or she may refer you for *psychotherapy* (p. 49).

**NO**

**Consult your physician** if you are unable to make a diagnosis from this chart and unexplained feelings of anxiety persists.

## WHAT IS STRESS?

Stress refers to physical or mental demands that require an increased response from the body. Stress can be caused by changes in daily routine, including changes for the better – getting married or having a baby – as well as for the worse – losing a job or getting divorced. The greater the change, the more stress you will suffer. A single major event such as the death of a close relative may, on its own, equal the stress resulting from an accumulation of smaller changes such as a change in job responsibilities, a move to a new house or a vacation overseas.

### The effects of stress

A certain amount of stress can be beneficial when it excites and stimulates the body and improves performance. However, as stress levels continue to rise, helpful stimulation becomes replaced by fatigue and, if stress is not reduced, may increase susceptibility to physical and mental illness. Everybody has a different level of toler-ance to stress; some people never seem to suffer harmful effects from seemingly high levels of stress in their lives, while others can cope with only a few changes at a time without becoming anxious, depressed or physically ill.

Some of the most common disorders that may be caused by or made worse by stress are:
- Mental and emotional problems, including anxiety and depression
- Asthma
- Mouth ulcers
- Angina and some other heart conditions
- Stomach or duodenal ulcers
- Ulcerative colitis; irritable bowel (see p.87)
- Stuttering
- Skin problems, including eczema and psoriasis
- Cessation of periods
- Certain forms of hair loss

## RELAXATION TECHNIQUES

Some people manage to remain relaxed and easygoing no matter how much strain they are under at work or at home. Others become tense and worried as a result of even minor stresses (see *What is stress?* above). If you are one of the latter type, learning to relax may help mitigate the harmful effects of stress and enable you to cope with problems more easily. Try practicing some of the simple relaxation techniques described below once or twice a day. See also *Preventing sleeplessness* (p. 29).

### Breathing exercises

Try taking deep rather than shallow breaths. To develop the habit, sit or lie in a comfortable position and breathe deeply and slowly for one minute, counting the number of breaths you take. Try to reduce your breathing rate so that you take half as many breaths as you normally do during a minute. Try this twice daily.

### Meditation

Meditation involves emptying the mind of all distractions, thoughts and worries. Try the following method:

**1** Find a quiet part of the house and sit in a comfortable chair with your eyes closed.

**2** Without moving your lips, repeat a word silently to yourself, paying attention only to this action. Do not choose a word that has any emotional overtones. If your mind wanders, do not fight this new train of thought but continue to focus your attention on the unspoken sound of the word. (Some people find it easier to concentrate on something visual – a door knob or a vase of flowers – rather than a word).

**3** Do this for 5 minutes twice a day for a week, then gradually increase the meditation period until you can manage about 20 minutes at each session.

**Muscle relaxation exercises**
Try these exercises each evening or at other times if you feel tense. Wear comfortable clothes that enable you to move freely.

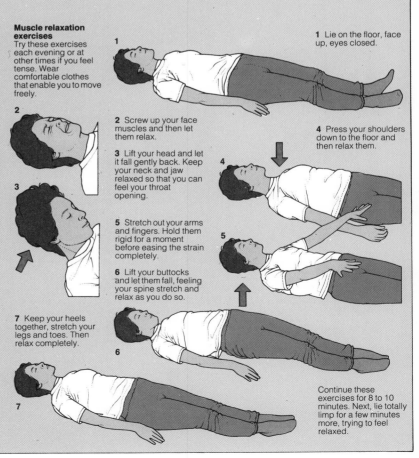

**1** Lie on the floor, face up, eyes closed.

**2** Screw up your face muscles and then let them relax.

**3** Lift your head and let it fall gently back. Keep your neck and jaw relaxed so that you can feel your throat opening.

**4** Press your shoulders down to the floor and then relax them.

**5** Stretch out your arms and fingers. Hold them rigid for a moment before easing the strain completely.

**6** Lift your buttocks and let them fall, feeling your spine stretch and relax as you do so.

**7** Keep your heels together, stretch your legs and toes. Then relax completely.

Continue these exercises for 8 to 10 minutes. Next, lie totally limp for a few minutes more, trying to feel relaxed.

# 21 Hair and scalp problems

Hair grows over the whole surface of the human body, except the palms and soles, and grows especially thickly on the head, in the armpits and in the genital area. Your hair color and type are inherited, but your hair's condition may be affected by your overall health, your diet and the environment. This chart pinpoints common problems affecting hair on the head and the condition of the scalp.

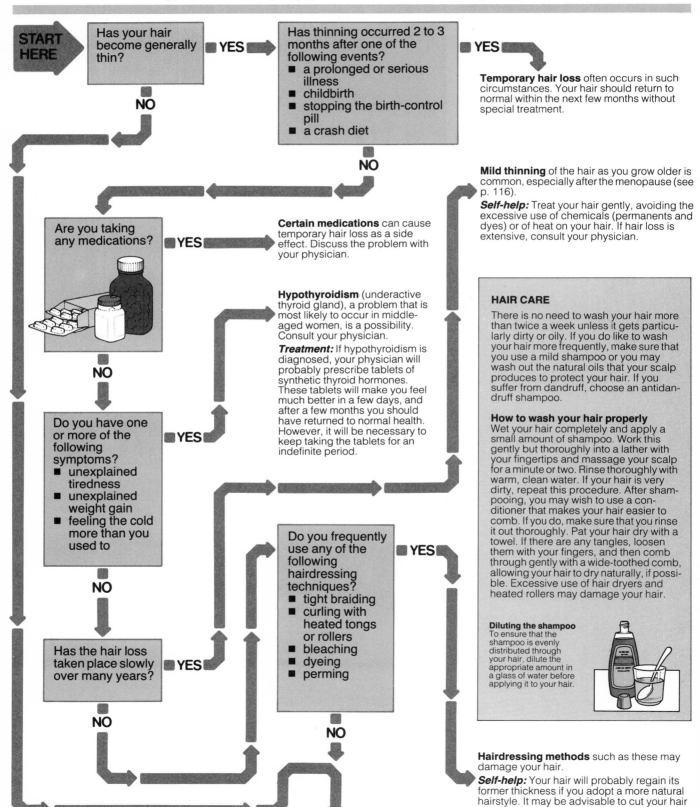

**START HERE**

**Has your hair become generally thin?**

**Has thinning occurred 2 to 3 months after one of the following events?**
- a prolonged or serious illness
- childbirth
- stopping the birth-control pill
- a crash diet

**YES** → **Temporary hair loss** often occurs in such circumstances. Your hair should return to normal within the next few months without special treatment.

**Mild thinning** of the hair as you grow older is common, especially after the menopause (see p. 116).

**Self-help:** Treat your hair gently, avoiding the excessive use of chemicals (permanents and dyes) or of heat on your hair. If hair loss is extensive, consult your physician.

**Are you taking any medications?**

**YES** → **Certain medications** can cause temporary hair loss as a side effect. Discuss the problem with your physician.

**Do you have one or more of the following symptoms?**
- unexplained tiredness
- unexplained weight gain
- feeling the cold more than you used to

**YES** → **Hypothyroidism** (underactive thyroid gland), a problem that is most likely to occur in middle-aged women, is a possibility. Consult your physician.

**Treatment:** If hypothyroidism is diagnosed, your physician will probably prescribe tablets of synthetic thyroid hormones. These tablets will make you feel much better in a few days, and after a few months you should have returned to normal health. However, it will be necessary to keep taking the tablets for an indefinite period.

**Has the hair loss taken place slowly over many years?**

**Do you frequently use any of the following hairdressing techniques?**
- tight braiding
- curling with heated tongs or rollers
- bleaching
- dyeing
- perming

**YES**

**NO**

### HAIR CARE

There is no need to wash your hair more than twice a week unless it gets particularly dirty or oily. If you do like to wash your hair more frequently, make sure that you use a mild shampoo or you may wash out the natural oils that your scalp produces to protect your hair. If you suffer from dandruff, choose an antidandruff shampoo.

**How to wash your hair properly**
Wet your hair completely and apply a small amount of shampoo. Work this gently but thoroughly into a lather with your fingertips and massage your scalp for a minute or two. Rinse thoroughly with warm, clean water. If your hair is very dirty, repeat this procedure. After shampooing, you may wish to use a conditioner that makes your hair easier to comb. If you do, make sure that you rinse it out thoroughly. Pat your hair dry with a towel. If there are any tangles, loosen them with your fingers, and then comb through gently with a wide-toothed comb, allowing your hair to dry naturally, if possible. Excessive use of hair dryers and heated rollers may damage your hair.

**Diluting the shampoo**
To ensure that the shampoo is evenly distributed through your hair, dilute the appropriate amount in a glass of water before applying it to your hair.

**Hairdressing methods** such as these may damage your hair.

**Self-help:** Your hair will probably regain its former thickness if you adopt a more natural hairstyle. It may be advisable to cut your hair short if it is severely damaged.

*Go to next page*

*Continued from previous page*

Have one or more bald patches suddenly developed?

**YES**

**Patchy hair loss** may be the result of fungal infection (especially if the scalp is inflamed and itchy) or of alopecia areata (a condition that may be related to emotional stress). Consult your physician.

**Treatment:** Fungal infection of the scalp is usually treated by an *antifungal* lotion and possibly a course of antifungal tablets. Alopecia areata often clears up without treatment and new hair grows within 6 to 9 months.

**NO**

Is your scalp flaky and/or itchy?

**YES**

**Dandruff** is the name used to describe excessive flaking and itching of the scalp. It may be caused by seborrheic dermatitis (see *Eczema,* p.57) or, less commonly, by psoriasis.

**Self-help:** Use one of the many over-the-counter *antidandruff* shampoos every 2 to 3 days. If this does not improve the condition, consult your physician, who may prescribe a different shampoo and/or a lotion to apply to your scalp.

**NO**

**Consult your physician** if you are unable to make a diagnosis from this chart.

# 22 Nail problems

Fingernails and toenails are made of hard, dead tissue called keratin that protects the sensitive tips of the fingers and toes from damage. Any abnormalities or diseases affecting the nails may be unsightly and irritating, but they are not harmful to health. Trim your nails regularly.

**START HERE**

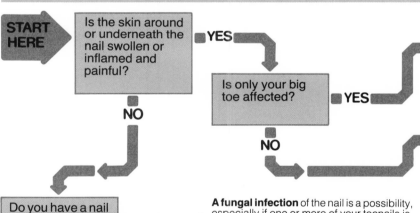

Is the skin around or underneath the nail swollen or inflamed and painful?

**YES**

Is only your big toe affected?

**YES**

**An ingrown toenail** may be the cause of the problem.

Go to chart

**62** **Foot problems.**

**NO**

**NO**

Do you have a nail that has become discolored, thickened and flaky?

**YES**

**A fungal infection** of the nail is a possibility, especially if one or more of your toenails is affected. Consult your physician.

**Treatment:** Your physician may send a sample of nail clippings to be examined in a laboratory to confirm the diagnosis. Treatment may include a long course of *antifungal* tablets.

**NO**

Have your nails become pitted or dimpled?

**YES**

**Psoriasis** of the nails may cause this. In severe cases, the nail is loosened from the nail bed. The skin may also be affected by the disease when thick patches of silvery-white, scaly skin appear. Consult your physician.

**Treatment:** Your physician will probably advise you to keep your nails short. Nail polish will disguise unsightly nails and may protect them from further damage. If your skin is affected by psoriasis, your physician may prescribe an *adrenal steroid* cream and ultraviolet treatment.

**NO**

**Paronychia,** an infection of the skin adjacent to the nail, may be the cause of this problem. This is particularly likely if you spend a lot of time with your hands in water – for instance, washing clothes or dishes. Consult your physician.

**Treatment:** Your physician may prescribe an *antibiotic* or *antifungal* cream or paint to apply to the affected nail after each time you wet your hands. Avoid putting your hands in water too often. Wear rubber gloves, if necessary. Your nails and cuticles should return to normal after a few months.

**A tendency to brittle nails** is usually inherited, but may be exacerbated by excessive exposure to water, detergents and harsh chemicals.

**Self-help:** Wear rubber gloves whenever you have to put your hands in water or handle chemicals or detergents. Keep your nails short and, if you like, apply a protective coat of nail polish. Regular applications of hand cream may also be helpful.

Do your nails crack or break easily?

**YES**

**NO**

**Consult your physician** if you are unable to make a diagnosis from this chart.

# 23 General skin problems

Many different types of disorders may affect the skin, including infections, inflammation, abnormal cell growth and abnormal skin coloration. Such disorders may be the result of an internal disease, exposure to an irritant or some other external factor. Symptoms may include blemishes, lumps, rashes, change in skin coloring or texture, itching or discomfort. Consult this chart if your symptom is not covered elsewhere in this book.

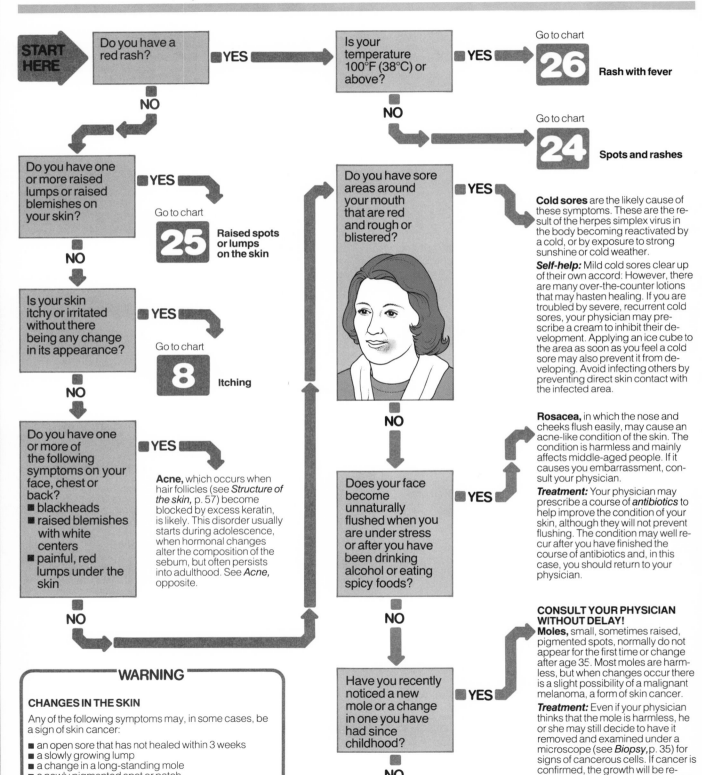

**START HERE**

**Do you have a red rash?**
— **YES** →

**Is your temperature 100°F (38°C) or above?**
— **YES** → Go to chart **26** **Rash with fever**

**NO** ↓ (from temperature) → Go to chart **24** **Spots and rashes**

**NO** ↓ (from red rash)

**Do you have one or more raised lumps or raised blemishes on your skin?**
— **YES** → Go to chart **25** **Raised spots or lumps on the skin**

**NO** ↓

**Is your skin itchy or irritated without there being any change in its appearance?**
— **YES** → Go to chart **8** **Itching**

**NO** ↓

**Do you have one or more of the following symptoms on your face, chest or back?**
- blackheads
- raised blemishes with white centers
- painful, red lumps under the skin

— **YES** → **Acne,** which occurs when hair follicles (see *Structure of the skin,* p. 57) become blocked by excess keratin, is likely. This disorder usually starts during adolescence, when hormonal changes alter the composition of the sebum, but often persists into adulthood. See *Acne,* opposite.

**NO** ↓

**Do you have sore areas around your mouth that are red and rough or blistered?**
— **YES** → **Cold sores** are the likely cause of these symptoms. These are the result of the herpes simplex virus in the body becoming reactivated by a cold, or by exposure to strong sunshine or cold weather.

*Self-help:* Mild cold sores clear up of their own accord: However, there are many over-the-counter lotions that may hasten healing. If you are troubled by severe, recurrent cold sores, your physician may prescribe a cream to inhibit their development. Applying an ice cube to the area as soon as you feel a cold sore may also prevent it from developing. Avoid infecting others by preventing direct skin contact with the infected area.

**NO** ↓

**Does your face become unnaturally flushed when you are under stress or after you have been drinking alcohol or eating spicy foods?**
— **YES** → **Rosacea,** in which the nose and cheeks flush easily, may cause an acne-like condition of the skin. The condition is harmless and mainly affects middle-aged people. If it causes you embarrassment, consult your physician.

*Treatment:* Your physician may prescribe a course of *antibiotics* to help improve the condition of your skin, although they will not prevent flushing. The condition may well recur after you have finished the course of antibiotics and, in this case, you should return to your physician.

**NO** ↓

**Have you recently noticed a new mole or a change in one you have had since childhood?**
— **YES** → **CONSULT YOUR PHYSICIAN WITHOUT DELAY!**
**Moles,** small, sometimes raised, pigmented spots, normally do not appear for the first time or change after age 35. Most moles are harmless, but when changes occur there is a slight possibility of a malignant melanoma, a form of skin cancer.

*Treatment:* Even if your physician thinks that the mole is harmless, he or she may still decide to have it removed and examined under a microscope (see *Biopsy,* p. 35) for signs of cancerous cells. If cancer is confirmed, the growth will be removed, together with a wide margin of adjacent skin. A skin graft to cover the whole area will probably be carried out at the same period.

**NO** ↓ *Go to next page*

---

**WARNING**

**CHANGES IN THE SKIN**

Any of the following symptoms may, in some cases, be a sign of skin cancer:

- an open sore that has not healed within 3 weeks
- a slowly growing lump
- a change in a long-standing mole
- a newly pigmented spot or patch

**Consult your physician without delay!**

*Continued from previous page*

**Have flat patches of very pale or very dark skin developed on your skin?**

▶YES◀

**Are you pregnant?**

▶YES◀

**NO**

Go to chart

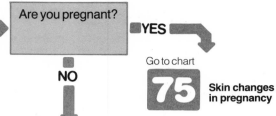

**75** **Skin changes in pregnancy**

**NO**

**Uneven skin pigmentation** is usually the result of abnormal formation of the cells that produce skin pigment or of an abnormal rate of pigment production. This may sometimes be caused by a fungal infection. Consult your physician.

**Treatment:** Most disorders of skin pigment are harmless and require no treatment. You can disguise any disfiguring patches with make-up. If your physician suspects a fungal infection, you will be prescribed an *antifungal* cream, which will soon clear up the condition.

---

## ACNE

Acne is the name used to describe a group of skin symptoms mainly affecting the face, chest and back, caused by blockage and infection of hair follicles (see *Structure of the skin,* p. 57). There are 3 main types of symptoms:

### Blackheads
These are tiny black spots caused by excess skin pigment overlying trapped sebum and skin debris in a hair follicle.

### Pustules
Pustules are tender, red blemishes that develop raised, white centers. They occur when excess keratin blocks a hair follicle and becomes inflamed (see below).

**The development of a pustule**

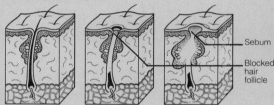

Sebum

Blocked hair follicle

### Cysts
These are painful, red, fluid-filled lumps under the skin. They persist for several weeks and are more likely than other types of blemishes to lead to scarring.

### Self-help
Mild acne with blackheads and the occasional pustule needs no special treatment other than ensuring that you wash your face thoroughly twice a day. Exposure to sunlight or careful use of an ultraviolet lamp often improves the condition. Avoid squeezing blemishes, as this is likely to increase the risk of infection and scarring. There are many over-the-counter preparations for acne. You may find some of these helpful. But you should avoid using anything too vigorously; this may lead to permanent skin damage.

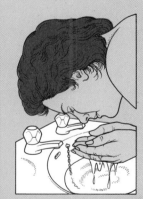

### Professional treatment
If your acne is severe enough to embarrass you, if you have cystic blemishes or if there is any sign of scarring, consult your physician. Various treatments may be advised, depending on the type of acne. You may be prescribed a lotion that gently removes the top layer of skin, clearing blocked pores and preventing further blemishes from forming. Or you may be prescribed a long course of low-dose *antibiotics* that counters bacterial activity in the skin. Less commonly, a medication that alters the composition of the sebum may be prescribed. This treatment needs to be monitored carefully because of possible side-effects.

---

**Do you have one or more red patches covered with silvery-white, flaky skin?**

▶YES◀

**Psoriasis,** a disorder in which the skin cells grow unusually rapidly and form scales, is a possibility. The most common sites for this to occur are the scalp, elbows and knees, though scaly patches can also appear in the armpits, on the trunk or around the anus. Consult your physician.

**Treatment:** Your physician will probably prescribe a *steroid* ointment or cream to apply to the affected area. This needs to be done carefully because it may thin the unaffected skin. Alternatively, a combination of ultraviolet light treatment and medication may be recommended, or medication may be prescribed to slow down the rate of cell growth in the skin.

**NO**

**Has a blistery rash appeared on one side of your body in a place in which there has been a burning sensation for a day or two?**

▶YES◀

**Shingles,** a virus infection of the nerves, is a possibility. Consult your physician. This is a matter of urgency if the rash is on your face because it may affect your eyes.

**Treatment:** Your physician will probably prescribe painkillers and a soothing ointment to put on the skin and, possibly, an antiviral agent. If there is any possibility of damage to the eyes, you will probably be referred to a specialist for treatment.

**NO**

**Do you have one or more open sores on your skin?**

▶YES◀

**Skin ulcers** are usually caused by injury or infection, but may in some cases be encouraged by an underlying disorder such as poor circulation or diabetes.

**Self-help:** Keep the sore area clean, dry and, if necessary, protect it with an adhesive bandage or light dressing. Consult your physician if the sore has not healed within 3 weeks or if ulcers recur. Tests may be needed to determine the underlying cause of the trouble and determine treatment.

**NO**

**Consult your physician** if you are unable to make a diagnosis from this chart.

# 24 Spots and rashes

Groups of inflamed spots or blisters, or larger areas of inflamed skin, are usually caused by infection, irritation or an allergic reaction. Such a rash may come up suddenly or develop over a period of days and may, or may not, cause discomfort or itching. If a rash persists for more than a day, it is wise to consult your physician for diagnosis and treatment. Scratching may extend or enlarge the rash or spread it to other areas.

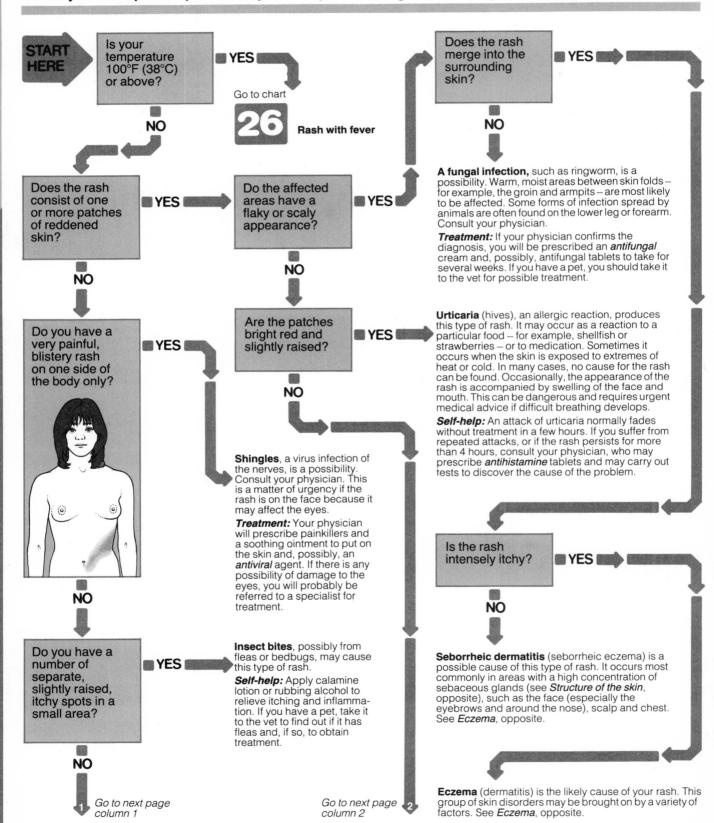

**START HERE**

**Is your temperature 100°F (38°C) or above?**

YES → Go to chart **26** **Rash with fever**

NO

**Does the rash consist of one or more patches of reddened skin?**

YES → **Do the affected areas have a flaky or scaly appearance?**

NO

**Do you have a very painful, blistery rash on one side of the body only?**

YES → **Are the patches bright red and slightly raised?**

NO → **Shingles,** a virus infection of the nerves, is a possibility. Consult your physician. This is a matter of urgency if the rash is on the face because it may affect the eyes.

*Treatment:* Your physician will prescribe painkillers and a soothing ointment to put on the skin and, possibly, an *antiviral* agent. If there is any possibility of damage to the eyes, you will probably be referred to a specialist for treatment.

NO

**Do you have a number of separate, slightly raised, itchy spots in a small area?**

YES → **Insect bites,** possibly from fleas or bedbugs, may cause this type of rash.

*Self-help:* Apply calamine lotion or rubbing alcohol to relieve itching and inflammation. If you have a pet, take it to the vet to find out if it has fleas and, if so, to obtain treatment.

NO

*Go to next page column 1*

**Does the rash merge into the surrounding skin?**

YES →

NO

**A fungal infection,** such as ringworm, is a possibility. Warm, moist areas between skin folds – for example, the groin and armpits – are most likely to be affected. Some forms of infection spread by animals are often found on the lower leg or forearm. Consult your physician.

*Treatment:* If your physician confirms the diagnosis, you will be prescribed an *antifungal* cream and, possibly, antifungal tablets to take for several weeks. If you have a pet, you should take it to the vet for possible treatment.

**Urticaria** (hives), an allergic reaction, produces this type of rash. It may occur as a reaction to a particular food – for example, shellfish or strawberries – or to medication. Sometimes it occurs when the skin is exposed to extremes of heat or cold. In many cases, no cause for the rash can be found. Occasionally, the appearance of the rash is accompanied by swelling of the face and mouth. This can be dangerous and requires urgent medical advice if difficult breathing develops.

*Self-help:* An attack of urticaria normally fades without treatment in a few hours. If you suffer from repeated attacks, or if the rash persists for more than 4 hours, consult your physician, who may prescribe *antihistamine* tablets and may carry out tests to discover the cause of the problem.

**Is the rash intensely itchy?**

YES →

NO

**Seborrheic dermatitis** (seborrheic eczema) is a possible cause of this type of rash. It occurs most commonly in areas with a high concentration of sebaceous glands (see *Structure of the skin,* opposite), such as the face (especially the eyebrows and around the nose), scalp and chest. See *Eczema,* opposite.

*Go to next page column 2*

**Eczema** (dermatitis) is the likely cause of your rash. This group of skin disorders may be brought on by a variety of factors. See *Eczema,* opposite.

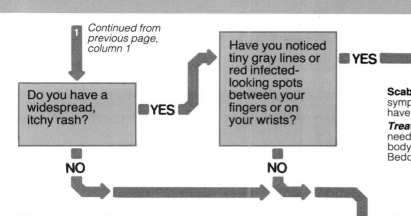

Continued from previous page, column 1

**Do you have a widespread, itchy rash?**

YES →

**Have you noticed tiny gray lines or red infected-looking spots between your fingers or on your wrists?**

YES →

Continued from previous page, column 2

**Scabies,** a parasitic infection, may be causing these symptoms. This is especially likely if others in the household have the same problem. Consult your physician.

***Treatment:*** If your physician diagnoses scabies, you will need to apply a prescribed insecticide to the whole of your body. The procedure should be repeated a few days later. Bedding and clothing should be thoroughly laundered.

NO

NO

**Have you recently started to take any medication?**

YES → **Certain medications** may cause rashes as a side effect. Discuss the problem with your physician.

NO

**Consult your physician** if you are unable to make a diagnosis from this chart.

## STRUCTURE OF THE SKIN

Skin consists of two layers. The surface layer is known as the epidermis. Active cells at its base are continuously dividing to produce new cells, which gradually die as they fill up with a hard substance, keratin. As each cell dies, it moves up toward the surface of the skin, to be shed or worn away. This production of cells at the base of the epidermis is carefully balanced with the loss of cells at the surface of the skin. If the rate of cell replacement is altered, a skin problem develops. For instance, in psoriasis there is an abnormal buildup of surface cells being produced and pushed up from the base of the epidermis.

The underlying layer, the dermis, contains the many specialized structures that allow the skin to function properly. Here, sebaceous glands produce sebum, a waxy substance that helps to keep the surface of the skin supple. Sweat glands produce perspiration to cool you when you are hot (see *Sweat glands,* p.33). And the small blood vessels dilate in hot weather (so that the body can lose heat) and contract in cold weather (to retain heat).

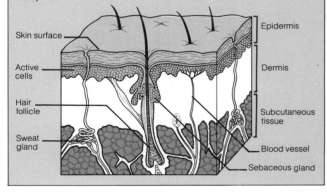

Skin surface — Epidermis
Active cells — Dermis
Hair follicle — Subcutaneous tissue
Sweat gland — Blood vessel — Sebaceous gland

## ECZEMA

Eczema (dermatitis) refers to a group of related conditions in which the skin becomes inflamed and itchy. The main types of eczema are described below.

### Infantile (atopic) eczema

This is an allergic condition that usually appears for the first time in early infancy. It tends to get less severe and may clear up completely by early adolescence. Infantile eczema usually affects the wrists, insides of the elbows and backs of the knees but, in severe cases, the whole body may be affected. The usual treatment is to avoid harsh soaps and detergents, to use a special soap substitute and to apply oil after the bath. A rich, moisturizing cream should be applied to the affected areas. If itching is severe, your physician may prescribe medication. Mild *steroid* creams are recommended in some cases and, if the eczema becomes infected, a mixed steroid and *antibiotic* cream or antibiotics by mouth may be necessary. Skin tests may be carried out to identify factors that trigger outbreaks. Going on a special diet may help.

### Contact eczema

This type of eczema is caused by a reaction to contact with a substance to which you are allergic. Certain plants, such as poison ivy or poison oak, are common causes. The skin becomes red and itchy and blisters (which break and crust over) may form. Milder forms of contact eczema may be caused by contact with certain metals – for example, nickel used in jewelry or on a watch. The rash will clear up in a week or so if the cause of the trouble is removed.

### Irritant eczema

As the name suggests, this type of rash is caused by contact with irritant chemicals – for example, harsh detergents or industrial chemicals in your place of work. The skin becomes dry, red, rough and itchy. The condition usually clears up if you avoid contact with the irritants by protecting your hands with gloves. A moisturizing hand cream should soothe the affected skin, but it is advisable to consult your physician, who may prescribe a mild steroid cream to clear up the rash.

### Seborrheic dermatitis

The tendency to develop this type of eczema is probably inherited. Flaky, red, but not especially itchy, patches appear in areas with a high concentration of sebaceous glands (see *Structure of the skin,* above left), such as around the nose, eyebrows or on the scalp and chest. Seborrheic dermatitis on the scalp is the most common cause of dandruff. Keep the affected skin clean and dry, but avoid using harsh soaps or detergents. Further treatment is often unnecessary but, if the rash is extensive, consult your physician, who may prescribe a mild cream or ointment.

## BRUISING

A bruise is a discolored area of skin caused by blood leaking into the dermis (see *Structure of the skin,* above) from a blood vessel damaged by injury. A bruise is usually blue, purple or black at first, but gradually fades to yellow before disappearing.

### Self-help

If you have a bruise, do not rub or massage the bruised area; this may make matters worse. Applying an ice bag (or an unopened packet of frozen vegetables) immediately after the injury may reduce the extent of bruising. If you have bruised your leg, resting with your feet up may assist healing.

### When to consult your physician

Consult your physician in any of the following circumstances:

- If you feel severe pain, or if movement is restricted.
- If bruises appear without injury.
- If you bruise frequently and easily.

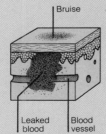

Bruise
Leaked blood — Blood vessel

**Formation of a bruise**
A bruise forms when blood from a damaged blood vessel leaks under the skin (above).

# 25 Raised spots or lumps on the skin

Consult this chart if you develop any raised lumps, whether they are skin colored or pigmented (brown). In the majority of cases, such lumps are the harmless result of virus infection. Your physician will be willing to give you advice on the problem if skin lumps persist or cause you discomfort or embarrassment.

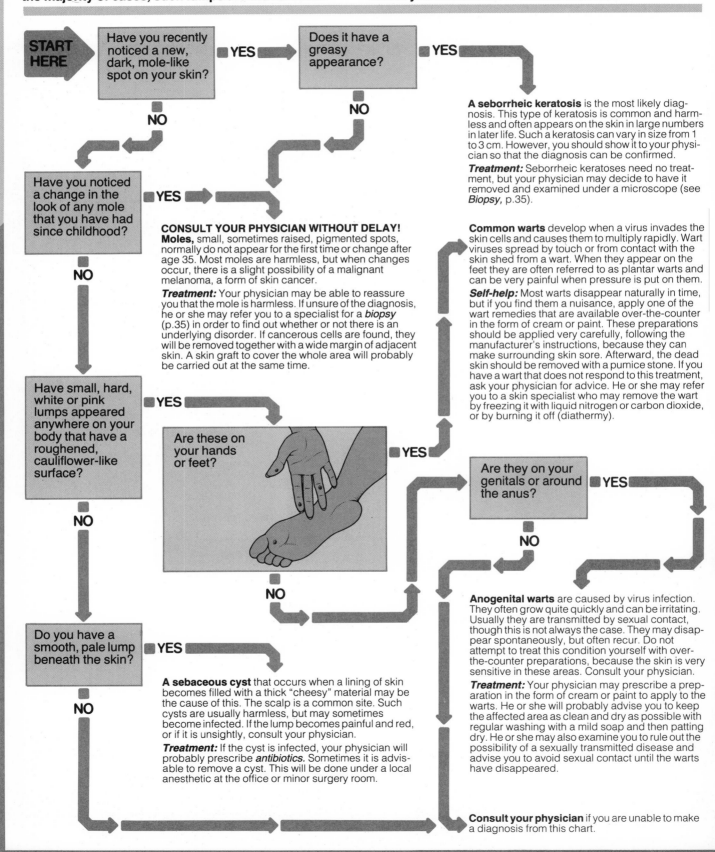

**START HERE**

**Have you recently noticed a new, dark, mole-like spot on your skin?** — NO / YES

**Does it have a greasy appearance?** — NO / YES

**A seborrheic keratosis** is the most likely diagnosis. This type of keratosis is common and harmless and often appears on the skin in large numbers in later life. Such a keratosis can vary in size from 1 to 3 cm. However, you should show it to your physician so that the diagnosis can be confirmed.

**Treatment:** Seborrheic keratoses need no treatment, but your physician may decide to have it removed and examined under a microscope (see *Biopsy,* p.35).

**Have you noticed a change in the look of any mole that you have had since childhood?** — NO / YES

**CONSULT YOUR PHYSICIAN WITHOUT DELAY!**
**Moles,** small, sometimes raised, pigmented spots, normally do not appear for the first time or change after age 35. Most moles are harmless, but when changes occur, there is a slight possibility of a malignant melanoma, a form of skin cancer.

**Treatment:** Your physician may be able to reassure you that the mole is harmless. If unsure of the diagnosis, he or she may refer you to a specialist for a *biopsy* (p.35) in order to find out whether or not there is an underlying disorder. If cancerous cells are found, they will be removed together with a wide margin of adjacent skin. A skin graft to cover the whole area will probably be carried out at the same time.

**Have small, hard, white or pink lumps appeared anywhere on your body that have a roughened, cauliflower-like surface?** — NO / YES

**Are these on your hands or feet?** — NO / YES

**Common warts** develop when a virus invades the skin cells and causes them to multiply rapidly. Wart viruses spread by touch or from contact with the skin shed from a wart. When they appear on the feet they are often referred to as plantar warts and can be very painful when pressure is put on them.

**Self-help:** Most warts disappear naturally in time, but if you find them a nuisance, apply one of the wart remedies that are available over-the-counter in the form of cream or paint. These preparations should be applied very carefully, following the manufacturer's instructions, because they can make surrounding skin sore. Afterward, the dead skin should be removed with a pumice stone. If you have a wart that does not respond to this treatment, ask your physician for advice. He or she may refer you to a skin specialist who may remove the wart by freezing it with liquid nitrogen or carbon dioxide, or by burning it off (diathermy).

**Are they on your genitals or around the anus?** — NO / YES

**Do you have a smooth, pale lump beneath the skin?** — NO / YES

**A sebaceous cyst** that occurs when a lining of skin becomes filled with a thick "cheesy" material may be the cause of this. The scalp is a common site. Such cysts are usually harmless, but may sometimes become infected. If the lump becomes painful and red, or if it is unsightly, consult your physician.

**Treatment:** If the cyst is infected, your physician will probably prescribe *antibiotics*. Sometimes it is advisable to remove a cyst. This will be done under a local anesthetic at the office or minor surgery room.

**Anogenital warts** are caused by virus infection. They often grow quite quickly and can be irritating. Usually they are transmitted by sexual contact, though this is not always the case. They may disappear spontaneously, but often recur. Do not attempt to treat this condition yourself with over-the-counter preparations, because the skin is very sensitive in these areas. Consult your physician.

**Treatment:** Your physician may prescribe a preparation in the form of cream or paint to apply to the warts. He or she will probably advise you to keep the affected area as clean and dry as possible with regular washing with a mild soap and then patting dry. He or she may also examine you to rule out the possibility of a sexually transmitted disease and advise you to avoid sexual contact until the warts have disappeared.

**Consult your physician** if you are unable to make a diagnosis from this chart.

# 26 Rash with fever

Consult this chart if you notice any blemishes or discolored areas of skin and also have a temperature of 100°F (38°C) or above. You may well have one of the infectious diseases that are more common in childhood.

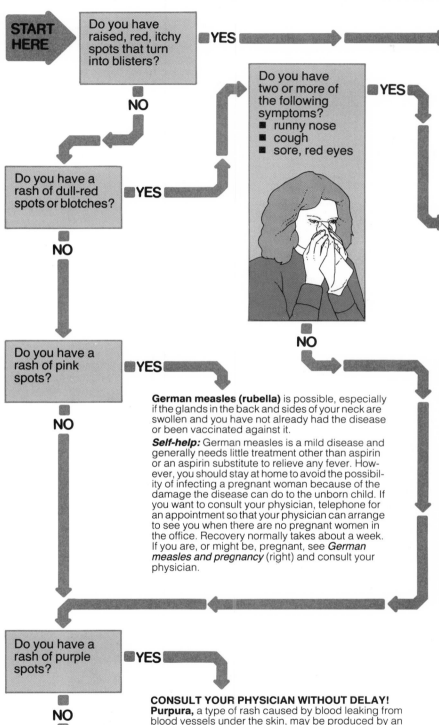

**START HERE**

**Do you have raised, red, itchy spots that turn into blisters?**
NO — **Do you have a rash of dull-red spots or blotches?**
NO — **Do you have a rash of pink spots?**
NO — **Do you have a rash of purple spots?**
NO — **Consult your physician** if you are unable to make a diagnosis from this chart.

YES → 

**Do you have two or more of the following symptoms?**
- runny nose
- cough
- sore, red eyes

YES →

**Chickenpox,** a childhood infectious disease caused by the herpes varicella-zoster virus, is the likely cause of such symptoms. The rash usually starts on the face and trunk, but later may spread to the limbs.
***Self-help:*** Drink plenty of fluids and take aspirin or an aspirin substitute to relieve any feverish symptoms. Apply calamine lotion to the rash to relieve itching. Try to resist the urge to scratch because scratching leads to scarring. Consult your physician if you are, or might be, pregnant, if your temperature rises above 104°F (40°C), if you develop a severe cough, if your eyes become painful, or if you find it hard not to scratch. You are infectious until all the blisters have formed scabs (after about a week).

**Measles (rubeola),** a highly contagious viral disease, may be the cause of such symptoms, especially if you did not have measles as a child.
***Self-help:*** There is no specific treatment for measles. Stay at home, drink plenty of fluids and take aspirin or an aspirin substitute to reduce fever. Consult your physician if you are, or might be, pregnant, if you develop a severe headache or earache, or if your cough starts to get worse.

NO ↓

**German measles (rubella)** is possible, especially if the glands in the back and sides of your neck are swollen and you have not already had the disease or been vaccinated against it.
***Self-help:*** German measles is a mild disease and generally needs little treatment other than aspirin or an aspirin substitute to relieve any fever. However, you should stay at home to avoid the possibility of infecting a pregnant woman because of the damage the disease can do to the unborn child. If you want to consult your physician, telephone for an appointment so that your physician can arrange to see you when there are no pregnant women in the office. Recovery normally takes about a week. If you are, or might be, pregnant, see *German measles and pregnancy* (right) and consult your physician.

**CONSULT YOUR PHYSICIAN WITHOUT DELAY!**
**Purpura,** a type of rash caused by blood leaking from blood vessels under the skin, may be produced by an allergic reaction to a food or medication, or by infection. Call your physician at once if your temperature rises to 104°F (40°C), or if you are suffering from a headache, stiff neck and/or are vomiting.
***Treatment:*** You will probably be admitted to the hospital for a blood test (see *Blood analysis,* p. 22) and possibly a *lumbar puncture* (p.30) to determine the exact nature of the disorder. Further treatment will depend on the results of these tests.

---

**GERMAN MEASLES AND PREGNANCY**

The virus responsible for German measles may cross the placenta of a pregnant woman and damage the developing fetus, causing defects such as deafness, blindness and heart problems. The likelihood of damage occurring is strongest if the disease develops in the first 12 weeks of pregnancy. If you are pregnant or trying to become pregnant, it is vitally important to avoid contracting this disease.

In most cases you will be given a blood test in early pregnancy to see whether you are immune. If this test shows that you are at risk of the disease, be careful to avoid anyone who has the disease or has recently been in contact with it.

**Rash and fever in pregnancy**
If you develop an unexplained rash during pregnancy, especially if you also feel feverish or sick, consult your physician at once. Analysis of blood samples will confirm whether or not you have had German measles. If a diagnosis of German measles is confirmed, your physician will discuss the risks to the baby in your case and, depending on factors such as the stage of pregnancy, your age and your religious and moral convictions, will advise you whether or not *elective abortion* (p.131) should be considered.

**Immunization**
If you have had German measles you are probably immune to the disease. However, it is advisable for any woman who has not been vaccinated against the disease in childhood to have a test to confirm whether or not she is immune and, if not, to be immunized. This is especially important if you are thinking of starting a family. Once you have been immunized, you should be sure to take effective contraceptive precautions for 3 months after the vaccination, because within this period the vaccine itself may possibly damage the fetus.

# 27 Painful or irritated eye

Pain or irritation in or around the eye may be caused by disorders of the eye or surrounding tissues or injury to the eye area. Infection and inflammation are the common causes of eye discomfort. Disorders that threaten sight or that endanger health are uncommon, but should always be ruled out by your physician.

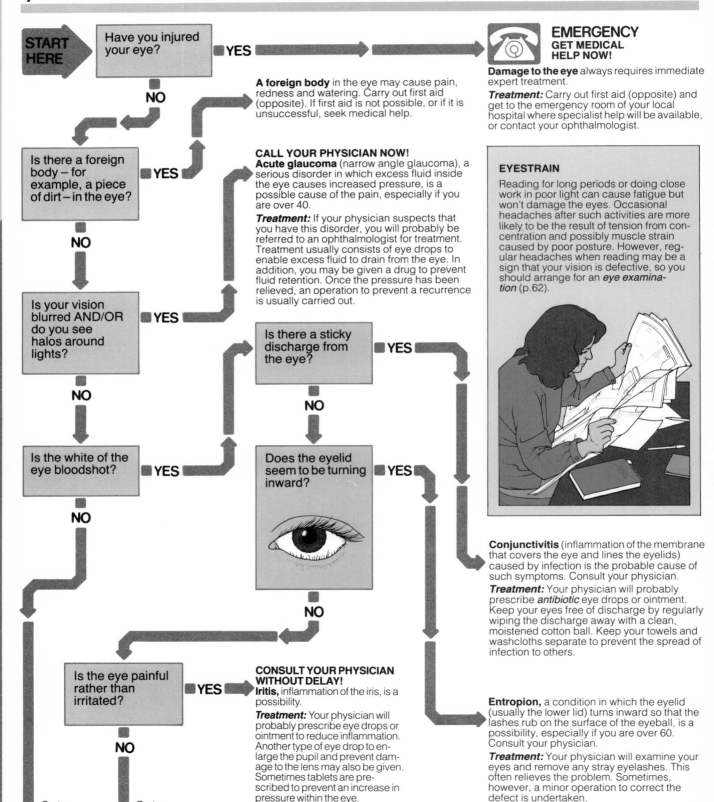

**START HERE**

**Have you injured your eye?** → **YES** →

**EMERGENCY GET MEDICAL HELP NOW!**

**Damage to the eye** always requires immediate expert treatment.

**Treatment:** Carry out first aid (opposite) and get to the emergency room of your local hospital where specialist help will be available, or contact your ophthalmologist.

**NO**

**Is there a foreign body – for example, a piece of dirt – in the eye?** → **YES** →

**A foreign body** in the eye may cause pain, redness and watering. Carry out first aid (opposite). If first aid is not possible, or if it is unsuccessful, seek medical help.

**NO**

**Is your vision blurred AND/OR do you see halos around lights?** → **YES** →

**CALL YOUR PHYSICIAN NOW!**
**Acute glaucoma** (narrow angle glaucoma), a serious disorder in which excess fluid inside the eye causes increased pressure, is a possible cause of the pain, especially if you are over 40.

**Treatment:** If your physician suspects that you have this disorder, you will probably be referred to an ophthalmologist for treatment. Treatment usually consists of eye drops to enable excess fluid to drain from the eye. In addition, you may be given a drug to prevent fluid retention. Once the pressure has been relieved, an operation to prevent a recurrence is usually carried out.

**NO**

**Is the white of the eye bloodshot?** → **YES** →

**Is there a sticky discharge from the eye?** → **YES** →

**NO**

**Does the eyelid seem to be turning inward?** → **YES** →

**NO**

**Is the eye painful rather than irritated?** → **YES** →

**CONSULT YOUR PHYSICIAN WITHOUT DELAY!**
**Iritis,** inflammation of the iris, is a possibility.

**Treatment:** Your physician will probably prescribe eye drops or ointment to reduce inflammation. Another type of eye drop to enlarge the pupil and prevent damage to the lens may also be given. Sometimes tablets are prescribed to prevent an increase in pressure within the eye.

**NO**

*Go to next page, column 1* **1**

*Go to next page, column 2* **2**

### EYESTRAIN

Reading for long periods or doing close work in poor light can cause fatigue but won't damage the eyes. Occasional headaches after such activities are more likely to be the result of tension from concentration and possibly muscle strain caused by poor posture. However, regular headaches when reading may be a sign that your vision is defective, so you should arrange for an *eye examination* (p.62).

**Conjunctivitis** (inflammation of the membrane that covers the eye and lines the eyelids) caused by infection is the probable cause of such symptoms. Consult your physician.

**Treatment:** Your physician will probably prescribe *antibiotic* eye drops or ointment. Keep your eyes free of discharge by regularly wiping the discharge away with a clean, moistened cotton ball. Keep your towels and washcloths separate to prevent the spread of infection to others.

**Entropion,** a condition in which the eyelid (usually the lower lid) turns inward so that the lashes rub on the surface of the eyeball, is a possibility, especially if you are over 60. Consult your physician.

**Treatment:** Your physician will examine your eyes and remove any stray eyelashes. This often relieves the problem. Sometimes, however, a minor operation to correct the defect is undertaken.

1 *Continued from previous page, column 1*

2 *Continued from previous page, column 2*

**Are your eyelids red and itchy?** ▪ YES

NO

**Blepharitis** (inflammation and scaling of the lid margins) may cause itchy eyelids and occurs with *dandruff* (p.53). Consult your physician.

**Treatment:** Your physician may prescribe ointment to apply to the lids; and recommend bathing the lids in warm salt water. Treat dandruff by using an antidandruff shampoo.

**Do you have a red lump on the eyelid?** ▪ YES

**A sty** (chalazion), a boil-like infection at the base of an eyelash, is likely.

**Self-help:** A sty will usually either burst, and release pus, or dry up within a week without special treatment other than warm soaks. If the sty bursts, carefully wipe away the pus using a clean moistened cotton ball each time you wipe. Consult your physician if a sty fails to heal within a week, the eye itself becomes red and painful, or if stys recur.

NO →

**Has your eye been watering?** ▪ YES

NO

**Dry eye,** a condition in which the eye fails to produce enough tears, is possible. Consult your physician.

**Treatment:** If dry eye is confirmed, your physician will prescribe eye drops of artificial tears, which you can use as frequently as you like in order to reduce discomfort.

**Eye irritation** may be caused by exposure to chemical fumes, or by an allergic reaction (for example, to eye make-up or to pollen), or it may be caused by viral conjunctivitis.

**Self-help:** There is no specific treatment for any of these conditions. Avoiding the irritant in the first two cases will bring relief. However, it may be difficult to trace an allergen. Your physician may be able to help. Viral conjunctivitis will get better without treatment, but while it persists you will need to be careful to avoid spreading the infection to others. So keep a separate towel and washcloth.

**Consult your physician** if you are unable to make a diagnosis from this chart.

---

## FIRST AID FOR EYE INJURIES

If you suffer an injury to your eye or eyelid, rapid action is essential. Except in the case of a foreign body that has been successfully removed, go to the emergency room of your local hospital or to an ophthalmologist by the fastest means possible, as soon as you have carried out first aid.

### Cuts to the eye or eyelid
Cover the eye with a clean pad (such as a folded handkerchief) and hold it lightly in place with a bandage. Apply no pressure. Cover the other eye as well to prevent movement of the eyeball. Seek medical help.

### Blows to the eye area
Carry out first aid as for a cut eye (above) but use a cold compress instead of a dry pad over the injured eye.

### Corrosive chemicals
If you spill any harsh chemical (for example, bleach or household cleaner) in the eye, immediately flood the eye with large quantities of cold running water. Tilt your head with the injured eye downward so that the water runs from the inside outward. Keep the eyelids apart with your fingers. When all traces of the chemical have been removed, lightly cover the eye with a clean pad and seek medical help.

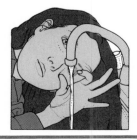

### Foreign body in the eye
Never attempt to remove any of the following:

- an object that is embedded in the eyeball
- a chip of metal
- a particle over the colored part of the eye

In any of these cases, cover both eyes as described for cuts to the eye or eyelid (left) and seek medical help. Other foreign bodies – for example, specks of dirt or eyelashes floating on the white of the eye or inside the lids – may be removed as follows:

1 If you can see the particle on the white of the eye or inside the lower lid, pick it off using the moistened corner of a clean handkerchief (below) or sterile cotton-tipped swab.

2 If you cannot see the particle, pull the upper lid down over the lower lid and hold it for a moment (far right). This may dislodge the particle. If the particle remains, it may be on the inside of the upper lid. If you are alone, seek medical help. Another person may be able to remove the foreign body as in step 3.

3 Ask the person to look down. Hold the lashes of the upper lid and pull it down. Place a match or cotton-tipped swab over the upper lid and fold the lid back over it (right). If the particle is now visible, pick it off as in step 1 (far right).

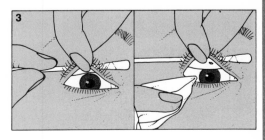

If you do not succeed in removing the foreign body, lightly cover the eye and seek medical help at once.

# 28 Disturbed or impaired vision

This chart deals with any change in your vision, including blurring, seeing double, seeing flashing lights or floating spots, and loss of part or all of your field of vision. Any such change in vision should be brought to your physician's attention promptly to rule out the possibility of a sight-threatening eye disorder. Successful treatment of many eye disorders may depend on catching the disease in its early stages.

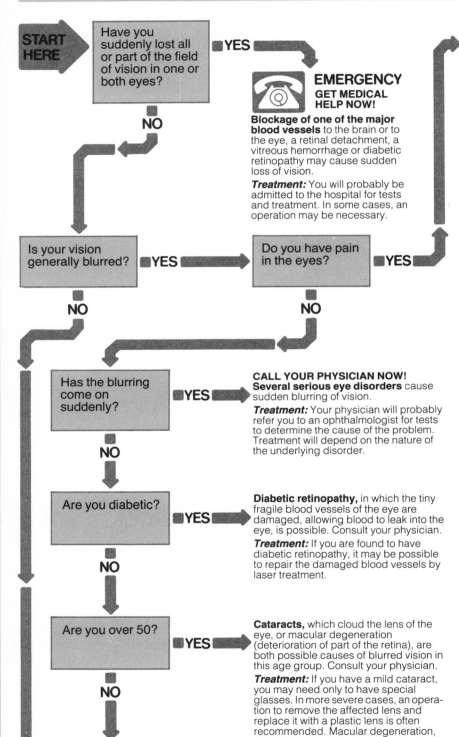

**START HERE**

**Have you suddenly lost all or part of the field of vision in one or both eyes?** — **YES** →

**EMERGENCY GET MEDICAL HELP NOW!**

**Blockage of one of the major blood vessels** to the brain or to the eye, a retinal detachment, a vitreous hemorrhage or diabetic retinopathy may cause sudden loss of vision.

*Treatment:* You will probably be admitted to the hospital for tests and treatment. In some cases, an operation may be necessary.

**NO** ↓

**Is your vision generally blurred?** — **YES** → **Do you have pain in the eyes?** — **YES** →

**CALL YOUR PHYSICIAN NOW!**
**Acute glaucoma** (narrow angle glaucoma) is a possibility, especially if you are over 40. This is a serious disorder in which obstruction to the normal draining mechanism causes a buildup of fluid, and a consequent increase of pressure in the eye.

*Treatment:* If your physician suspects this disorder, you will probably be referred to an ophthalmologist for treatment. Treatment usually consists of drugs to help lower the pressure within the eye and to relieve pain. You will also probably be given eye drops to help fluid drain from the eye. Later on you may need to have an operation to prevent a recurrence of the problem.

**NO** ↓ (blurred) **NO** ↓ (pain)

**Has the blurring come on suddenly?** — **YES** →

**CALL YOUR PHYSICIAN NOW!**
**Several serious eye disorders** cause sudden blurring of vision.

*Treatment:* Your physician will probably refer you to an ophthalmologist for tests to determine the cause of the problem. Treatment will depend on the nature of the underlying disorder.

**NO** ↓

**Are you diabetic?** — **YES** →

**Diabetic retinopathy,** in which the tiny fragile blood vessels of the eye are damaged, allowing blood to leak into the eye, is possible. Consult your physician.

*Treatment:* If you are found to have diabetic retinopathy, it may be possible to repair the damaged blood vessels by laser treatment.

**NO** ↓

**Are you over 50?** — **YES** →

**Cataracts,** which cloud the lens of the eye, or macular degeneration (deterioration of part of the retina), are both possible causes of blurred vision in this age group. Consult your physician.

*Treatment:* If you have a mild cataract, you may need only to have special glasses. In more severe cases, an operation to remove the affected lens and replace it with a plastic lens is often recommended. Macular degeneration, another cause of impaired vision, can, in some cases, be halted by laser treatment. In other cases, special glasses may improve vision.

**NO** ↓

**A variety of eye disorders** may cause blurring of vision. Consult your physician, who may refer you to an ophthalmologist for tests and treatment.

*Go to next page*

---

**EYE TESTING**

You should have your eyes tested routinely every 2 years. The ophthalmologist will test your sight in various ways. He or she will test the sharpness of your vision by asking you to read letters on a Snellen chart (named after its inventor) (below). The result of the test is given as two figures. The first refers to the distance in feet – usually 20 feet – at which you are asked to read the letters. The second figure refers to the lowermost row of letters that you were able to read correctly, and indicates the optimum distance in feet at which a person with normal vision could read that row. So the result 20/40 means that the lowest row of letters that you were able to read at a distance of 20 feet is one that a person with normal vision would read at 40 feet.

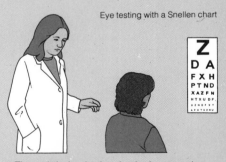

Eye testing with a Snellen chart

The ophthalmologist also looks at each eye through an instrument called an ophthalmoscope (below) to check that the back of the eye looks normal and make sure that there are no signs suggestive of a general disorder, such as high blood pressure or diabetes. Also, he or she will test the balance of the muscles that control the movements of the eyes to detect any eye muscle disorder.

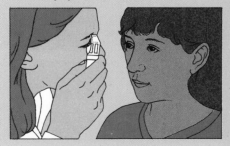

*Continued from previous page*

**Have you developed double vision?** → ■ **YES** → **Do your eyes seem to be bulging or staring?** → ■ **YES** →

**Exophthalmos,** a condition in which the eyes protrude, is a possibility. Consult your physician.

***Treatment:*** Your physician will probably arrange for tests to find out if an underlying disorder, such as an overactive thyroid gland (thyrotoxicosis), is causing this condition. Treatment of thyrotoxicosis (p. 24) may consist of radioactive iodine, other medications or surgery.

↓ **NO** (under "Have you developed double vision?")

↓ **NO** (under "Do your eyes seem to be bulging or staring?")

**An eye muscle problem** may have developed. This is the result of a lack of coordination between the muscles responsible for the movement of both eyes. Consult your physician.

***Treatment:*** Your physician will probably arrange for you to have tests to find the underlying cause for the problem. These may include measuring your blood pressure, blood and urine analysis, a skull X ray, and possibly a *CAT (computerized axial tomography) scan* (p. 39) of the brain. While you are awaiting the results of such tests, your physician may suggest that you wear a patch over one eye to prevent double vision. Long-term treatment will depend on the underlying cause of the strabismus.

**Have you been seeing flashing lights, floating spots AND/OR suffering other visual disturbances?** → ■ **YES** → **Has this happened before AND did a severe headache follow?** → ■ **YES** →

↓ **NO** (under "Has this happened before AND did a severe headache follow?")

**CONSULT YOUR PHYSICIAN WITHOUT DELAY!**
**Retinal detachment,** a disorder in which the lining of the back of the eye is torn, may cause such symptoms in its early stages.

***Treatment:*** The earlier treatment of this problem is started, the greater the chance of success. If the disorder is in its early stages, cryosurgery or sometimes laser treatment may be possible. Otherwise conventional surgery may be necessary. Following retinal detachment in one eye, there is a considerable risk of it developing in the other. Your other eye will therefore also be examined and treatment carried out if necessary.

**Migraine** (recurrent severe headaches) may be preceded by a warning period in which you may experience visual disturbances. Consult your physician.

***Treatment:*** If you suffer from migraines regularly, try to find out if any particular food or other factor seems to trigger the headaches, so that you can avoid it. The self-help measures suggested on p. 38 may help to relieve the pain. Your physician will be able to offer more effective drug treatment if the attacks recur.

↓ **NO** (under "Have you been seeing flashing lights...")

**Consult your physician** if you are unable to make a diagnosis from this chart.

---

## THE STRUCTURE OF THE EYE

The eye is a complex and delicate structure. The eyeball itself consists of 3 layers:

**The sclera,** the tough outer layer, is visible as the white of the eye. It is protected at the front by the conjunctiva, a clear membrane that also lines the inner surface of the eyelids. The colored part of the eye, the iris, is covered by the cornea.

**The choroid layer** beneath the sclera is rich in blood vessels that supply the retina (the light-sensitive inner lining of the eyeball) with oxygen. At the front of the eye, the choroid layer thickens to form the ciliary body, a circle of muscles that supports and controls the lens. In front of the ciliary body lies the iris, which contains muscular fibers that control the amount of light that passes through the lens. The area between the iris and the cornea is filled with watery fluid known as the aqueous humor.

**The retina** is the innermost layer of the eyeball. This contains the light-sensitive nerve cells that pick up images and transmit the information through the optic nerve to the brain. The inner part of the eyeball is filled with a thick, jelly-like substance called the vitreous humor.

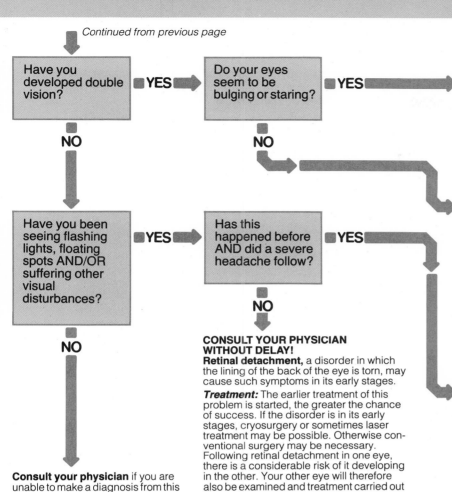

Labels: Eye muscles, Retina, Sclera, Conjunctiva, Eyelids, Aqueous humor, Cornea, Pupil, Eyelashes, Iris, Ciliary body, Vitreous humor, Optic nerve, Lens, Choroid layer

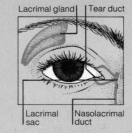

Labels: Lacrimal gland, Tear duct, Lacrimal sac, Nasolacrimal duct

**Tear glands and ducts**
Tears are produced in the lacrimal glands above each eyeball and drain away along tear ducts in the inner corners of the lids, into the lacrimal sac, and via the nasolacrimal duct into the nose.

## CONTACT LENSES

In recent years, contact lenses have become a popular alternative to eyeglasses as a means of correcting defects in vision such as nearsightedness or farsightedness. There are 2 main types of lens: the hard lens, which is made of hard-wearing plastic, but may be uncomfortable for some people; and the soft lens, which is often more comfortable, but is more easily damaged and not so long-lasting. Your ophthalmologist will help you decide which type of lens is most suitable.

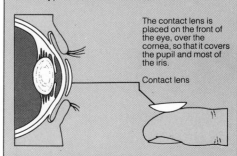

The contact lens is placed on the front of the eye, over the cornea, so that it covers the pupil and most of the iris.

Contact lens

**Care of contact lenses**
All types of contact lenses need regular and careful cleaning to remove dirt and prevent the buildup of protein deposits on the lens. If this is not done there is a danger of infection and permanent damage to the eye. Always use the special cleaning and soaking solutions recommended for your type of lens, and follow your ophthalmologist's detailed advice on the care of your lenses precisely.

# 29 Earache

Earache may vary from a dull, throbbing sensation to a sharp, stabbing pain that can be most distressing. It is a common symptom in childhood, but occurs much less frequently in adults. Pain in the ear is usually caused by infection and normally requires medical attention and antibiotic treatment.

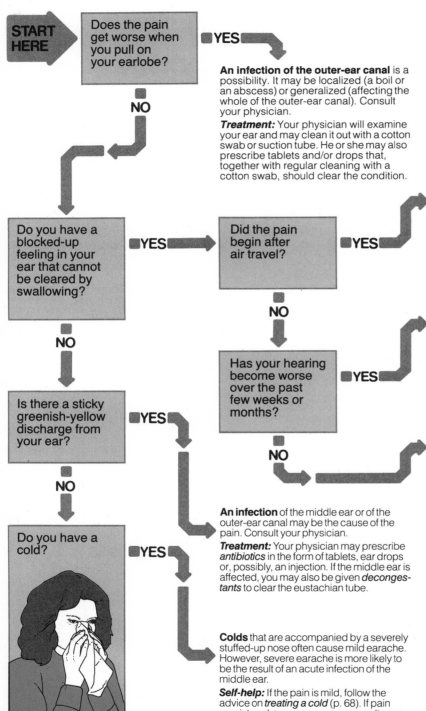

**START HERE**

**Does the pain get worse when you pull on your earlobe?**

**YES** →

**An infection of the outer-ear canal** is a possibility. It may be localized (a boil or an abscess) or generalized (affecting the whole of the outer-ear canal). Consult your physician.

*Treatment:* Your physician will examine your ear and may clean it out with a cotton swab or suction tube. He or she may also prescribe tablets and/or drops that, together with regular cleaning with a cotton swab, should clear the condition.

**NO**

**Do you have a blocked-up feeling in your ear that cannot be cleared by swallowing?**

**YES** →

**Did the pain begin after air travel?**

**YES** →

**Barotrauma,** in which the air-pressure balance between the middle and outer ears is disrupted, is a possibility, especially if you had a cold or a stuffy nose when you traveled.

*Self-help:* Try blowing through your nose while pinching the nostrils closed. In many cases, this brings relief. If the trouble persists for more than 24 hours, consult your physician.

**NO**

**Has your hearing become worse over the past few weeks or months?**

**YES** →

**Wax blockage** may be causing the pain.

*Self-help:* To remove wax yourself, soften it with over-the-counter ear drops or warm oil for several days. Then lie in a warm bath with your ears submerged to loosen it. The wax should work its way out of the outer-ear canal by itself. If you cannot remove the wax yourself, or if pain persists, consult your physician, who may flush (syringe) the ear with warm water to wash away the blockage. Never attempt to lever the wax out yourself by poking a pointed instrument into your ear, as this may tear a hole in the eardrum or canal skin.

**NO**

**Is there a sticky greenish-yellow discharge from your ear?**

**YES** →

**An infection** of the middle ear or of the outer-ear canal may be the cause of the pain. Consult your physician.

*Treatment:* Your physician may prescribe *antibiotics* in the form of tablets, ear drops or, possibly, an injection. If the middle ear is affected, you may also be given *decongestants* to clear the eustachian tube.

**NO**

**Do you have a cold?**

**YES** →

**Colds** that are accompanied by a severely stuffed-up nose often cause mild earache. However, severe earache is more likely to be the result of an acute infection of the middle ear.

*Self-help:* If the pain is mild, follow the advice on *treating a cold* (p. 68). If pain persists or becomes severe, consult your physician, who may prescribe *decongestant* nose drops or spray and, possibly, *antibiotics.*

**NO**

**An acute infection of the middle ear** is a possibility. This may have occurred as a result of blockage of the eustachian tube. Consult your physician.

*Treatment:* Your physician may prescribe *decongestant* nose drops or spray, to help unblock the eustachian tube and to allow restoration of normal ear pressure. In addition, you may be given *antibiotics* to clear up a bacterial infection.

**Consult your physician** if you are unable to make a diagnosis from this chart.

---

### HOW TO RELIEVE AN EARACHE

In any case of earache, you will be able to relieve the pain by taking the recommended dose of aspirin or an aspirin substitute. It may also be comforting to place a warm heating pad against the ear. But remember that these measures alone will not cure the underlying disorder. With persistent cases of earache, you should always consult your physician.

---

### EAR PIERCING

Many woman have holes pierced in their earlobes for earrings. If done properly, this is a perfectly safe and painless procedure, but unfortunately, in many cases it is carried out inexpertly, leading to discomfort and sometimes infection. If you want to have your ears pierced, go to a reputable jeweler or department store. Ask what method of ear piercing they use. The usual technique is to use a special ear punch along with a local anesthetic. Other methods may not be reliable. Make sure that the conditions look clean and that all the instruments and earrings are sterilized before use. When you have had your ears pierced, you should wear only earrings of high-carat gold for the first month and these should not be removed for the first two weeks. You will need to bathe the earlobe with hydrogen peroxide or isopropyl (rubbing) alcohol twice a day during this time. Do not have your ears pierced if you have any skin infection affecting the earlobes. If either earlobe becomes inflamed or if there is any pus after having your ears pierced, consult your physician.

# 30 Noises in the ear

If you sometimes hear noises inside your ears, such as buzzing, ringing or hissing, you are probably suffering from a symptom known as tinnitus. This symptom can indicate a variety of ear disorders.

**START HERE** → **Did the noises start during or after air travel?** — **YES** →

**Barotrauma,** in which the air-pressure balance between the middle and outer ears is disrupted, is a possibility, especially if you had a cold or a blocked nose when you traveled.

***Self-help:*** Try blowing through your nose while pinching the nostrils closed. In many cases, this restores hearing to normal. If the trouble persists for more than 24 hours, consult your physician.

**NO** ↓

**Have you noticed any loss of hearing?** — **YES** →

**Deafness** often occurs together with noises in the ear.

Go to chart

**31** **Deafness**

**NO** ↓

**Are you taking, or have you recently taken, any prescribed or over-the-counter medications?** — **YES** →

**Certain drugs** can cause noises in the ear as a side effect. Discuss the problem with your physician.

**NO** ↓

**Do you have a tickling sensation in the ear?** — **YES** →

**An insect,** or other foreign body, may have become trapped in your outer-ear canal.

***Self-help:*** Carry out the first-aid suggestions described above. If these are not effective, consult your physician. Never attempt to remove anything by inserting an object into the ear.

**NO** ↓

**Consult your physician** if you are unable to make a diagnosis from this chart, especially if associated with hearing loss, dizziness, headache or ear pressure.

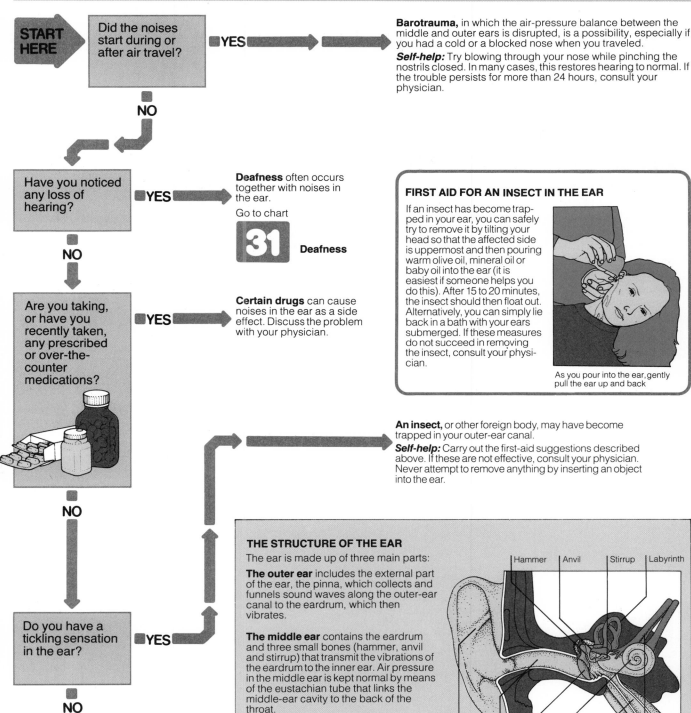

**FIRST AID FOR AN INSECT IN THE EAR**

If an insect has become trapped in your ear, you can safely try to remove it by tilting your head so that the affected side is uppermost and then pouring warm olive oil, mineral oil or baby oil into the ear (it is easiest if someone helps you do this). After 15 to 20 minutes, the insect should then float out. Alternatively, you can simply lie back in a bath with your ears submerged. If these measures do not succeed in removing the insect, consult your physician.

As you pour into the ear, gently pull the ear up and back

**THE STRUCTURE OF THE EAR**

The ear is made up of three main parts:

**The outer ear** includes the external part of the ear, the pinna, which collects and funnels sound waves along the outer-ear canal to the eardrum, which then vibrates.

**The middle ear** contains the eardrum and three small bones (hammer, anvil and stirrup) that transmit the vibrations of the eardrum to the inner ear. Air pressure in the middle ear is kept normal by means of the eustachian tube that links the middle-ear cavity to the back of the throat.

**The inner ear** is filled with fluid and contains the cochlea, which converts the vibrations from the middle ear into nerve impulses. These are passed to the brain by the auditory nerve. The inner ear also contains the labyrinth (semicircular canals), which controls the body's balance.

Hammer · Anvil · Stirrup · Labyrinth · Cochlea · Eustachian tube · Auditory nerve · Pinna · Outer-ear canal · Eardrum

# 31 Deafness

**Deafness – decreased ability to hear some or all sounds – may come on gradually over a period of months or years, or may occur suddenly over a matter of days or** hours. One or both ears may be affected. In most cases, deafness is the result of infection or wax blockage and can be treated.

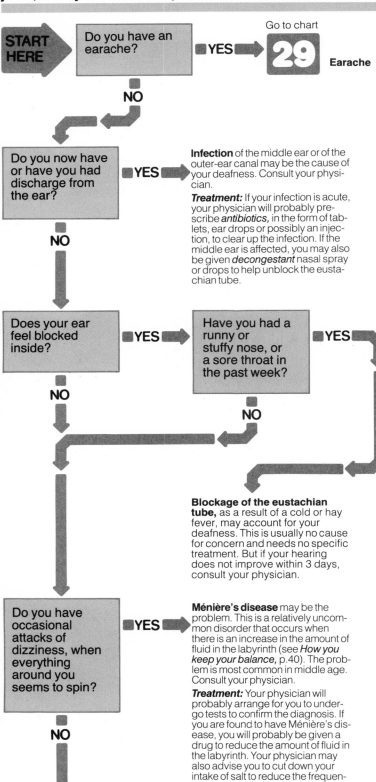

**START HERE** ➡ **Do you have an earache?** ➡ **YES** ➡ Go to chart **29** Earache

**NO**

**Do you now have or have you had discharge from the ear?** ➡ **YES** ➡

**Infection** of the middle ear or of the outer-ear canal may be the cause of your deafness. Consult your physician.

**Treatment:** If your infection is acute, your physician will probably prescribe *antibiotics,* in the form of tablets, ear drops or possibly an injection, to clear up the infection. If the middle ear is affected, you may also be given *decongestant* nasal spray or drops to help unblock the eustachian tube.

**NO**

**Does your ear feel blocked inside?** ➡ **YES** ➡ **Have you had a runny or stuffy nose, or a sore throat in the past week?** ➡ **YES** ➡

**NO**

**NO**

**Blockage of the eustachian tube,** as a result of a cold or hay fever, may account for your deafness. This is usually no cause for concern and needs no specific treatment. But if your hearing does not improve within 3 days, consult your physician.

**Do you have occasional attacks of dizziness, when everything around you seems to spin?** ➡ **YES** ➡

**Ménière's disease** may be the problem. This is a relatively uncommon disorder that occurs when there is an increase in the amount of fluid in the labyrinth (see *How you keep your balance,* p.40). The problem is most common in middle age. Consult your physician.

**Treatment:** Your physician will probably arrange for you to undergo tests to confirm the diagnosis. If you are found to have Ménière's disease, you will probably be given a drug to reduce the amount of fluid in the labyrinth. Your physician may also advise you to cut down your intake of salt to reduce the frequency of future attacks. Sometimes an operation is recommended.

**NO**

*Go to next page*

---

**HEARING TESTS**

If, after examining you, your physician suspects that your hearing is impaired, he or she may refer you for specialized hearing tests known as audiometry and acoustic impedance testing.

**Audiometry**
The first part of this test measures your ability to hear sounds conducted through the air. You are asked to listen through headphones, one ear at a time, to different pitches of sound. Each sound is played first at an inaudible level, then the volume is gradually increased until you signal that you can hear it.

The second part of the test measures your ability to hear the same sounds conducted through the bones in your head. For this test you wear a special headset that vibrates against your skull, usually behind the ear.

The third part of the test measures your ability to understand and repeat certain words.

The results of the tests are recorded on an audiogram and show what sounds you have difficulty hearing.

In the first part of the test, your ability to hear sound through headphones is measured (above). In the second part of the test, you wear a special headset behind your ears that transmits vibrations through the bones in your skull (right).

**Acoustic impedance testing**
Acoustic impedance testing is used to assess the movement of the eardrum, which may be impaired as a result of a disorder of the middle ear. A special probe containing a sound transmitter and receiver is inserted into the outer-ear canal. Air is pumped through the probe and the ability of the eardrum to reflect sound emitted by the sound transmitter at different air pressure levels is measured. From the results it is possible to determine the ease with which sound is transmitted through the eardrum and into the inner ear.

*Continued from previous page*

**Do you regularly spend time listening to loud music, for example, at rock concerts or discos, or through headphones; are you often exposed to loud noise at work; or are you exposed to loud noise through hobbies involving power tools or firearms?**

■YES■▶

**Repeated exposure to loud noise** has probably caused your hearing loss. Even noise levels that do not cause discomfort can result in permanent damage to your hearing. Headphones can be particularly dangerous, since it is easy to have the volume too high (to overcome external noises such as traffic) without realizing it.

*Self-help:* Take appropriate steps to avoid noise exposure. Keep well away from the speakers at rock concerts and discos, and reduce the volume on your headphones so that others in the same room cannot hear the music. If you work in noisy surroundings (in a factory, for example), your employer should supply you with ear protectors, or you can buy your own earplugs. You should consult your physician, who may arrange for you to have special hearing tests and, if necessary, recommend a hearing aid.

**NO**
▼

**Have you recently taken any prescribed or over-the-counter medications?**

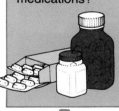

■YES■▶

**Certain drugs** can cause deafness as a side effect. Discuss the problem with your physician.

**Have other members of your family suffered from gradual hearing loss?**

■YES■▶

**NO**
▼

**Wax blockage** may be the cause of your deafness.

*Self-help:* To remove wax yourself, soften it with over-the-counter ear drops or warm oil for several days. Then lie in a warm bath with your ears submerged to loosen the wax, which should work its way out of the outer ear by itself. If you cannot remove the wax this way, do not attempt to lever it out by poking a pointed instrument into your ear. Consult your physician, who will flush (syringe) the ear with warm water to wash away the blockage.

**NO**
▼

**Has your hearing been getting worse over a period of several weeks or more?**

■YES■

**NO**
▼

**Consult your physician** if you are unable to make a diagnosis from this chart.

### STAPEDECTOMY

Stapedectomy is an operation on the stirup bone in the middle ear that is often carried out in severe cases of otosclerosis. Usually the operation produces a marked improvement in hearing but, unfortunately, in a small proportion of cases it results in complete deafness in that ear.

**The operation**
During the operation, the eardrum is moved aside and the stirrup, one of the three tiny bones in the middle ear that is immobilized by the disease, is replaced by a metal or plastic substitute. This improves the conduction of sound through the middle ear.

Stapedectomy usually involves a hospital stay of 2 to 3 days and convalescence at home for another week or so. You may feel dizzy for a few days following the operation.

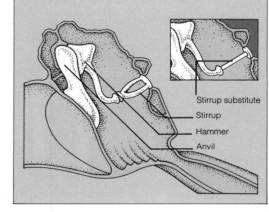

Stirrup substitute
Stirrup
Hammer
Anvil

**Are you over 50 years old?**

■YES■▶

**NO**
▼

**Otosclerosis,** a disorder that affects the working of the bones in the middle ear, may be the problem. This type of deafness usually affects young adults and is especially common in women. The disorder may get worse during pregnancy (see *Deafness and pregnancy,* below left). Consult your physician.

*Treatment:* If your physician suspects otosclerosis, he or she will probably arrange for you to undergo *hearing tests* (opposite). If you have serious loss of hearing in one or both ears, a *stapedectomy* (above) may be recommended.

### DEAFNESS AND PREGNANCY

If you notice any loss of hearing during pregnancy, you should always seek your physician's advice. This is because otosclerosis, a middle-ear disorder resulting in progressive deafness, can sometimes appear for the first time or get worse during pregnancy. The disorder tends to run in families.

**Presbycusis,** gradual loss of hearing as you get older, is common, especially if other members of your family have become deaf in old age. Consult your physician.

*Treatment:* Your physician may refer you for *hearing tests* (opposite). If these confirm the diagnosis, you will probably be offered a hearing aid.

# 32 Runny nose

Blockage of the nose by a thick or watery discharge is probably one of the most familiar symptoms. It is nearly always caused by irritation of the mucous membrane lining of the nose. This is usually the result of infection, but may sometimes occur as an allergic reaction. A runny nose rarely indicates serious disorder.

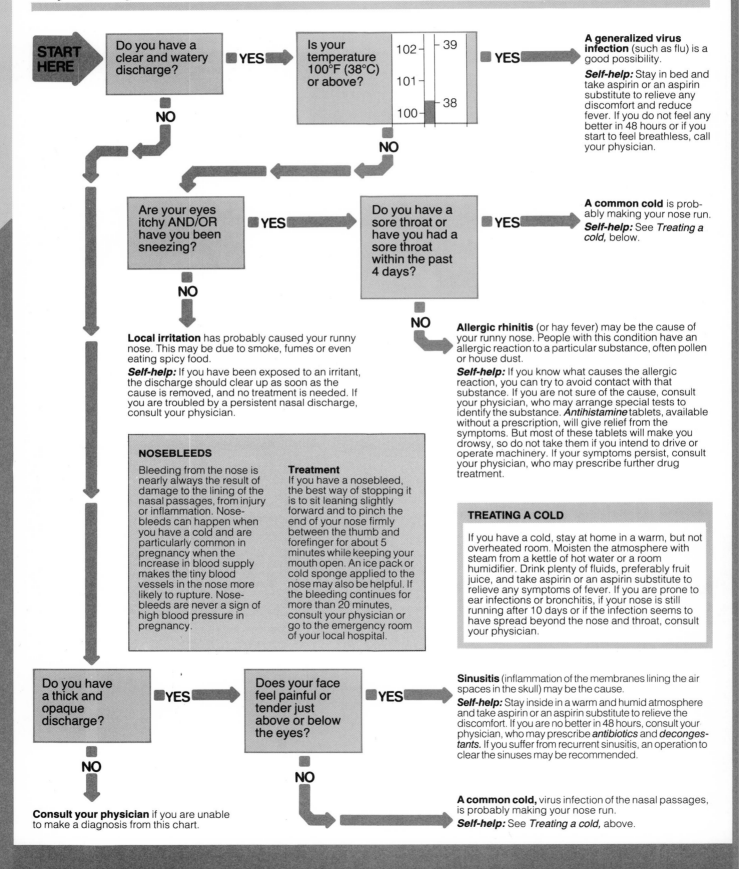

**START HERE**

**Do you have a clear and watery discharge?**

**YES** → **Is your temperature 100°F (38°C) or above?**

| | |
|---|---|
| 102 | 39 |
| 101 | 38 |
| 100 | |

**YES** → **A generalized virus infection** (such as flu) is a good possibility.

*Self-help:* Stay in bed and take aspirin or an aspirin substitute to relieve any discomfort and reduce fever. If you do not feel any better in 48 hours or if you start to feel breathless, call your physician.

**NO**

**NO**

**Are your eyes itchy AND/OR have you been sneezing?**

**YES** → **Do you have a sore throat or have you had a sore throat within the past 4 days?**

**YES** → **A common cold** is probably making your nose run.
*Self-help:* See *Treating a cold,* below.

**NO**

**NO**

**Local irritation** has probably caused your runny nose. This may be due to smoke, fumes or even eating spicy food.

*Self-help:* If you have been exposed to an irritant, the discharge should clear up as soon as the cause is removed, and no treatment is needed. If you are troubled by a persistent nasal discharge, consult your physician.

**Allergic rhinitis** (or hay fever) may be the cause of your runny nose. People with this condition have an allergic reaction to a particular substance, often pollen or house dust.

*Self-help:* If you know what causes the allergic reaction, you can try to avoid contact with that substance. If you are not sure of the cause, consult your physician, who may arrange special tests to identify the substance. *Antihistamine* tablets, available without a prescription, will give relief from the symptoms. But most of these tablets will make you drowsy, so do not take them if you intend to drive or operate machinery. If your symptoms persist, consult your physician, who may prescribe further drug treatment.

### NOSEBLEEDS

Bleeding from the nose is nearly always the result of damage to the lining of the nasal passages, from injury or inflammation. Nosebleeds can happen when you have a cold and are particularly common in pregnancy when the increase in blood supply makes the tiny blood vessels in the nose more likely to rupture. Nosebleeds are never a sign of high blood pressure in pregnancy.

**Treatment**
If you have a nosebleed, the best way of stopping it is to sit leaning slightly forward and to pinch the end of your nose firmly between the thumb and forefinger for about 5 minutes while keeping your mouth open. An ice pack or cold sponge applied to the nose may also be helpful. If the bleeding continues for more than 20 minutes, consult your physician or go to the emergency room of your local hospital.

### TREATING A COLD

If you have a cold, stay at home in a warm, but not overheated room. Moisten the atmosphere with steam from a kettle of hot water or a room humidifier. Drink plenty of fluids, preferably fruit juice, and take aspirin or an aspirin substitute to relieve any symptoms of fever. If you are prone to ear infections or bronchitis, if your nose is still running after 10 days or if the infection seems to have spread beyond the nose and throat, consult your physician.

**Do you have a thick and opaque discharge?**

**YES** → **Does your face feel painful or tender just above or below the eyes?**

**YES** → **Sinusitis** (inflammation of the membranes lining the air spaces in the skull) may be the cause.

*Self-help:* Stay inside in a warm and humid atmosphere and take aspirin or an aspirin substitute to relieve the discomfort. If you are no better in 48 hours, consult your physician, who may prescribe *antibiotics* and *decongestants.* If you suffer from recurrent sinusitis, an operation to clear the sinuses may be recommended.

**NO**

**NO**

**Consult your physician** if you are unable to make a diagnosis from this chart.

**A common cold,** virus infection of the nasal passages, is probably making your nose run.
*Self-help:* See *Treating a cold,* above.

# 33 Sore throat

Most people suffer from a painful, rough or raw feeling in the throat at times. This is usually the result of a minor infection or local irritation, and almost always disappears within a day or so without treatment.

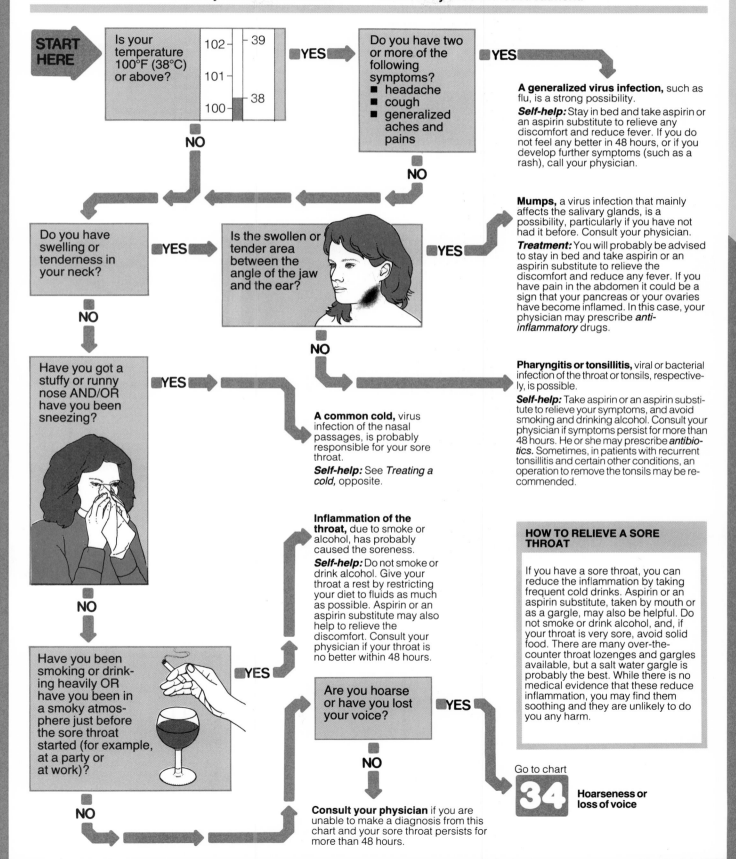

**START HERE**

**Is your temperature 100°F (38°C) or above?**

102 — 39
101 —
100 — 38

**YES** → **Do you have two or more of the following symptoms?**
- headache
- cough
- generalized aches and pains

**YES** →

**A generalized virus infection,** such as flu, is a strong possibility.
***Self-help:*** Stay in bed and take aspirin or an aspirin substitute to relieve any discomfort and reduce fever. If you do not feel any better in 48 hours, or if you develop further symptoms (such as a rash), call your physician.

**NO**

**NO**

**Do you have swelling or tenderness in your neck?**

**YES** → **Is the swollen or tender area between the angle of the jaw and the ear?**

**YES** →

**Mumps,** a virus infection that mainly affects the salivary glands, is a possibility, particularly if you have not had it before. Consult your physician.
***Treatment:*** You will probably be advised to stay in bed and take aspirin or an aspirin substitute to relieve the discomfort and reduce any fever. If you have pain in the abdomen it could be a sign that your pancreas or your ovaries have become inflamed. In this case, your physician may prescribe *anti-inflammatory* drugs.

**NO**

**NO**

**Have you got a stuffy or runny nose AND/OR have you been sneezing?**

**YES** →

**Pharyngitis or tonsillitis,** viral or bacterial infection of the throat or tonsils, respectively, is possible.
***Self-help:*** Take aspirin or an aspirin substitute to relieve your symptoms, and avoid smoking and drinking alcohol. Consult your physician if symptoms persist for more than 48 hours. He or she may prescribe *antibiotics.* Sometimes, in patients with recurrent tonsillitis and certain other conditions, an operation to remove the tonsils may be recommended.

**A common cold,** virus infection of the nasal passages, is probably responsible for your sore throat.
***Self-help:*** See *Treating a cold,* opposite.

**NO**

**Inflammation of the throat,** due to smoke or alcohol, has probably caused the soreness.
***Self-help:*** Do not smoke or drink alcohol. Give your throat a rest by restricting your diet to fluids as much as possible. Aspirin or an aspirin substitute may also help to relieve the discomfort. Consult your physician if your throat is no better within 48 hours.

**Have you been smoking or drinking heavily OR have you been in a smoky atmosphere just before the sore throat started (for example, at a party or at work)?**

**YES** →

**NO**

### HOW TO RELIEVE A SORE THROAT

If you have a sore throat, you can reduce the inflammation by taking frequent cold drinks. Aspirin or an aspirin substitute, taken by mouth or as a gargle, may also be helpful. Do not smoke or drink alcohol, and, if your throat is very sore, avoid solid food. There are many over-the-counter throat lozenges and gargles available, but a salt water gargle is probably the best. While there is no medical evidence that these reduce inflammation, you may find them soothing and they are unlikely to do you any harm.

**Are you hoarse or have you lost your voice?**

**YES** →

Go to chart
**34** Hoarseness or loss of voice

**NO**

**Consult your physician** if you are unable to make a diagnosis from this chart and your sore throat persists for more than 48 hours.

# 34 Hoarseness or loss of voice

Hoarseness, huskiness or loss of voice is almost always caused by laryngitis – inflammation and swelling of the vocal cords that interferes with their ability to vibrate normally to produce sounds. There can be a variety of underlying causes for this inflammation, including infections or irritations, most of which are minor and easily treated at home. However, persistent or recurrent hoarseness or loss of voice may have a more serious cause and should always be brought to your physician's attention without delay.

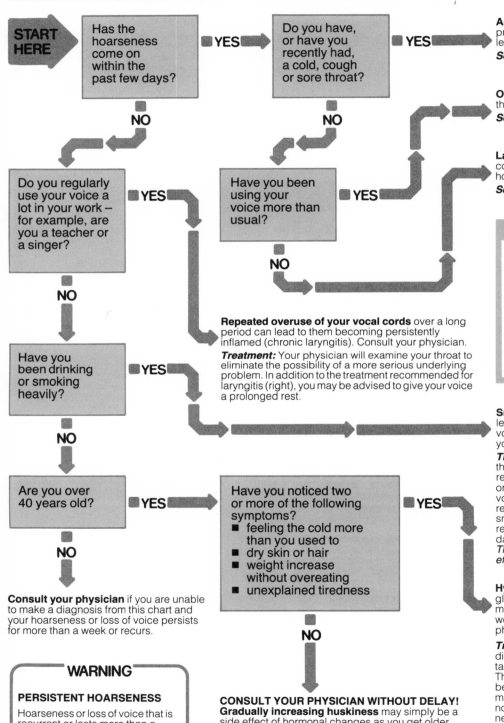

**START HERE**

**Has the hoarseness come on within the past few days?** — **YES** → **Do you have, or have you recently had, a cold, cough or sore throat?** — **YES** →

**An infection affecting the throat** has probably inflamed your vocal cords, leading to laryngitis.
*Self-help:* See *Treating laryngitis*, below.

**Overuse of the vocal cords** can inflame them, leading to laryngitis.
*Self-help:* See *Treating laryngitis*, below.

**Laryngitis** (inflammation of the vocal cords) is the most likely cause of sudden hoarseness or loss of voice.
*Self-help:* See *Treating laryngitis*, below.

**Do you have, or have you recently had, a cold, cough or sore throat?** → **NO** → **Have you been using your voice more than usual?** — **YES** →

**Have you been using your voice more than usual?** → **NO**

**Has the hoarseness come on within the past few days?** → **NO** → **Do you regularly use your voice a lot in your work – for example, are you a teacher or a singer?** — **YES** →

**Do you regularly use your voice a lot in your work – for example, are you a teacher or a singer?** → **NO** → **Have you been drinking or smoking heavily?** — **YES** →

**Repeated overuse of your vocal cords** over a long period can lead to them becoming persistently inflamed (chronic laryngitis). Consult your physician.
*Treatment:* Your physician will examine your throat to eliminate the possibility of a more serious underlying problem. In addition to the treatment recommended for laryngitis (right), you may be advised to give your voice a prolonged rest.

---

### TREATING LARYNGITIS

If you have laryngitis, the following self-help measures should help your voice to return to normal within a week:

- Do not smoke or drink alcohol.
- Rest your voice as much as possible.
- Drink plenty of fluids and take aspirin or an aspirin substitute to relieve any cold-like symptoms.

---

**Smoking and heavy drinking** can both lead to persistent inflammation of the vocal cords (chronic laryngitis). Consult your physician.

*Treatment:* If your physician confirms the diagnosis, he or she will probably recommend that you stop smoking and/or give up alcohol, at least until your voice has recovered. If, however, you return to your former drinking and/or smoking habits, the problem is likely to recur and in time may lead to permanent damage to your vocal cords. See also *The dangers of smoking*, p. 72, and *The effects of alcohol*, p. 22.

**Have you been drinking or smoking heavily?** → **NO** → **Are you over 40 years old?** — **YES** → **Have you noticed two or more of the following symptoms?**
- feeling the cold more than you used to
- dry skin or hair
- weight increase without overeating
- unexplained tiredness

— **YES** →

**Are you over 40 years old?** → **NO**

**Consult your physician** if you are unable to make a diagnosis from this chart and your hoarseness or loss of voice persists for more than a week or recurs.

**Hypothyroidism** (underactive thyroid gland), an uncommon problem that is most likely to occur in middle-aged women, is a possibility. Consult your physician.

*Treatment:* If hypothyroidism is diagnosed, your physician will prescribe tablets of synthetic thyroid hormones. These tablets will make you feel much better in a few days, and after a few months you should have returned to normal health. However, it will be necessary to continue taking the tablets.

**Have you noticed two or more of the following symptoms?** → **NO**

---

### WARNING

**PERSISTENT HOARSENESS**

Hoarseness or loss of voice that is recurrent or lasts more than a week may be a sign of a tumor in the voice box, especially if you are over 40 and smoke.
**Consult your physician without delay!**

---

**CONSULT YOUR PHYSICIAN WITHOUT DELAY!**
**Gradually increasing huskiness** may simply be a side effect of hormonal changes as you get older. However, hoarseness that lasts longer than a week may, in rare cases, be a sign of a tumor in the voice box, particularly if you smoke.

*Treatment:* Your physician will probably examine your throat and may arrange for you to have a *biopsy* (p. 35) of the voice box. Many growths can be removed.

# 35 Wheezing

Wheezing sometimes occurs when breathing out if you have a chest cold, and this is no cause for concern as long as breathing is otherwise normal. Such wheezing can usually be heard only through a stethoscope, but it may become more apparent to you when you exhale violently (during exercise, for example). Loud wheezing, especially if you also feel breathless or if breathing is painful, may be a sign of a number of more serious conditions, including congestive heart failure, asthma and bronchitis, which require medical attention.

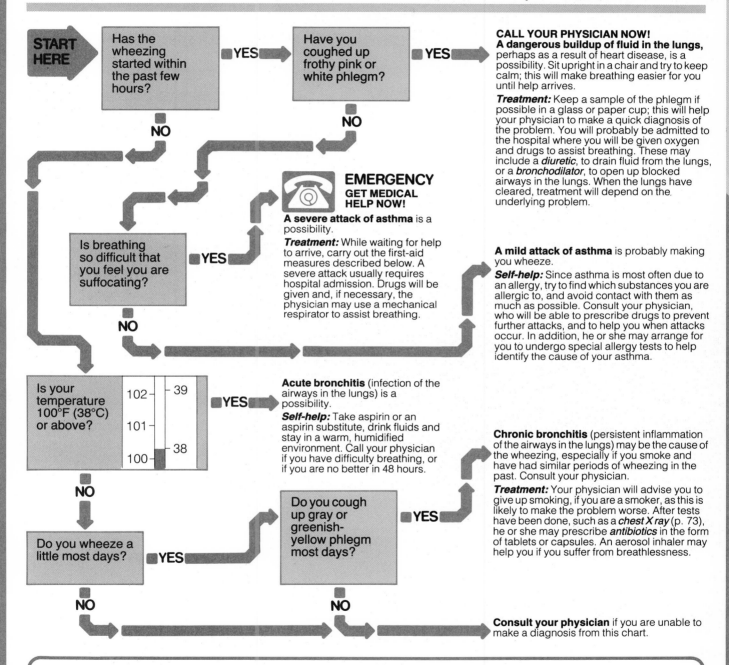

**START HERE**

**Has the wheezing started within the past few hours?** — **YES** → **Have you coughed up frothy pink or white phlegm?** — **YES** →

**CALL YOUR PHYSICIAN NOW!**
**A dangerous buildup of fluid in the lungs,** perhaps as a result of heart disease, is a possibility. Sit upright in a chair and try to keep calm; this will make breathing easier for you until help arrives.

*Treatment:* Keep a sample of the phlegm if possible in a glass or paper cup; this will help your physician to make a quick diagnosis of the problem. You will probably be admitted to the hospital where you will be given oxygen and drugs to assist breathing. These may include a *diuretic*, to drain fluid from the lungs, or a *bronchodilator*, to open up blocked airways in the lungs. When the lungs have cleared, treatment will depend on the underlying problem.

**NO** (from wheezing question)
**NO** (from frothy phlegm question)

**Is breathing so difficult that you feel you are suffocating?** — **YES** →

**EMERGENCY GET MEDICAL HELP NOW!**
**A severe attack of asthma** is a possibility.
*Treatment:* While waiting for help to arrive, carry out the first-aid measures described below. A severe attack usually requires hospital admission. Drugs will be given and, if necessary, the physician may use a mechanical respirator to assist breathing.

**A mild attack of asthma** is probably making you wheeze.
*Self-help:* Since asthma is most often due to an allergy, try to find which substances you are allergic to, and avoid contact with them as much as possible. Consult your physician, who will be able to prescribe drugs to prevent further attacks, and to help you when attacks occur. In addition, he or she may arrange for you to undergo special allergy tests to help identify the cause of your asthma.

**NO**

**Is your temperature 100°F (38°C) or above?**

| 102 | 39 |
| 101 | |
| 100 | 38 |

— **YES** →

**Acute bronchitis** (infection of the airways in the lungs) is a possibility.
*Self-help:* Take aspirin or an aspirin substitute, drink fluids and stay in a warm, humidified environment. Call your physician if you have difficulty breathing, or if you are no better in 48 hours.

**Chronic bronchitis** (persistent inflammation of the airways in the lungs) may be the cause of the wheezing, especially if you smoke and have had similar periods of wheezing in the past. Consult your physician.
*Treatment:* Your physician will advise you to give up smoking, if you are a smoker, as this is likely to make the problem worse. After tests have been done, such as a *chest X ray* (p. 73), he or she may prescribe *antibiotics* in the form of tablets or capsules. An aerosol inhaler may help you if you suffer from breathlessness.

**NO**

**Do you wheeze a little most days?** — **YES** →

**Do you cough up gray or greenish-yellow phlegm most days?** — **YES** →

**NO** **NO**

**Consult your physician** if you are unable to make a diagnosis from this chart.

---

## FIRST AID FOR ASTHMA

A severe attack of asthma, in which the person is fighting for breath and/or becomes pale and clammy with a blue tinge to the tongue or lips, is an emergency and admission to the hospital is essential. Call an ambulance or go to the emergency room of your local hospital immediately. Most people with asthma already have drugs or an inhaling apparatus, both of which should be administered. If one dose of inhalant does not quickly relieve the wheezing, it should be repeated only once.

In all cases, help the asthmatic to find the most comfortable position while you are waiting for medical help. The best position is sitting up, leaning forward on the back of a chair, and taking some of the weight on the arms (right). Plenty of fresh air will also help. A sudden severe attack of asthma can be very frightening for the family as well as the asthmatic. However, anxiety can make the attack worse, so only one other person should remain with the asthmatic and this person should be calm until help is provided.

# 36 Coughing

A cough may produce phlegm or be "dry." It is the body's response to any foreign body, congestion or irritation in the lungs or the throat (for instance, as a result of a cold, smoking or an allergy). Sometimes, however, coughing signals a more serious disorder in the respiratory tract and requires medical attention.

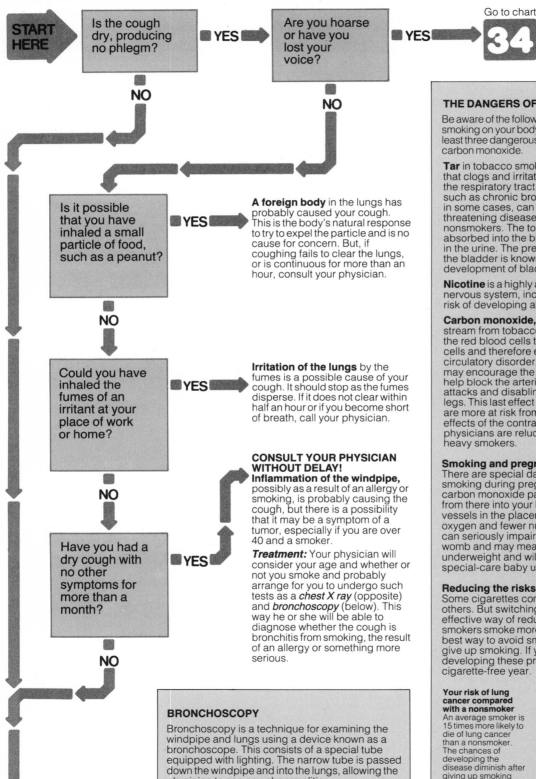

**START HERE** → Is the cough dry, producing no phlegm?

→ **YES** → Are you hoarse or have you lost your voice? → **YES** → Go to chart **34** Hoarseness or loss of voice

**NO** ↓ (from first box)

**NO** ↓ (from second box)

Is it possible that you have inhaled a small particle of food, such as a peanut? → **YES** → **A foreign body** in the lungs has probably caused your cough. This is the body's natural response to try to expel the particle and is no cause for concern. But, if coughing fails to clear the lungs, or is continuous for more than an hour, consult your physician.

**NO** ↓

Could you have inhaled the fumes of an irritant at your place of work or home? → **YES** → **Irritation of the lungs** by the fumes is a possible cause of your cough. It should stop as the fumes disperse. If it does not clear within half an hour or if you become short of breath, call your physician.

**NO** ↓

Have you had a dry cough with no other symptoms for more than a month? → **YES** → **CONSULT YOUR PHYSICIAN WITHOUT DELAY!**
**Inflammation of the windpipe,** possibly as a result of an allergy or smoking, is probably causing the cough, but there is a possibility that it may be a symptom of a tumor, especially if you are over 40 and a smoker.

*Treatment:* Your physician will consider your age and whether or not you smoke and probably arrange for you to undergo such tests as a *chest X ray* (opposite) and *bronchoscopy* (below). This way he or she will be able to diagnose whether the cough is bronchitis from smoking, the result of an allergy or something more serious.

**NO** ↓

*Go to next page*

## BRONCHOSCOPY

Bronchoscopy is a technique for examining the windpipe and lungs using a device known as a bronchoscope. This consists of a special tube equipped with lighting. The narrow tube is passed down the windpipe and into the lungs, allowing the physician to see any abnormalities.

## THE DANGERS OF SMOKING

Be aware of the following facts about the effects of smoking on your body. Tobacco smoke contains at least three dangerous substances: tar, nicotine and carbon monoxide.

**Tar** in tobacco smoke collects as a sticky deposit that clogs and irritates the lungs and other parts of the respiratory tract. This can lead to diseases such as chronic bronchitis and emphysema and, in some cases, can cause lung cancer, a life-threatening disease that is almost unknown in nonsmokers. The toxic chemicals in tar are also absorbed into the bloodstream and then excreted in the urine. The presence of such substances in the bladder is known to contribute to the development of bladder cancer.

**Nicotine** is a highly addictive drug that acts on the nervous system, increasing the heart rate and the risk of developing abnormal heart rhythms.

**Carbon monoxide,** absorbed into the bloodstream from tobacco smoke, reduces the ability of the red blood cells to carry oxygen to the body cells and therefore exaggerates the effects of any circulatory disorder. In addition, carbon monoxide may encourage the formation of substances that help block the arteries and cause fatal heart attacks and disabling circulation problems in the legs. This last effect means that women who smoke are more at risk from possible dangerous side effects of the contraceptive pill and many physicians are reluctant to prescribe the pill to heavy smokers.

**Smoking and pregnancy**
There are special dangers associated with smoking during pregnancy because nicotine and carbon monoxide pass into your bloodstream and from there into your baby's. This makes the blood vessels in the placenta constrict so that less oxygen and fewer nutrients reach your baby. This can seriously impair the growth of your baby in the womb and may mean that he or she will be born underweight and will have to spend time in a special-care baby unit after the birth.

**Reducing the risks**
Some cigarettes contain less tar and nicotine than others. But switching to a low-tar brand is not an effective way of reducing the risks. Most heavy smokers smoke more and inhale more deeply. The best way to avoid smoking-related disease is to give up smoking. If you succeed, the chances of developing these problems diminish with every cigarette-free year.

**Your risk of lung cancer compared with a nonsmoker**
An average smoker is 15 times more likely to die of lung cancer than a nonsmoker. The chances of developing the disease diminish after giving up smoking until after 15 years the risk is equal to that of a nonsmoker.

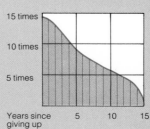

*Continued from previous page*

**Has the cough started within the past week?** — **YES** → **Is your temperature 100°F (38°C) or above?**

| | |
|---|---|
| 102 — | 39 |
| 101 — | |
| 100 — | 38 |

→ **YES** → **Are you short of breath?**

**Has the cough started within the past week?** — **NO** ↓

**Is your temperature 100°F (38°C) or above?** — **NO** ↓

**Are you short of breath?** — **NO** ↓

**Do you have a runny nose AND/OR a sore throat?** — **YES** →

**A common cold,** a viral infection of the nasal passages, has probably caused these symptoms.

***Self-help:*** For advice on the treatment of colds, see p. 68.

**Acute bronchitis** (infection of the airways in the lungs) is a possibility.

***Self-help:*** Take aspirin or an aspirin substitute and cough medicine following the instructions on the labels. Stay in a humid environment but it is not necessary to go to bed. Call your physician if you have difficulty in breathing, or if you are no better in 48 hours.

**Do you have a runny nose AND/OR a sore throat?** — **NO** ↓

**Are you short of breath, even when you have not been exercising?** — **YES** →

Go to chart

**37** **Difficulty breathing**

**CALL YOUR PHYSICIAN NOW!**
**Pneumonia** is a possibility. This is an infection of the lungs that can be dangerous, especially for the elderly and those in poor health.

***Treatment:*** Your physician will probably recommend that you take aspirin or an aspirin substitute to reduce your fever and relieve any discomfort. He or she may prescribe ***antibiotics*** and, in a severe case, may advise admission to a hospital.

**Are you short of breath, even when you have not been exercising?** — **NO** ↓

**Do you cough up thick, gray or greenish-yellow phlegm most days?** — **YES** →

**Chronic bronchitis,** persistent inflammation of the airways to the lungs, may be the cause of a cough, especially if you smoke and have had similar periods of persistent coughing in the past. Consult your physician.

***Treatment:*** Your physician may prescribe ***antibiotics*** in the form of tablets or capsules. An aerosol inhaler may help you if you are suffering from shortness of breath. However, the problem is likely to get worse over the years unless you stop smoking.

**Do you cough up thick, gray or greenish-yellow phlegm most days?** — **NO** ↓

**CONSULT YOUR PHYSICIAN WITHOUT DELAY!**
**A serious lung disorder,** such as tuberculosis or lung cancer, may cause persistent coughing although a simpler explanation, such as an allergy or chronic bronchitis, is more likely.

***Treatment:*** Your physician will probably arrange for tests to find out which underlying disorder is causing the symptoms. You may be asked to give blood and phlegm samples for analysis. A ***chest X ray*** (below) and ***bronchoscopy*** (opposite) may also be necessary.

**Have you had your cough for several weeks or months AND has it been getting more severe?** — **YES** →

**CHEST X RAY**

A chest X ray is an effective way of examining the lungs and is used by chest specialists as their main diagnostic test. It will show up infections, tumors, other lung disorders, fluid or air in the chest cavity and damage to the rib cage.

This chest x ray shows a condition called pericardial effusion, in which fluid collects around the heart.

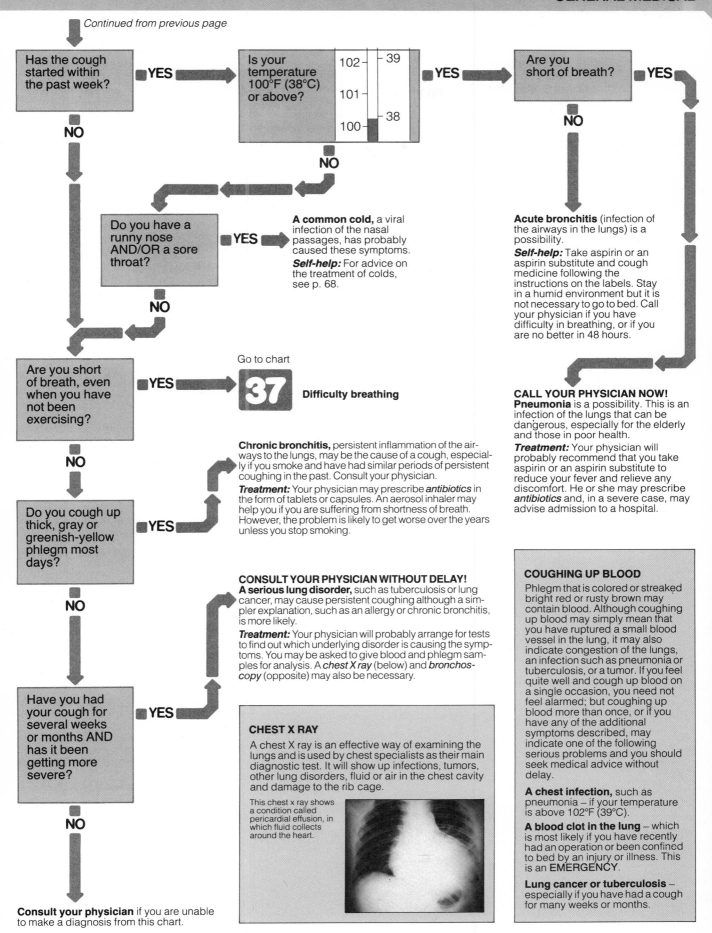

**Have you had your cough for several weeks or months AND has it been getting more severe?** — **NO** ↓

**Consult your physician** if you are unable to make a diagnosis from this chart.

**COUGHING UP BLOOD**

Phlegm that is colored or streaked bright red or rusty brown may contain blood. Although coughing up blood may simply mean that you have ruptured a small blood vessel in the lung, it may also indicate congestion of the lungs, an infection such as pneumonia or tuberculosis, or a tumor. If you feel quite well and cough up blood on a single occasion, you need not feel alarmed; but coughing up blood more than once, or if you have any of the additional symptoms described, may indicate one of the following serious problems and you should seek medical advice without delay.

**A chest infection,** such as pneumonia – if your temperature is above 102°F (39°C).

**A blood clot in the lung** – which is most likely if you have recently had an operation or been confined to bed by an injury or illness. This is an EMERGENCY.

**Lung cancer or tuberculosis** – especially if you have had a cough for many weeks or months.

# 37 Difficulty breathing

If you have the feeling that you cannot get enough air or are breathless to the extent that you are breathing rapidly or "puffing," either at rest or after gentle exercise, this suggests the possibility of a problem affecting the heart or the respiratory system. The sudden onset of difficult breathing while eating is more likely to be caused by choking, and you should immediately carry out first aid as described in the box opposite. Because of the possibility of a disorder that may threaten the supply of oxygen to the body, it is important to seek medical advice promptly if you notice any of the symptoms mentioned in this diagnostic chart.

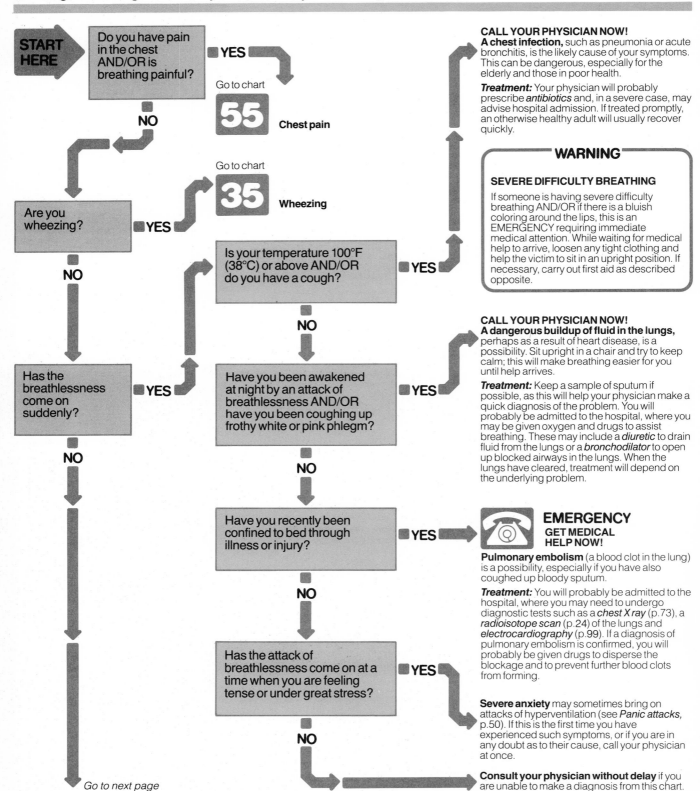

**START HERE**

**Do you have pain in the chest AND/OR is breathing painful?**

YES → Go to chart **55** Chest pain

NO

**Are you wheezing?**

YES → Go to chart **35** Wheezing

NO

**Is your temperature 100°F (38°C) or above AND/OR do you have a cough?**

YES →

NO

**CALL YOUR PHYSICIAN NOW!**
**A chest infection,** such as pneumonia or acute bronchitis, is the likely cause of your symptoms. This can be dangerous, especially for the elderly and those in poor health.

*Treatment:* Your physician will probably prescribe *antibiotics* and, in a severe case, may advise hospital admission. If treated promptly, an otherwise healthy adult will usually recover quickly.

---

**WARNING**

**SEVERE DIFFICULTY BREATHING**

If someone is having severe difficulty breathing AND/OR if there is a bluish coloring around the lips, this is an EMERGENCY requiring immediate medical attention. While waiting for medical help to arrive, loosen any tight clothing and help the victim to sit in an upright position. If necessary, carry out first aid as described opposite.

---

**Has the breathlessness come on suddenly?**

YES →

NO

**Have you been awakened at night by an attack of breathlessness AND/OR have you been coughing up frothy white or pink phlegm?**

YES →

NO

**CALL YOUR PHYSICIAN NOW!**
**A dangerous buildup of fluid in the lungs,** perhaps as a result of heart disease, is a possibility. Sit upright in a chair and try to keep calm; this will make breathing easier for you until help arrives.

*Treatment:* Keep a sample of sputum if possible, as this will help your physician make a quick diagnosis of the problem. You will probably be admitted to the hospital, where you may be given oxygen and drugs to assist breathing. These may include a *diuretic* to drain fluid from the lungs or a *bronchodilator* to open up blocked airways in the lungs. When the lungs have cleared, treatment will depend on the underlying problem.

**Have you recently been confined to bed through illness or injury?**

YES →

NO

**EMERGENCY GET MEDICAL HELP NOW!**

**Pulmonary embolism** (a blood clot in the lung) is a possibility, especially if you have also coughed up bloody sputum.

*Treatment:* You will probably be admitted to the hospital, where you may need to undergo diagnostic tests such as a *chest X ray* (p.73), a *radioisotope scan* (p.24) of the lungs and *electrocardiography* (p.99). If a diagnosis of pulmonary embolism is confirmed, you will probably be given drugs to disperse the blockage and to prevent further blood clots from forming.

**Has the attack of breathlessness come on at a time when you are feeling tense or under great stress?**

YES →

NO

**Severe anxiety** may sometimes bring on attacks of hyperventilation (see *Panic attacks,* p.50). If this is the first time you have experienced such symptoms, or if you are in any doubt as to their cause, call your physician at once.

**Consult your physician without delay** if you are unable to make a diagnosis from this chart.

*Go to next page*

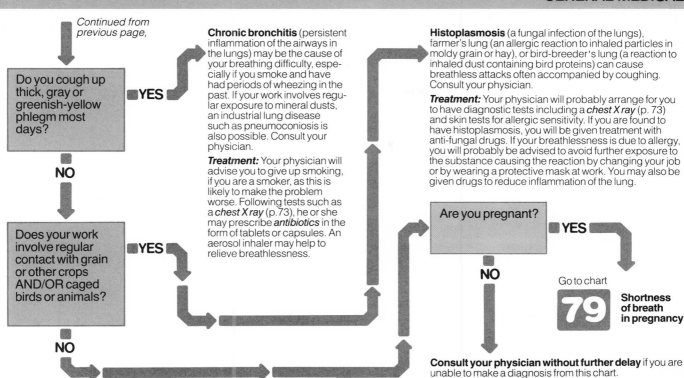

*Continued from previous page,*

**Do you cough up thick, gray or greenish-yellow phlegm most days?** — ▶**YES**

**NO**

**Does your work involve regular contact with grain or other crops AND/OR caged birds or animals?** — ▶**YES**

**NO**

**Chronic bronchitis** (persistent inflammation of the airways in the lungs) may be the cause of your breathing difficulty, especially if you smoke and have had periods of wheezing in the past. If your work involves regular exposure to mineral dusts, an industrial lung disease such as pneumoconiosis is also possible. Consult your physician.

**Treatment:** Your physician will advise you to give up smoking, if you are a smoker, as this is likely to make the problem worse. Following tests such as a *chest X ray* (p.73), he or she may prescribe *antibiotics* in the form of tablets or capsules. An aerosol inhaler may help to relieve breathlessness.

**Histoplasmosis** (a fungal infection of the lungs), farmer's lung (an allergic reaction to inhaled particles in moldy grain or hay), or bird-breeder's lung (a reaction to inhaled dust containing bird proteins) can cause breathless attacks often accompanied by coughing. Consult your physician.

**Treatment:** Your physician will probably arrange for you to have diagnostic tests including a *chest X ray* (p. 73) and skin tests for allergic sensitivity. If you are found to have histoplasmosis, you will be given treatment with anti-fungal drugs. If your breathlessness is due to allergy, you will probably be advised to avoid further exposure to the substance causing the reaction by changing your job or by wearing a protective mask at work. You may also be given drugs to reduce inflammation of the lung.

**Are you pregnant?** — ▶**YES**

**NO**

Go to chart **79** **Shortness of breath in pregnancy**

**Consult your physician without further delay** if you are unable to make a diagnosis from this chart.

## FIRST AID FOR STOPPED BREATHING

If someone stops breathing, carry out first aid as described below before summoning emergency medical help.

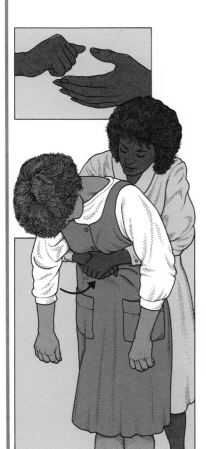

**Suspected choking**
When severe breathing difficulty comes on while eating, and if the victim is unable to cough up the obstruction, carry out the following steps:

**1** Hold the victim up from behind in a standing position, pressing one fist (with thumb inward) against the waist. Hold your other hand over the fist and thrust hard in and up under the rib cage. If this does not clear the blockage, repeat 3 more times.

**2** If this does not clear the obstruction, lay the victim on his or her back. Tilt the head back (chin up), open the mouth and sweep deeply into the mouth with hooked finger (you may need to remove dentures).

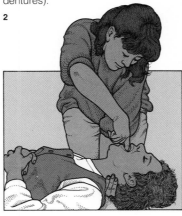

**3** If obstruction is still not dislodged, repeat steps 1 and 2.

**4** If breathing does not restart following removal of the blockage, carry out mouth-to-mouth resuscitation (right).

**Mouth-to-mouth resuscitation**
If a person has actually stopped breathing (whether as a result of an accident such as near drowning or electric shock, or from a medical condition such as a suspected heart attack), immediately start mouth-to-mouth resuscitation.

**1** Lay the victim face upward. Support the back of the neck and tip the head well back. Clear the mouth with your finger to remove any blockage from the windpipe.

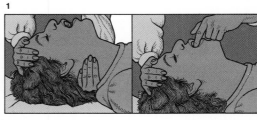

**2** Pinch the nose shut, take a deep breath and seal your mouth around the mouth. Blow strongly into the lungs 4 times.

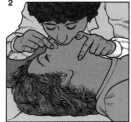

**3** Continue to give a breath every 5 seconds. After each breath remove your mouth. Listen for air leaving the lungs and watch the chest fall. Continue until medical help arrives or until the victim is able to breathe on his own.

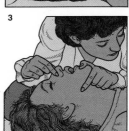

# 38 Toothache

Teeth are just as much living structures as any other part of the body, despite their tough appearance. They are constantly under threat from our diet because of the high level of sugar we consume. Bacteria act on sugar to produce acids that attack enamel, the tooth's protective layer. When this happens, bacterial destruction (decay) spreads down the root canal to the nerve, causing inflammation and pain. Any pain in one tooth or from teeth and gums in general, whether it is a dull throb or a sharp twinge, should be brought to your dentist's attention.

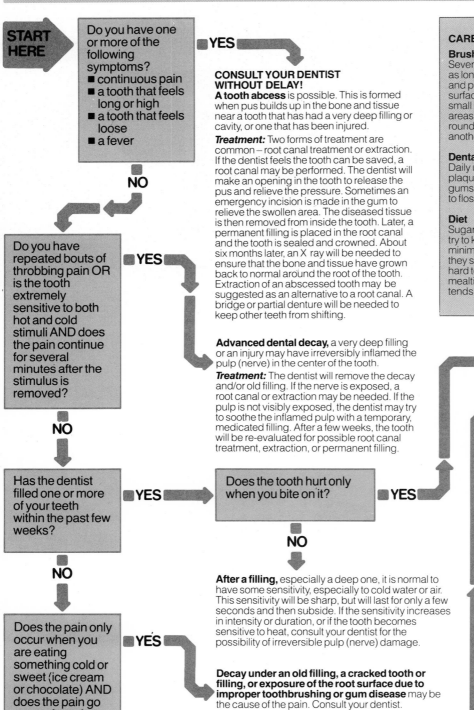

**START HERE**

**Do you have one or more of the following symptoms?**
- continuous pain
- a tooth that feels long or high
- a tooth that feels loose
- a fever

**YES**

**CONSULT YOUR DENTIST WITHOUT DELAY!**
**A tooth abcess** is possible. This is formed when pus builds up in the bone and tissue near a tooth that has had a very deep filling or cavity, or one that has been injured.

*Treatment:* Two forms of treatment are common – root canal treatment or extraction. If the dentist feels the tooth can be saved, a root canal may be performed. The dentist will make an opening in the tooth to release the pus and relieve the pressure. Sometimes an emergency incision is made in the gum to relieve the swollen area. The diseased tissue is then removed from inside the tooth. Later, a permanent filling is placed in the root canal and the tooth is sealed and crowned. About six months later, an X ray will be needed to ensure that the bone and tissue have grown back to normal around the root of the tooth. Extraction of an abscessed tooth may be suggested as an alternative to a root canal. A bridge or partial denture will be needed to keep other teeth from shifting.

**NO**

**Do you have repeated bouts of throbbing pain OR is the tooth extremely sensitive to both hot and cold stimuli AND does the pain continue for several minutes after the stimulus is removed?**

**YES**

**Advanced dental decay,** a very deep filling or an injury may have irreversibly inflamed the pulp (nerve) in the center of the tooth.

*Treatment:* The dentist will remove the decay and/or old filling. If the nerve is exposed, a root canal or extraction may be needed. If the pulp is not visibly exposed, the dentist may try to soothe the inflamed pulp with a temporary, medicated filling. After a few weeks, the tooth will be re-evaluated for possible root canal treatment, extraction, or permanent filling.

**NO**

**Has the dentist filled one or more of your teeth within the past few weeks?**

**YES**

**Does the tooth hurt only when you bite on it?**

**YES**

**An uneven or "high" filling** can cause discomfort. Your dentist will adjust the filling if necessary.

**Does the tooth hurt only when you bite or chew on it?**

**YES**

**NO**

**Dental decay** may have caused a hole (or cavity) to form in your tooth. Consult your dentist.
*Treatment:* Your dentist will probably clean out the affected tooth and put in a filling.

**NO**

**After a filling,** especially a deep one, it is normal to have some sensitivity, especially to cold water or air. This sensitivity will be sharp, but will last for only a few seconds and then subside. If the sensitivity increases in intensity or duration, or if the tooth becomes sensitive to heat, consult your dentist for the possibility of irreversible pulp (nerve) damage.

**NO**

**Does the pain only occur when you are eating something cold or sweet (ice cream or chocolate) AND does the pain go away after a few seconds?**

**YES**

**Decay under an old filling, a cracked tooth or filling, or exposure of the root surface due to improper toothbrushing or gum disease** may be the cause of the pain. Consult your dentist.

*Treatment:* Your dentist may recommend replacing an old filling or remove any decay. If the problem is sensitivity, the dentist may recommend a special desensitizing toothpaste, protective fluoride applications or bonding to seal the sensitive root area.

**A cracked filling or a cracked or fractured tooth** is probably the cause of the pain. Consult your dentist.

*Treatment:* You may need to have the affected tooth crowned (capped) or have a root canal if the pain becomes more severe. The tooth may need to be extracted if the crack is too deep into the tooth. Pain may also be caused by acute sinus problems that make the upper back teeth ache and tender to bite on. If this is the case, you may need to see a physician for further treatment.

**NO**

**CARE OF YOUR TEETH**

**Brushing**
Several tooth brushing techniques are acceptable as long as you manage to remove all traces of food and plaque from the back, front, and biting surfaces of your teeth. If you use a toothbrush with a small head you will be able to get at the difficult areas more easily. The toothbrush should have soft, rounded bristles unless your dentist suggests another type of brush.

**Dental floss**
Daily use of dental floss helps to remove debris and plaque from between your teeth and under your gums. Your dentist or hygienist will teach you how to floss your teeth correctly.

**Diet**
Sugary foods are the main cause of tooth decay, so try to keep your consumption of sweet foods to a minimum. If you need to eat snacks during the day, they should consist of cheese or nuts. If you find it hard to do without sweet foods, confine them to mealtimes and finish the meal with cheese, as this tends to neutralize acid formation.

# 39 Difficulty swallowing

Difficulty swallowing is most often the result of an infection causing soreness, swelling and excess mucus at the back of the throat. Difficulty or pain when swallowing that is not related to a sore throat may be a sign of a more serious disorder affecting the esophagus and should be brought to your physician's attention.

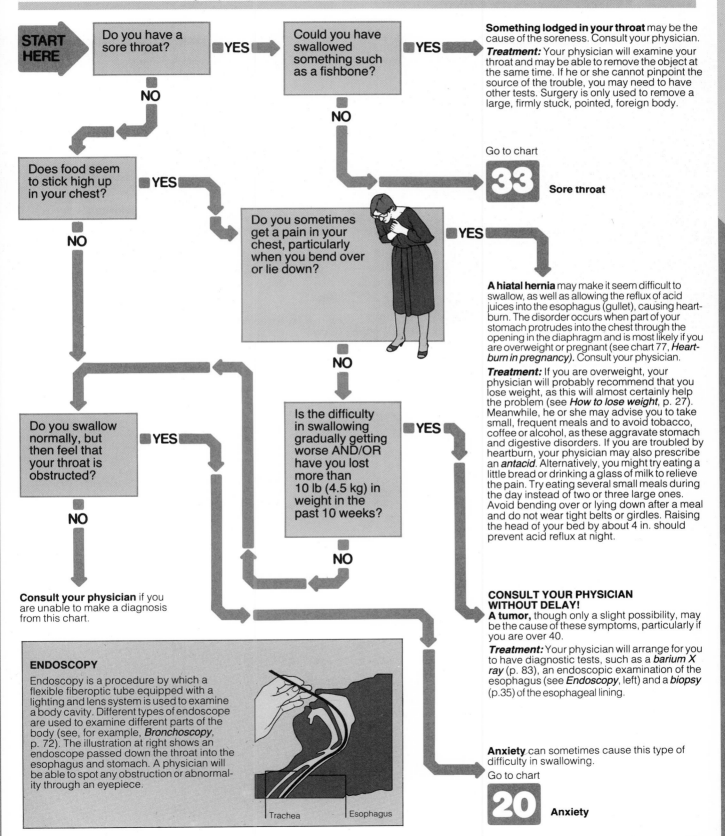

**START HERE**

**Do you have a sore throat?**

**Could you have swallowed something such as a fishbone?**

**Something lodged in your throat** may be the cause of the soreness. Consult your physician.

**Treatment:** Your physician will examine your throat and may be able to remove the object at the same time. If he or she cannot pinpoint the source of the trouble, you may need to have other tests. Surgery is only used to remove a large, firmly stuck, pointed, foreign body.

Go to chart

**33** **Sore throat**

**Does food seem to stick high up in your chest?**

**Do you sometimes get a pain in your chest, particularly when you bend over or lie down?**

**A hiatal hernia** may make it seem difficult to swallow, as well as allowing the reflux of acid juices into the esophagus (gullet), causing heartburn. The disorder occurs when part of your stomach protrudes into the chest through the opening in the diaphragm and is most likely if you are overweight or pregnant (see chart 77, *Heartburn in pregnancy).* Consult your physician.

**Treatment:** If you are overweight, your physician will probably recommend that you lose weight, as this will almost certainly help the problem (see *How to lose weight*, p. 27). Meanwhile, he or she may advise you to take small, frequent meals and to avoid tobacco, coffee or alcohol, as these aggravate stomach and digestive disorders. If you are troubled by heartburn, your physician may also prescribe an *antacid.* Alternatively, you might try eating a little bread or drinking a glass of milk to relieve the pain. Try eating several small meals during the day instead of two or three large ones. Avoid bending over or lying down after a meal and do not wear tight belts or girdles. Raising the head of your bed by about 4 in. should prevent acid reflux at night.

**Do you swallow normally, but then feel that your throat is obstructed?**

**Is the difficulty in swallowing gradually getting worse AND/OR have you lost more than 10 lb (4.5 kg) in weight in the past 10 weeks?**

**Consult your physician** if you are unable to make a diagnosis from this chart.

**CONSULT YOUR PHYSICIAN WITHOUT DELAY!**
**A tumor,** though only a slight possibility, may be the cause of these symptoms, particularly if you are over 40.

**Treatment:** Your physician will arrange for you to have diagnostic tests, such as a *barium X ray* (p. 83), an endoscopic examination of the esophagus (see *Endoscopy,* left) and a *biopsy* (p.35) of the esophageal lining.

## ENDOSCOPY

Endoscopy is a procedure by which a flexible fiberoptic tube equipped with a lighting and lens system is used to examine a body cavity. Different types of endoscope are used to examine different parts of the body (see, for example, *Bronchoscopy,* p. 72). The illustration at right shows an endoscope passed down the throat into the esophagus and stomach. A physician will be able to spot any obstruction or abnormality through an eyepiece.

Trachea    Esophagus

**Anxiety** can sometimes cause this type of difficulty in swallowing.
Go to chart

**20** **Anxiety**

# 40 Sore mouth or tongue

Most painful areas on the lips or tongue or around the teeth are symptoms of minor conditions. You will be able to tell the mild from the serious by the length of time they take to heal. Any condition lasting longer than 3 weeks should be seen by your physician or dentist. It is important to keep the delicate mucous membrane that lines the mouth healthy by maintaining good oral hygiene at all times (see Care of your teeth, p.76).

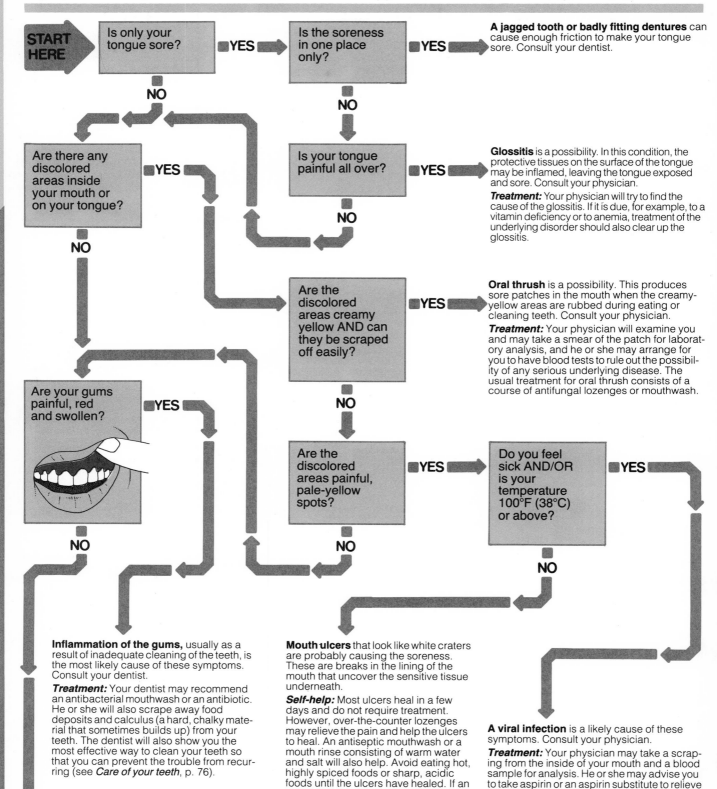

**START HERE**

**Is only your tongue sore?**

**Is the soreness in one place only?**

**A jagged tooth or badly fitting dentures** can cause enough friction to make your tongue sore. Consult your dentist.

**Are there any discolored areas inside your mouth or on your tongue?**

**Is your tongue painful all over?**

**Glossitis** is a possibility. In this condition, the protective tissues on the surface of the tongue may be inflamed, leaving the tongue exposed and sore. Consult your physician.

*Treatment:* Your physician will try to find the cause of the glossitis. If it is due, for example, to a vitamin deficiency or to anemia, treatment of the underlying disorder should also clear up the glossitis.

**Are the discolored areas creamy yellow AND can they be scraped off easily?**

**Oral thrush** is a possibility. This produces sore patches in the mouth when the creamy-yellow areas are rubbed during eating or cleaning teeth. Consult your physician.

*Treatment:* Your physician will examine you and may take a smear of the patch for laboratory analysis, and he or she may arrange for you to have blood tests to rule out the possibility of any serious underlying disease. The usual treatment for oral thrush consists of a course of antifungal lozenges or mouthwash.

**Are your gums painful, red and swollen?**

**Are the discolored areas painful, pale-yellow spots?**

**Do you feel sick AND/OR is your temperature 100°F (38°C) or above?**

**Inflammation of the gums,** usually as a result of inadequate cleaning of the teeth, is the most likely cause of these symptoms. Consult your dentist.

*Treatment:* Your dentist may recommend an antibacterial mouthwash or an antibiotic. He or she will also scrape away food deposits and calculus (a hard, chalky material that sometimes builds up) from your teeth. The dentist will also show you the most effective way to clean your teeth so that you can prevent the trouble from recurring (see *Care of your teeth*, p. 76).

**Mouth ulcers** that look like white craters are probably causing the soreness. These are breaks in the lining of the mouth that uncover the sensitive tissue underneath.

*Self-help:* Most ulcers heal in a few days and do not require treatment. However, over-the-counter lozenges may relieve the pain and help the ulcers to heal. An antiseptic mouthwash or a mouth rinse consisting of warm water and salt will also help. Avoid eating hot, highly spiced foods or sharp, acidic foods until the ulcers have healed. If an ulcer fails to heal within 3 weeks, consult your physician.

**A viral infection** is a likely cause of these symptoms. Consult your physician.

*Treatment:* Your physician may take a scraping from the inside of your mouth and a blood sample for analysis. He or she may advise you to take aspirin or an aspirin substitute to relieve your symptoms.

*Go to next page*

*Continued from previous page*

**Do you have sore places on or around the lips?**

→ **YES** →

**Did the sores start as painful blisters?**

→ **YES** →

**Cold sores** are the likely cause of these symptoms. They are the result of a virus in the body becoming reactivated by a cold, or exposure to strong sunshine or cold weather.

*Self-help:* Mild cases of cold sores clear up on their own. However, there are many over-the-counter preparations that may relieve symptoms. If you are troubled by severe, recurrent cold sores, your physician may prescribe a cream for you to apply when a sore is in its early stages to inhibit its development.

**NO** ↓ (under first box)

**NO** ↓

**Do you have cracks at the corners of your mouth?**

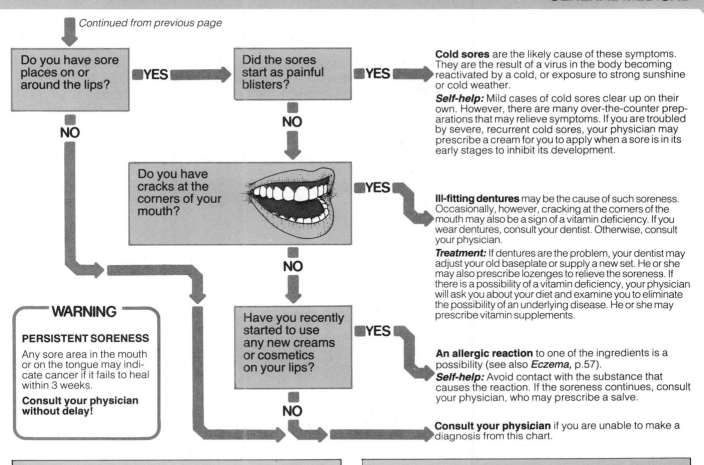

→ **YES** →

**Ill-fitting dentures** may be the cause of such soreness. Occasionally, however, cracking at the corners of the mouth may also be a sign of a vitamin deficiency. If you wear dentures, consult your dentist. Otherwise, consult your physician.

*Treatment:* If dentures are the problem, your dentist may adjust your old baseplate or supply a new set. He or she may also prescribe lozenges to relieve the soreness. If there is a possibility of a vitamin deficiency, your physician will ask you about your diet and examine you to eliminate the possibility of an underlying disease. He or she may prescribe vitamin supplements.

**NO** ↓

**Have you recently started to use any new creams or cosmetics on your lips?**

→ **YES** →

**An allergic reaction** to one of the ingredients is a possibility (see also *Eczema,* p.57).
*Self-help:* Avoid contact with the substance that causes the reaction. If the soreness continues, consult your physician, who may prescribe a salve.

**NO** ↓

**Consult your physician** if you are unable to make a diagnosis from this chart.

---

**WARNING**

**PERSISTENT SORENESS**

Any sore area in the mouth or on the tongue may indicate cancer if it fails to heal within 3 weeks.

**Consult your physician without delay!**

---

## BAD BREATH

You are unlikely to notice that you have bad breath unless it is pointed out to you by a friend. The following are the most common causes of bad breath and are easily remedied:

### Sore mouth
Infection or ulceration of the mouth, gums or tongue may cause bad breath. Rinsing out your mouth with an antiseptic mouthwash usually clears up the problem within a few days. If the problem persists, consult your physician.

### Inadequately cleaned teeth or dentures
If you do not clean your teeth (or dentures, if you wear them) thoroughly at least twice a day, this may be the cause of your bad breath. Decaying food particles lodge between the teeth or stick to the dentures (see *Care of your teeth*, p. 76, and *Caring for your dentures*, right).

### Garlic, onions and alcohol
These foods contain volatile substances that, when absorbed into the bloodstream and then released into the lungs, may cause bad breath. Alcohol may also be responsible for bad breath in much the same way. Your breath should return to normal within 24 hours after consuming these foods.

### Smoking
Smoking always causes a form of bad breath (see also *The dangers of smoking*, p. 72).

If your bad breath continues for some time, it may be a symptom of something more serious such as a mouth infection or a lung disease. Consult your physician.

## CARING FOR YOUR DENTURES

Always remove your dentures at night and keep them in a glass of water containing a cleansing agent so that they do not dry out and warp. This will also give the gum tissues a regular rest period. Brush your dentures thoroughly every day. Your dentist will show you the best way to do this. It is also important to remember to clean any remaining natural teeth thoroughly, especially where teeth and gums meet. Partial dentures may feel a little tight when inserted in the morning, but this is normal and the feeling disappears in a few minutes. The useful life of dentures varies greatly – from 6 months to 5 years or more – depending on how well your gums and jaws keep their shape. If you have a full set of dentures, you should visit the dentist every 2 years. If you still have some natural teeth, you should go for a check-up every 6 months.

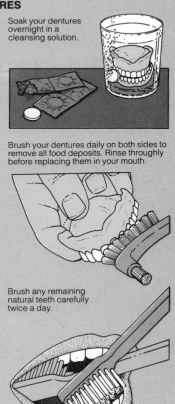

Soak your dentures overnight in a cleansing solution.

Brush your dentures daily on both sides to remove all food deposits. Rinse throughly before replacing them in your mouth.

Brush any remaining natural teeth carefully twice a day.

# 41 Vomiting

Vomiting occurs when the muscles around the stomach suddenly contract and "throw up" the stomach contents. This is usually the result of irritation of the stomach from infection or overindulgence in rich food or alcohol, but may also occur as a result of disturbance elsewhere in the digestive tract. Occasionally, a dis- order affecting the nerve signals from the brain, or from the balance mechanism in the inner ear (p. 40), can also produce vomiting. Most cases of vomiting can be treated at home, but vomiting that is accompanied by severe abdominal pain, or by severe headache or eye pain, requires urgent medical attention.

**For attacks of vomiting, see chart 42, Recurrent vomiting**

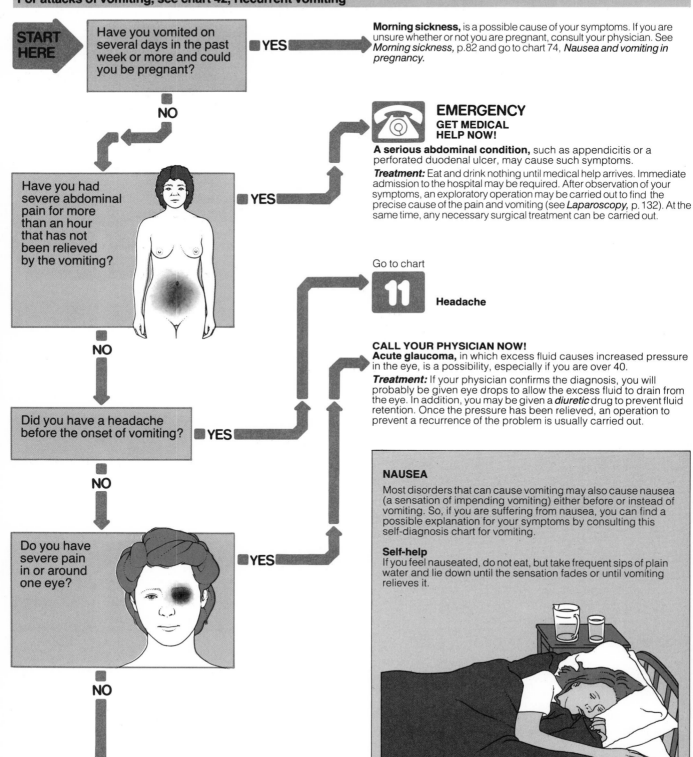

**START HERE**

**Have you vomited on several days in the past week or more and could you be pregnant?**

**YES** — **Morning sickness,** is a possible cause of your symptoms. If you are unsure whether or not you are pregnant, consult your physician. See *Morning sickness,* p.82 and go to chart 74, *Nausea and vomiting in pregnancy.*

**NO**

**Have you had severe abdominal pain for more than an hour that has not been relieved by the vomiting?**

**YES** — **EMERGENCY GET MEDICAL HELP NOW!**

**A serious abdominal condition,** such as appendicitis or a perforated duodenal ulcer, may cause such symptoms.

***Treatment:*** Eat and drink nothing until medical help arrives. Immediate admission to the hospital may be required. After observation of your symptoms, an exploratory operation may be carried out to find the precise cause of the pain and vomiting (see *Laparoscopy,* p. 132). At the same time, any necessary surgical treatment can be carried out.

**NO**

Go to chart

**11** Headache

**Did you have a headache before the onset of vomiting?**

**YES**

**CALL YOUR PHYSICIAN NOW!**
**Acute glaucoma,** in which excess fluid causes increased pressure in the eye, is a possibility, especially if you are over 40.

***Treatment:*** If your physician confirms the diagnosis, you will probably be given eye drops to allow the excess fluid to drain from the eye. In addition, you may be given a ***diuretic*** drug to prevent fluid retention. Once the pressure has been relieved, an operation to prevent a recurrence of the problem is usually carried out.

**NO**

**Do you have severe pain in or around one eye?**

**YES**

**NAUSEA**

Most disorders that can cause vomiting may also cause nausea (a sensation of impending vomiting) either before or instead of vomiting. So, if you are suffering from nausea, you can find a possible explanation for your symptoms by consulting this self-diagnosis chart for vomiting.

**Self-help**
If you feel nauseated, do not eat, but take frequent sips of plain water and lie down until the sensation fades or until vomiting relieves it.

**NO**

*Go to next page*

*Continued from previous page*

**Do you have diarrhea AND/OR is your temperature 100°F (38°C) or above?**

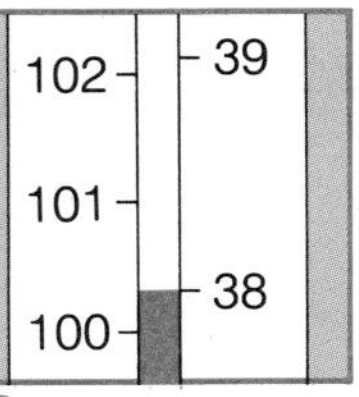

102 — 39
101 —
100 — 38

**YES** → **Gastroenteritis** (inflammation of the digestive tract caused by infection or food poisoning) is probable.
*Self-help:* See *Self-help for gastroenteritis*, p. 90. If you are no better in 24 hours, call your physician. He or she may prescribe drugs to relieve your symptoms.

**NO** ↓

**In the past few hours, have you done any of the following?**
- overeaten
- eaten anything spicy or rich (containing buttery or creamy sauces)
- drunk a large amount of alcohol

**YES** →

**NO** ↓

**Have you eaten anything that may have gone bad or to which you may be allergic — for example, shellfish or fruit?**

**YES** → **Food poisoning,** either from food contaminated by bacteria or by poisonous chemicals, or from food to which you are allergic, may be responsible for your vomiting.
*Self-help:* Follow the advice on treating vomiting (above right). If you are no better in 24 hours, or if you develop further symptoms, consult your physician.

**NO** ↓

**Before you vomited, did you feel so dizzy that everything around you seemed to spin?**

**YES** → **A disorder of the inner ear** may cause vomiting and dizzy spells. Consult your physician.
*Treatment:* Your physician may order balance tests. If you are found to have an inner-ear disorder, you will probably be given medication to relieve the symptoms.

**NO** ↓

**Are you taking any medication?**

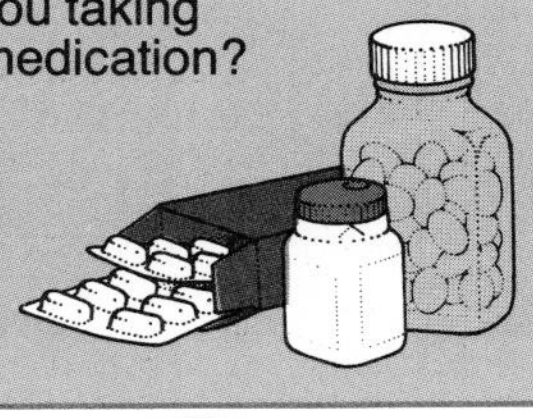

**YES** →

**NO** ↓

**Gastritis,** inflammation of the stomach lining, can easily occur as a result of such overindulgence.
*Self-help:* Follow the advice on treating vomiting (above). An over-the-counter *antacid* medicine should help to relieve any pain. Consult your physician if you are no better in 24 hours.

**Does your skin or do the whites of your eyes look yellow?**

**YES** →

**NO** ↓

**Jaundice,** as a result of a liver or gallbladder disorder, is a possibility. Consult your physician.
*Treatment:* Your physician may arrange for you to have blood tests (see *Blood analysis,* p. 22) and possibly an *ultrasound scan* (p. 136) or a *CAT (computerized axial tomography) scan* (p. 39) may be required in order to find the cause of the trouble. Treatment will depend on the nature of the underlying disorder.

---

## TREATMENT FOR VOMITING

If you have been vomiting, providing you suspect no serious cause, try the following self-help measures:

- Eat no solid food until your nausea and vomiting subside.
- Drink plenty of clear (non-alcoholic) fluids in small sips even if you cannot keep anything down for long.
- Do not smoke.
- Do not take aspirin.

If you vomit repeatedly for more than 24 hours, or if you develop further symptoms, consult your physician.

---

### VOMITING AND THE PILL

If you are taking birth control pills, and suffer from an attack of vomiting, your protection against conception may be reduced. Continue to take your pills as usual, but use an alternative form of contraception as well until you start a new packet.

**Certain medications** can cause vomiting as a side effect. Discuss the problem with your physician.

**Consult your physician** if you are unable to make a diagnosis from this chart.

---

## WARNING

### RED OR BLACK BLOOD IN VOMIT

Violent or recurrent vomiting can cause damage to the lining of the esophagus (gullet) and this can result in streaks of red blood appearing in your vomit. Consult your physician if this happens to you. If your vomit contains large quantities of red blood or any black or dark brown matter like coffee grounds (partly digested blood), seek medical help at once; you may have a serious abdominal condition such as a bleeding stomach or duodenal ulcer. It will assist rapid diagnosis of the problem if you keep the vomit containing the blood for the physician to examine.

# 42 Recurrent vomiting

Consult this chart if you have vomited (or felt nauseated) for several days in the past week. Apart from the nausea and vomiting of early pregnancy, most cases of recurrent vomiting are caused by persistent inflammation of the stomach lining or ulceration and are not serious. However, it is important to seek medical advice so that you can obtain effective treatment and to eliminate the slight possibility of a more serious underlying disorder.

**For isolated attacks of vomiting, see chart 41, Vomiting**

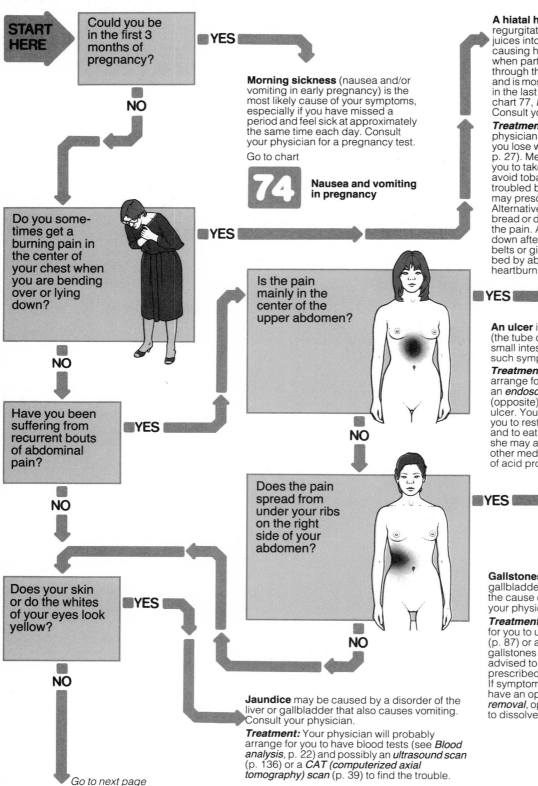

**START HERE**

**Could you be in the first 3 months of pregnancy?**

**YES**

**Morning sickness** (nausea and/or vomiting in early pregnancy) is the most likely cause of your symptoms, especially if you have missed a period and feel sick at approximately the same time each day. Consult your physician for a pregnancy test.

Go to chart

**74** **Nausea and vomiting in pregnancy**

**NO**

**Do you sometimes get a burning pain in the center of your chest when you are bending over or lying down?**

**YES**

**A hiatal hernia** with reflux causes regurgitation of food and leakage of acid juices into the esophagus (gullet), causing heartburn. The disorder occurs when part of the stomach protrudes through the opening in the diaphragm and is most likely if you are overweight or in the last months of pregnancy (see chart 77, *Heartburn in pregnancy*). Consult your physician.

**Treatment:** If you are overweight, your physician will probably recommend that you lose weight (see *How to lose weight*, p. 27). Meanwhile, he or she may advise you to take small, frequent meals and to avoid tobacco and alcohol. If you are troubled by heartburn, your physician may prescribe an *antacid* medication. Alternatively you might try eating a little bread or drinking a glass of milk to relieve the pain. Avoid bending over or lying down after meals and do not wear tight belts or girdles. Raising the head of your bed by about 4 in. should prevent heartburn.

**NO**

**Is the pain mainly in the center of the upper abdomen?**

**YES**

**An ulcer** in the stomach or duodenum (the tube connecting the stomach to the small intestine) is a common cause of such symptoms. Consult your physician.

**Treatment:** Your physician will probably arrange for you to undergo tests such as an *endoscopy* (p. 77) or a *barium X ray* (opposite) to locate the exact site of the ulcer. Your physician is likely to advise you to rest, to avoid tobacco and alcohol and to eat small, frequent meals. He or she may also prescribe an *antacid* or other medications to reduce the amount of acid produced in your stomach.

**Have you been suffering from recurrent bouts of abdominal pain?**

**YES**

**NO**

**NO**

**Does the pain spread from under your ribs on the right side of your abdomen?**

**YES**

**Gallstones** in the tube connecting the gallbladder to the digestive tract may be the cause of such symptoms. Consult your physician.

**Treatment:** Your physician may arrange for you to undergo *cholecystography* (p. 87) or an *ultrasound scan* (p. 136). If gallstones are diagnosed, you will be advised to avoid fatty foods and may be prescribed muscle relaxants for the pain. If symptoms persist, you may need to have an operation (see *Gallbladder removal*, opposite). In some cases, drugs to dissolve the stones may be given.

**Does your skin or do the whites of your eyes look yellow?**

**YES**

**NO**

**NO**

**Jaundice** may be caused by a disorder of the liver or gallbladder that also causes vomiting. Consult your physician.

**Treatment:** Your physician will probably arrange for you to have blood tests (see *Blood analysis*, p. 22) and possibly an *ultrasound scan* (p. 136) or a *CAT (computerized axial tomography) scan* (p. 39) to find the trouble.

*Go to next page*

*Continued from previous page*

**Have you lost your appetite AND/OR more than 10 lb (4.5 kg) in weight within the past 10 weeks?**

→ **YES** →

**CONSULT YOUR PHYSICIAN WITHOUT DELAY!**
**An ulcer** in the stomach or duodenum or gastritis are the most likely causes of your symptoms, but there is a slight possibility of stomach cancer.

***Treatment:*** Your physician will probably arrange for you to have a barium meal (see *Barium X rays*, right) and possibly an *endoscopy* (p. 77). Treatment will depend on the underlying disorder. Treatments for an ulcer are described opposite and treatments for gastritis are described below. If stomach cancer is diagnosed, the affected part of the stomach may be removed.

**NO** ↓

**Does vomiting usually occur a few hours after drinking alcohol?**

→ **YES** →

**Chronic gastritis** (persistent inflammation of the lining of the stomach), a disorder that is aggravated by drinking alcohol, is a possibility (see also *The effects of alcohol*, p. 22). Consult your physician.

***Treatment:*** Your physician will probably advise you to eat nothing while vomiting persists and to drink plenty of clear (non-alcoholic) fluids (see *Treatment for vomiting*, p. 81). As you start to feel better, he or she will probably suggest that you gradually introduce some bland foods. If you suffer from abdominal pain, your physician will probably prescribe an *antacid*. And he or she may advise you to cut down on your regular alcohol intake.

**NO** ↓

**Have you been suffering from recurrent headaches?**

→ **YES** →

**Do you vomit without preceding nausea?**

→ **YES** →

**NO** ↓ (loops back)

**NO** ↓

**Are you taking any medications?**

→ **YES** →

**Certain drugs** can cause nausea and vomiting as a side effect. Discuss the problem with your physician.

**NO** ↓

**Consult your physician** if you are unable to make a diagnosis from this chart.

**CONSULT YOUR PHYSICIAN WITHOUT DELAY!**
**Pressure on the brain** as a result of bleeding or a tumor is possible.

***Treatment:*** Your physician will probably arrange for tests such as a *CAT (computerized axial tomography) scan* (p. 39) and a *radioisotope scan* (p. 24) of the brain tissues. Treatment usually consists of either surgery or drugs to reduce the pressure and relieve symptoms.

---

### BARIUM X RAYS

Barium sulfate is a metallic compound that is visible on X-ray pictures and is used to show up areas of the digestive tract under investigation. If you need to have an X ray of the esophagus (gullet), stomach or small intestine, you will probably be given barium in the form of a drink (a barium swallow or meal). X rays will then be taken when the liquid reaches the relevant part of the digestive tract (after about 10 minutes for the esophagus, after 2 to 3 hours for the small intestine). If the large intestine (colon and rectum) is being examined, barium will be given in the form of an enema and the X rays will be taken immediately. Normally, you will be told to eat nothing after midnight on the day before your barium meal or enema. If you are having an enema, you may also be given a laxative to clear the bowel..

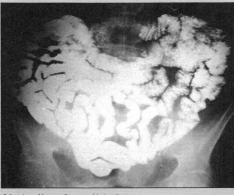

A barium X ray of normal intestines

---

### WARNING

#### RED OR BLACK BLOOD IN VOMIT

Violent or recurrent vomiting can cause damage to the lining of the esophagus (gullet) and this can result in streaks of red blood appearing in your vomit. Consult your physician if this happens to you. If your vomit contains large quantities of red blood or any black or dark brown matter like coffee grounds (partly digested blood), you should *seek medical help at once*; you may have a serious abdominal condition such as a bleeding stomach or duodenal ulcer. It will assist rapid diagnosis of the problem if you keep the vomit containing the blood for the physician to examine.

---

### GALLBLADDER REMOVAL

When gallstones or another disorder of the gallbladder cause serious symptoms, the gallbladder is often removed surgically. The operation is performed under general anesthetic, and the surgeon will also explore the bile duct and remove any stones found there.

Immediately after the operation, you probably will have intravenous fluid feedings, but after a few days you will be able to eat and drink normally. You should be able to return home about 7 to 10 days after the operation.

**The operation**
A cut is made in the right side of the abdomen (right). The gallbladder is then removed by cutting the cystic duct near where it joins the bile duct as shown in the diagram (above right). After the operation, bile drains straight into the intestine instead of first collecting in the gallbladder.

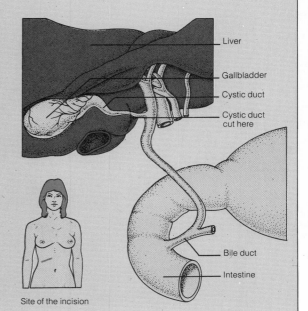

Liver
Gallbladder
Cystic duct
Cystic duct cut here
Bile duct
Intestine

Site of the incision

# 43 Abdominal pain

Pain between the bottom of the rib cage and the groin can be a sign of a wide number of different disorders of the digestive tract, urinary tract or reproductive organs.

Most cases of abdominal pain are due to minor digestive upsets, but severe and persistent pain should always receive prompt medical attention.

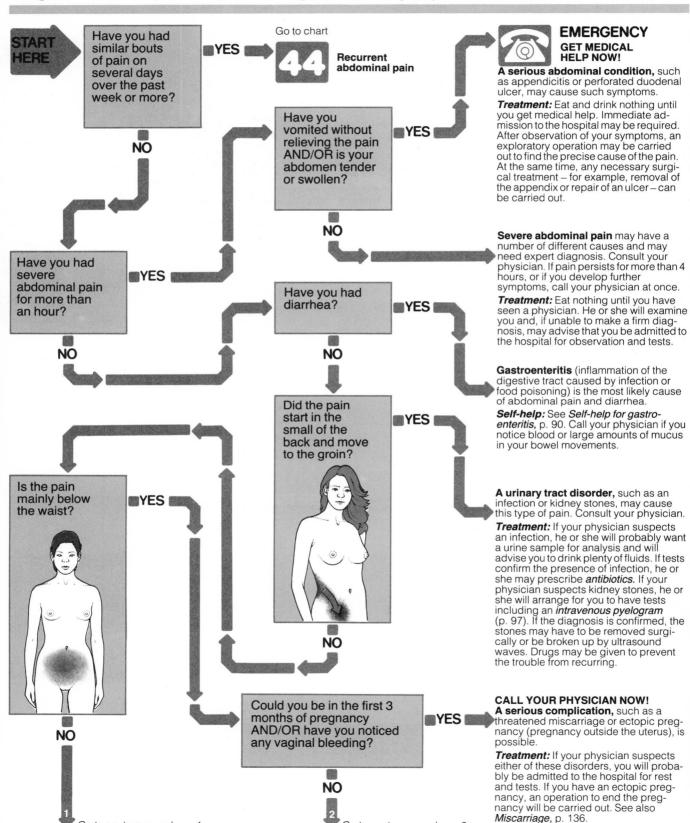

**START HERE**

Have you had similar bouts of pain on several days over the past week or more?

**YES** → Go to chart **44** Recurrent abdominal pain

**NO**

Have you had severe abdominal pain for more than an hour?

**YES**

**NO**

Is the pain mainly below the waist?

**YES**

**NO**

1 *Go to next page, column 1*

Have you vomited without relieving the pain AND/OR is your abdomen tender or swollen?

**YES**

**NO**

Have you had diarrhea?

**YES**

**NO**

Did the pain start in the small of the back and move to the groin?

**YES**

**NO**

Could you be in the first 3 months of pregnancy AND/OR have you noticed any vaginal bleeding?

**YES**

**NO**

2 *Go to next page, column 2*

### EMERGENCY
**GET MEDICAL HELP NOW!**

**A serious abdominal condition,** such as appendicitis or perforated duodenal ulcer, may cause such symptoms.

*Treatment:* Eat and drink nothing until you get medical help. Immediate admission to the hospital may be required. After observation of your symptoms, an exploratory operation may be carried out to find the precise cause of the pain. At the same time, any necessary surgical treatment – for example, removal of the appendix or repair of an ulcer – can be carried out.

**Severe abdominal pain** may have a number of different causes and may need expert diagnosis. Consult your physician. If pain persists for more than 4 hours, or if you develop further symptoms, call your physician at once.

*Treatment:* Eat nothing until you have seen a physician. He or she will examine you and, if unable to make a firm diagnosis, may advise that you be admitted to the hospital for observation and tests.

**Gastroenteritis** (inflammation of the digestive tract caused by infection or food poisoning) is the most likely cause of abdominal pain and diarrhea.

*Self-help:* See *Self-help for gastroenteritis*, p. 90. Call your physician if you notice blood or large amounts of mucus in your bowel movements.

**A urinary tract disorder,** such as an infection or kidney stones, may cause this type of pain. Consult your physician.

*Treatment:* If your physician suspects an infection, he or she will probably want a urine sample for analysis and will advise you to drink plenty of fluids. If tests confirm the presence of infection, he or she may prescribe *antibiotics.* If your physician suspects kidney stones, he or she will arrange for you to have tests including an *intravenous pyelogram* (p. 97). If the diagnosis is confirmed, the stones may have to be removed surgically or be broken up by ultrasound waves. Drugs may be given to prevent the trouble from recurring.

**CALL YOUR PHYSICIAN NOW!**
**A serious complication,** such as a threatened miscarriage or ectopic pregnancy (pregnancy outside the uterus), is possible.

*Treatment:* If your physician suspects either of these disorders, you will probably be admitted to the hospital for rest and tests. If you have an ectopic pregnancy, an operation to end the pregnancy will be carried out. See also *Miscarriage,* p. 136.

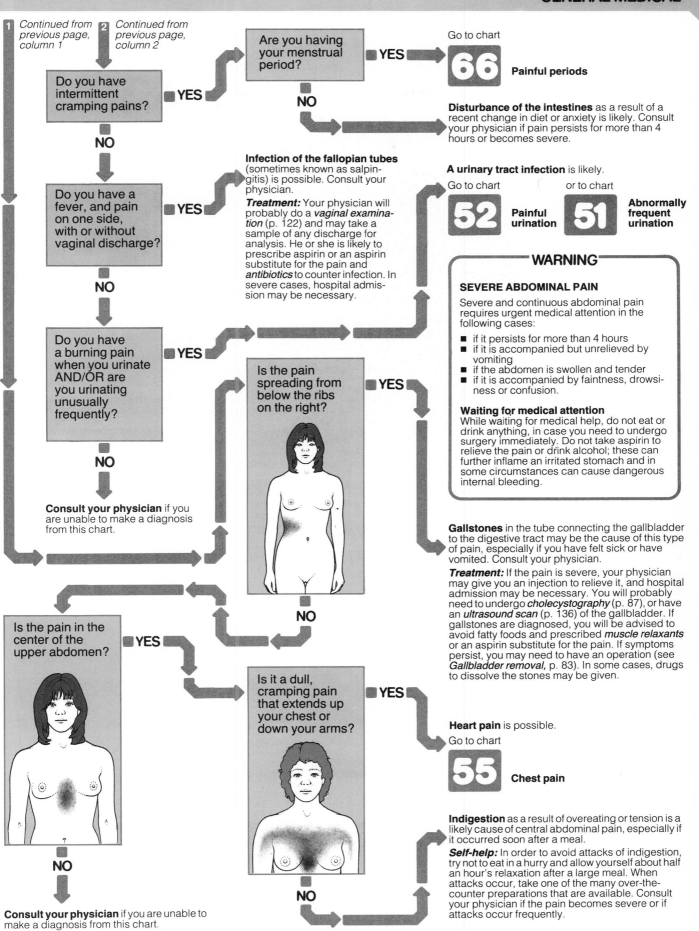

**1** *Continued from previous page, column 1*

**2** *Continued from previous page, column 2*

**Do you have intermittent cramping pains?**

**YES** →

**Are you having your menstrual period?**

**YES** → Go to chart

**66** **Painful periods**

**NO** →

**Disturbance of the intestines** as a result of a recent change in diet or anxiety is likely. Consult your physician if pain persists for more than 4 hours or becomes severe.

**NO** ↓

**Do you have a fever, and pain on one side, with or without vaginal discharge?**

**YES** → **Infection of the fallopian tubes** (sometimes known as salpingitis) is possible. Consult your physician.
**Treatment:** Your physician will probably do a *vaginal examination* (p. 122) and may take a sample of any discharge for analysis. He or she is likely to prescribe aspirin or an aspirin substitute for the pain and *antibiotics* to counter infection. In severe cases, hospital admission may be necessary.

**A urinary tract infection** is likely.

Go to chart

**52** **Painful urination**

or to chart

**51** **Abnormally frequent urination**

**NO** ↓

**Do you have a burning pain when you urinate AND/OR are you urinating unusually frequently?**

**YES** →

**Is the pain spreading from below the ribs on the right?**

**YES** →

> ### WARNING
>
> **SEVERE ABDOMINAL PAIN**
>
> Severe and continuous abdominal pain requires urgent medical attention in the following cases:
>
> ■ if it persists for more than 4 hours
> ■ if it is accompanied but unrelieved by vomiting
> ■ if the abdomen is swollen and tender
> ■ if it is accompanied by faintness, drowsiness or confusion.
>
> **Waiting for medical attention**
> While waiting for medical help, do not eat or drink anything, in case you need to undergo surgery immediately. Do not take aspirin to relieve the pain or drink alcohol; these can further inflame an irritated stomach and in some circumstances can cause dangerous internal bleeding.

**NO** ↓

**Consult your physician** if you are unable to make a diagnosis from this chart.

**NO**

**Gallstones** in the tube connecting the gallbladder to the digestive tract may be the cause of this type of pain, especially if you have felt sick or have vomited. Consult your physician.

**Treatment:** If the pain is severe, your physician may give you an injection to relieve it, and hospital admission may be necessary. You will probably need to undergo *cholecystography* (p. 87), or have an *ultrasound scan* (p. 136) of the gallbladder. If gallstones are diagnosed, you will be advised to avoid fatty foods and prescribed *muscle relaxants* or an aspirin substitute for the pain. If symptoms persist, you may need to have an operation (see *Gallbladder removal*, p. 83). In some cases, drugs to dissolve the stones may be given.

**Is the pain in the center of the upper abdomen?**

**YES** →

**Is it a dull, cramping pain that extends up your chest or down your arms?**

**YES** →

**Heart pain** is possible.

Go to chart

**55** **Chest pain**

**NO** ↓

**Consult your physician** if you are unable to make a diagnosis from this chart.

**NO**

**Indigestion** as a result of overeating or tension is a likely cause of central abdominal pain, especially if it occurred soon after a meal.

**Self-help:** In order to avoid attacks of indigestion, try not to eat in a hurry and allow yourself about half an hour's relaxation after a large meal. When attacks occur, take one of the many over-the-counter preparations that are available. Consult your physician if the pain becomes severe or if attacks occur frequently.

# 44 Recurrent abdominal pain

Consult this chart if you have pain in the abdomen (between the bottom of the rib cage and the groin) of a similar type on several days in the course of a week or more. Most cases of recurrent abdominal pain are the result of long-standing digestive problems that can be remedied by drugs from your physician, possibly combined with a change in eating habits. However, early diagnosis is always necessary to eliminate the slight possibility of serious underlying disease of the stomach, bowel or reproductive organs.

**For isolated attacks of abdominal pain, see chart 43, Abdominal pain**

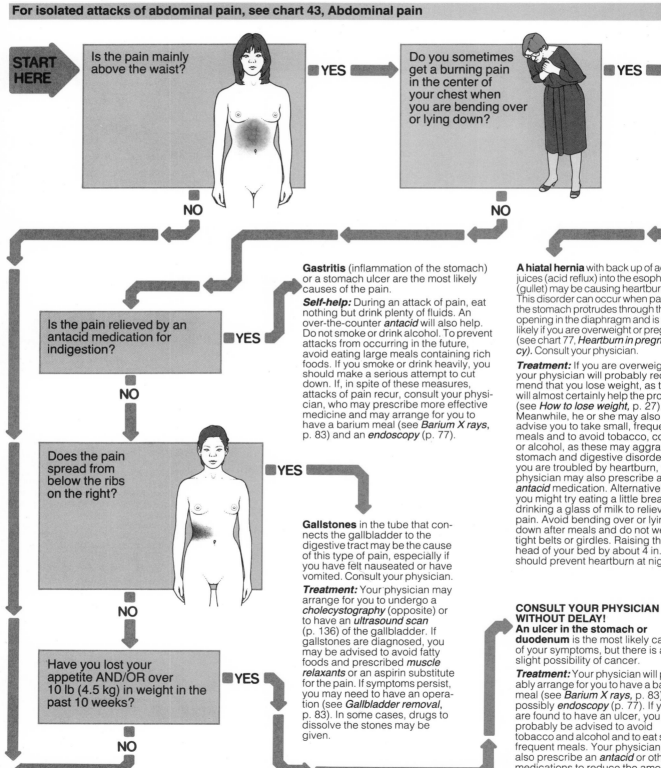

**START HERE**

Is the pain mainly above the waist? **YES** → Do you sometimes get a burning pain in the center of your chest when you are bending over or lying down? **YES**

**NO** / **NO**

Is the pain relieved by an antacid medication for indigestion? **YES**

**NO**

Does the pain spread from below the ribs on the right? **YES**

**NO**

Have you lost your appetite AND/OR over 10 lb (4.5 kg) in weight in the past 10 weeks? **YES**

**NO**

**Gastritis** (inflammation of the stomach) or a stomach ulcer are the most likely causes of the pain.

***Self-help:*** During an attack of pain, eat nothing but drink plenty of fluids. An over-the-counter *antacid* will also help. Do not smoke or drink alcohol. To prevent attacks from occurring in the future, avoid eating large meals containing rich foods. If you smoke or drink heavily, you should make a serious attempt to cut down. If, in spite of these measures, attacks of pain recur, consult your physician, who may prescribe more effective medicine and may arrange for you to have a barium meal (see *Barium X rays*, p. 83) and an *endoscopy* (p. 77).

**Gallstones** in the tube that connects the gallbladder to the digestive tract may be the cause of this type of pain, especially if you have felt nauseated or have vomited. Consult your physician.

***Treatment:*** Your physician may arrange for you to undergo a *cholecystography* (opposite) or to have an *ultrasound scan* (p. 136) of the gallbladder. If gallstones are diagnosed, you may be advised to avoid fatty foods and prescribed *muscle relaxants* or an aspirin substitute for the pain. If symptoms persist, you may need to have an operation (see *Gallbladder removal*, p. 83). In some cases, drugs to dissolve the stones may be given.

**A hiatal hernia** with back up of acid juices (acid reflux) into the esophagus (gullet) may be causing heartburn. This disorder can occur when part of the stomach protrudes through the opening in the diaphragm and is most likely if you are overweight or pregnant (see chart 77, *Heartburn in pregnancy).* Consult your physician.

***Treatment:*** If you are overweight, your physician will probably recommend that you lose weight, as this will almost certainly help the problem (see *How to lose weight,* p. 27). Meanwhile, he or she may also advise you to take small, frequent meals and to avoid tobacco, coffee or alcohol, as these may aggravate stomach and digestive disorders. If you are troubled by heartburn, your physician may also prescribe an *antacid* medication. Alternatively, you might try eating a little bread or drinking a glass of milk to relieve the pain. Avoid bending over or lying down after meals and do not wear tight belts or girdles. Raising the head of your bed by about 4 in. should prevent heartburn at night.

**CONSULT YOUR PHYSICIAN WITHOUT DELAY!**
**An ulcer in the stomach or duodenum** is the most likely cause of your symptoms, but there is a slight possibility of cancer.

***Treatment:*** Your physician will probably arrange for you to have a barium meal (see *Barium X rays,* p. 83) and possibly *endoscopy* (p. 77). If you are found to have an ulcer, you will probably be advised to avoid tobacco and alcohol and to eat small, frequent meals. Your physician will also prescribe an *antacid* or other medications to reduce the amount of acid in your stomach. Stomach cancer is usually treated surgically.

*Go to next page*

*Continued from previous page*

**Is the pain mainly below the waist?**

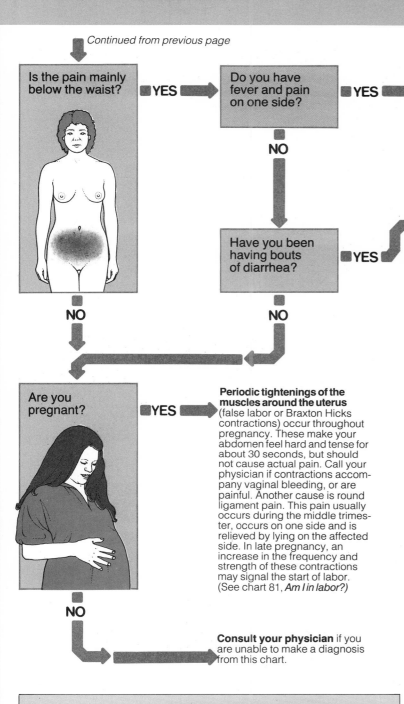

▶ **YES** ▶ **Do you have fever and pain on one side?** ▶ **YES** ▶ **Infection of the fallopian tubes** (sometimes known as salpingitis) is possible. Consult your physician.
**Treatment:** Your physician will probably do a *vaginal examination* (p. 122) and take a sample of the discharge from your vagina for analysis. You may also need to have a *D and C* (p. 118) and/or *laparoscopy* (p. 132). If the diagnosis is confirmed, your physician is likely to prescribe aspirin or an aspirin substitute for the pain and *antibiotics* to counter infection. In severe cases, admission to the hospital may be necessary.

**NO**

**Have you been having bouts of diarrhea?** ▶ **YES** ▶ **Have you also been intermittently constipated?** ▶ **YES**

**NO**

**NO**

**NO**

**Are you pregnant?**

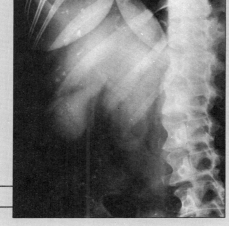

▶ **YES** ▶ **Periodic tightenings of the muscles around the uterus** (false labor or Braxton Hicks contractions) occur throughout pregnancy. These make your abdomen feel hard and tense for about 30 seconds, but should not cause actual pain. Call your physician if contractions accompany vaginal bleeding, or are painful. Another cause is round ligament pain. This pain usually occurs during the middle trimester, occurs on one side and is relieved by lying on the affected side. In late pregnancy, an increase in the frequency and strength of these contractions may signal the start of labor. (See chart 81, *Am I in labor?*)

**NO**

**Consult your physician** if you are unable to make a diagnosis from this chart.

**Crohn's disease or ulcerative colitis** may cause lower abdominal pain and diarrhea. The former is a patchy inflammation of the intestines, the latter is inflammation and ulceration of only the large intestine. Consult your physician. Seek medical help without delay if you have passed blood in your stools.
**Treatment:** A severe attack of ulcerative colitis may require hospital admission. In any case, you will probably need to have tests such as a *barium X ray* (p. 83), *sigmoidoscopy* (p. 92) and analysis of samples of your stools. If you are found to have either Crohn's disease or ulcerative colitis, you will probably be put on a bland diet and may be given a course of *anti-inflammatory* drugs.

**CONSULT YOUR PHYSICIAN WITHOUT DELAY!**
**Irritable colon** (see below) or diverticular disease (in which swellings develop on the walls of the large intestine) may be the cause of your symptoms. However, the slight possibility of bowel cancer also needs to be ruled out.
**Treatment:** To make an exact diagnosis, your physician may need to arrange for tests such as a barium enema (see *Barium X rays*, p. 83) and an *endoscopy* (p. 77). The long-term treatment for both irritable colon and diverticular disease is based on a high-fiber diet (p. 91). Your physician may also prescribe drugs to relieve your symptoms.

---

**CHOLECYSTOGRAPHY**

This is a special procedure for diagnosing disorders of the gallbladder and bile duct. A substance visible on X rays is taken as a tablet and photographed as it passes through the gallbladder and bile duct. The X-ray pictures produced are called cholecystograms. The cholecystogram (right) shows a gallbladder filled with gallstones.

Gallbladder ———

Gallstones ———

**IRRITABLE COLON**

Many people who suffer from recurrent cramping pains in the lower abdomen with or without intermittent diarrhea and/or constipation have no serious underlying disorder and are diagnosed as having an irritable colon (or irritable bowel syndrome). It is thought that the disorder is caused by abnormally strong and irregular muscle contractions in the colon. This may be due to sensitivity to the passage of matter through the intestines, but it may also be linked to psychological stress (see *What is stress?* p. 51). A large proportion of those with this complaint are anxious, and attacks seem to be made worse by worry. Most sufferers learn to live with the problem without specific treatment. A high-fiber diet (p. 91) often relieves the symptoms. Those who suffer from severe pain may be prescribed *antispasmodic* drugs.

# 45 Swollen abdomen

A generalized swelling over the whole abdomen (the area between the bottom of the rib cage and the groin) suggests a condition affecting the digestive or repro- ductive organs. If your abdomen is painful as well as swollen, this is an emergency and you should seek medical advice immediately.

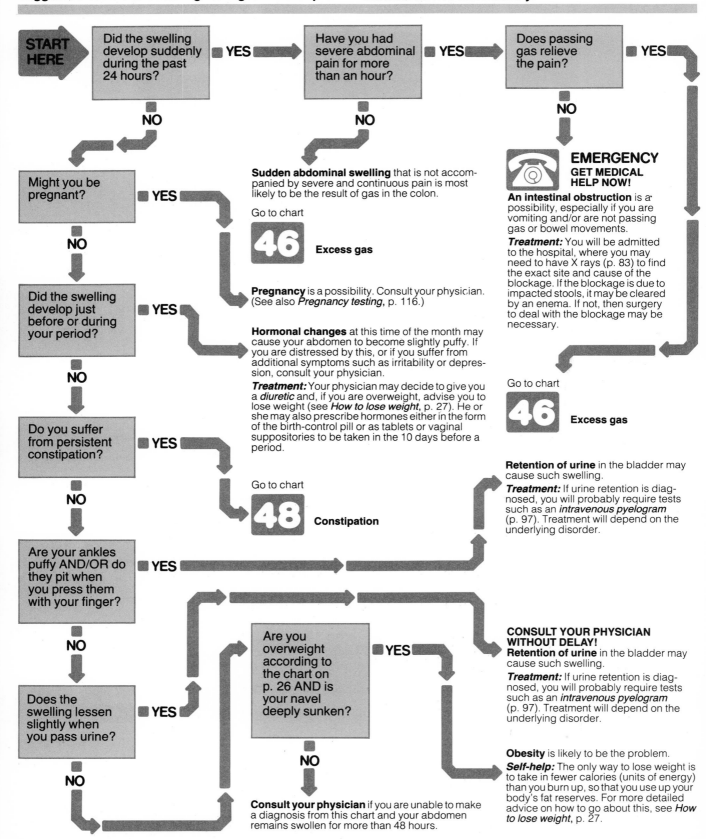

**START HERE**

**Did the swelling develop suddenly during the past 24 hours?** — **YES** → **Have you had severe abdominal pain for more than an hour?** — **YES** → **Does passing gas relieve the pain?** — **YES**

**NO** ↓

**Might you be pregnant?** — **YES**

**NO** ↓

**Did the swelling develop just before or during your period?** — **YES**

**NO** ↓

**Do you suffer from persistent constipation?** — **YES**

**NO** ↓

**Are your ankles puffy AND/OR do they pit when you press them with your finger?** — **YES**

**NO** ↓

**Does the swelling lessen slightly when you pass urine?** — **YES**

**NO** ↓

**Have you had severe abdominal pain for more than an hour?** — **NO** ↓

**Sudden abdominal swelling** that is not accompanied by severe and continuous pain is most likely to be the result of gas in the colon.

Go to chart

**46** **Excess gas**

**Pregnancy** is a possibility. Consult your physician. (See also *Pregnancy testing*, p. 116.)

**Hormonal changes** at this time of the month may cause your abdomen to become slightly puffy. If you are distressed by this, or if you suffer from additional symptoms such as irritability or depression, consult your physician.
***Treatment:*** Your physician may decide to give you a *diuretic* and, if you are overweight, advise you to lose weight (see *How to lose weight*, p. 27). He or she may also prescribe hormones either in the form of the birth-control pill or as tablets or vaginal suppositories to be taken in the 10 days before a period.

Go to chart

**48** **Constipation**

**Does passing gas relieve the pain?** — **NO** ↓

## EMERGENCY
### GET MEDICAL HELP NOW!

**An intestinal obstruction** is a possibility, especially if you are vomiting and/or are not passing gas or bowel movements.
***Treatment:*** You will be admitted to the hospital, where you may need to have X rays (p. 83) to find the exact site and cause of the blockage. If the blockage is due to impacted stools, it may be cleared by an enema. If not, then surgery to deal with the blockage may be necessary.

Go to chart

**46** **Excess gas**

**Retention of urine** in the bladder may cause such swelling.
***Treatment:*** If urine retention is diagnosed, you will probably require tests such as an *intravenous pyelogram* (p. 97). Treatment will depend on the underlying disorder.

**Are you overweight according to the chart on p. 26 AND is your navel deeply sunken?** — **YES**

**NO** ↓

## CONSULT YOUR PHYSICIAN WITHOUT DELAY!
**Retention of urine** in the bladder may cause such swelling.

***Treatment:*** If urine retention is diagnosed, you will probably require tests such as an *intravenous pyelogram* (p. 97). Treatment will depend on the underlying disorder.

**Obesity** is likely to be the problem.
***Self-help:*** The only way to lose weight is to take in fewer calories (units of energy) than you burn up, so that you use up your body's fat reserves. For more detailed advice on how to go about this, see *How to lose weight*, p. 27.

**Consult your physician** if you are unable to make a diagnosis from this chart and your abdomen remains swollen for more than 48 hours.

# 46 Excess gas

Excess gas in the digestive system may cause an uncomfortable, distended feeling in the abdomen and may produce rumbling noises in the intestines. Expulsion of gas, either through the mouth or the anus, generally relieves these symptoms temporarily. Although it may be embarrassing, passing gas is rarely a sign of an underlying disease. In most cases, gas is caused by swallowing air or by certain foods not being properly digested, leaving a residue that ferments, producing gas in the intestines. Different foods affect different people – though onions, cabbage and beans are common causes of gas.

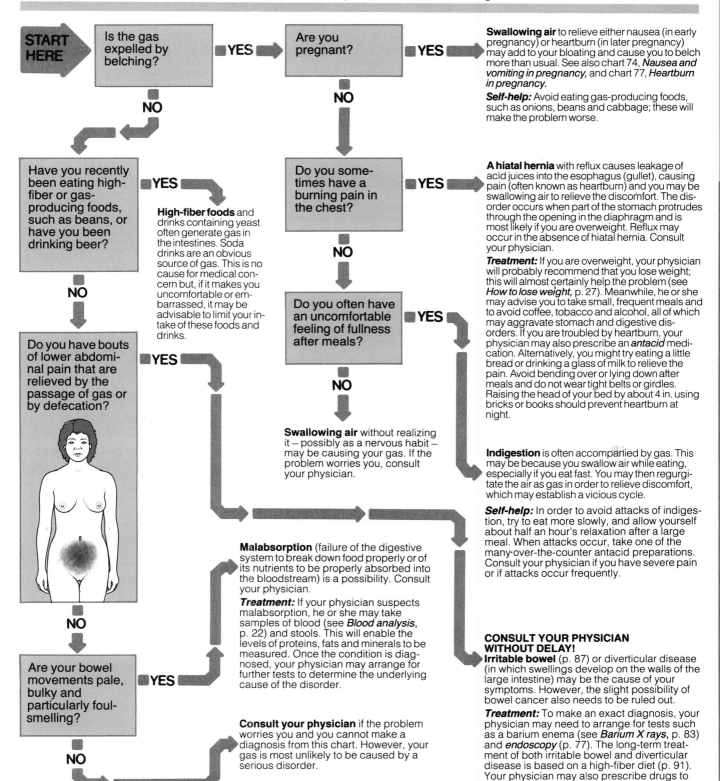

**START HERE**

**Is the gas expelled by belching?**

**YES** → **Are you pregnant?**

**YES** → **Swallowing air** to relieve either nausea (in early pregnancy) or heartburn (in later pregnancy) may add to your bloating and cause you to belch more than usual. See also chart 74, *Nausea and vomiting in pregnancy,* and chart 77, *Heartburn in pregnancy.*

**Self-help:** Avoid eating gas-producing foods, such as onions, beans and cabbage; these will make the problem worse.

**NO**

**Have you recently been eating high-fiber or gas-producing foods, such as beans, or have you been drinking beer?**

**YES** → **High-fiber foods** and drinks containing yeast often generate gas in the intestines. Soda drinks are an obvious source of gas. This is no cause for medical concern but, if it makes you uncomfortable or embarrassed, it may be advisable to limit your intake of these foods and drinks.

**NO**

**Do you sometimes have a burning pain in the chest?**

**YES** → **A hiatal hernia** with reflux causes leakage of acid juices into the esophagus (gullet), causing pain (often known as heartburn) and you may be swallowing air to relieve the discomfort. The disorder occurs when part of the stomach protrudes through the opening in the diaphragm and is most likely if you are overweight. Reflux may occur in the absence of hiatal hernia. Consult your physician.

**Treatment:** If you are overweight, your physician will probably recommend that you lose weight; this will almost certainly help the problem (see *How to lose weight,* p. 27). Meanwhile, he or she may advise you to take small, frequent meals and to avoid coffee, tobacco and alcohol, all of which may aggravate stomach and digestive disorders. If you are troubled by heartburn, your physician may also prescribe an *antacid* medication. Alternatively, you might try eating a little bread or drinking a glass of milk to relieve the pain. Avoid bending over or lying down after meals and do not wear tight belts or girdles. Raising the head of your bed by about 4 in. using bricks or books should prevent heartburn at night.

**NO**

**Do you have bouts of lower abdominal pain that are relieved by the passage of gas or by defecation?**

**Do you often have an uncomfortable feeling of fullness after meals?**

**YES** →

**NO**

**Swallowing air** without realizing it – possibly as a nervous habit – may be causing your gas. If the problem worries you, consult your physician.

**Indigestion** is often accompanied by gas. This may be because you swallow air while eating, especially if you eat fast. You may then regurgitate the air as gas in order to relieve discomfort, which may establish a vicious cycle.

**Self-help:** In order to avoid attacks of indigestion, try to eat more slowly, and allow yourself about half an hour's relaxation after a large meal. When attacks occur, take one of the many over-the-counter antacid preparations. Consult your physician if you have severe pain or if attacks occur frequently.

**YES**

**Malabsorption** (failure of the digestive system to break down food properly or of its nutrients to be properly absorbed into the bloodstream) is a possibility. Consult your physician.

**Treatment:** If your physician suspects malabsorption, he or she may take samples of blood (see *Blood analysis,* p. 22) and stools. This will enable the levels of proteins, fats and minerals to be measured. Once the condition is diagnosed, your physician may arrange for further tests to determine the underlying cause of the disorder.

**NO**

**Are your bowel movements pale, bulky and particularly foul-smelling?**

**YES**

**Consult your physician** if the problem worries you and you cannot make a diagnosis from this chart. However, your gas is most unlikely to be caused by a serious disorder.

**CONSULT YOUR PHYSICIAN WITHOUT DELAY!**
**Irritable bowel** (p. 87) or diverticular disease (in which swellings develop on the walls of the large intestine) may be the cause of your symptoms. However, the slight possibility of bowel cancer also needs to be ruled out.

**Treatment:** To make an exact diagnosis, your physician may need to arrange for tests such as a barium enema (see *Barium X rays,* p. 83) and *endoscopy* (p. 77). The long-term treatment of both irritable bowel and diverticular disease is based on a high-fiber diet (p. 91). Your physician may also prescribe drugs to relieve pain.

**NO**

# 47 Diarrhea

Diarrhea is the passing of unusually loose and frequent bowel movements. It is rarely a dangerous symptom, but it may cause discomfort and is often accompanied or preceded by cramping pains in the lower abdomen. In this country, most attacks of diarrhea are the result of infection and last no more than 48 hours. No special treatment is usually needed other than ensuring that you drink enough fluids. However, if diarrhea persists or recurs, it should be reported to your physician. Remember, if you are taking a birth-control pill and have diarrhea for more than 24 hours, your protection against pregnancy may be reduced and you should use another means of contraception for the remainder of your cycle (see chart 72, Choosing a contraceptive method).

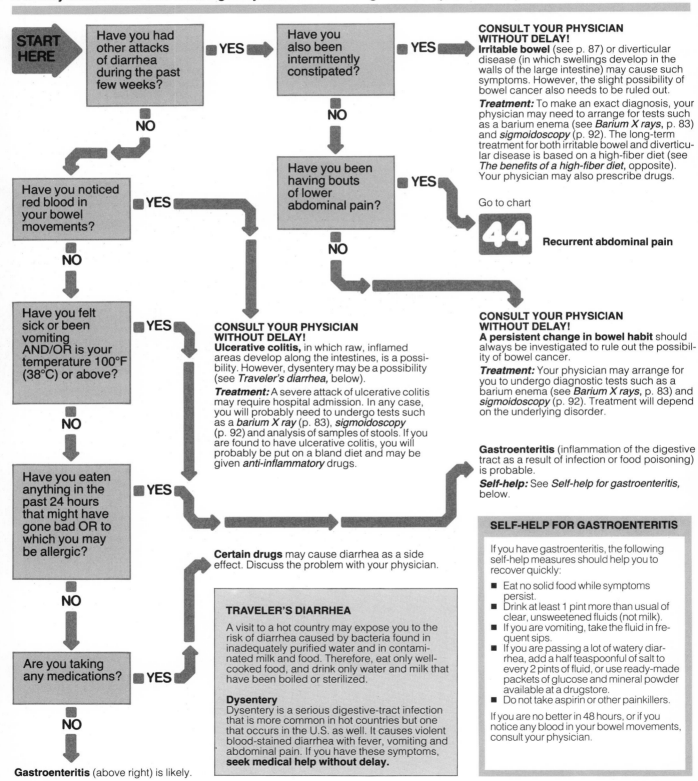

**START HERE**

Have you had other attacks of diarrhea during the past few weeks?

**YES** → Have you also been intermittently constipated?

**YES** →

**CONSULT YOUR PHYSICIAN WITHOUT DELAY!**
**Irritable bowel** (see p. 87) or diverticular disease (in which swellings develop in the walls of the large intestine) may cause such symptoms. However, the slight possibility of bowel cancer also needs to be ruled out.

*Treatment:* To make an exact diagnosis, your physician may need to arrange for tests such as a barium enema (see *Barium X rays*, p. 83) and *sigmoidoscopy* (p. 92). The long-term treatment for both irritable bowel and diverticular disease is based on a high-fiber diet (see *The benefits of a high-fiber diet*, opposite). Your physician may also prescribe drugs.

**NO** ↓

**NO** ↓

Have you been having bouts of lower abdominal pain?

**YES** → Go to chart **44** Recurrent abdominal pain

Have you noticed red blood in your bowel movements?

**YES** →

**NO** ↓

**NO** ↓

Have you felt sick or been vomiting AND/OR is your temperature 100°F (38°C) or above?

**YES** →

**CONSULT YOUR PHYSICIAN WITHOUT DELAY!**
**Ulcerative colitis,** in which raw, inflamed areas develop along the intestines, is a possibility. However, dysentery may be a possibility (see *Traveler's diarrhea,* below).

*Treatment:* A severe attack of ulcerative colitis may require hospital admission. In any case, you will probably need to undergo tests such as a barium X ray (p. 83), *sigmoidoscopy* (p. 92) and analysis of samples of stools. If you are found to have ulcerative colitis, you will probably be put on a bland diet and may be given *anti-inflammatory* drugs.

**CONSULT YOUR PHYSICIAN WITHOUT DELAY!**
**A persistent change in bowel habit** should always be investigated to rule out the possibility of bowel cancer.

*Treatment:* Your physician may arrange for you to undergo diagnostic tests such as a barium enema (see *Barium X rays*, p. 83) and *sigmoidoscopy* (p. 92). Treatment will depend on the underlying disorder.

**NO** ↓

**Gastroenteritis** (inflammation of the digestive tract as a result of infection or food poisoning) is probable.

*Self-help:* See *Self-help for gastroenteritis*, below.

Have you eaten anything in the past 24 hours that might have gone bad OR to which you may be allergic?

**YES** →

**Certain drugs** may cause diarrhea as a side effect. Discuss the problem with your physician.

### SELF-HELP FOR GASTROENTERITIS

If you have gastroenteritis, the following self-help measures should help you to recover quickly:

- Eat no solid food while symptoms persist.
- Drink at least 1 pint more than usual of clear, unsweetened fluids (not milk).
- If you are vomiting, take the fluid in frequent sips.
- If you are passing a lot of watery diarrhea, add a half teaspoonful of salt to every 2 pints of fluid, or use ready-made packets of glucose and mineral powder available at a drugstore.
- Do not take aspirin or other painkillers.

If you are no better in 48 hours, or if you notice any blood in your bowel movements, consult your physician.

**NO** ↓

### TRAVELER'S DIARRHEA

A visit to a hot country may expose you to the risk of diarrhea caused by bacteria found in inadequately purified water and in contaminated milk and food. Therefore, eat only well-cooked food, and drink only water and milk that have been boiled or sterilized.

### Dysentery
Dysentery is a serious digestive-tract infection that is more common in hot countries but one that occurs in the U.S. as well. It causes violent blood-stained diarrhea with fever, vomiting and abdominal pain. If you have these symptoms, **seek medical help without delay.**

Are you taking any medications?

**YES** →

**NO** ↓

**Gastroenteritis** (above right) is likely.

# 48 Constipation

Normal bowel habits vary from person to person – many people have one or more bowel movements a day, but a few have four or five a day. Constipation occurs only when the stools are dry, hard and painful or difficult to pass. This is more likely to occur when stools are passed more infrequently than you are used to.

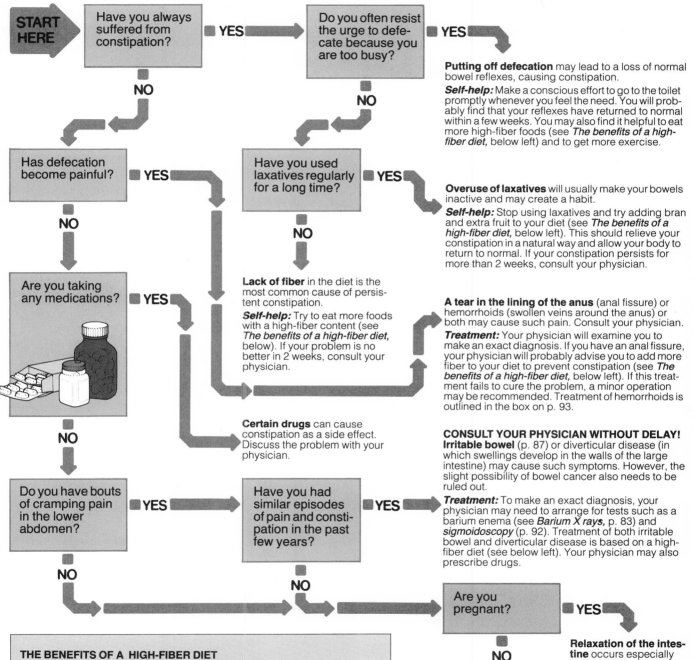

**START HERE**

**Have you always suffered from constipation?** — YES → **Do you often resist the urge to defecate because you are too busy?** — YES →

**Putting off defecation** may lead to a loss of normal bowel reflexes, causing constipation.
***Self-help:*** Make a conscious effort to go to the toilet promptly whenever you feel the need. You will probably find that your reflexes have returned to normal within a few weeks. You may also find it helpful to eat more high-fiber foods (see *The benefits of a high-fiber diet,* below left) and to get more exercise.

NO ↓ (from "always suffered")

NO ↓ (from "often resist")

**Has defecation become painful?** — YES →

**Have you used laxatives regularly for a long time?** — YES →

**Overuse of laxatives** will usually make your bowels inactive and may create a habit.
***Self-help:*** Stop using laxatives and try adding bran and extra fruit to your diet (see *The benefits of a high-fiber diet,* below left). This should relieve your constipation in a natural way and allow your body to return to normal. If your constipation persists for more than 2 weeks, consult your physician.

NO ↓ (from "defecation painful")

NO ↓ (from "laxatives")

**Are you taking any medications?** — YES →

**Lack of fiber** in the diet is the most common cause of persistent constipation.
***Self-help:*** Try to eat more foods with a high-fiber content (see *The benefits of a high-fiber diet,* below). If your problem is no better in 2 weeks, consult your physician.

**A tear in the lining of the anus** (anal fissure) or hemorrhoids (swollen veins around the anus) or both may cause such pain. Consult your physician.
***Treatment:*** Your physician will examine you to make an exact diagnosis. If you have an anal fissure, your physician will probably advise you to add more fiber to your diet to prevent constipation (see *The benefits of a high-fiber diet,* below left). If this treatment fails to cure the problem, a minor operation may be recommended. Treatment of hemorrhoids is outlined in the box on p. 93.

**Certain drugs** can cause constipation as a side effect. Discuss the problem with your physician.

**CONSULT YOUR PHYSICIAN WITHOUT DELAY!**
**Irritable bowel** (p. 87) or diverticular disease (in which swellings develop in the walls of the large intestine) may cause such symptoms. However, the slight possibility of bowel cancer also needs to be ruled out.
***Treatment:*** To make an exact diagnosis, your physician may need to arrange for tests such as a barium enema (see *Barium X rays,* p. 83) and *sigmoidoscopy* (p. 92). Treatment of both irritable bowel and diverticular disease is based on a high-fiber diet (see below left). Your physician may also prescribe drugs.

NO ↓ (from "taking medications")

**Do you have bouts of cramping pain in the lower abdomen?** — YES →

**Have you had similar episodes of pain and constipation in the past few years?** — YES →

NO ↓ (from "cramping pain")

NO ↓ (from "similar episodes")

**Are you pregnant?** — YES →

**Relaxation of the intestine** occurs especially during early pregnancy and can lead to constipation. An increase in your daily intake of fluid and fiber should relieve the problem. If constipation persists, avoid taking laxatives and consult your physician.

NO ↓ (from "pregnant")

**Lack of fiber** in the diet is the most likely cause of constipation (see *The benefits of a high-fiber diet,* left). If your bowel habits have not returned to normal within 2 weeks, consult your physician.

---

## THE BENEFITS OF A HIGH-FIBER DIET

Most plant matter contains a proportion of indigestible material known as fiber (or roughage). This is very important in our diet. It provides the bulk that helps the large intestine carry away body waste and keeps the stools soft. Those who eat plenty of fiber in their diet are less likely to develop cancer of the large intestine and other bowel problems. Finally, a high-fiber diet may help you to lose weight, because fiber fills you up without providing extra calories.

**High-fiber foods**
The foods listed below all contain a high proportion of fiber.

- unrefined cereals and cereal products, such as bran and whole-grain bread
- fruit and vegetables
- beans and other legumes

# 49 Abnormal-looking bowel movements

**Most minor changes in the color, shape and consistency of your bowel movements are due to a recent change in diet. But if the stools are black or significantly lighter** than usual, or if they are streaked with blood, this may indicate something more serious and you should consult your physician.

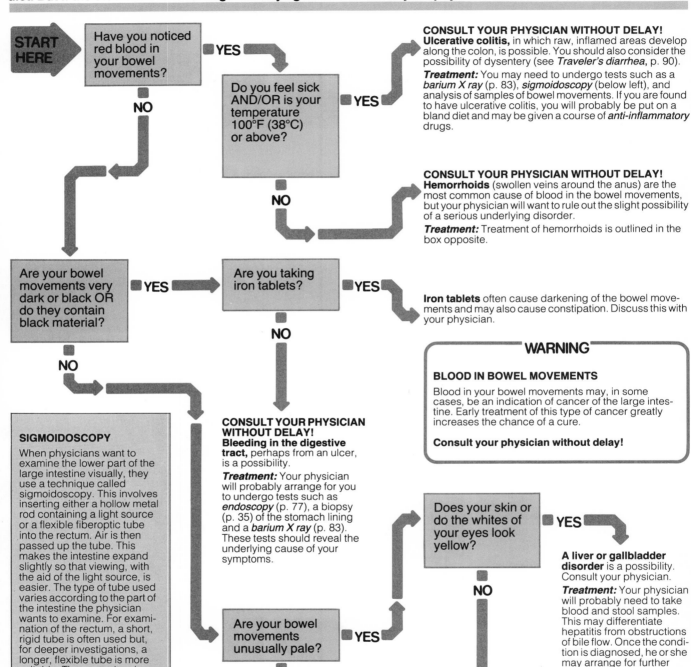

**START HERE**

**Have you noticed red blood in your bowel movements?**

**YES** → **Do you feel sick AND/OR is your temperature 100°F (38°C) or above?**

**YES** →

**CONSULT YOUR PHYSICIAN WITHOUT DELAY!**
**Ulcerative colitis,** in which raw, inflamed areas develop along the colon, is possible. You should also consider the possibility of dysentery (see *Traveler's diarrhea,* p. 90).

***Treatment:*** You may need to undergo tests such as a *barium X ray* (p. 83), *sigmoidoscopy* (below left), and analysis of samples of bowel movements. If you are found to have ulcerative colitis, you will probably be put on a bland diet and may be given a course of *anti-inflammatory* drugs.

**NO** →

**CONSULT YOUR PHYSICIAN WITHOUT DELAY!**
**Hemorrhoids** (swollen veins around the anus) are the most common cause of blood in the bowel movements, but your physician will want to rule out the slight possibility of a serious underlying disorder.

***Treatment:*** Treatment of hemorrhoids is outlined in the box opposite.

**NO** ↓

**Are your bowel movements very dark or black OR do they contain black material?**

**YES** → **Are you taking iron tablets?**

**YES** →

**Iron tablets** often cause darkening of the bowel movements and may also cause constipation. Discuss this with your physician.

**NO** ↓

**CONSULT YOUR PHYSICIAN WITHOUT DELAY!**
**Bleeding in the digestive tract,** perhaps from an ulcer, is a possibility.

***Treatment:*** Your physician will probably arrange for you to undergo tests such as *endoscopy* (p. 77), a biopsy (p. 35) of the stomach lining and a *barium X ray* (p. 83). These tests should reveal the underlying cause of your symptoms.

**NO** ↓

## SIGMOIDOSCOPY

When physicians want to examine the lower part of the large intestine visually, they use a technique called sigmoidoscopy. This involves inserting either a hollow metal rod containing a light source or a flexible fiberoptic tube into the rectum. Air is then passed up the tube. This makes the intestine expand slightly so that viewing, with the aid of the light source, is easier. The type of tube used varies according to the part of the intestine the physician wants to examine. For examination of the rectum, a short, rigid tube is often used but, for deeper investigations, a longer, flexible tube is more suitable. The procedure is uncomfortable rather than painful, takes only a few minutes and is helpful in diagnosing serious bowel problems at an early stage. Your physician may suggest that you have an enema before the investigation.

### WARNING

**BLOOD IN BOWEL MOVEMENTS**

Blood in your bowel movements may, in some cases, be an indication of cancer of the large intestine. Early treatment of this type of cancer greatly increases the chance of a cure.

**Consult your physician without delay!**

**Does your skin or do the whites of your eyes look yellow?**

**YES** →

**A liver or gallbladder disorder** is a possibility. Consult your physician.

***Treatment:*** Your physician will probably need to take blood and stool samples. This may differentiate hepatitis from obstructions of bile flow. Once the condition is diagnosed, he or she may arrange for further tests to determine the underlying cause of the disorder.

**NO** ↓

**Are your bowel movements unusually pale?**

**YES** →

**NO** ↓

**Consult your physician** if you are unable to make a diagnosis from this chart.

**Malabsorption** exists when your digestive system fails to break down food properly or its nutrients fail to be properly absorbed into the bloodstream. However, pale bowel movements may also occur normally for a few days after a bout of diarrhea and/or vomiting. Consult your physician.

***Treatment:*** If malabsorption is suspected, your physician may ask for samples of blood (see *Blood analysis,* p. 22) and bowel movements. This will enable the levels of proteins, fats and minerals to be measured. Once the condition is diagnosed, he or she may arrange for further tests to determine the underlying cause of the disorder.

# 50 Anal problems

The anus is a short tube that leads from the rectum to the outside. The anus is closed by a ring of muscles (or sphincter). The most common disorder affecting this area is swelling or plugging from clots of the veins around the anus (hemorrhoids). This is often caused by and associated with painful constipation.

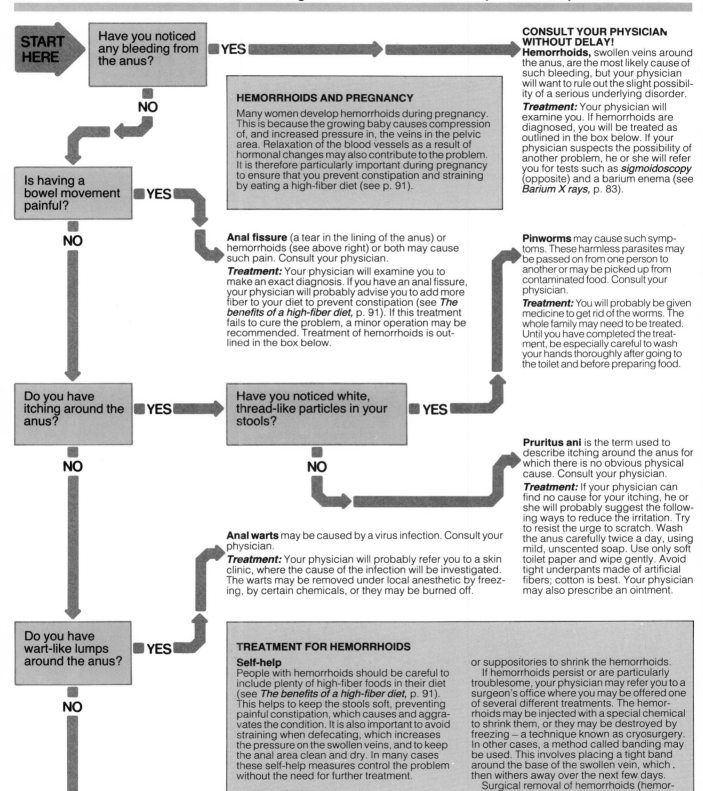

**START HERE**

**Have you noticed any bleeding from the anus?** — YES →

**CONSULT YOUR PHYSICIAN WITHOUT DELAY!**
**Hemorrhoids,** swollen veins around the anus, are the most likely cause of such bleeding, but your physician will want to rule out the slight possibility of a serious underlying disorder.
***Treatment:*** Your physician will examine you. If hemorrhoids are diagnosed, you will be treated as outlined in the box below. If your physician suspects the possibility of another problem, he or she will refer you for tests such as *sigmoidoscopy* (opposite) and a barium enema (see *Barium X rays,* p. 83).

NO ↓

**Is having a bowel movement painful?** — YES →

### HEMORRHOIDS AND PREGNANCY

Many women develop hemorrhoids during pregnancy. This is because the growing baby causes compression of, and increased pressure in, the veins in the pelvic area. Relaxation of the blood vessels as a result of hormonal changes may also contribute to the problem. It is therefore particularly important during pregnancy to ensure that you prevent constipation and straining by eating a high-fiber diet (see p. 91).

**Anal fissure** (a tear in the lining of the anus) or hemorrhoids (see above right) or both may cause such pain. Consult your physician.
***Treatment:*** Your physician will examine you to make an exact diagnosis. If you have an anal fissure, your physician will probably advise you to add more fiber to your diet to prevent constipation (see *The benefits of a high-fiber diet,* p. 91). If this treatment fails to cure the problem, a minor operation may be recommended. Treatment of hemorrhoids is outlined in the box below.

NO ↓

**Do you have itching around the anus?** — YES → **Have you noticed white, thread-like particles in your stools?** — YES →

**Pinworms** may cause such symptoms. These harmless parasites may be passed on from one person to another or may be picked up from contaminated food. Consult your physician.
***Treatment:*** You will probably be given medicine to get rid of the worms. The whole family may need to be treated. Until you have completed the treatment, be especially careful to wash your hands thoroughly after going to the toilet and before preparing food.

NO ↓ (itching)    NO ↓ (white particles)

**Pruritus ani** is the term used to describe itching around the anus for which there is no obvious physical cause. Consult your physician.
***Treatment:*** If your physician can find no cause for your itching, he or she will probably suggest the following ways to reduce the irritation. Try to resist the urge to scratch. Wash the anus carefully twice a day, using mild, unscented soap. Use only soft toilet paper and wipe gently. Avoid tight underpants made of artificial fibers; cotton is best. Your physician may also prescribe an ointment.

**Anal warts** may be caused by a virus infection. Consult your physician.
***Treatment:*** Your physician will probably refer you to a skin clinic, where the cause of the infection will be investigated. The warts may be removed under local anesthetic by freezing, by certain chemicals, or they may be burned off.

**Do you have wart-like lumps around the anus?** — YES →

NO ↓

### TREATMENT FOR HEMORRHOIDS

**Self-help**
People with hemorrhoids should be careful to include plenty of high-fiber foods in their diet (see *The benefits of a high-fiber diet,* p. 91). This helps to keep the stools soft, preventing painful constipation, which causes and aggravates the condition. It is also important to avoid straining when defecating, which increases the pressure on the swollen veins, and to keep the anal area clean and dry. In many cases these self-help measures control the problem without the need for further treatment.

**Professional treatment**
Your physician will probably prescribe a cream or suppositories to shrink the hemorrhoids.
If hemorrhoids persist or are particularly troublesome, your physician may refer you to a surgeon's office where you may be offered one of several different treatments. The hemorrhoids may be injected with a special chemical to shrink them, or they may be destroyed by freezing – a technique known as cryosurgery. In other cases, a method called banding may be used. This involves placing a tight band around the base of the swollen vein, which then withers away over the next few days.
Surgical removal of hemorrhoids (hemorrhoidectomy) under general anesthetic is generally not necessary.

**Consult your physician** if you are unable to make a diagnosis from this chart.

# 51 Abnormally frequent urination

The number of times you need to pass urine each day depends on a number of factors, including habit, the amount of fluid consumed and the strength of your bladder muscles. Most women need to pass urine between 2 and 6 times a day. You will know what is normal for you. Consult this chart if you find that you are having to pass urine more frequently than you are used to. This is rarely a symptom of serious disease, but simple treatment can often clear up this disruptive and sometimes embarrassing symptom.

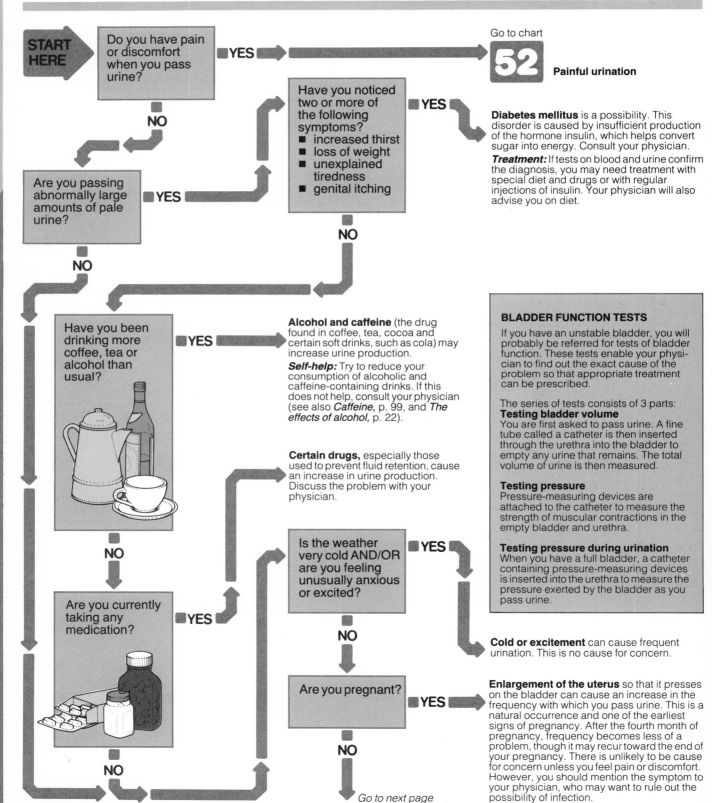

**START HERE**

**Do you have pain or discomfort when you pass urine?**

YES → **Go to chart 52 Painful urination**

NO ↓

**Are you passing abnormally large amounts of pale urine?**

YES →

**Have you noticed two or more of the following symptoms?**
- increased thirst
- loss of weight
- unexplained tiredness
- genital itching

YES →

**Diabetes mellitus** is a possibility. This disorder is caused by insufficient production of the hormone insulin, which helps convert sugar into energy. Consult your physician.
*Treatment:* If tests on blood and urine confirm the diagnosis, you may need treatment with special diet and drugs or with regular injections of insulin. Your physician will also advise you on diet.

NO ↓

**Have you been drinking more coffee, tea or alcohol than usual?**

YES →

**Alcohol and caffeine** (the drug found in coffee, tea, cocoa and certain soft drinks, such as cola) may increase urine production.
*Self-help:* Try to reduce your consumption of alcoholic and caffeine-containing drinks. If this does not help, consult your physician (see also *Caffeine,* p. 99, and *The effects of alcohol,* p. 22).

**Certain drugs,** especially those used to prevent fluid retention, cause an increase in urine production. Discuss the problem with your physician.

NO ↓

**Are you currently taking any medication?**

YES →

**Is the weather very cold AND/OR are you feeling unusually anxious or excited?**

YES →

**Cold or excitement** can cause frequent urination. This is no cause for concern.

NO ↓

**Are you pregnant?**

YES →

**Enlargement of the uterus** so that it presses on the bladder can cause an increase in the frequency with which you pass urine. This is a natural occurrence and one of the earliest signs of pregnancy. After the fourth month of pregnancy, frequency becomes less of a problem, though it may recur toward the end of your pregnancy. There is unlikely to be cause for concern unless you feel pain or discomfort. However, you should mention the symptom to your physician, who may want to rule out the possibility of infection.

NO ↓ *Go to next page*

---

**BLADDER FUNCTION TESTS**

If you have an unstable bladder, you will probably be referred for tests of bladder function. These tests enable your physician to find out the exact cause of the problem so that appropriate treatment can be prescribed.

The series of tests consists of 3 parts:
**Testing bladder volume**
You are first asked to pass urine. A fine tube called a catheter is then inserted through the urethra into the bladder to empty any urine that remains. The total volume of urine is then measured.

**Testing pressure**
Pressure-measuring devices are attached to the catheter to measure the strength of muscular contractions in the empty bladder and urethra.

**Testing pressure during urination**
When you have a full bladder, a catheter containing pressure-measuring devices is inserted into the urethra to measure the pressure exerted by the bladder as you pass urine.

*Continued from previous page*

**Do you often have a sudden, strong urge to pass urine, but pass only a small amount?**

■YES➤

**NO**

**Unstable bladder** is a condition in which even small amounts of urine in the bladder produce a strong urge to urinate, and urine may be passed before you can reach the toilet. Consult your physician.

*Treatment:* Your physician will examine you and will probably ask you to provide a urine specimen for tests to exclude the possibility of infection. You may also be referred for *bladder function tests* (opposite). Sometimes bladder control can be improved by practicing holding your urine for as long as possible. The *pelvic-floor exercises* on p.98 may also be helpful. Your physician may prescribe a drug to relax your bladder muscles and to calm the nerves that control bladder contraction. In rare cases, an operation may be recommended.

**Do you sometimes have difficulty controlling your bladder?**

■YES➤

Go to chart

**53**

**Poor bladder control**

**NO**

**Consult your physician** if you are unable to make a diagnosis from this chart and the frequency of urination is such that it wakes you at night or continues for more than a week.

## THE STRUCTURE OF THE URINARY TRACT

The organs that comprise the urinary tract are responsible for filtering the blood and expelling the resulting waste fluid from the body. The tract is made up of the following elements: the 2 kidneys, which lie at the back of the abdomen just above the waist on either side of the spinal column; the 2 ureters, which connect the kidneys to the bladder; the bladder itself; and the tube that leads from the bladder to the outside, the urethra.

**How the tract works**
The outer part of the kidney, the cortex, contains tiny tubes that filter waste substances from the blood. The filtered liquid passes into the central section of the kidney, the medulla, where tubules reabsorb water and certain chemicals from the fluid. The remaining liquid (urine) flows down the ureters into the bladder, which is kept closed by a ring of muscles (sphincter). Periodically, the accumulated urine is released through the urethra.

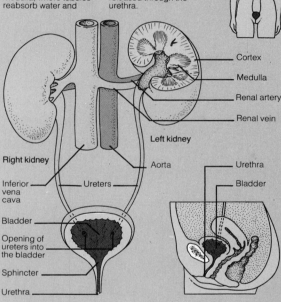

Cortex
Medulla
Renal artery
Renal vein
Left kidney
Right kidney
Aorta
Urethra
Inferior vena cava
Ureters
Bladder
Bladder
Opening of ureters into the bladder
Sphincter
Urethra

### ABNORMAL-LOOKING URINE

| Color of urine | Possible causes | What action is necessary |
|---|---|---|
| Pink, red or smoky | There is a chance that you may have blood in the urine, possibly caused by infection, inflammation or a growth in the urinary tract. However, natural or artificial red food colorings can also pass into the urine. | Consult your physician without delay. He or she may need to take samples of urine and blood for analysis (see *Blood analysis,* p. 22) in order to make a firm diagnosis. Treatment will depend on the underlying problem. |
| Dark yellow or orange | If you have not been drinking much fluid, your urine has become concentrated. Loss of fluid caused by diarrhea, vomiting or sweating can make your urine more concentrated and therefore darker than usual. Certain substances in senna-based laxatives and in rhubarb can also darken your urine. | This is no cause for concern. As soon as you compensate for any loss of fluid by drinking, your urine will return to its normal color. Substances in laxatives and rhubarb will pass through your system within 24 hours. |
| Clear and dark brown | Jaundice caused by a disorder of the liver (most commonly hepatitis) or gallbladder is a possibility, especially if your bowel movements are very pale and your skin or eyes look yellow. | Consult your physician. He or she will need to take samples of urine and blood for analysis (see *Blood analysis,* p. 22) in order to make a firm diagnosis. Treatment will depend on the underlying problem. |
| Green or blue | Artificial coloring in food or medicines is almost certainly the cause of this. | This is no cause for concern; the coloring will pass through without harmful effects. |

# 52 Painful urination

A burning or stinging pain or discomfort when you pass urine is usually the result of infection in the lower urinary tract or inflammation around the urethral opening. Such disorders are more common in women and in most cases are easily cured by a combination of home and professional treatments.

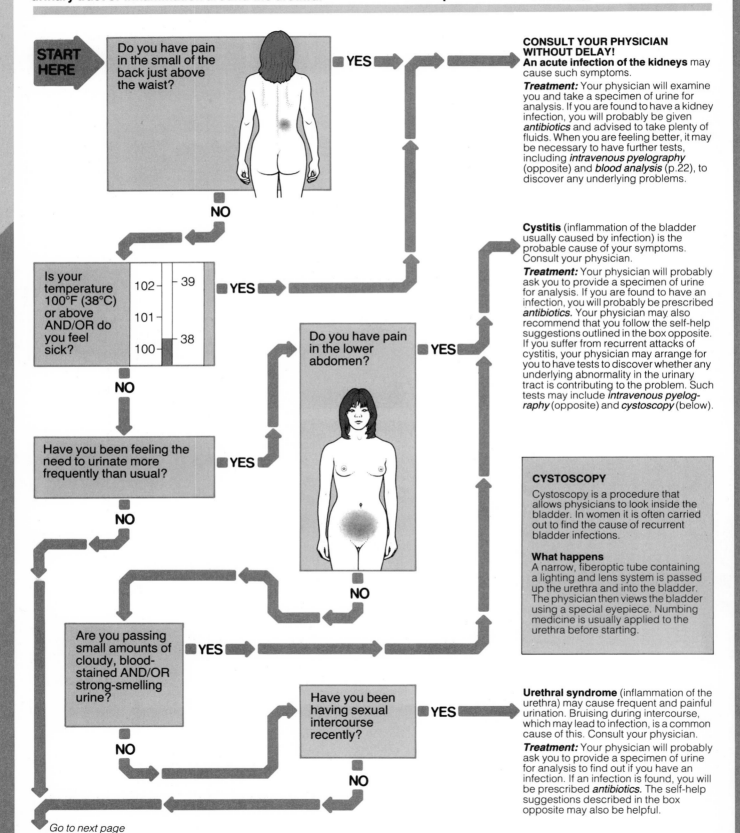

**START HERE**

Do you have pain in the small of the back just above the waist?

NO

**YES →**

**CONSULT YOUR PHYSICIAN WITHOUT DELAY!**
**An acute infection of the kidneys** may cause such symptoms.

*Treatment:* Your physician will examine you and take a specimen of urine for analysis. If you are found to have a kidney infection, you will probably be given *antibiotics* and advised to take plenty of fluids. When you are feeling better, it may be necessary to have further tests, including *intravenous pyelography* (opposite) and *blood analysis* (p.22), to discover any underlying problems.

Is your temperature 100°F (38°C) or above AND/OR do you feel sick?

| 102 | 39 |
| 101 | |
| 100 | 38 |

**YES →**

NO

**Cystitis** (inflammation of the bladder usually caused by infection) is the probable cause of your symptoms. Consult your physician.

*Treatment:* Your physician will probably ask you to provide a specimen of urine for analysis. If you are found to have an infection, you will probably be prescribed *antibiotics*. Your physician may also recommend that you follow the self-help suggestions outlined in the box opposite. If you suffer from recurrent attacks of cystitis, your physician may arrange for you to have tests to discover whether any underlying abnormality in the urinary tract is contributing to the problem. Such tests may include *intravenous pyelography* (opposite) and *cystoscopy* (below).

Do you have pain in the lower abdomen?

**YES →**

NO

Have you been feeling the need to urinate more frequently than usual?

NO

**YES**

### CYSTOSCOPY

Cystoscopy is a procedure that allows physicians to look inside the bladder. In women it is often carried out to find the cause of recurrent bladder infections.

**What happens**
A narrow, fiberoptic tube containing a lighting and lens system is passed up the urethra and into the bladder. The physician then views the bladder using a special eyepiece. Numbing medicine is usually applied to the urethra before starting.

Are you passing small amounts of cloudy, blood-stained AND/OR strong-smelling urine?

**YES →**

NO

Have you been having sexual intercourse recently?

**YES →**

NO

**Urethral syndrome** (inflammation of the urethra) may cause frequent and painful urination. Bruising during intercourse, which may lead to infection, is a common cause of this. Consult your physician.

*Treatment:* Your physician will probably ask you to provide a specimen of urine for analysis to find out if you have an infection. If an infection is found, you will be prescribed *antibiotics*. The self-help suggestions described in the box opposite may also be helpful.

*Go to next page*

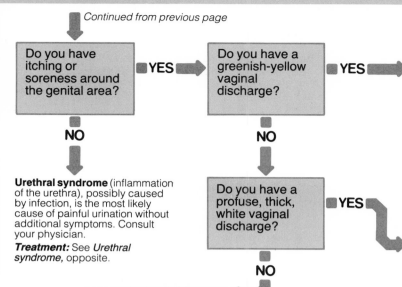

*Continued from previous page*

**Do you have itching or soreness around the genital area?** → **YES** → **Do you have a greenish-yellow vaginal discharge?** → **YES**

↓ **NO**

**Urethral syndrome** (inflammation of the urethra), possibly caused by infection, is the most likely cause of painful urination without additional symptoms. Consult your physician.

*Treatment:* See *Urethral syndrome,* opposite.

↓ **NO**

**Do you have a profuse, thick, white vaginal discharge?** → **YES**

↓ **NO**

**Vaginal thrush,** a fungal (yeast) infection, is a likely cause of such symptoms. Consult your physician.

*Treatment:* Your physician will examine you and may take a swab of the discharge from the inside of the vagina for analysis (see *Vaginal examination,* p.122). If the diagnosis of thrush is confirmed, you will probably be prescribed *antifungal* vaginal suppositories. If you have a regular sexual partner, you will also be given cream for him to apply daily to his penis to prevent him from reinfecting you. If you suffer from recurrent bouts of thrush and you also take the birth control pill, you may be advised to change to another method of contraception. This is because the pill sometimes causes an increase in vaginal secretions, which makes fungal infection more likely. See also chart 72, *Choosing a contraceptive method.*

**Trichomonal vaginitis,** a vaginal infection that may be transmitted sexually, is a possibility. Consult your physician.

*Treatment:* Your physician will examine you and will probably take a sample of the discharge from the vagina for analysis (see *Vaginal examination,* p.122). If trichomonal vaginitis is confirmed, you will be prescribed a course of *antibiotics.* It is important that your sexual partner(s) also receive treatment, even if no symptoms are apparent. Otherwise, it is possible that you will be reinfected. See also *Sexually transmitted diseases,* p.123.

**Pruritis vulvae** (irritation of the vulva) may cause urination to become painful. There is often no obvious cause for this condition, but, in women who are past the menopause, it may be linked to a drop in hormone levels, causing the vagina to become dry. In younger women, an allergic reaction – to soap, for example – or irritation may be responsible.

*Self-help:* Try not to scratch the irritated area; this will only aggravate the condition. Wash the genital area gently once a day and apply a soothing cream. Do not use soap, talcum powder, vaginal deodorants or douches because these may increase irritation. Wear cotton underwear and avoid nylon pantyhose and close-fitting pants that restrict ventilation. If your vagina feels dry during intercourse, use a lubricating jelly. If the problem persists for more than a few days, consult your physician.

## INTRAVENOUS PYELOGRAPHY

Intravenous pyelography (excretory urography) is a procedure that provides physicians with a series of X-ray pictures of the urinary tract. A dye that shows up on X rays is injected into the bloodstream. It travels around the body until it is absorbed by the kidneys. This process may take an hour or so. X-ray pictures are taken as the chemical works its way through the kidneys, down the ureters, and into the bladder.

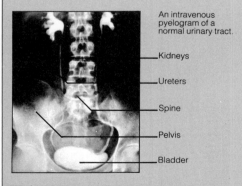

An intravenous pyelogram of a normal urinary tract.

– Kidneys
– Ureters
– Spine
– Pelvis
– Bladder

**Micturating cystogram or voiding cystourethrogram**
This is a series of X rays that show the action of the bladder during urination. This is often done following an intravenous pyelogram when dye is already in the bladder. However, sometimes the dye is passed directly into the bladder through a fine tube (catheter) inserted into the urethra.

## SELF-HELP FOR INFECTIONS OF THE BLADDER AND URETHRA

If you are suffering from cystitis or the urethral syndrome, the following self-help suggestions, in addition to whatever treatment your physician may prescribe, will help to relieve your symptoms, hasten recovery, and prevent the trouble from recurring.

- To relieve abdominal pain and fever, take aspirin or an aspirin substitute. A hot-water bottle wrapped in a towel or a heating pad on the abdomen is often comforting. Sitz baths two or three times daily are beneficial.
- Make sure that you drink plenty of fluids and urinate frequently.
- Cranberry juice or vitamin C will acidify the urine, thereby inhibiting the growth of many of the cystitis-causing bacteria.

- Try to empty your bladder completely each time you pass urine to prevent a residue from remaining in the bladder, which could encourage infection.
- If sexual intercourse is sometimes painful, use a vaginal lubricant and experiment with different positions.
- Always empty your bladder after sexual intercourse.

- If you use a diaphragm, ask your physician or clinic to check that it fits properly; ill-fitting diaphragms may bruise the urethra, leading to infection.

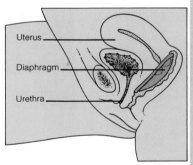

Uterus
Diaphragm
Urethra

- Keep the genital area clean and dry, but do not use vaginal douches or deodorants, or heavily scented soaps.
- When you go to the toilet, always wipe from front to back to keep germs from the bowel away from the urethral opening.
- Avoid wearing nylon pantyhose or underpants. Cotton underpants are preferable. No undergarment should be too tight-fitting or snug.

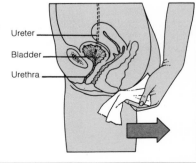

Ureter
Bladder
Urethra

# 53 Poor bladder control

**Difficulty controlling your bladder or involuntary passing of urine may be a sign of infection in the urinary** tract or it may be due to weak muscle control. Always seek your physician's advice about this symptom.

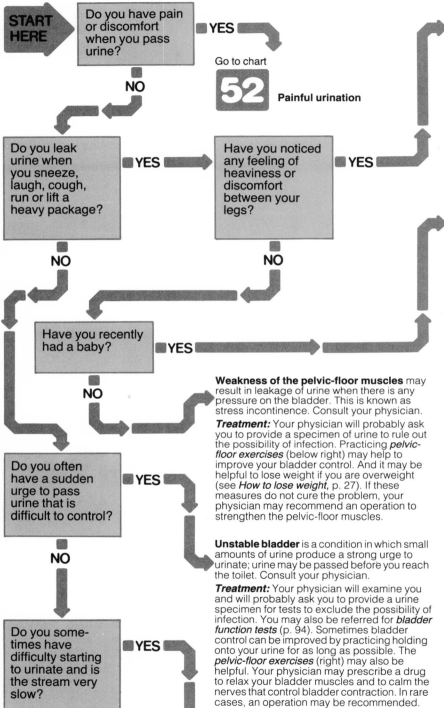

**START HERE**

Do you have pain or discomfort when you pass urine?

**YES** → Go to chart **52** Painful urination

**NO**

Do you leak urine when you sneeze, laugh, cough, run or lift a heavy package?

**YES** → Have you noticed any feeling of heaviness or discomfort between your legs?

**YES** →

**NO** (leak) → Have you recently had a baby?

**YES** →

**NO** (heaviness)

**NO** (baby)

Do you often have a sudden urge to pass urine that is difficult to control?

**YES** →

**NO**

Do you sometimes have difficulty starting to urinate and is the stream very slow?

**YES** →

**NO**

**Consult your physician** if you are unable to make a diagnosis from this chart.

---

**Prolapse of the uterus or vagina** may be causing these symptoms. This occurs when the muscles and ligaments supporting the uterus become weak and slack. This is particularly likely if you are over 50. Consult your physician.

**Treatment:** Your physician will examine you and may ask you to provide a specimen of urine for analysis to rule out the possibility of infection. If you are suffering from prolapse, your physician will probably recommend that you try *pelvic-floor exercises* (below). If you are overweight, you will also be advised to lose weight (see *How to lose weight,* p. 27). In some cases, a specially designed vaginal pessary will also be fitted. If these measures do not improve your condition, you may need to have an operation.

**Childbirth** may have temporarily weakened your pelvic-floor muscles. This is a common occurrence and nearly always improves within a few months without special treatment. Consult your physician.

**Treatment:** Your physician will examine you and may ask you to provide a urine sample for tests to rule out the possibility of infection. In most cases, no treatment is necessary. However, *pelvic-floor exercises* (below) may help your muscle tone return to normal more quickly. Your condition will also improve if you lose any excess weight you may have gained during pregnancy (see *How to lose weight,* p. 27).

**Weakness of the pelvic-floor muscles** may result in leakage of urine when there is any pressure on the bladder. This is known as stress incontinence. Consult your physician.

**Treatment:** Your physician will probably ask you to provide a specimen of urine to rule out the possibility of infection. Practicing *pelvic-floor exercises* (below right) may help to improve your bladder control. And it may be helpful to lose weight if you are overweight (see *How to lose weight,* p. 27). If these measures do not cure the problem, your physician may recommend an operation to strengthen the pelvic-floor muscles.

**Unstable bladder** is a condition in which small amounts of urine produce a strong urge to urinate; urine may be passed before you reach the toilet. Consult your physician.

**Treatment:** Your physician will examine you and will probably ask you to provide a urine specimen for tests to exclude the possibility of infection. You may also be referred for *bladder function tests* (p. 94). Sometimes bladder control can be improved by practicing holding onto your urine for as long as possible. The *pelvic-floor exercises* (right) may also be helpful. Your physician may prescribe a drug to relax your bladder muscles and to calm the nerves that control bladder contraction. In rare cases, an operation may be recommended.

**Narrowing of the urethra** as a result of a difficult childbirth in the past or recurrent urinary-tract infections may cause such symptoms. Consult your physician.

**Treatment:** You will probably be referred for tests. If you are found to have a narrow urethra, a dilatation may be carried out.

---

## WARNING

**INABILITY TO PASS URINE**

If you find that you are unable to urinate even though you feel the urge to urinate, you need urgent medical attention. Try taking a warm bath, which may enable you to pass some urine.

**SUDDEN LOSS OF BLADDER CONTROL**

Sudden inability to control urination may be a sign of damage to the spinal cord or nervous system, especially if you have recently had a back injury or have experienced weakness in your legs.

**Seek medical help at once!**

---

**PELVIC-FLOOR EXERCISES**

These exercises are useful for toning up the pelvic floor muscles that support the bladder and reproductive organs. While the exercises are particularly useful during pregnancy, after childbirth or if you are suffering from weak bladder control, they are worth practicing at any time. When you go to the toilet to pass urine, follow this procedure at least twice a day:

1 Contract the muscles around the vagina upward and inward so that you can stop the flow of urine.
2 Hold this position for a count of 6.
3 Now let the flow of urine continue for another count of 6.
4 Finally, interrupt the flow of urine again for the count of 6, before totally emptying your bladder of urine.

# 54 Palpitations

Palpitations is a term used to describe unusually rapid, strong or irregular beating of the heart. It is normal for the heart rate to speed up during strenuous exercise and to feel your heart "thumping" for some minutes after. This is no cause for concern. Consult this chart if you have palpitations unconnected with physical exertion. In most cases such palpitations are caused by consumption of nicotine or caffeine, or by anxiety. However, in a small proportion of cases, they are a symptom of an underlying illness. Palpitations that recur on several days or that are connected with pain or breathlessness should always be brought to your physician's attention.

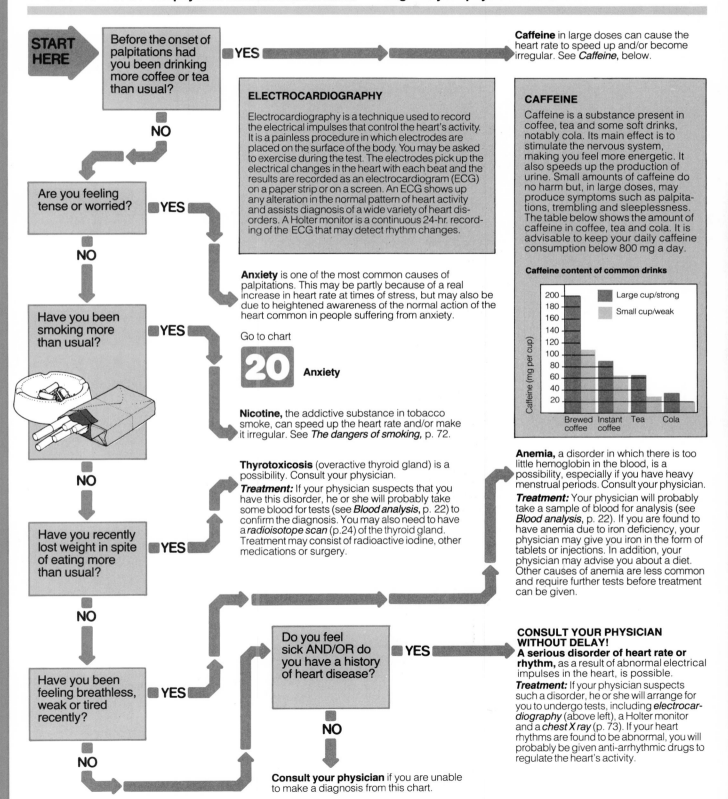

**START HERE**

**Before the onset of palpitations had you been drinking more coffee or tea than usual?**

YES → **Caffeine** in large doses can cause the heart rate to speed up and/or become irregular. See *Caffeine*, below.

NO

**Are you feeling tense or worried?**

YES

NO

**Have you been smoking more than usual?**

YES

NO

**Have you recently lost weight in spite of eating more than usual?**

YES

NO

**Have you been feeling breathless, weak or tired recently?**

YES

NO

**Do you feel sick AND/OR do you have a history of heart disease?**

YES → **CONSULT YOUR PHYSICIAN WITHOUT DELAY!**

NO

**Consult your physician** if you are unable to make a diagnosis from this chart.

### ELECTROCARDIOGRAPHY

Electrocardiography is a technique used to record the electrical impulses that control the heart's activity. It is a painless procedure in which electrodes are placed on the surface of the body. You may be asked to exercise during the test. The electrodes pick up the electrical changes in the heart with each beat and the results are recorded as an electrocardiogram (ECG) on a paper strip or on a screen. An ECG shows up any alteration in the normal pattern of heart activity and assists diagnosis of a wide variety of heart disorders. A Holter monitor is a continuous 24-hr. recording of the ECG that may detect rhythm changes.

**Anxiety** is one of the most common causes of palpitations. This may be partly because of a real increase in heart rate at times of stress, but may also be due to heightened awareness of the normal action of the heart common in people suffering from anxiety.

Go to chart

**20** Anxiety

**Nicotine,** the addictive substance in tobacco smoke, can speed up the heart rate and/or make it irregular. See *The dangers of smoking*, p. 72.

**Thyrotoxicosis** (overactive thyroid gland) is a possibility. Consult your physician.

***Treatment:*** If your physician suspects that you have this disorder, he or she will probably take some blood for tests (see *Blood analysis*, p. 22) to confirm the diagnosis. You may also need to have a *radioisotope scan* (p.24) of the thyroid gland. Treatment may consist of radioactive iodine, other medications or surgery.

### CAFFEINE

Caffeine is a substance present in coffee, tea and some soft drinks, notably cola. Its main effect is to stimulate the nervous system, making you feel more energetic. It also speeds up the production of urine. Small amounts of caffeine do no harm but, in large doses, may produce symptoms such as palpitations, trembling and sleeplessness. The table below shows the amount of caffeine in coffee, tea and cola. It is advisable to keep your daily caffeine consumption below 800 mg a day.

**Caffeine content of common drinks**

Caffeine (mg per cup)

- Large cup/strong
- Small cup/weak

200 180 160 140 120 100 80 60 40 20

Brewed coffee · Instant coffee · Tea · Cola

**Anemia,** a disorder in which there is too little hemoglobin in the blood, is a possibility, especially if you have heavy menstrual periods. Consult your physician.

***Treatment:*** Your physician will probably take a sample of blood for analysis (see *Blood analysis*, p. 22). If you are found to have anemia due to iron deficiency, your physician may give you iron in the form of tablets or injections. In addition, your physician may advise you about a diet. Other causes of anemia are less common and require further tests before treatment can be given.

**CONSULT YOUR PHYSICIAN WITHOUT DELAY!**
**A serious disorder of heart rate or rhythm,** as a result of abnormal electrical impulses in the heart, is possible.
***Treatment:*** If your physician suspects such a disorder, he or she will arrange for you to undergo tests, including *electrocardiography* (above left), a Holter monitor and a *chest X ray* (p. 73). If your heart rhythms are found to be abnormal, you will probably be given anti-arrhythmic drugs to regulate the heart's activity.

# 55 Chest pain

Pain in the chest (anywhere between the neck and the bottom of the rib cage) may be dull and persistent, sharp and stabbing, or crushing. Although it may be alarming, most chest pain does not have a serious cause. However, severe, crushing central chest pain, or pain that is associated with breathlessness or irregular heartbeat, may be a sign of a serious disorder of the heart or lungs and may warrant emergency treatment.

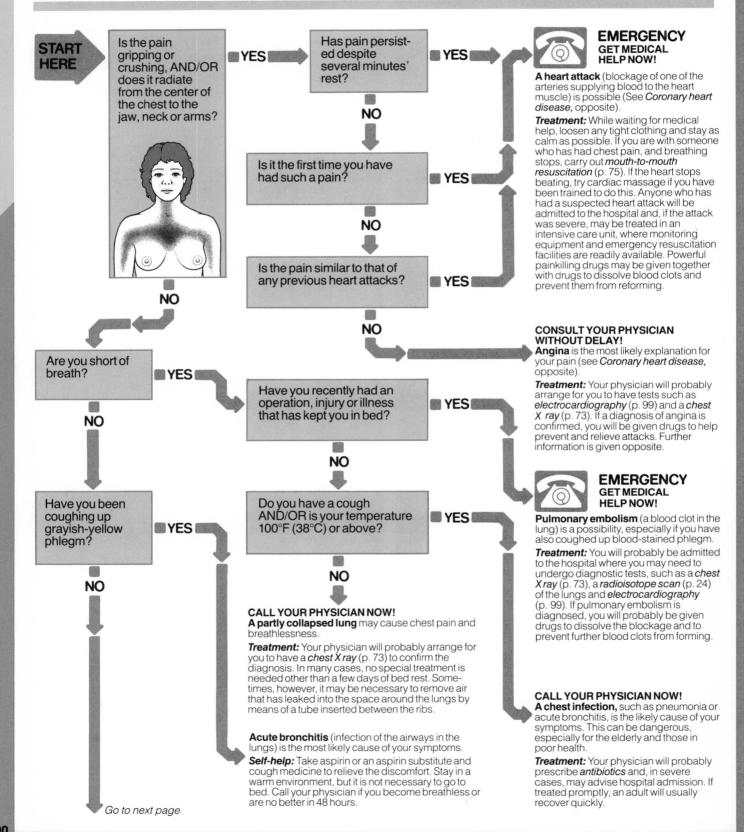

**START HERE**

Is the pain gripping or crushing, AND/OR does it radiate from the center of the chest to the jaw, neck or arms?

**YES** → Has pain persisted despite several minutes' rest?

**YES** → **EMERGENCY GET MEDICAL HELP NOW!**

Has pain persisted despite several minutes' rest? — **NO** → Is it the first time you have had such a pain? — **YES** →

Is it the first time you have had such a pain? — **NO** → Is the pain similar to that of any previous heart attacks? — **YES** →

Is the pain similar to that of any previous heart attacks? — **NO** → CONSULT YOUR PHYSICIAN WITHOUT DELAY!

Is the pain gripping or crushing...? — **NO** → Are you short of breath?

Are you short of breath? — **YES** → Have you recently had an operation, injury or illness that has kept you in bed?

Have you recently had an operation, injury or illness that has kept you in bed? — **YES** → EMERGENCY GET MEDICAL HELP NOW!

Have you recently had an operation, injury or illness that has kept you in bed? — **NO** → Do you have a cough AND/OR is your temperature 100°F (38°C) or above?

Do you have a cough AND/OR is your temperature 100°F (38°C) or above? — **YES** → CALL YOUR PHYSICIAN NOW!

Do you have a cough AND/OR is your temperature 100°F (38°C) or above? — **NO** → CALL YOUR PHYSICIAN NOW!

Are you short of breath? — **NO** → Have you been coughing up grayish-yellow phlegm?

Have you been coughing up grayish-yellow phlegm? — **YES** → (Acute bronchitis)

Have you been coughing up grayish-yellow phlegm? — **NO** → *Go to next page*

## EMERGENCY GET MEDICAL HELP NOW!

**A heart attack** (blockage of one of the arteries supplying blood to the heart muscle) is possible (See *Coronary heart disease,* opposite).

**Treatment:** While waiting for medical help, loosen any tight clothing and stay as calm as possible. If you are with someone who has had chest pain, and breathing stops, carry out *mouth-to-mouth resuscitation* (p. 75). If the heart stops beating, try cardiac massage if you have been trained to do this. Anyone who has had a suspected heart attack will be admitted to the hospital and, if the attack was severe, may be treated in an intensive care unit, where monitoring equipment and emergency resuscitation facilities are readily available. Powerful painkilling drugs may be given together with drugs to dissolve blood clots and prevent them from reforming.

## CONSULT YOUR PHYSICIAN WITHOUT DELAY!

**Angina** is the most likely explanation for your pain (see *Coronary heart disease,* opposite).

**Treatment:** Your physician will probably arrange for you to have tests such as *electrocardiography* (p. 99) and a *chest X ray* (p. 73). If a diagnosis of angina is confirmed, you will be given drugs to help prevent and relieve attacks. Further information is given opposite.

## EMERGENCY GET MEDICAL HELP NOW!

**Pulmonary embolism** (a blood clot in the lung) is a possibility, especially if you have also coughed up blood-stained phlegm.

**Treatment:** You will probably be admitted to the hospital where you may need to undergo diagnostic tests, such as a *chest X ray* (p. 73), a *radioisotope scan* (p. 24) of the lungs and *electrocardiography* (p. 99). If pulmonary embolism is diagnosed, you will probably be given drugs to dissolve the blockage and to prevent further blood clots from forming.

## CALL YOUR PHYSICIAN NOW!

**A partly collapsed lung** may cause chest pain and breathlessness.

**Treatment:** Your physician will probably arrange for you to have a *chest X ray* (p. 73) to confirm the diagnosis. In many cases, no special treatment is needed other than a few days of bed rest. Sometimes, however, it may be necessary to remove air that has leaked into the space around the lungs by means of a tube inserted between the ribs.

**Acute bronchitis** (infection of the airways in the lungs) is the most likely cause of your symptoms.

**Self-help:** Take aspirin or an aspirin substitute and cough medicine to relieve the discomfort. Stay in a warm environment, but it is not necessary to go to bed. Call your physician if you become breathless or are no better in 48 hours.

## CALL YOUR PHYSICIAN NOW!

**A chest infection,** such as pneumonia or acute bronchitis, is the likely cause of your symptoms. This can be dangerous, especially for the elderly and those in poor health.

**Treatment:** Your physician will probably prescribe *antibiotics* and, in severe cases, may advise hospital admission. If treated promptly, an adult will usually recover quickly.

*Continued from previous page*

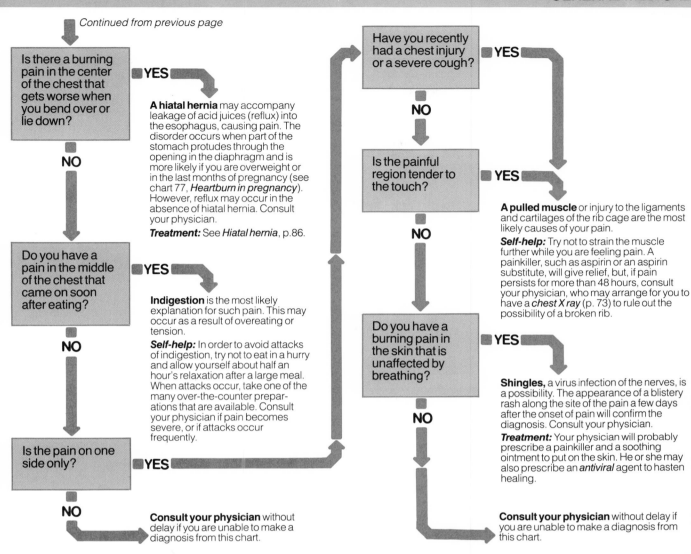

**Is there a burning pain in the center of the chest that gets worse when you bend over or lie down?**

**YES** → **A hiatal hernia** may accompany leakage of acid juices (reflux) into the esophagus, causing pain. The disorder occurs when part of the stomach protudes through the opening in the diaphragm and is more likely if you are overweight or in the last months of pregnancy (see chart 77, *Heartburn in pregnancy*). However, reflux may occur in the absence of hiatal hernia. Consult your physician.

**Treatment:** See *Hiatal hernia*, p.86.

**NO** ↓

**Do you have a pain in the middle of the chest that came on soon after eating?**

**YES** → **Indigestion** is the most likely explanation for such pain. This may occur as a result of overeating or tension.

**Self-help:** In order to avoid attacks of indigestion, try not to eat in a hurry and allow yourself about half an hour's relaxation after a large meal. When attacks occur, take one of the many over-the-counter preparations that are available. Consult your physician if pain becomes severe, or if attacks occur frequently.

**NO** ↓

**Is the pain on one side only?**

**YES** →

**NO** → **Consult your physician** without delay if you are unable to make a diagnosis from this chart.

**Have you recently had a chest injury or a severe cough?**

**YES** →

**NO** ↓

**Is the painful region tender to the touch?**

**YES** → **A pulled muscle** or injury to the ligaments and cartilages of the rib cage are the most likely causes of your pain.

**Self-help:** Try not to strain the muscle further while you are feeling pain. A painkiller, such as aspirin or an aspirin substitute, will give relief, but, if pain persists for more than 48 hours, consult your physician, who may arrange for you to have a *chest X ray* (p. 73) to rule out the possibility of a broken rib.

**NO** ↓

**Do you have a burning pain in the skin that is unaffected by breathing?**

**YES** → **Shingles,** a virus infection of the nerves, is a possibility. The appearance of a blistery rash along the site of the pain a few days after the onset of pain will confirm the diagnosis. Consult your physician.

**Treatment:** Your physician will probably prescribe a painkiller and a soothing ointment to put on the skin. He or she may also prescribe an *antiviral* agent to hasten healing.

**NO** → **Consult your physician** without delay if you are unable to make a diagnosis from this chart.

---

## CORONARY HEART DISEASE

Coronary heart disease occurs when fatty deposits, or plaques, called atheroma, build up on the inside walls of the arteries that supply oxygenated blood to the heart muscle. This causes them to become narrowed and disturbs the flow of blood.

Coronary heart disease may cause chest pain (angina). This can occur after exertion or emotional stress, when the increased oxygen needs of the heart cannot be supplied through the narrowed coronary arteries. However, many people with coronary heart disease have no symptoms. Often their first indication of the disease is when they experience a heart attack, which occurs when a blood clot or buildup of atheroma blocks a coronary artery, cutting off the blood supply to part of the heart muscle. This can be fatal and even if it is not usually results in some permanent damage to the heart muscle.

### What is the treatment?

If you are found to have coronary heart disease, you will probably be advised to change any aspects of your life-style that seem to be contributing to the disease (see *Preventing coronary heart disease,* right). You will probably be given medication to reduce the likelihood of angina attacks and others to take if attacks do occur. If you are found to have high blood pressure, this may also need drug treatment.

### Coronary artery bypass surgery

If your coronary arteries are found to be dangerously narrowed, you may be advised to have an operation in which the diseased sections of the coronary arteries are bypassed using healthy veins from the leg or an artery in the chest wall. This is a major operation, but the prospects for an active life and relief of chest pain are good.

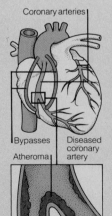

Coronary arteries

Bypasses | Diseased coronary artery

Atheroma

If surgery is necessary, the diseased sections of the coronary arteries containing atheroma are bypassed, usually with multiple bypass sections.

### Preventing coronary heart disease

There are many factors that are known to increase the risk of developing coronary heart disease – notably, the tendency for the disease to run in families. But anyone who has a family history of heart disease can reduce the risk of developing serious problems by avoiding the factors listed below.

- **Smoking** Smokers are at least twice as likely to die of a heart attack than nonsmokers. This is because substances in tobacco smoke increase the level of atheroma-forming fats in the bloodstream.

- **Obesity** Overweight people tend to eat higher-than-average amounts of fat, increasing the risk of atheroma build up. Carrying too much weight places an increased strain on the heart, making it less able to withstand any restriction of its blood supply.

- **Too much fat in the diet** The tendency for atheroma to form in the arteries seems to be related to the level of certain types of fat in the bloodstream, which in turn is related partly to heredity, and partly to the amount of fat in the diet. Cutting down on all types of fat should help to reduce your risk of developing coronary heart disease.

- **Lack of exercise** Regular strenuous exercise increases the efficiency of the heart, so that it needs less oxygen to function well. If you gradually increase your physical fitness, your heart will be under less strain should its blood supply be reduced by coronary heart disease.

# 56 Back pain

Your backbone (or spine) extends from the base of your skull to the buttocks. It consists of the spinal column, which is made up of more than 30 separate bones called vertebrae stacked on top of one another. In between each pair of vertebrae is an elastic disc. The vertebrae and discs are held together by ligaments. Along the length of the spinal column is a space containing the spinal cord and the nerves that run from it to the rest of the body. Most people suffer from mild back pain from time to time, the exact cause of which may be difficult to diagnose. It is usually a sign that you have damaged one or more joints, ligaments or discs by overstretching or twisting your back into an awkward position. Severe pain, however, may be the result of pressure on the nerves from malalignment of the bones or discs in the back. Consult your physician.

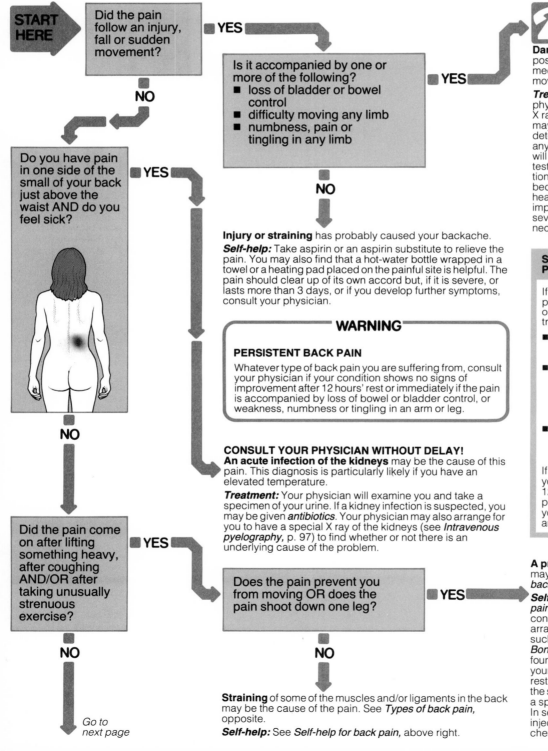

**START HERE**

**Did the pain follow an injury, fall or sudden movement?**

**NO**

**YES**

**Is it accompanied by one or more of the following?**
- **loss of bladder or bowel control**
- **difficulty moving any limb**
- **numbness, pain or tingling in any limb**

**YES**

**NO**

**Do you have pain in one side of the small of your back just above the waist AND do you feel sick?**

**YES**

**NO**

**Injury or straining** has probably caused your backache.

*Self-help:* Take aspirin or an aspirin substitute to relieve the pain. You may also find that a hot-water bottle wrapped in a towel or a heating pad placed on the painful site is helpful. The pain should clear up of its own accord but, if it is severe, or lasts more than 3 days, or if you develop further symptoms, consult your physician.

---

### WARNING

**PERSISTENT BACK PAIN**

Whatever type of back pain you are suffering from, consult your physician if your condition shows no signs of improvement after 12 hours' rest or immediately if the pain is accompanied by loss of bowel or bladder control, or weakness, numbness or tingling in an arm or leg.

---

**CONSULT YOUR PHYSICIAN WITHOUT DELAY!**
**An acute infection of the kidneys** may be the cause of this pain. This diagnosis is particularly likely if you have an elevated temperature.

*Treatment:* Your physician will examine you and take a specimen of your urine. If a kidney infection is suspected, you may be given **antibiotics**. Your physician may also arrange for you to have a special X ray of the kidneys (see *Intravenous pyelography,* p. 97) to find whether or not there is an underlying cause of the problem.

**Did the pain come on after lifting something heavy, after coughing AND/OR after taking unusually strenuous exercise?**

**YES**

**NO**

*Go to next page*

**Does the pain prevent you from moving OR does the pain shoot down one leg?**

**YES**

**NO**

**Straining** of some of the muscles and/or ligaments in the back may be the cause of the pain. See *Types of back pain,* opposite.

*Self-help:* See *Self-help for back pain,* above right.

## EMERGENCY
**GET MEDICAL HELP NOW!**

**Damage to the spinal cord** is possible. While waiting for medical help to arrive, do not move. Keep warm and stay calm.

*Treatment:* In the hospital, a physical examination and spine X rays (see *Bone X rays,* p. 105) may be carried out in order to determine the site and extent of any damage. Further treatment will depend on the results of these tests and the physician's observations. In some cases, resting in bed will be sufficient to allow healing. If there is little or no improvement, or if damage is severe, surgery may be necessary.

---

### SELF-HELP FOR BACK PAIN

If you are suffering from back pain caused by a minor strain or that has no obvious cause, try these measures:

- Take the recommended dose of aspirin or an aspirin substitute.
- Rest on your back (or whichever position is most comfortable) on a firm mattress for as long as pain persists, getting up only when necessary.
- A hot-water bottle or heating pad on the back may help to relieve pain.

If pain becomes severe, or if your condition is no better in 12 hours, consult your physician, who will examine you and may order X rays and recommend treatment.

---

**A prolapsed (or slipped) disc** may cause sciatica (see *Types of back pain,* opposite).

*Self-help:* See *Self-help for back pain* (above). If pain persists, consult your physician, who may arrange for you to undergo tests such as an X ray of the spine (see *Bone X rays,* p. 105). If you are found to have a prolapsed disc, your physician may simply advise rest, recommend manipulation of the spine or suggest that you wear a specially fitted support corset. In severe cases, surgery or injection of the disc with a special chemical may be recommended.

*Continued from previous page*

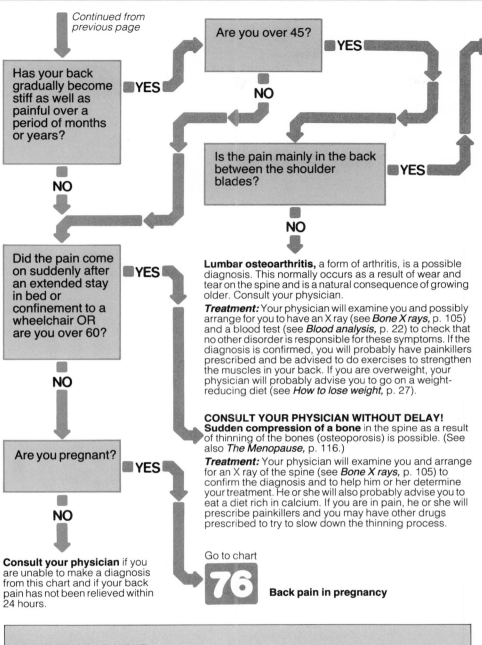

**Has your back gradually become stiff as well as painful over a period of months or years?**

■ **YES**

**NO**

**Are you over 45?**

■ **YES**

**NO**

**Is the pain mainly in the back between the shoulder blades?**

■ **YES**

**NO**

**Did the pain come on suddenly after an extended stay in bed or confinement to a wheelchair OR are you over 60?**

■ **YES**

**NO**

**Are you pregnant?**

■ **YES**

**NO**

**Consult your physician** if you are unable to make a diagnosis from this chart and if your back pain has not been relieved within 24 hours.

**Cervical osteoarthritis,** arthritis of the joints and bones in the neck as a result of wear and tear, may be the cause of this pain. Consult your physician.

***Treatment:*** Your physician will examine you and may arrange for you to have an X ray of the bones in your neck (see *Bone X rays,* p. 105). If he or she thinks that the symptoms are due to this disorder, you may be given a supportive collar to wear to reduce neck mobility. Aspirin or an aspirin substitute can be taken to relieve the discomfort. If these measures fail to help the condition, your physician may send you to a physical or occupational therapist for further treatment.

**Lumbar osteoarthritis,** a form of arthritis, is a possible diagnosis. This normally occurs as a result of wear and tear on the spine and is a natural consequence of growing older. Consult your physician.

***Treatment:*** Your physician will examine you and possibly arrange for you to have an X ray (see *Bone X rays,* p. 105) and a blood test (see *Blood analysis,* p. 22) to check that no other disorder is responsible for these symptoms. If the diagnosis is confirmed, you will probably have painkillers prescribed and be advised to do exercises to strengthen the muscles in your back. If you are overweight, your physician will probably advise you to go on a weight-reducing diet (see *How to lose weight,* p. 27).

**CONSULT YOUR PHYSICIAN WITHOUT DELAY!**
**Sudden compression of a bone** in the spine as a result of thinning of the bones (osteoporosis) is possible. (See also *The Menopause,* p. 116.)

***Treatment:*** Your physician will examine you and arrange for an X ray of the spine (see *Bone X rays,* p. 105) to confirm the diagnosis and to help him or her determine your treatment. He or she will also probably advise you to eat a diet rich in calcium. If you are in pain, he or she will prescribe painkillers and you may have other drugs prescribed to try to slow down the thinning process.

Go to chart

## 76

**Back pain in pregnancy**

## TYPES OF BACK PAIN

**Nonspecific back pain**
If back pain has no obvious cause, it is "nonspecific." Such pain is probably the result of strained ligaments or a strained or slightly misplaced vertebral joint that has caused the surrounding muscles to go into spasm. Or it may be fibrositis (stiffness and pain within the muscles). Some people tend to develop nonspecific back pain when they are under stress. Follow the self-help measures opposite.

**Low back pain**
Low back pain is centered in the small of the back and there is often a tender spot. In severe cases, the sufferer is unable to move his or her back. It may develop suddenly or come on overnight. It is usually brought on by unaccustomed strenuous activity. Follow the self-help measures opposite.

**Sciatica**
This is a pain that is caused by pressure on one of the nerves where it leaves the spinal cord. It is usually the result of pressure on a nerve from a prolapsed (slipped) vertebral disc. A severe pain shoots through the buttocks and along the back of the thigh down toward the ankle. If you cough, sneeze or try to bend your back, the pain becomes worse. Mild sciatica may be relieved by self-help treatment (opposite) but, if it persists or is severe, consult your physician.

**Coccygodynia**
Coccygodynia is a condition affecting the coccyx, at the base of the spinal column. It is a localized ache that is made worse when you sit down. It may be caused by a heavy blow on the buttocks or a fall. Some women suffer from coccygodynia during or after childbirth. Sitting on a cushion or resting on your side may help to relieve the pain.

**Sites of back pain**

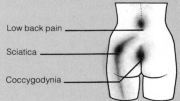

Low back pain ___

Sciatica ___

Coccygodynia ___

## PREVENTING BACKACHE

There are several practical ways in which you can minimize the amount of strain on your back. Feeling comfortable in any movement or position is a general guide to whether or not you are putting strain on your back. Below are some suggestions on specific precautions you can take.

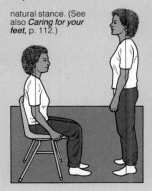

**Sitting correctly**
When sitting for any length of time, try to keep your back straight and avoid slumping. Choose a chair that has a firm, upright back that will support the length of your spine. You should be able to rest your feet flat on the floor with your knees bent at a right angle.

**Posture**
To avoid placing unnecessary strain on your back, stand with your head, trunk and legs aligned. Avoid wearing high heels, which force an un- natural stance. (See also *Caring for your feet,* p. 112.)

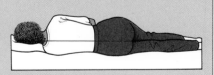

**Sleeping**
Sleep on a firm mattress or put a board under your existing mattress. Use a flat pillow to support your head (or use none at all). These measures will support your back and prevent your spine from sagging.

**Lifting**
When lifting a heavy object, get as close to it as possible. Keep your back straight and bend your knees so that your leg muscles, not the weaker back muscles, take the strain.

# 57 Painful or stiff neck

A stiff or painful neck is most often the result of a muscle stiffness brought on by sitting in a cold draft, sleeping in an uncomfortable position or doing some form of exercise or activity to which you are not accustomed.

This type of problem should resolve itself within a day or so. If pain and/or stiffness persist, ask your physician for advice. Occasionally, a stiff or painful neck may be a sign of a disorder that requires medical treatment.

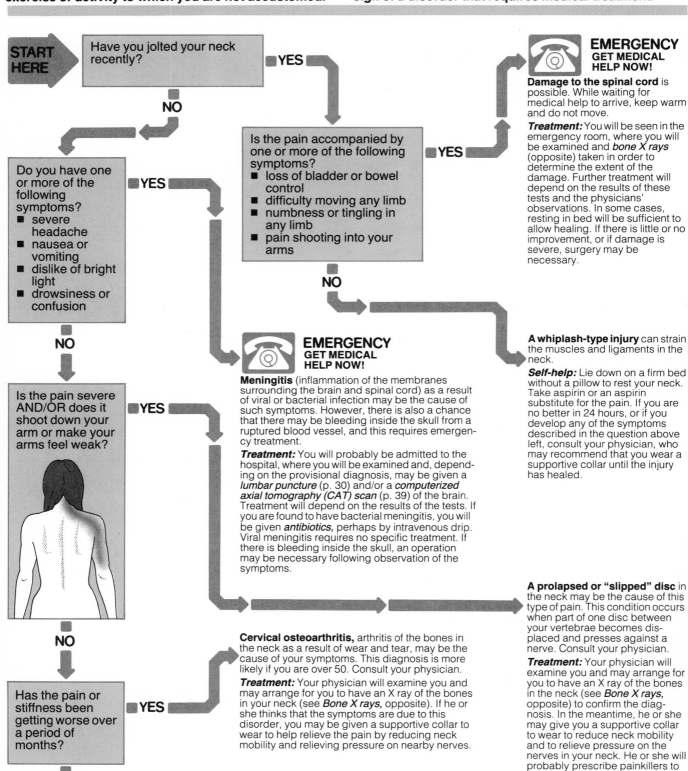

**START HERE**

**Have you jolted your neck recently?**

NO · YES

**Do you have one or more of the following symptoms?**
- severe headache
- nausea or vomiting
- dislike of bright light
- drowsiness or confusion

YES · NO

**Is the pain accompanied by one or more of the following symptoms?**
- loss of bladder or bowel control
- difficulty moving any limb
- numbness or tingling in any limb
- pain shooting into your arms

YES · NO

**EMERGENCY GET MEDICAL HELP NOW!**

**Damage to the spinal cord** is possible. While waiting for medical help to arrive, keep warm and do not move.

**Treatment:** You will be seen in the emergency room, where you will be examined and *bone X rays* (opposite) taken in order to determine the extent of the damage. Further treatment will depend on the results of these tests and the physicians' observations. In some cases, resting in bed will be sufficient to allow healing. If there is little or no improvement, or if damage is severe, surgery may be necessary.

**Is the pain severe AND/OR does it shoot down your arm or make your arms feel weak?**

YES · NO

**EMERGENCY GET MEDICAL HELP NOW!**

**Meningitis** (inflammation of the membranes surrounding the brain and spinal cord) as a result of viral or bacterial infection may be the cause of such symptoms. However, there is also a chance that there may be bleeding inside the skull from a ruptured blood vessel, and this requires emergency treatment.

**Treatment:** You will probably be admitted to the hospital, where you will be examined and, depending on the provisional diagnosis, may be given a *lumbar puncture* (p. 30) and/or a *computerized axial tomography (CAT) scan* (p. 39) of the brain. Treatment will depend on the results of the tests. If you are found to have bacterial meningitis, you will be given *antibiotics,* perhaps by intravenous drip. Viral meningitis requires no specific treatment. If there is bleeding inside the skull, an operation may be necessary following observation of the symptoms.

**A whiplash-type injury** can strain the muscles and ligaments in the neck.

**Self-help:** Lie down on a firm bed without a pillow to rest your neck. Take aspirin or an aspirin substitute for the pain. If you are no better in 24 hours, or if you develop any of the symptoms described in the question above left, consult your physician, who may recommend that you wear a supportive collar until the injury has healed.

**A prolapsed or "slipped" disc** in the neck may be the cause of this type of pain. This condition occurs when part of one disc between your vertebrae becomes displaced and presses against a nerve. Consult your physician.

**Treatment:** Your physician will examine you and may arrange for you to have an X ray of the bones in the neck (see *Bone X rays,* opposite) to confirm the diagnosis. In the meantime, he or she may give you a supportive collar to wear to reduce neck mobility and to relieve pressure on the nerves in your neck. He or she will probably prescribe painkillers to ease any pain or discomfort that you may feel. In some cases, surgery may be necessary.

**Cervical osteoarthritis,** arthritis of the bones in the neck as a result of wear and tear, may be the cause of your symptoms. This diagnosis is more likely if you are over 50. Consult your physician.

**Treatment:** Your physician will examine you and may arrange for you to have an X ray of the bones in your neck (see *Bone X rays,* opposite). If he or she thinks that the symptoms are due to this disorder, you may be given a supportive collar to wear to help relieve the pain by reducing neck mobility and relieving pressure on nearby nerves.

**Has the pain or stiffness been getting worse over a period of months?**

YES · NO

**Consult your physician** if you are unable to make a diagnosis from this chart.

# 58 Painful arm

Pain in the arm is almost always the result of injury or straining of the muscles and ligaments that hold the various bones and joints in place. Such injuries are particularly likely to occur after any unaccustomed strenuous physical activity, such as participating in a sport for the first time. The pain should disappear if you rest your arm. If any pain in your arm is recurrent or persistent, consult your physician.

**START HERE**

**Did the pain immediately follow an injury, fall or sudden movement?**

YES →

**Are you unable to move your arm AND/OR is the pain severe, even when resting?**

YES →

NO ↓

**Is the pain mainly in the upper arm and does it come on only when you move your arm in a certain way?**

YES →

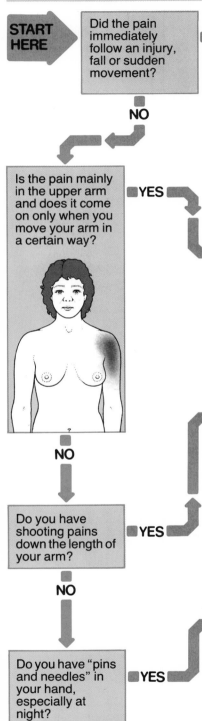

NO ↓

**Do you have shooting pains down the length of your arm?**

YES →

NO ↓

**Do you have "pins and needles" in your hand, especially at night?**

YES →

NO ↓

**EMERGENCY**
**GET MEDICAL HELP NOW!**

**A fracture, dislocation or serious injury** to the muscles or ligaments may be causing this pain (see *First aid for suspected broken bones and dislocated joints,* p. 109).

***Treatment:*** The limb will be examined and probably X-rayed (see *Bone X rays,* below) to discover the extent of the damage. Depending on the nature of the injury, you may need to wear a plaster cast or a firm bandage. Sometimes an operation is necessary to reposition the bones.

NO ↓

**Injury to the soft tissues** (muscles, ligaments and cartilages), such as a sprain or strain or bruising of the arm, is probably causing this pain.

***Self-help:*** Follow the advice on treating such injuries given in the box on p. 111. Consult your physician if the pain is severe or is no better the following day (see also *Sports injuries,* p. 107).

**Inflammation of the soft tissues or tendons of the shoulder joint** (bursitis or tendonitis) as a result of injury or strain is the most likely cause of such pain, although certain forms of arthritis may also cause such symptoms.

***Self-help:*** Take aspirin, an aspirin substitute or an over-the-counter *anti-inflammatory* drug to relieve the pain. Rest the arm while pain persists. Consult your physician if you are no better in 3 days.

**CONSULT YOUR PHYSICIAN WITHOUT DELAY**
**Displacement of a disc** between the bones in the neck (see *Prolapsed disc,* opposite) may cause such pain as a result of pressure on a nerve (see *Cervical osteoarthritis,* opposite). There is also likely to be some numbness in the hand.

***Treatment:*** You may be referred for an X ray (see *Bone X rays,* right) of the neck. Your physician will probably prescribe painkillers and may recommend that you wear a supportive collar. In some cases, traction may be necessary.

**Carpal tunnel syndrome,** a disorder in which a nerve (the median nerve) in the wrist is pinched due to swelling of surrounding tissues, is possible. This condition is particularly common during pregnancy. Consult your physician.

***Treatment:*** The condition often clears up of its own accord. Your physician may refer you for tests to confirm the diagnosis and you may be given injections of *steroids* into the wrist. If the condition is particularly painful and persistent, a simple operation will relieve it.

---

**BONE X RAYS**

Because X rays pass through soft tissues such as muscle and fat and clearly show up areas of bone, X-ray pictures are often used to diagnose the extent and nature of any damage to any bones from injury or disease. This helps physicians decide on the best form of treatment and, in the case of a broken (fractured) bone, whether or not an operation is necessary to reposition the pieces.

This bone X ray shows a fracture in one of the bones in the lower arm. This type of break is difficult to diagnose without an X ray.

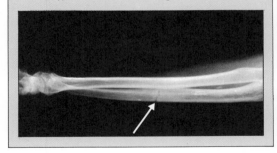

**Does the pain mainly affect your joints – for example, your shoulder, elbow or finger joints?**

YES →

Go to chart

**61** **Painful or swollen joints**

NO ↓

**Consult your physician** if you are unable to make a diagnosis from this chart and if the pain is severe or persists for more than 24 hours.

# 59 Painful knee

The knee is one of the principal weight-bearing joints in the body and is subject to much wear and tear. If your work involves a great deal of bending or squatting, the risk of damage to the bones, ligaments and cartilages through overuse and/or injury is increased. Consult this chart if you experience pain in one or both knees.

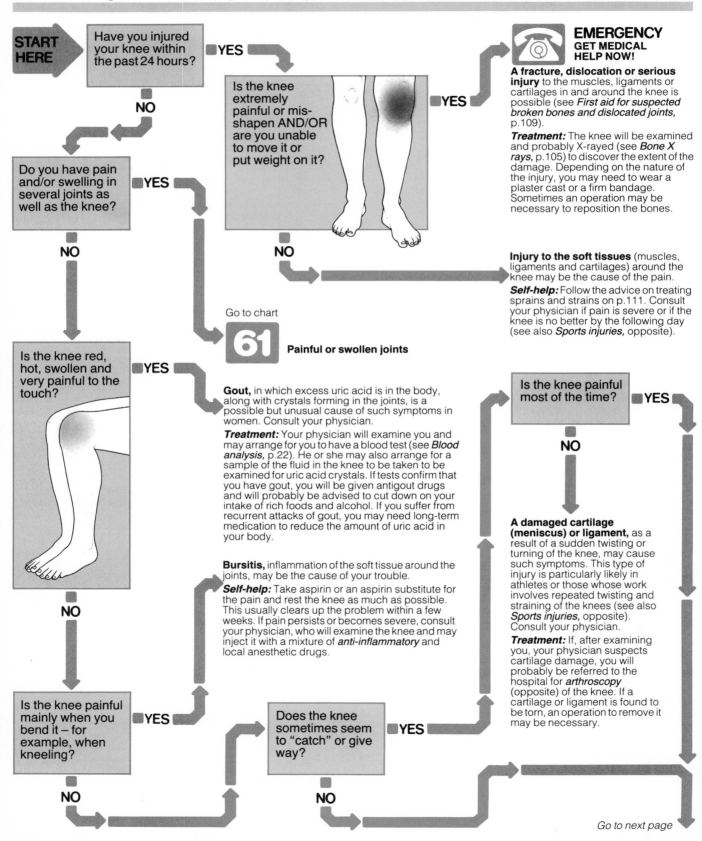

**START HERE**

**Have you injured your knee within the past 24 hours?** → **YES**

**NO**

**Do you have pain and/or swelling in several joints as well as the knee?** → **YES**

**NO**

**Is the knee extremely painful or mis-shapen AND/OR are you unable to move it or put weight on it?** → **YES**

**NO**

Go to chart

**61** **Painful or swollen joints**

**Is the knee red, hot, swollen and very painful to the touch?** → **YES**

**NO**

**Is the knee painful mainly when you bend it — for example, when kneeling?** → **YES**

**NO**

**Does the knee sometimes seem to "catch" or give way?** → **YES**

**NO**

**Is the knee painful most of the time?** → **YES**

**NO**

## EMERGENCY
### GET MEDICAL HELP NOW!

**A fracture, dislocation or serious injury** to the muscles, ligaments or cartilages in and around the knee is possible (see *First aid for suspected broken bones and dislocated joints*, p.109).

***Treatment:*** The knee will be examined and probably X-rayed (see *Bone X rays*, p.105) to discover the extent of the damage. Depending on the nature of the injury, you may need to wear a plaster cast or a firm bandage. Sometimes an operation may be necessary to reposition the bones.

**Injury to the soft tissues** (muscles, ligaments and cartilages) around the knee may be the cause of the pain.

***Self-help:*** Follow the advice on treating sprains and strains on p.111. Consult your physician if pain is severe or if the knee is no better by the following day (see also *Sports injuries,* opposite).

**Gout,** in which excess uric acid is in the body, along with crystals forming in the joints, is a possible but unusual cause of such symptoms in women. Consult your physician.

***Treatment:*** Your physician will examine you and may arrange for you to have a blood test (see *Blood analysis,* p.22). He or she may also arrange for a sample of the fluid in the knee to be taken to be examined for uric acid crystals. If tests confirm that you have gout, you will be given antigout drugs and will probably be advised to cut down on your intake of rich foods and alcohol. If you suffer from recurrent attacks of gout, you may need long-term medication to reduce the amount of uric acid in your body.

**Bursitis,** inflammation of the soft tissue around the joints, may be the cause of your trouble.

***Self-help:*** Take aspirin or an aspirin substitute for the pain and rest the knee as much as possible. This usually clears up the problem within a few weeks. If pain persists or becomes severe, consult your physician, who will examine the knee and may inject it with a mixture of *anti-inflammatory* and local anesthetic drugs.

**A damaged cartilage (meniscus) or ligament,** as a result of a sudden twisting or turning of the knee, may cause such symptoms. This type of injury is particularly likely in athletes or those whose work involves repeated twisting and straining of the knees (see also *Sports injuries,* opposite). Consult your physician.

***Treatment:*** If, after examining you, your physician suspects cartilage damage, you will probably be referred to the hospital for *arthroscopy* (opposite) of the knee. If a cartilage or ligament is found to be torn, an operation to remove it may be necessary.

*Go to next page*

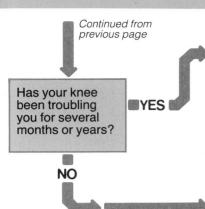

*Continued from previous page*

Has your knee been troubling you for several months or years?

**YES**

**Osteoarthritis,** as a result of injury or wear and tear on the knee, is a possible cause of such pain, especially if you are over 50, or if you have regularly overused the joint at work or participating in sports. Consult your physician.

*Treatment:* Your physician will examine you and may arrange for you to have a blood test (see *Blood analysis,* p.22) to exclude other possible causes of pain, and you may need to have an X ray (see *Bone X rays,* p.105) of the knee. If these investigations confirm the diagnosis, your physician will prescribe painkillers. If you are overweight, it will help relieve the strain on your knee if you try to lose weight (see *How to lose weight,* p.27). In some cases, physical or occupational therapy and/or heat treatment may be helpful.

**NO**

**Consult your physician** if you are unable to make a diagnosis from this chart and your knee is no better after 24 hours' rest.

### ARTHROSCOPY

Arthroscopy allows the physician to examine the interior of a joint using an arthroscope. This is a flexible fiberoptic tube with a lighting and lens system that is passed through a small incision into the joint. It is then possible to discover the abnormality by looking through an eyepiece. A local or general anesthetic will be given. Many common knee problems can be surgically corrected using arthroscopy.

---

### SPORTS INJURIES

Sports and other forms of physical exercise are important for maintaining health and general fitness, but an overambitious program may lead to injuries and other health problems. Injuries may also be the result of inadequate warm-ups before exercise, or failure to use the correct safety equipment or clothing. Make sure that you are aware of the risks of any exercise activities you undertake so that you can balance these against the likely health benefits, and so that you can take reasonable precautions to prevent injury.

Regular exercise will help you control your weight (see *Exercise and weight loss,* p.25) and help you to build up your stamina – that is, your staying power and endurance – which will in turn improve your physical and mental capacity for everyday activities. Some recent research has shown that regular, strenuous, physical activity can help prevent and alleviate minor depression. And there is evidence that regular exercise can help slow down bone thinning (osteoporosis), a disorder that is common in women past the *menopause* (see p.116). Most importantly, regular exercise has been proven to help prevent *coronary heart disease* (p.101).

#### Sensible precautions
If you are thinking of starting a new sport or other form of fitness training, and if you are not used to regular exercise, remember the following points:

- Do not be overambitious at first in the goals you set; it is safer to increase your level of fitness gradually.
- Make sure that your clothing and equipment is suitable (see right).
- Always do some warm-up exercises before each exercise session to reduce the likelihood of sprains and strains.
- If any exercise or movement becomes painful or causes other forms of discomfort, stop at once. Pain is a sign of damage (see *Common injuries,* right).

If you belong to any of the following categories, consult your physician before taking up any sort of strenuous activity for the first time:

- If you are over 50 years of age, or if you are over 40 and have not exercised regularly since early adulthood.
- If you are a heavy smoker (more than 20 cigarettes a day).
- If you are overweight (see *Weight chart,* p.26).
- If you have a long-term health problem such as high blood pressure, heart disease, diabetes or kidney disease.
- If you are pregnant (see above right).

#### Exercise and pregnancy
If you are used to exercising regularly, and providing you do not overtire yourself, there is no reason why you should not continue to participate in most sports until well into pregnancy, when your increasing size may make certain movements difficult or uncomfortable. However, activities that carry a risk of injury, such as horseback-riding, skiing or mountain climbing, may not be advisable. It is also unwise to take up a strenuous physical activity for the first time during pregnancy. But gentle forms of exercise, such as swimming or yoga-style stretching exercises, may increase your feeling of well-being and help to relieve the minor aches and pains of pregnancy.

#### Safety equipment
In some sports you can reduce the risk of injury by the use of special safety equipment – for example, eyeguards for racquet-ball players and helmets for cyclists. Make sure that any equipment you buy is of good quality and that it meets your individual requirements; if you are unsure what equipment is necessary, seek advice from a sports club or from the appropriate sporting organization. Borrowed equipment may not be suitable.

#### Clothing
For most sporting activities, choose clothes that are comfortable and that do not restrict your movement. Natural fibers such as cotton are best for shirts, shorts and socks, because they allow air to circulate more freely, reducing the likelihood of chafing and blisters. Most women feel more comfortable if they wear a bra for support. Special sports bras with a high-cotton content and that allow free movement are available. Wash your sports gear regularly to reduce the risk of fungal infection. Some sports require specialized protective clothing and, if you are unsure what to buy, seek advice from an expert.

#### Shoes
Wearing the correct shoes is essential if you are to avoid minor foot problems such as blisters. Make sure that your sports shoes fit well, allowing room for your feet to expand slightly during exercise.

#### Common injuries
**Minor injuries:** Chafing (soreness that can result from friction between clothes, equipment and skin) may be prevented by rubbing petroleum jelly into susceptible areas, or by wearing protective bandages. Blisters on the feet are usually the result of poorly fitting shoes. Apply an adhesive

bandage to protect against further rubbing.

**Strains, sprains and pulled muscles and ligaments:** Such injuries are most common in those just starting exercise after a long period of inactivity and those who have not undertaken adequate warm-up exercises. Serious injuries of this type can be very painful and require first aid and professional medical attention (see *First aid for sprains and strains,* p.111). Never attempt to continue exercise after such an injury, as you may do further damage. Minor muscle and ligament strain causing tenderness and stiffness may only be noticeable some hours after exercise. In such cases, resting the affected part for a few days and gradually returning to a vigorous exercise program is advisable.

**Shin splints:** Shin splints are pains along the shin bone that may occur during or after exercise. Shin splints may be the result of a stress fracture, swelling of the muscles, or inflammation of the lining of the bone. If you have pain, apply an ice bag, elevate your leg and rest it as much as possible. Wrapping the leg with an elastic bandage may also help. If after 2 to 3 weeks the pain persists, consult your physician.

**Stress fractures:** Bones that are constantly under stress – for example, those of the foot in runners – may develop hair-line cracks known as stress fractures. Pain may only be slight, so there is a danger that the injury may go unnoticed and that further exercise may increase the damage. If you suspect a stress fracture, consult your physician, who will arrange for you to be X-rayed (see *Bone X rays,* p.105). Rest and bandaging of the affected part are the usual treatments.

**Osteoarthritis:** The main long-term health problem associated with regular vigorous exercise is osteoarthritis of joints that are used excessively; the knee is particularly susceptible. Osteoarthritis often develops in later life as a result of wear and tear on joints, even in those who do not exercise excessively, but it is more likely to occur at a younger age in professional athletes.

#### After an injury
Following treatment of an injury, be careful not to strain the injured part by returning to your former exercise routine too quickly. A program of special exercises may help to restore your strength gradually. If you have any doubts as to what you can do safely, or if pain or swelling persists or recurs, consult your physician.

# 60 Painful leg

Pain in the leg is almost always the result of injury or straining of the muscles and ligaments that hold the joints in place. Such injuries are likely if you take part in any unaccustomed activity, such as participating in a sport for the first time. Such pain should disappear if you rest your leg. However, any pain in your leg that is persistent or recurrent may indicate an underlying disorder, so consult your physician.

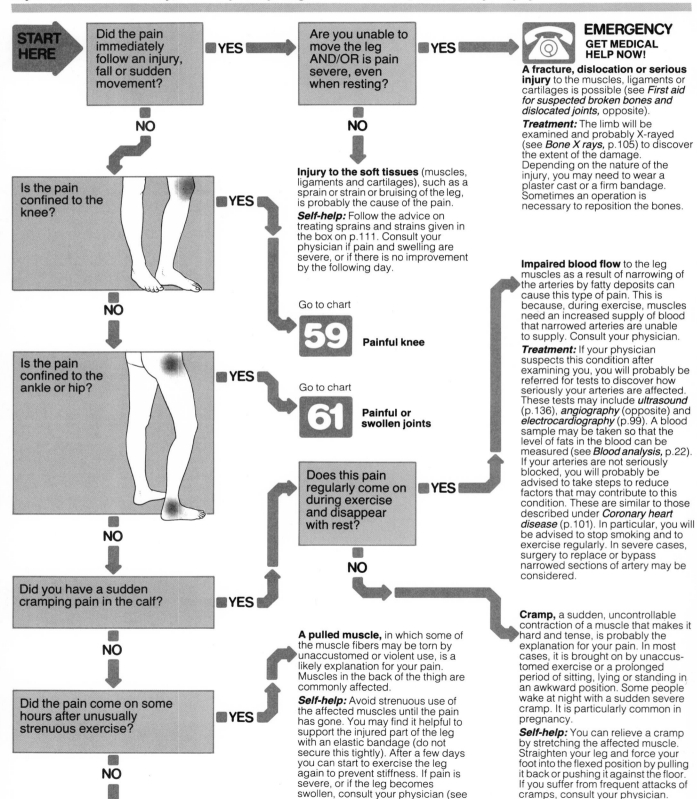

**START HERE**

**Did the pain immediately follow an injury, fall or sudden movement?**

**YES** →

**Are you unable to move the leg AND/OR is pain severe, even when resting?**

**YES** →

## EMERGENCY
**GET MEDICAL HELP NOW!**

**A fracture, dislocation or serious injury** to the muscles, ligaments or cartilages is possible (see *First aid for suspected broken bones and dislocated joints,* opposite).

***Treatment:*** The limb will be examined and probably X-rayed (see *Bone X rays,* p.105) to discover the extent of the damage. Depending on the nature of the injury, you may need to wear a plaster cast or a firm bandage. Sometimes an operation is necessary to reposition the bones.

**NO** ↓

**NO** ↓

**Is the pain confined to the knee?**

**YES** →

**Injury to the soft tissues** (muscles, ligaments and cartilages), such as a sprain or strain or bruising of the leg, is probably the cause of the pain.

***Self-help:*** Follow the advice on treating sprains and strains given in the box on p.111. Consult your physician if pain and swelling are severe, or if there is no improvement by the following day.

Go to chart

## 59
**Painful knee**

**Impaired blood flow** to the leg muscles as a result of narrowing of the arteries by fatty deposits can cause this type of pain. This is because, during exercise, muscles need an increased supply of blood that narrowed arteries are unable to supply. Consult your physician.

***Treatment:*** If your physician suspects this condition after examining you, you will probably be referred for tests to discover how seriously your arteries are affected. These tests may include *ultrasound* (p.136), *angiography* (opposite) and *electrocardiography* (p.99). A blood sample may be taken so that the level of fats in the blood can be measured (see *Blood analysis,* p.22). If your arteries are not seriously blocked, you will probably be advised to take steps to reduce factors that may contribute to this condition. These are similar to those described under *Coronary heart disease* (p.101). In particular, you will be advised to stop smoking and to exercise regularly. In severe cases, surgery to replace or bypass narrowed sections of artery may be considered.

**NO** ↓

**Is the pain confined to the ankle or hip?**

**YES** →

Go to chart

## 61
**Painful or swollen joints**

**Does this pain regularly come on during exercise and disappear with rest?**

**YES** →

**NO** ↓

**NO** ↓

**Did you have a sudden cramping pain in the calf?**

**YES** →

**A pulled muscle,** in which some of the muscle fibers may be torn by unaccustomed or violent use, is a likely explanation for your pain. Muscles in the back of the thigh are commonly affected.

***Self-help:*** Avoid strenuous use of the affected muscles until the pain has gone. You may find it helpful to support the injured part of the leg with an elastic bandage (do not secure this tightly). After a few days you can start to exercise the leg again to prevent stiffness. If pain is severe, or if the leg becomes swollen, consult your physician (see also *Sports injuries,* p.107).

**Cramp,** a sudden, uncontrollable contraction of a muscle that makes it hard and tense, is probably the explanation for your pain. In most cases, it is brought on by unaccustomed exercise or a prolonged period of sitting, lying or standing in an awkward position. Some people wake at night with a sudden severe cramp. It is particularly common in pregnancy.

***Self-help:*** You can relieve a cramp by stretching the affected muscle. Straighten your leg and force your foot into the flexed position by pulling it back or pushing it against the floor. If you suffer from frequent attacks of cramps, consult your physician.

**NO** ↓

**Did the pain come on some hours after unusually strenuous exercise?**

**YES** →

**NO** ↓

*Go to next page*

*Continued from previous page*

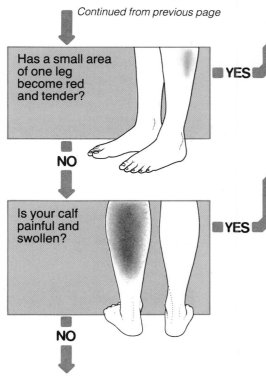

**Has a small area of one leg become red and tender?**

**YES** ▸ **Thrombophlebitis** (inflammation of a superficial vein) is the likely cause of such symptoms. Consult your physician.

*Treatment:* If your physician confirms the diagnosis, he or she will probably prescribe painkillers and, possibly, other medications. A sample of blood may be taken for analysis (see *Blood analysis*, p.22) to find out if there is an underlying reason you have developed this disorder.

**NO** ↓

**Is your calf painful and swollen?**

**YES** ▸ **CONSULT YOUR PHYSICIAN WITHOUT DELAY!**
**Deep-vein thrombosis,** a condition in which a blood clot blocks a vein in the leg, may be the cause of such symptoms. This disorder is also likely to cause swelling of the ankle. Those taking birth control pills, receiving post menopausal hormone therapy (see *The menopause*, p.116) or who have been immobilized by injury or illness for a long period are particularly susceptible.

*Treatment:* Your physician will examine you and, if he or she confirms the possibility of deep-vein thrombosis, will probably arrange for you to be admitted to the hospital for blood-flow tests, and venography (see *Angiography,* below right). Treatment for the condition consists of *anticoagulant* drugs to help dissolve and prevent blood clots. These drugs are usually taken for several months. If you are taking the birth control pill, see chart 72, *Choosing a contraceptive method.*

**NO** ↓

**Consult your physician** if you are unable to make a diagnosis from this chart.

---

## VARICOSE VEINS

Varicose veins are swollen leg veins causing poor circulation in the legs, usually as a result of damage to the valves in the veins. The veins in the back of the calf and along the inside of the leg are most commonly affected. Varicose veins are likely to cause aching of the leg and swelling of the ankle, especially after long periods of standing. Women often develop varicose veins during pregnancy because of pressure on the pelvic veins from the growing baby.

**Self-help measures**
If you think that you may be susceptible to varicose veins, especially if you are pregnant, or if you already have swollen veins in the leg, try to keep your weight off your feet as much as possible. Sit with your legs up whenever you can, to help the blood to flow back up your leg. If you have to spend long periods standing up, flex your calf muscles occasionally to help blood circulate in your leg. Wear support stockings or specially prescribed hose. Consult your physician if your varicose veins trouble you, or if the surrounding skin is cracked or sore.

**Professional treatment**
Your physician may arrange for you to have tests such as venography (see *Angiography,* below). If varicose veins are severe and the self-help measures are not helpful, your physician may recommend surgery to remove the affected veins, or they may be injected with a chemical that seals the vein.

---

## FIRST AID FOR SUSPECTED BROKEN BONES AND DISLOCATED JOINTS

A limb or joint that is very painful or looks misshapen and that will not move following an injury or fall may be broken and/or dislocated. Go to your hospital emergency room. If no help is readily available and/or if you are unable to move, call an ambulance.

**General points**
- If there is bleeding from the wound, cover it firmly with a clean dressing or cloth.
- Do not try to manipulate the bone or joint back into position yourself; this should only be attempted by a physician.
- While waiting for medical help to arrive, a helper should try to keep the injured person warm and as calm as possible.
- A person with a suspected broken bone or dislocated joint should not eat or drink anything in case a general anesthetic is needed later in order to reset the bone.
- If you have to wait some time for medical attention, immobilize the limb in the most comfortable position, using bandages and splints as described here.

**Arm injury**
Gently place the injured arm in the most comfortable position across the chest. Some padding, such as a pillow, should be placed between the arm and chest. Support the weight of the arm along its length together with the padding. If the arm cannot be bent, use bandages or tape to secure the arm to the side of the body. A splint (right) may help provide increased support.

**Shoulder, collarbone or elbow injury**
Support the weight of the arm in a sling in the most comfortable position.

**Leg injury**
Secure the injured leg to the undamaged one. If possible, place a well-padded splint (below) between them.

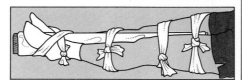

**Knee injury**
Support the joint in the most comfortable position. If the knee is bent, support it in the bent position. If the knee is unable to bend, support the leg along its length from underneath, using a board or something similar as a splint. Place padding between the knee and the splint and around the heel.

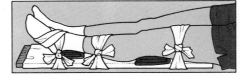

**Splints**
A splint is a support used to immobilize an injured part of the body (usually an arm or a leg) to reduce pain and the likelihood of further damage. Always secure a splint in at least 2 places not too close to the injury, preferably on either side of it. Use wide lengths of material or tape to do this (not string or rope) and do not secure it too tightly.

---

## ANGIOGRAPHY

Angiography is a procedure that allows physicians to take X-ray pictures of blood vessels that may have become narrowed or blocked. When an artery is under investigation, the procedure is known as arteriography; when it is a vein being examined, it is called venography.

**What happens**
During angiography, for which you may be sedated, a solution that is visible on X rays is injected into the bloodstream. This is done either by injecting directly into the blood vessel concerned or by means of a fine tube (catheter) inserted through an incision in an accessible blood vessel. The catheter is passed along the blood vessel until it reaches the area where an examination is required. The solution is then released and X rays taken.

# 61 Painful or swollen joints

Joints occur at the junction of two or more bones and usually allow movement between those bones. The degree and type of movement allowed depends on the structure of the joint. Major joints such as the hips, knees and ankles undergo constant wear and tear, so minor degrees of discomfort or stiffness may occur from time to time. However, severe pain, swelling or limitation of movement may be the result of damage to the bones or soft tissues of the joint from injury, or may indicate an underlying disorder of the joints or skeletal system. Consult this chart if you suffer to any extent from pain, stiffness and/or swelling in or around a joint.

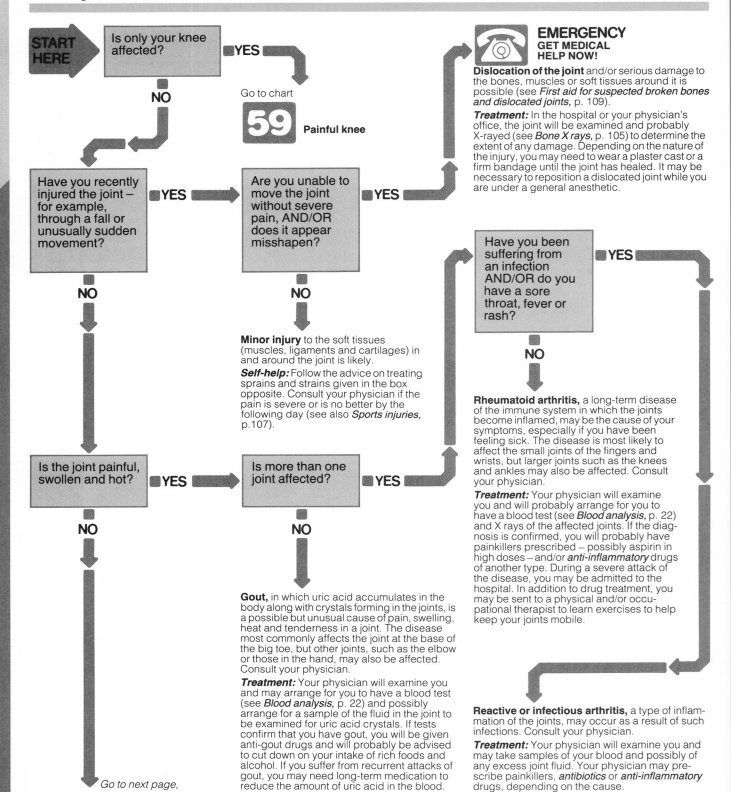

**START HERE**

**Is only your knee affected?**

NO

YES

Go to chart

**59** Painful knee

**Have you recently injured the joint — for example, through a fall or unusually sudden movement?**

YES

NO

**Are you unable to move the joint without severe pain, AND/OR does it appear misshapen?**

YES

NO

**EMERGENCY GET MEDICAL HELP NOW!**

**Dislocation of the joint** and/or serious damage to the bones, muscles or soft tissues around it is possible (see *First aid for suspected broken bones and dislocated joints,* p. 109).

**Treatment:** In the hospital or your physician's office, the joint will be examined and probably X-rayed (see *Bone X rays,* p. 105) to determine the extent of any damage. Depending on the nature of the injury, you may need to wear a plaster cast or a firm bandage until the joint has healed. It may be necessary to reposition a dislocated joint while you are under a general anesthetic.

**Have you been suffering from an infection AND/OR do you have a sore throat, fever or rash?**

YES

NO

**Minor injury** to the soft tissues (muscles, ligaments and cartilages) in and around the joint is likely.

**Self-help:** Follow the advice on treating sprains and strains given in the box opposite. Consult your physician if the pain is severe or is no better by the following day (see also *Sports injuries,* p.107).

**Rheumatoid arthritis,** a long-term disease of the immune system in which the joints become inflamed, may be the cause of your symptoms, especially if you have been feeling sick. The disease is most likely to affect the small joints of the fingers and wrists, but larger joints such as the knees and ankles may also be affected. Consult your physician.

**Treatment:** Your physician will examine you and will probably arrange for you to have a blood test (see *Blood analysis,* p. 22) and X rays of the affected joints. If the diagnosis is confirmed, you will probably have painkillers prescribed – possibly aspirin in high doses – and/or *anti-inflammatory* drugs of another type. During a severe attack of the disease, you may be admitted to the hospital. In addition to drug treatment, you may be sent to a physical and/or occupational therapist to learn exercises to help keep your joints mobile.

**Is the joint painful, swollen and hot?**

YES

NO

**Is more than one joint affected?**

YES

NO

**Gout,** in which uric acid accumulates in the body along with crystals forming in the joints, is a possible but unusual cause of pain, swelling, heat and tenderness in a joint. The disease most commonly affects the joint at the base of the big toe, but other joints, such as the elbow or those in the hand, may also be affected. Consult your physician.

**Treatment:** Your physician will examine you and may arrange for you to have a blood test (see *Blood analysis,* p. 22) and possibly arrange for a sample of the fluid in the joint to be examined for uric acid crystals. If tests confirm that you have gout, you will be given anti-gout drugs and will probably be advised to cut down on your intake of rich foods and alcohol. If you suffer from recurrent attacks of gout, you may need long-term medication to reduce the amount of uric acid in the blood.

**Reactive or infectious arthritis,** a type of inflammation of the joints, may occur as a result of such infections. Consult your physician.

**Treatment:** Your physician will examine you and may take samples of your blood and possibly any excess joint fluid. Your physician may prescribe painkillers, *antibiotics* or *anti-inflammatory* drugs, depending on the cause.

*Go to next page,*

*Continued from previous page*

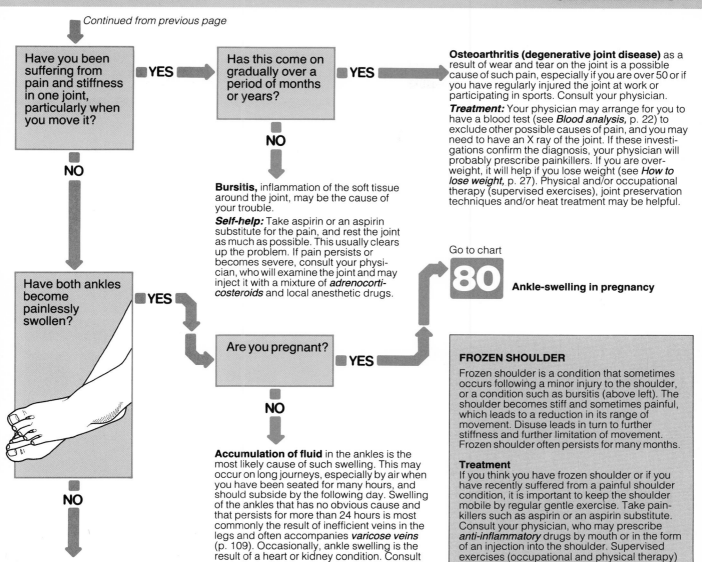

**Have you been suffering from pain and stiffness in one joint, particularly when you move it?**

→ **YES** →

**Has this come on gradually over a period of months or years?**

→ **YES** →

**Osteoarthritis (degenerative joint disease)** as a result of wear and tear on the joint is a possible cause of such pain, especially if you are over 50 or if you have regularly injured the joint at work or participating in sports. Consult your physician.

***Treatment:*** Your physician may arrange for you to have a blood test (see ***Blood analysis,*** p. 22) to exclude other possible causes of pain, and you may need to have an X ray of the joint. If these investigations confirm the diagnosis, your physician will probably prescribe painkillers. If you are overweight, it will help if you lose weight (see ***How to lose weight,*** p. 27). Physical and/or occupational therapy (supervised exercises), joint preservation techniques and/or heat treatment may be helpful.

**NO** (below "Have you been suffering")

**NO** (below "Has this come on")

**Bursitis,** inflammation of the soft tissue around the joint, may be the cause of your trouble.

***Self-help:*** Take aspirin or an aspirin substitute for the pain, and rest the joint as much as possible. This usually clears up the problem. If pain persists or becomes severe, consult your physician, who will examine the joint and may inject it with a mixture of ***adrenocorticosteroids*** and local anesthetic drugs.

Go to chart

**80**  **Ankle-swelling in pregnancy**

**Have both ankles become painlessly swollen?**

→ **YES** →

**Are you pregnant?**

→ **YES** →

**NO** (below "Have both ankles")

**NO** (below "Are you pregnant?")

**Accumulation of fluid** in the ankles is the most likely cause of such swelling. This may occur on long journeys, especially by air when you have been seated for many hours, and should subside by the following day. Swelling of the ankles that has no obvious cause and that persists for more than 24 hours is most commonly the result of inefficient veins in the legs and often accompanies ***varicose veins*** (p. 109). Occasionally, ankle swelling is the result of a heart or kidney condition. Consult your physician about any persistent ankle swelling. Do this without delay if you have noticed additional symptoms such as breathlessness, unusual fatigue or swelling in any other part of the body.

**Consult your physician** if you are unable to make a diagnosis from this chart and the pain or swelling is severe or persists for more than 48 hours.

**FROZEN SHOULDER**

Frozen shoulder is a condition that sometimes occurs following a minor injury to the shoulder, or a condition such as bursitis (above left). The shoulder becomes stiff and sometimes painful, which leads to a reduction in its range of movement. Disuse leads in turn to further stiffness and further limitation of movement. Frozen shoulder often persists for many months.

**Treatment**
If you think you have frozen shoulder or if you have recently suffered from a painful shoulder condition, it is important to keep the shoulder mobile by regular gentle exercise. Take painkillers such as aspirin or an aspirin substitute. Consult your physician, who may prescribe ***anti-inflammatory*** drugs by mouth or in the form of an injection into the shoulder. Supervised exercises (occupational and physical therapy) may also be recommended.

---

**FIRST AID FOR SPRAINS AND STRAINS**

A joint is said to be sprained when it is wrenched or twisted beyond its normal range of movement – in a fall, for example – thus tearing some or all of the ligaments that support it. Ankles are especially prone to this type of injury. The main symptoms, which may be indistinguishable from those of a minor strain, are pain, swelling and bruising. If you are unable to move the injured part, or if it looks misshapen, a broken bone or dislocated joint is possible and you should carry out first aid as described on p. 109. In other cases, try the following first-aid treatment:

**1** For the first 24 hours after the injury, cool the injured part (below).

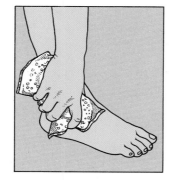

**2** Support an injured joint or limb with a firm, but not overtight bandage (below). An arm or wrist may be more comfortable in a sling.

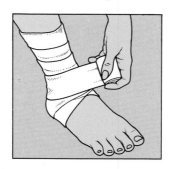

If you have a badly sprained ankle that is still painful the day after the injury, go to your physician, local hospital emergency room or urgent care center to have the joint firmly bandaged to prevent movement while the joint is healing. In this case, you should make sure that you rest the joint for at least a week.

**Cooling an injury**
Applying cold to any injury causing pain, swelling and/or bruising will help to reduce swelling and relieve pain. This can be done by using an ice bag, a cloth pad soaked in cold water or an unopened packet of frozen vegetables. After the first 24 hours, you should apply warmth to the affected part to reduce inflammation.

**3** Rest the injured part for a day or so. If it is a foot, leg or ankle that is injured, keep it raised whenever possible.

# 62 Foot problems

Problems with feet rarely indicate any serious underlying disorder or disease. Most foot problems are the result of injury or failure to take good care of the feet (see Caring for your feet, below). Consult this chart if you have any pain, irritation or itching of your feet, or if they become deformed in any way.

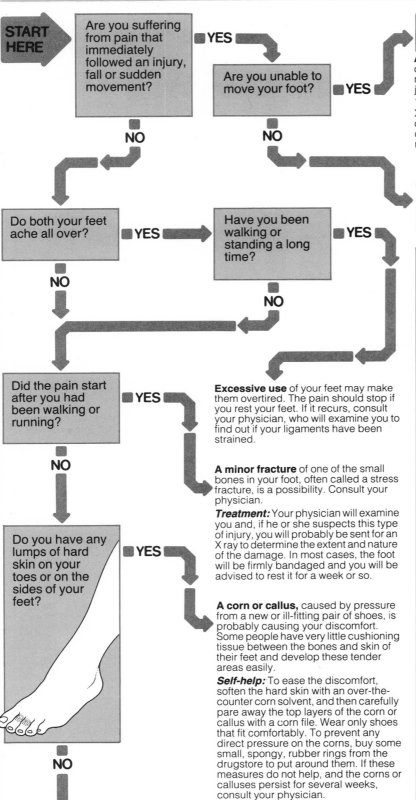

**START HERE**

Are you suffering from pain that immediately followed an injury, fall or sudden movement? — **YES**

**NO**

Are you unable to move your foot? — **YES**

**NO**

Do both your feet ache all over? — **YES**

**NO**

Have you been walking or standing a long time? — **YES**

**NO**

Did the pain start after you had been walking or running? — **YES**

**NO**

Do you have any lumps of hard skin on your toes or on the sides of your feet? — **YES**

**NO**

*Go to next page*

## EMERGENCY
### GET MEDICAL HELP NOW!

**A fracture, dislocation or serious injury** to the ligaments or muscles may be causing this pain. Carry out the first-aid measures for suspected broken bones and dislocated joints as described on p.109 until medical help arrives.

***Treatment:*** The foot will be examined and probably X-rayed to discover the extent of the damage. Depending on the nature of the injury, you may need to wear a plaster cast or a firm bandage. Sometimes an operation to reposition the bones is necessary.

**A soft tissue injury,** such as a sprain, strain or bruising, is probably causing this pain.

***Self-help:*** Follow the advice on treating such injuries given in the box on p.111. Consult your physician if the pain is severe or is no better the following day.

**Excessive use** of your feet may make them overtired. The pain should stop if you rest your feet. If it recurs, consult your physician, who will examine you to find out if your ligaments have been strained.

**A minor fracture** of one of the small bones in your foot, often called a stress fracture, is a possibility. Consult your physician.

***Treatment:*** Your physician will examine you and, if he or she suspects this type of injury, you will probably be sent for an X ray to determine the extent and nature of the damage. In most cases, the foot will be firmly bandaged and you will be advised to rest it for a week or so.

**A corn or callus,** caused by pressure from a new or ill-fitting pair of shoes, is probably causing your discomfort. Some people have very little cushioning tissue between the bones and skin of their feet and develop these tender areas easily.

***Self-help:*** To ease the discomfort, soften the hard skin with an over-the-counter corn solvent, and then carefully pare away the top layers of the corn or callus with a corn file. Wear only shoes that fit comfortably. To prevent any direct pressure on the corns, buy some small, spongy, rubber rings from the drugstore to put around them. If these measures do not help, and the corns or calluses persist for several weeks, consult your physician.

### CARING FOR YOUR FEET

Ill-fitting shoes can lead to distortion of the toes and may lead to the development of painful conditions such as bunions and corns. When buying shoes, take care to ensure that they fit properly, allowing enough space for the toes to spread. Shoes with pointed toes and high heels should be worn only when you do not expect to be standing or walking for long periods. These shoes are more likely to damage the feet and make you adopt an unnatural posture that may lead to backaches and headaches.

To avoid distorting the toes (right), choose a low-heeled, round-toed shoe (below).

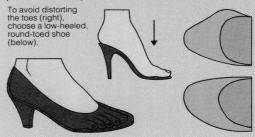

**Foot hygiene**
Wash your feet daily, drying thoroughly between the toes to reduce the risk of fungal infection (athlete's foot). If your feet are particularly sweaty, wear socks and pantyhose made of natural fibers such as cotton. If the skin of your feet is dry or cracked, apply a hand cream to the affected area.

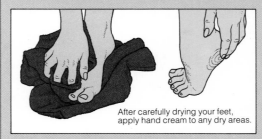

After carefully drying your feet, apply hand cream to any dry areas.

**Toenails**
Trim your toenails regularly, but do not cut them too short, as this may damage the skin underneath. Always cut your toenails straight across.

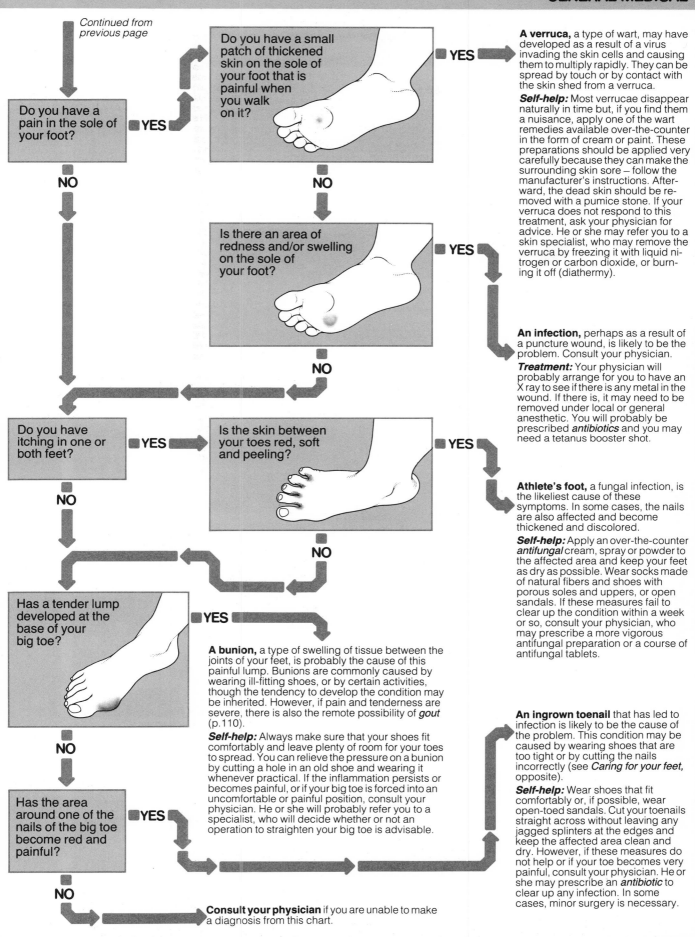

*Continued from previous page*

**Do you have a pain in the sole of your foot?**

**YES** ➤

**Do you have a small patch of thickened skin on the sole of your foot that is painful when you walk on it?**

**YES** ➤

**A verruca,** a type of wart, may have developed as a result of a virus invading the skin cells and causing them to multiply rapidly. They can be spread by touch or by contact with the skin shed from a verruca.

*Self-help:* Most verrucae disappear naturally in time but, if you find them a nuisance, apply one of the wart remedies available over-the-counter in the form of cream or paint. These preparations should be applied very carefully because they can make the surrounding skin sore – follow the manufacturer's instructions. Afterward, the dead skin should be removed with a pumice stone. If your verruca does not respond to this treatment, ask your physician for advice. He or she may refer you to a skin specialist, who may remove the verruca by freezing it with liquid nitrogen or carbon dioxide, or burning it off (diathermy).

**NO** ⬇ **NO** ⬇

**Is there an area of redness and/or swelling on the sole of your foot?**

**YES** ➤

**NO** ⬇

**An infection,** perhaps as a result of a puncture wound, is likely to be the problem. Consult your physician.

*Treatment:* Your physician will probably arrange for you to have an X ray to see if there is any metal in the wound. If there is, it may need to be removed under local or general anesthetic. You will probably be prescribed *antibiotics* and you may need a tetanus booster shot.

**Do you have itching in one or both feet?**

**YES** ➤

**Is the skin between your toes red, soft and peeling?**

**YES** ➤

**NO** ⬇ **NO** ⬇

**Athlete's foot,** a fungal infection, is the likeliest cause of these symptoms. In some cases, the nails are also affected and become thickened and discolored.

*Self-help:* Apply an over-the-counter *antifungal* cream, spray or powder to the affected area and keep your feet as dry as possible. Wear socks made of natural fibers and shoes with porous soles and uppers, or open sandals. If these measures fail to clear up the condition within a week or so, consult your physician, who may prescribe a more vigorous antifungal preparation or a course of antifungal tablets.

**Has a tender lump developed at the base of your big toe?**

**YES** ➤

**A bunion,** a type of swelling of tissue between the joints of your feet, is probably the cause of this painful lump. Bunions are commonly caused by wearing ill-fitting shoes, or by certain activities, though the tendency to develop the condition may be inherited. However, if pain and tenderness are severe, there is also the remote possibility of *gout* (p.110).

*Self-help:* Always make sure that your shoes fit comfortably and leave plenty of room for your toes to spread. You can relieve the pressure on a bunion by cutting a hole in an old shoe and wearing it whenever practical. If the inflammation persists or becomes painful, or if your big toe is forced into an uncomfortable or painful position, consult your physician. He or she will probably refer you to a specialist, who will decide whether or not an operation to straighten your big toe is advisable.

**An ingrown toenail** that has led to infection is likely to be the cause of the problem. This condition may be caused by wearing shoes that are too tight or by cutting the nails incorrectly (see *Caring for your feet,* opposite).

*Self-help:* Wear shoes that fit comfortably or, if possible, wear open-toed sandals. Cut your toenails straight across without leaving any jagged splinters at the edges and keep the affected area clean and dry. However, if these measures do not help or if your toe becomes very painful, consult your physician. He or she may prescribe an *antibiotic* to clear up any infection. In some cases, minor surgery is necessary.

**NO** ⬇

**Has the area around one of the nails of the big toe become red and painful?**

**YES** ➤

**NO** ⬇

**Consult your physician** if you are unable to make a diagnosis from this chart.

# 63 Breast problems

Each breast consists mainly of fatty tissue in which groups of milk-producing glands are embedded. The size and shape of each breast is determined by the amount of fatty tissue and the condition of the muscles and ligaments that support it. It is common for a woman to have one breast that is slightly larger than the other. Problems affecting the breasts may include pain, tenderness, changes in shape or general appearance (including that of the overlying skin) or the development of one or more lumps in the usually soft breast tissue. Although most breast problems are minor and easily treated, it is essential to watch for any changes (see *Breast self-examination,* below) and to report any change or obvious abnormality to your physician so that the possibility of breast cancer (one of the most common cancers affecting women) can be ruled out.

**START HERE**

Have you had a baby in the past 4 months?

**YES** → Go to chart **82** **Breast-feeding problems**

**NO** ↓

Have you recently noticed one or more lumps in your breast?

**YES** →

**NO** ↓

**CONSULT YOUR PHYSICIAN WITHOUT DELAY!**
**Any lump in the breast should be examined by a physician to exclude the possibility of breast cancer** (opposite), although it is much more likely that there is a less alarming cause for the lump(s), such as a harmless cyst or a thickening of the fibrous breast tissue (fibroadenosis).

*Treatment:* Your physician will examine you and, if he or she thinks that there is any cause for concern, will refer you for tests, such as those described under *Breast cancer* (opposite). If you are found to have a cyst, it will be examined by drawing off the fluid through a syringe (aspiration). Fibroadenosis often needs no treatment but, if it causes discomfort before periods, you may be offered treatment as described under *Premenstrual breast tenderness* (opposite). Treatments for breast cancer are described in the box opposite.

## BREAST SELF-EXAMINATION

Every woman should make breast self-examination a part of her routine. It helps you to become familiar with the shape and feel of your breasts so that any changes will be quickly noticed and any problem dealt with promptly. Follow the routine described here monthly, ideally at the end of each period. Some physicians suggest the 5th day after the onset of the period.

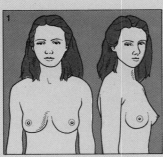

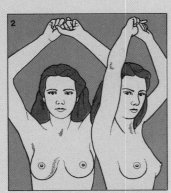

**1** Stand in front of a good mirror with your arms by your sides and look at your breasts and nipples from the front and sides for any change in their shape or in the appearance of the skin.

**2** Look again with your arms raised.

**3** With the left arm still raised, feel all around the left breast using the flat of the fingers of the right hand. Repeat using the left hand to examine the right breast.

**4** Lie down with a pillow under your left shoulder and with your left arm behind your head. Using the right hand as before, feel around the left breast, working from the outside toward the nipple at the center.

**5** Check the area between the breast and the armpit and into the armpit itself, first with the left arm raised and then with it by your side.

**6** Gently squeeze the nipple to check for any discharge.

Repeat 4, 5 and 6 using the left hand to examine the right breast.

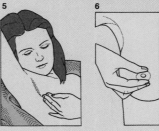

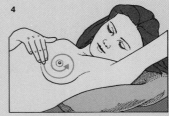

**When to consult your physician**
If you notice any of the following during the course of your regular breast self-examination – or at any other time – consult your physician without delay:

- a lump in the breast or armpit.
- a change in the outline of the breast.
- discharge from the nipple.
- retraction (indentation) of the nipple.
- any change in the skin of the breast – for example, puckering or dimpling.

Remember, the first few times you examine yourself, you are still becoming familiar with your breasts and many of the lumps you find will be perfectly normal. However, if you are worried that you have found something abnormal, consult your physician.

*Go to next page*

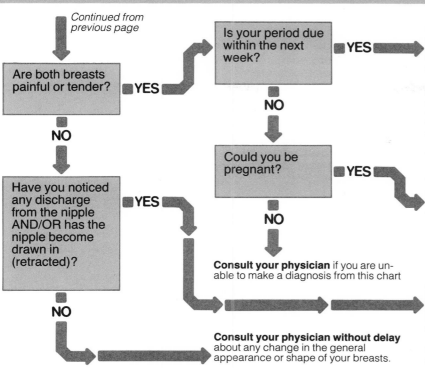

*Continued from previous page*

**Are both breasts painful or tender?** → **YES**

**NO** ↓

**Have you noticed any discharge from the nipple AND/OR has the nipple become drawn in (retracted)?** → **YES**

**NO** ↓

**Is your period due within the next week?** → **YES**

**NO** ↓

**Could you be pregnant?** → **YES**

**NO** ↓

**Consult your physician** if you are unable to make a diagnosis from this chart

**Consult your physician without delay** about any change in the general appearance or shape of your breasts.

**Premenstrual breast tenderness** is a common occurrence, and is most likely to affect women who have naturally lumpy breasts – a condition known as fibroadenosis (see also *The menstrual cycle,* p. 117). Consult your physician.

*Treatment:* Your physician will examine you. If he or she confirms the diagnosis, depending on the severity of your symptoms and whether you suffer from other unpleasant menstrual symptoms such as irritability or fluid retention, hormone treatment may be suggested (see *Treatment for menstrual problems,* p. 119). Wearing a firm-support bra may also help reduce discomfort.

**Tenderness of the breasts and nipples** is often one of the earliest signs of pregnancy and may continue for several months while your breasts prepare themselves to produce milk. If discomfort is severe, or you are not sure whether or not you are pregnant, consult your physician (see also *Diagnosis of pregnancy,* p. 116).

**CONSULT YOUR PHYSICIAN WITHOUT DELAY!**
**Most nipple discharges** are due to a glandular disorder, a breast infection or a benign growth. However, some may be a sign of *breast cancer* (below) and should be brought to your physician's attention.

*Treatment:* If your physician thinks there is any cause for concern, he or she will arrange for you to undergo the tests described below.

## BREAST CANCER

Breast cancer is the most common cancer affecting women; about 1 woman in 11 develops the disease. It occurs when abnormal (cancerous) cells develop and multiply in the breast, forming a tumor. If untreated, the cancer may spread to other parts of the body. There are several different types of breast cancer; the outlook for anyone affected by the disease depends on the type of cancer present in her case, as well as on how early treatment is started.

### Risk factors
Several factors are known to increase the risk of cancer of the breast. The following women may have a higher risk:

- Women who have no children, or who had their first child late in life.
- Women who are overweight.
- Women with close relatives who have had the disease.
- Women who started their periods early.

### Screening
Most of the risk factors for developing breast cancer are outside your control, but you can try to ensure that the disease is diagnosed early by regular screening for the disease. The basic form of screening that every adult woman should undertake is monthly breast self-examination (opposite). However, women in high-risk groups may also be advised to undergo regular mammography (below). Even women who are not in high-risk groups are wise to be screened with mammography by age 40. The recommended guidelines are: By 40 years old, at least once; 40 to 50, every 1 or 2 years; and over 50 years, once a year.

### Symptoms
The most common sign of breast cancer is the appearance of a painless lump in the breast or armpit. However, any of the symptoms listed in the box on breast self-examination (opposite) could indicate cancer.

### Confirming the diagnosis
If you notice any change in your breast, you should consult your physician without delay.

**Mammography:** A low-radiation X ray of the breast.
**Aspiration:** Used when a cyst is suspected. A fine needle is inserted into the lump to draw off a sample of fluid for examination.
**Needle biopsy:** A thick needle is inserted into the breast and a sample of tissue is removed for microscopic examination.
**Frozen-section biopsy:** Carried out under general anesthetic. An incision is made in the breast and all or part of the lump is removed and a section of the lump is frozen and examined under a microscope (see *Breast surgery,* right).

### Treatment
Any woman undergoing tests for breast cancer should be aware of all the treatment options for the disease and discuss these fully with her physicians. The best treatment will depend on the nature of the cancer and the stage at which it is discovered, but the final choice is a joint decision between the woman and her physicians. The main forms of treatment are listed below:

### Breast surgery

  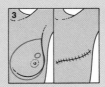 

**1 Lumpectomy:** Removal of the growth alone.
**2 Partial mastectomy:** Removal of the growth and some of the surrounding breast tissue.
**3 Simple mastectomy:** Removal of the growth together with the whole breast.
**4 Radical mastectomy:** Removal of the growth, the breast, the underlying tissue and the nearby lymph nodes in the armpit.
**5 Subcutaneous mastectomy:** Occasionally, partial or simple mastectomies may be carried out leaving the overlying skin. Later on, silicone can be implanted to restore breast appearance.

### Radiotherapy
This may be used on its own or in conjunction with other treatments. The breast and armpit are exposed to radiation to kill cancer cells.

### Chemotherapy
Chemotherapy – treatment with anticancer drugs that inhibit multiplication of cancer cells – may be the only treatment used or it may be used with breast surgery and/or radiotherapy. Other drugs, including some that affect hormone activity, may also be given. Some forms of chemotherapy can produce feelings of nausea, reduce the blood count, or cause hair loss as side effects.

### After breast surgery
Any woman who loses a breast as a result of breast cancer is naturally upset and worried that it may affect her appearance and femininity. Physicians who treat breast cancer will ensure that as much breast tissue is preserved as possible and may arrange for an implant to preserve breast shape. After a mastectomy you will be advised on the types of artificial breast that are available. These are undetectable under most types of clothing. Many hospitals have counselors with whom you can discuss your feelings and who will advise about problems before and after breast surgery. Outside support groups also exist for these purposes.

# 64 Absent periods

Menstrual periods normally start between the ages of 11 and 14. However, for some girls it is normal to start menstruating as early as 10 or as late as 17. Once periods start they may be irregular for the first few years and may not settle down to a regular monthly cycle until the late teens. Once the menstrual cycle is established, it may vary in length from woman to woman from as little as 24 days to about 35 days between periods. Both extremes are normal. Absence of periods (amenorrhea) may occur in healthy women for a variety of reasons, the most common of which is pregnancy. Other factors that may affect your monthly cycle include illness and stress. Strenuous physical activity also may be associated with amenorrhea. Only rarely is absence of periods a sign of an underlying disorder. It is normal for periods to cease permanently as you approach middle age. Consult this chart if you have never had a period or if your period is more than 2 weeks late.

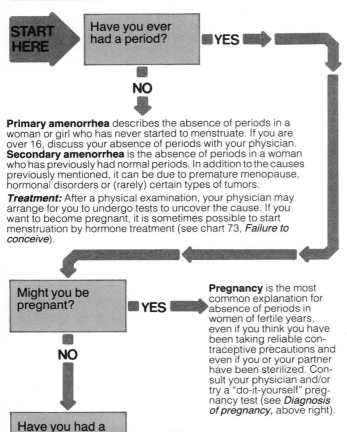

**START HERE** → Have you ever had a period? → **YES** →

**NO** ↓

**Primary amenorrhea** describes the absence of periods in a woman or girl who has never started to menstruate. If you are over 16, discuss your absence of periods with your physician.
**Secondary amenorrhea** is the absence of periods in a woman who has previously had normal periods. In addition to the causes previously mentioned, it can be due to premature menopause, hormonal disorders or (rarely) certain types of tumors.

*Treatment:* After a physical examination, your physician may arrange for you to undergo tests to uncover the cause. If you want to become pregnant, it is sometimes possible to start menstruation by hormone treatment (see chart 73, *Failure to conceive*).

Might you be pregnant? — **YES** →

**NO** ↓

**Pregnancy** is the most common explanation for absence of periods in women of fertile years, even if you think you have been taking reliable contraceptive precautions and even if you or your partner have been sterilized. Consult your physician and/or try a "do-it-yourself" pregnancy test (see *Diagnosis of pregnancy,* above right).

Have you had a baby recently? — **YES** →

**NO** ↓

**After childbirth** it is normal for a delay of a month or so before periods begin again. This period-free time may be extended if you are breast-feeding. Consult your physician if you have not had a period within 3 months following the birth of your baby (unless you are breast feeding).

Have you been sick, under stress or have you undergone an upheaval (such as moving to a new house)? — **YES** →

**NO** ↓

**Major physical or emotional upsets** often interfere with the chain of hormonal interactions that control the menstrual cycle (opposite), causing periods to cease temporarily. This is no cause for concern, but see your physician if you are feeling sick, anxious or depressed (see also chart 1, *Feeling under the weather;* chart 20, *Anxiety;* or chart 19, *Depression*).

*Go to next page*

---

### DIAGNOSIS OF PREGNANCY
For most women, the first indication of pregnancy is missing a menstrual period. However, you may also notice:

- tenderness of the breasts or nipples
- increased frequency of urination
- unusual tiredness
- nausea and/or vomiting

**Pregnancy testing**
If you think that you may be pregnant, you can either go to your physician (or family planning clinic) for a pregnancy test or try one of the "do-it-yourself" pregnancy testing kits. If you go to your physician, you are likely to be asked for a sample of the first urine you pass in the morning or a blood sample. This will be sent for tests that reveal the presence of certain hormones that occur only during pregnancy. Do-it-yourself pregnancy tests usually work in the same way. Tubal pregnancies can be dangerous and they may not register on a urine pregnancy test.

### THE MENOPAUSE
The menopause is signaled by the end of menstrual periods and marks the time when a woman ceases to be fertile. The years surrounding this event are often referred to as the climacteric. The menopause usually occurs around the age of 50 but can happen earlier or later. In general, you can consider that you have reached the menopause if you are over 45 years old and you have not had a period for 6 months. Hormonal fluctuations before and after the menopause often (but not always) give rise to a variety of physical and emotional symptoms. Emotional difficulties may be complicated by social factors that necessitate psychological adjustments as you approach middle age.

**Principal symptoms of the menopause**
The most common menopausal symptoms are listed below. These normally disappear within a year or so of the cessation of periods.

- irregularity and eventual cessation of periods
- hot flashes (attacks of increased heat and sweating)
- night sweats
- dryness of the vagina as a result of thinning of the vaginal secretions (which may make intercourse uncomfortable)
- emotional upset, including depression and irritability

**Treatment for menopausal symptoms**
If your symptoms cause you no distress, you probably don't need medical treatment. However, much can be done to alleviate symptoms if they are uncomfortable or embarrassing.

**Hormone-replacement therapy**
Supplements of estrogen and progesterone may be prescribed for women who are suffering from menopausal symptoms. However, because of the increased risk of blood clots, heart attacks and strokes, such treatment is not suitable for all women. For this reason, your physician may also be unwilling to continue hormone treatment for more than a few years.

**Other treatments**
Hormone cream or lubricating jelly (for vaginal dryness), *antidepressants* or *antianxiety* drugs (for psychological symptoms) and nonhormonal drugs (to control hot flashes) may also be prescribed in addition to or as an alternative to *hormone*-replacement therapy.

*Continued from previous page*

Are you underweight according to the chart on p.26 AND/OR have you recently lost more than 9 lb (4 kg) in weight?

**▶ YES**

**NO**

Have you recently undertaken a rigorous program of exercise?

**▶ YES**

**Loss of weight or regular strenuous exercise** often results in cessation of periods. In these circumstances, absence of periods is not in itself a cause for concern, but it is advisable to discuss the problem with your physician so that he or she can check your general health.

See also chart

**3** Loss of weight

**Re-adjustment of your hormone balance** after stopping the birth-control pill may take a month or so. Consult your physician if normal menstruation has not started again after 3 months.

**NO**

Have you recently stopped taking the birth-control pill?

**▶ YES**

**Irregular periods** are normal in the years preceding the menopause (opposite). Most women find that periods become increasingly infrequent until they stop altogether. Occasionally, periods continue normally until they suddenly cease. Remember that while you continue to have periods you are probably still fertile. So, if you are sexually active and have missed a period, you should also consider the possibility of pregnancy. You may want to keep a record of your periods to discuss during your medical visits to see if your pattern seems normal for your age.

**NO**

Are you over 40 years old?

**▶ YES**

**NO**

**Consult your physician** if you are unable to make a diagnosis from this chart.

## THE MENSTRUAL CYCLE

The menstrual cycle refers to the hormonal interactions that occur approximately every month in women during their childbearing years. This chain of events enables an egg to be released and, if it is fertilized, ensures that the uterus provides a suitable environment for the egg to implant and for the fetus to develop. The most noticeable outward sign of the menstrual cycle is vaginal bleeding – menstruation – during which the lining of the uterus is shed when the previous month's egg is not fertilized. However, many more body changes also take place during the course of the cycle.

### A typical cycle
The typical menstrual cycle takes about 28 days, although this varies. The first day of menstrual bleeding is counted as day 1.

### Days 1 to 4
Falling levels of the hormone progesterone in the body trigger the start of menstruation – the shedding of the lining of the uterus. During this time, hormones produced in the pituitary gland, prompted by signals from the hypothalamus (part of the brain), stimulate the ripening of an egg in the ovary, which in turn produces increasing levels of another hormone, estrogen.

### Days 5 to 14
Menstrual bleeding normally ceases by day 5. For the next few days you may notice a slight vaginal discharge of mucus from the cervix. Between days 9 and 13, estrogen levels reach their peak and the cervical mucus becomes clear and runny. This is the start of the potentially fertile period. On day 13 the levels of the pituitary hormones that stimulate the ripening and release of the egg also reach a peak, temperature rises by about 1°F (½°C), and ovulation takes place on day 14, or approximately 2 weeks before the next menstrual period.

### Days 15 to 23
Following ovulation, and if the egg is not fertilized, estrogen levels drop markedly, and the follicle from which the egg has been released forms into a gland called the corpus luteum, which secretes progesterone. On days 15 to 16 you may notice thick, jelly-like cervical mucus, after which there is likely to be little if any mucus for the remainder of the cycle, or the mucus will be pasty rather than jelly-like.

### Days 24 to 28
The activity of the corpus luteum begins to decline as the gland degenerates, and progesterone levels begin to fall. Some women may begin to notice premenstrual symptoms such as breast tenderness and mood changes – especially irritability and depression. There may be slight bloating due to fluid retention. The onset of menstruation may be signaled by a drop in temperature of about 1°F (½°C).

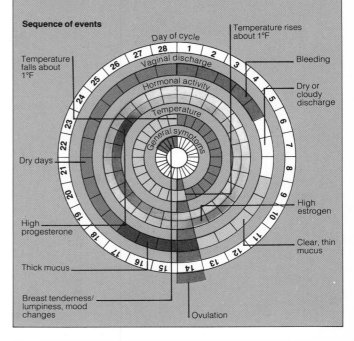

Sequence of events

# 65 Heavy periods

Heavy periods, a condition sometimes called menor-rhagia, are periods in which more than the average amount of blood is lost. Some women naturally lose more blood than others, but for most women bleeding lasts about 5 days, with the heaviest blood loss occurring in the first 3 days. Consult this chart if your periods last longer than this, if normal sanitary napkins or tampons are not sufficient, or if your periods suddenly become heavier than you are used to. Various disorders or devices may cause unusually heavy periods, including disorders of the lining of the uterus and the use of intrauterine contraceptive devices (IUDs). However, whichever reason you suspect for your heavy periods, consult your physician for treatment because there is a risk that regular heavy bleeding may lead to iron-deficiency anemia.

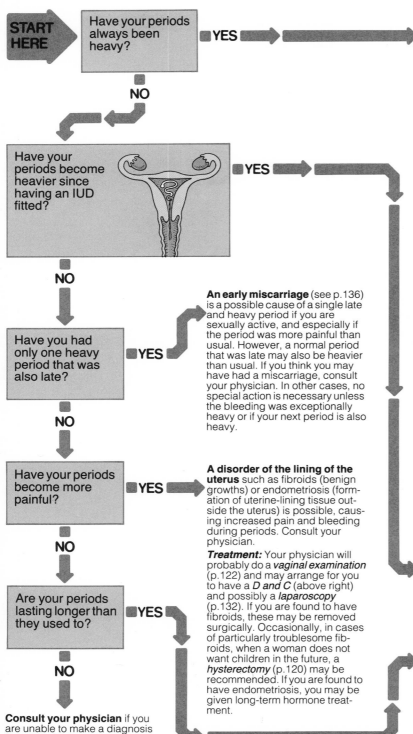

**START HERE** → Have your periods always been heavy? → **YES** →

**NO** ↓

Have your periods become heavier since having an IUD fitted? → **YES** →

**NO** ↓

Have you had only one heavy period that was also late? → **YES**

**NO** ↓

Have your periods become more painful? → **YES**

**NO** ↓

Are your periods lasting longer than they used to? → **YES**

**NO** ↓

**Consult your physician** if you are unable to make a diagnosis from this chart.

**A thicker-than-usual lining of the uterus** may explain why some women have heavier periods than others. This in itself is no cause for concern, but you should discuss the problem with your physician, who may want to rule out the possibility of anemia, and may suggest treatment.

**Treatment:** If, after examining you, your physician suspects the possibility of anemia, he or she will probably take a blood sample for analysis (see p.22). If you are found to be anemic, your physician will probably prescribe iron tablets and may advise you on a diet. Your physician will also discuss the possibility of treating the heaviness of your periods. In some cases, hormone treatment is suitable. Or you may be advised to have a *D and C* (below).

## D AND C

D and C (dilatation and curettage) is a minor operation that is used to discover the cause of heavy periods and may in some cases cure the problem. The technique may also be used for investigation of infertility and for early elective abortion (see p.131). D and C is carried out under general anesthetic. The opening of the cervix (neck of the uterus) is dilated (widened) and an instrument called a curette is used to scrape out the lining of the uterus. These scrapings are then taken for laboratory examination. Following the operation, you will have bleeding from the uterus for a few days, and you are likely to experience backache and/or lower abdominal pain. You will probably be advised not to use tampons and to refrain from sexual intercourse for a week or so.

**Position of the curette scraping out the uterine lining**

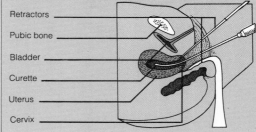

Retractors
Pubic bone
Bladder
Curette
Uterus
Cervix

**An early miscarriage** (see p.136) is a possible cause of a single late and heavy period if you are sexually active, and especially if the period was more painful than usual. However, a normal period that was late may also be heavier than usual. If you think you may have had a miscarriage, consult your physician. In other cases, no special action is necessary unless the bleeding was exceptionally heavy or if your next period is also heavy.

**A disorder of the lining of the uterus** such as fibroids (benign growths) or endometriosis (formation of uterine-lining tissue outside the uterus) is possible, causing increased pain and bleeding during periods. Consult your physician.

**Treatment:** Your physician will probably do a *vaginal examination* (p.122) and may arrange for you to have a *D and C* (above right) and possibly a *laparoscopy* (p.132). If you are found to have fibroids, these may be removed surgically. Occasionally, in cases of particularly troublesome fibroids, when a woman does not want children in the future, a *hysterectomy* (p.120) may be recommended. If you are found to have endometriosis, you may be given long-term hormone treatment.

**The IUD** (intrauterine contraceptive device) may cause heavier periods as a side effect. This is no cause for concern if the increase in bleeding is slight. If the bleeding is much heavier than usual or if it distresses you, consult your physician, who may suggest that you change to an alternative method of contraception (see chart 72, *Choosing a contraceptive method*).

**Fibroids** (benign growths inside the uterus) may cause periods to become heavier and longer. This is especially likely if you are over 35 years old. Consult your physician.

**Treatment:** A physician will usually be able to detect fibroids by a *vaginal examination* (p.122). If the diagnosis is confirmed you may be prescribed hormone treatment to reduce bleeding. If this does not control your symptoms you may need to have a *D and C* (above). Large, troublesome fibroids may need to be removed surgically. Occasionally, a *hysterectomy* (p.120) is advised.

# 66 Painful periods

Many women experience some degree of pain or discomfort during menstrual periods. The pain – called dysmenorrhea – is usually cramping and is felt in the lower abdomen. In most cases painful periods are not a sign of ill health and do not disrupt everyday activities. However, if you suffer from severe pain or if your periods suddenly start to become much more painful than previously, consult your physician.

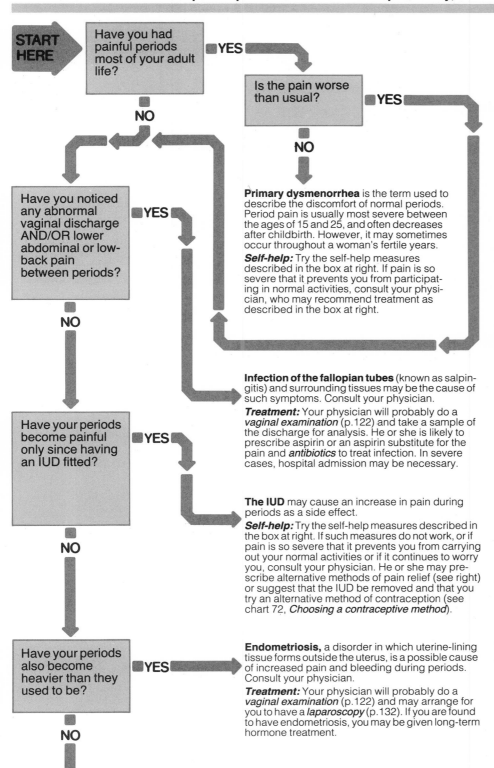

**START HERE**

**Have you had painful periods most of your adult life?**

YES → **Is the pain worse than usual?**

NO ↓

YES →

NO ↓

**Primary dysmenorrhea** is the term used to describe the discomfort of normal periods. Period pain is usually most severe between the ages of 15 and 25, and often decreases after childbirth. However, it may sometimes occur throughout a woman's fertile years.
***Self-help:*** Try the self-help measures described in the box at right. If pain is so severe that it prevents you from participating in normal activities, consult your physician, who may recommend treatment as described in the box at right.

**Have you noticed any abnormal vaginal discharge AND/OR lower abdominal or low-back pain between periods?**

YES →

NO ↓

**Infection of the fallopian tubes** (known as salpingitis) and surrounding tissues may be the cause of such symptoms. Consult your physician.
***Treatment:*** Your physician will probably do a ***vaginal examination*** (p.122) and take a sample of the discharge for analysis. He or she is likely to prescribe aspirin or an aspirin substitute for the pain and ***antibiotics*** to treat infection. In severe cases, hospital admission may be necessary.

**Have your periods become painful only since having an IUD fitted?**

YES →

NO ↓

**The IUD** may cause an increase in pain during periods as a side effect.
***Self-help:*** Try the self-help measures described in the box at right. If such measures do not work, or if pain is so severe that it prevents you from carrying out your normal activities or if it continues to worry you, consult your physician. He or she may prescribe alternative methods of pain relief (see right) or suggest that the IUD be removed and that you try an alternative method of contraception (see chart 72, *Choosing a contraceptive method*).

**Have your periods also become heavier than they used to be?**

YES →

NO ↓

**Endometriosis,** a disorder in which uterine-lining tissue forms outside the uterus, is a possible cause of increased pain and bleeding during periods. Consult your physician.
***Treatment:*** Your physician will probably do a ***vaginal examination*** (p.122) and may arrange for you to have a ***laparoscopy*** (p.132). If you are found to have endometriosis, you may be given long-term hormone treatment.

**Consult your physician** if you are unable to make a diagnosis from this chart.

---

## TREATMENT FOR MENSTRUAL PROBLEMS

Unpleasant menstrual symptoms, including premenstrual syndrome (see below), period pain and excessive bleeding, can often be relieved by medical treatment. It is worthwhile to seek your physician's advice if you are distressed by such symptoms.

**Premenstrual syndrome**
In the week or so before a period, many women experience a variety of symptoms including tension, irritability, depression, a feeling of being bloated – especially in the breasts and abdomen – and headaches. Treatment will depend on your individual symptoms and their severity, but may include one or more of the following:

**Counseling** may be offered. This may be in the form of sympathetic discussion with your family physician, or through self-help discussion groups.
**Progesterone (hormone supplements)** may be given in the last part of your *menstrual cycle* (p.117).
**Pyridoxine** (vitamin B6) is sometimes given daily to relieve premenstrual symptoms.
**Diuretics or dietary sodium restriction** (see p.15) may be prescribed in the last half of your menstrual cycle to relieve bloating.
**Regular exercise and a diet low in sugar** with emphasis on protein and fiber seems to help many women.

**Period pain**
If you have painful periods, first try the following self-help suggestions:
- Take the recommended dose of aspirin or an aspirin substitute.
- When pain is severe, rest in bed with a well-wrapped hot-water bottle or heating-pad on your abdomen.

If pain continues to trouble you, consult your physician, who may prescribe tablets to inhibit the muscle cramps that lead to period pain. Alternatively, you may be given hormone tablets. If you also require contraception and there is no medical reason that makes it inadvisable, your physician may suggest that you start taking the birth-control pill (see also chart 72, *Choosing a contraceptive method*).

**Excessive bleeding**
If you suffer from excessive blood loss during periods (menorrhagia), consult your physician, who may advise a *D and C* (opposite) or may prescribe hormone treatment in the form of the birth-control pill (see above) or in another form.

# 67 Irregular vaginal bleeding

Irregular vaginal bleeding includes irregular menstrual periods and blood loss between normal periods. The latter type of bleeding may consist only of slight "spotting" on one or two days, or it may be heavier. Sometimes, irregular periods may be the result of hor- monal fluctuations – for example, in adolescence or as you approach the menopause. However, bleeding between periods, especially if accompanied by pain (or in an older woman), may be a sign of a serious under- lying disorder and should be investigated.

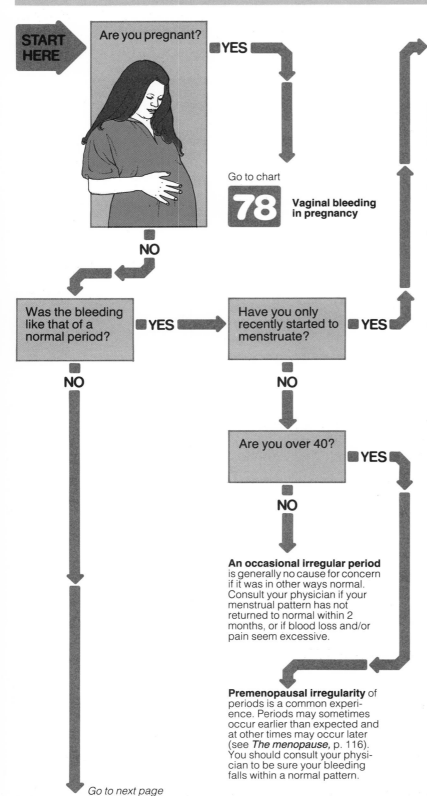

START HERE

**Are you pregnant?**

**YES** → Go to chart

**78** Vaginal bleeding in pregnancy

**NO**

**Was the bleeding like that of a normal period?**

**YES** → **Have you only recently started to menstruate?**

**NO**

**NO**

**YES**

**Are you over 40?**

**YES**

**NO**

**An occasional irregular period** is generally no cause for concern if it was in other ways normal. Consult your physician if your menstrual pattern has not returned to normal within 2 months, or if blood loss and/or pain seem excessive.

**Premenopausal irregularity** of periods is a common experi- ence. Periods may sometimes occur earlier than expected and at other times may occur later (see *The menopause,* p. 116). You should consult your physi- cian to be sure your bleeding falls within a normal pattern.

*Go to next page*

**Irregular periods** are common in the first years of menstruation. They may occur sometimes as often as every two weeks, and then perhaps you may not have a period for several months. This is usually no cause for concern and a regular pattern will gradually establish itself. If you are worried, however, consult your physician.

## HYSTERECTOMY

Removal of the uterus is a major operation. It is a usual part of the treatment for cancer of the uterus, but may also be carried out in cases of cervical cancer, severe fibroids (benign growths in the uterus), or abnormal menstrual bleeding that cannot be controlled by other means.

There are several types of hysterectomy, depend- ing on the site of the incision (vaginal or abdominal) and whether or not the fallopian tubes and/or ovaries are also removed. Whether the ovaries are removed or left in place will depend on a woman's age, the condition of the ovaries themselves, and whether there is a family history of ovarian cancer. Whenever possible, in women under 40, physicians try to leave at least one ovary in place to prevent hormonal disturbance after the operation.

**Simple hysterectomy**
Removal of the uterus only. It may be done through an incision in the lower abdomen or through the vagina (this leaves no scar).

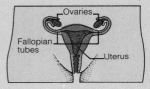

**Hysterectomy with salpingectomy**
Removal of the uterus and fallopian tubes, usually through an incision in the lower abdomen.

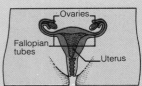

**Hysterectomy with salpingo-oophorectomy**
Removal of the uterus, fallopian tubes and ovaries, usually through an incision in the lower abdomen.

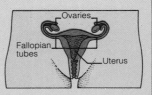

**After a hysterectomy**
After a hysterectomy you will no longer be able to have children and you will cease to menstruate. However, you will be able to have a normal sex life, and most physicians encourage women who have had hysterectomies to resume sexual relations as soon as they have recovered from the operation. If you have had both ovaries removed and have not yet passed the menopause, you will experience symptoms of a premature menopause. You may receive hormone replacement treatment to prevent this (see *The menopause,* p.116). Many (especially younger) women find that it takes some time for them to adjust mentally and emotionally to the loss of their uterus. Your physician will be sympathetic to such feelings and may be able to offer counseling after the operation to help you overcome any depression or other difficulties.

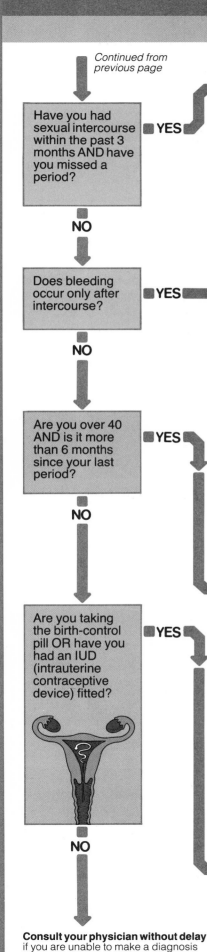

*Continued from previous page*

**Have you had sexual intercourse within the past 3 months AND have you missed a period?**

YES

**CALL YOUR PHYSICIAN NOW!**
**A serious complication of early pregnancy,** such as an ectopic pregnancy (pregnancy outside the uterus), is possible, especially if you also have abdominal pain.

***Treatment:*** If your physician suspects an ectopic pregnancy, you will probably be admitted to the hospital. If the diagnosis is confirmed, you will need to have an urgent operation to end the pregnancy.

NO

**Does bleeding occur only after intercourse?**

YES

**CONSULT YOUR PHYSICIAN WITHOUT DELAY!**
**Postcoital bleeding** may be a sign of a minor abnormality of the cervix (neck of the uterus) but it can also be a sign of other diseases of the cervix.

***Treatment:*** Your physician will do a *vaginal examination* (p.122). If the smear shows the presence of abnormal cells, you may need to have further tests, such as *colposcopy* (below right). Some cervical abnormalities can be treated by laser surgery, freezing, or a minor operation (cone biopsy). However, cancer that seems to have spread may require a *hysterectomy* (opposite) and/or radiotherapy (either in the form of X-ray treatment or by insertion of a radium pellet into the vagina). Treatment of cancer of the cervix is often successful if started early.

NO

**Are you over 40 AND is it more than 6 months since your last period?**

YES

**CONSULT YOUR PHYSICIAN WITHOUT DELAY!**
**Postmenopausal bleeding** may be caused by a minor vaginal disorder, but it could also be a sign of cancer of the uterus or cervix (neck of the uterus).

***Treatment:*** Your physician will do a *vaginal examination* (p.122) and will probably take a smear of the cervix (see *Cervical screening,* right). He or she may also arrange for you to have a *D and C* (p.118). If cancer is diagnosed, you will probably need to have a *hysterectomy* (opposite). Radiotherapy or the insertion of a radium pellet into the vagina may also be part of your treatment. Hormones may also be given. The earlier treatment is started, the greater the chances of a complete cure.

NO

**Are you taking the birth-control pill OR have you had an IUD (intrauterine contraceptive device) fitted?**

YES

**Both these contraceptive methods may cause spotting between periods.** This is unlikely to be a cause for concern, but you should discuss the symptom with your physician, who may suggest a change of pill, or an alternative form of contraception. (See also chart 72, *Choosing a contraceptive method.*)

NO

**Consult your physician without delay** if you are unable to make a diagnosis from this chart.

---

**CERVICAL SCREENING**

The cells that make up the outer surface of the cervix (neck of the uterus) may sometimes undergo changes for reasons that are not yet fully understood. Such cell abnormalities often present no risk to general health, but in a small proportion of cases the abnormal cells may become cancerous. Cancer of the cervix, although rare compared with other cervical abnormalities, is one of the most common cancers affecting women. It is, however, also one of the most easily treated cancers if diagnosed early. For these reasons it is important for every adult woman to make sure that she has regular screening so that any change in the cells of the cervix can be detected and, when necessary, treated as soon as possible.

**Cervical smear test (Pap smear)**
The standard method of screening is the cervical smear. It is recommended that every woman have this test at least every 3 years unless suspicious cells are found; then it should be done more often. The test can be carried out by your family physician or at a family planning clinic. In the test, the vagina is held open by a speculum, and a spatula is used to scrape away a sample of cells from the surface of the cervix. The sample is then sent for examination.

If the smear shows a mild abnormality, you may simply be asked to return for another smear test in a few months. This is because minor abnormalities often heal without the need for further treatment. If the trouble persists or the smear is suggestive of cancer or precancerous cells, you will probably be referred for a colposcopy.

For a cervical smear you will need to lie on your back with your knees apart as for a *vaginal examination* (p.122).

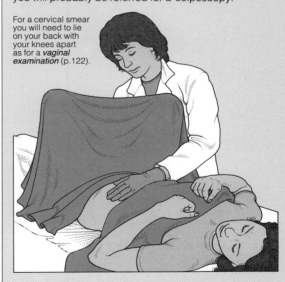

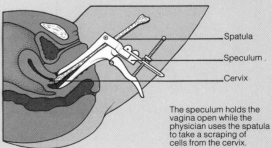

Spatula
Speculum
Cervix

The speculum holds the vagina open while the physician uses the spatula to take a scraping of cells from the cervix.

**Colposcopy**
This is a technique that allows the physician to take a close look at the surface of the cervix. An instrument with a magnifying lens and an eyepiece is inserted into the vagina. While the physician is viewing the cervix, he or she will probably also take a *biopsy* (p.35) of the cervical tissue for further examination. Minor abnormalities can often be treated during colposcopy by laser beam, burning or freezing. More serious abnormalities may require surgery.

# 68 Abnormal vaginal discharge

The vagina is normally kept moist and clean by secretions from the tissue lining the vagina. Such secretions may be apparent as a thin, whitish discharge from the vagina. This normal discharge may vary in quantity and consistency according to the time of your menstrual cycle, and may increase at times of sexual arousal, during pregnancy and in women using the birth-control pill or intrauterine contraceptive device (IUD). A discharge that looks abnormal, especially if it is accompanied by itching or burning around the vagina, may be a sign of infection and needs medical diagnosis and treatment. Consult this chart if you notice any increase in vaginal discharge or change in its color or consistency.

**For discharge containing blood, see chart 67, Irregular vaginal bleeding.**

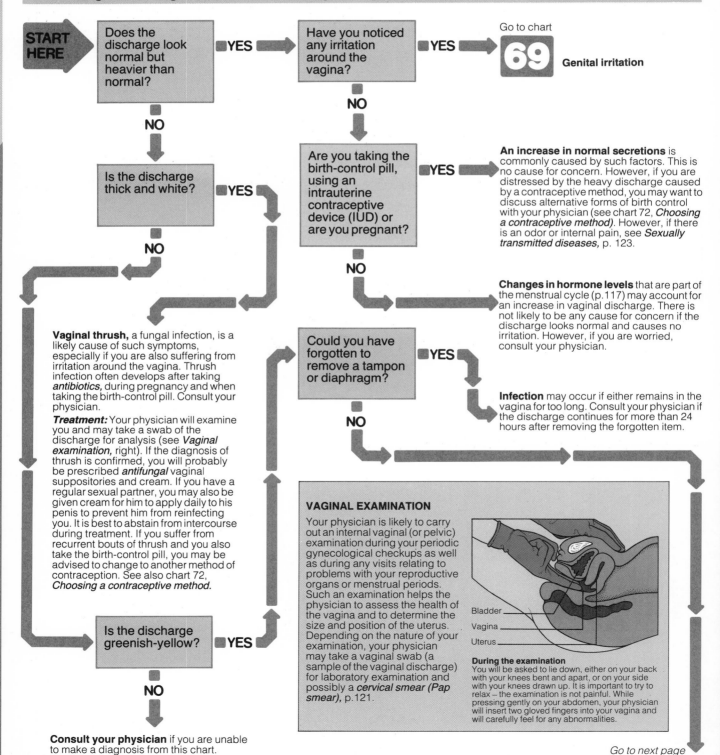

**START HERE**

**Does the discharge look normal but heavier than normal?**

YES →

**Have you noticed any irritation around the vagina?**

YES →

Go to chart **69** **Genital irritation**

NO ↓ (from discharge look normal)

**Is the discharge thick and white?**

YES →

NO ↓ (from irritation)

**Are you taking the birth-control pill, using an intrauterine contraceptive device (IUD) or are you pregnant?**

YES →

**An increase in normal secretions** is commonly caused by such factors. This is no cause for concern. However, if you are distressed by the heavy discharge caused by a contraceptive method, you may want to discuss alternative forms of birth control with your physician (see chart 72, *Choosing a contraceptive method*). However, if there is an odor or internal pain, see *Sexually transmitted diseases,* p. 123.

NO ↓ (from birth-control pill)

**Changes in hormone levels** that are part of the menstrual cycle (p.117) may account for an increase in vaginal discharge. There is not likely to be any cause for concern if the discharge looks normal and causes no irritation. However, if you are worried, consult your physician.

**Vaginal thrush,** a fungal infection, is a likely cause of such symptoms, especially if you are also suffering from irritation around the vagina. Thrush infection often develops after taking *antibiotics,* during pregnancy and when taking the birth-control pill. Consult your physician.

**Treatment:** Your physician will examine you and may take a swab of the discharge for analysis (see *Vaginal examination,* right). If the diagnosis of thrush is confirmed, you will probably be prescribed *antifungal* vaginal suppositories and cream. If you have a regular sexual partner, you may also be given cream for him to apply daily to his penis to prevent him from reinfecting you. It is best to abstain from intercourse during treatment. If you suffer from recurrent bouts of thrush and you also take the birth-control pill, you may be advised to change to another method of contraception. See also chart 72, *Choosing a contraceptive method.*

**Could you have forgotten to remove a tampon or diaphragm?**

YES →

**Infection** may occur if either remains in the vagina for too long. Consult your physician if the discharge continues for more than 24 hours after removing the forgotten item.

NO ↓

**Is the discharge greenish-yellow?**

YES →

NO ↓

**Consult your physician** if you are unable to make a diagnosis from this chart.

## VAGINAL EXAMINATION

Your physician is likely to carry out an internal vaginal (or pelvic) examination during your periodic gynecological checkups as well as during any visits relating to problems with your reproductive organs or menstrual periods. Such an examination helps the physician to assess the health of the vagina and to determine the size and position of the uterus. Depending on the nature of your examination, your physician may take a vaginal swab (a sample of the vaginal discharge) for laboratory examination and possibly a *cervical smear (Pap smear),* p.121.

Bladder
Vagina
Uterus

**During the examination**
You will be asked to lie down, either on your back with your knees bent and apart, or on your side with your knees drawn up. It is important to try to relax – the examination is not painful. While pressing gently on your abdomen, your physician will insert two gloved fingers into your vagina and will carefully feel for any abnormalities.

*Go to next page*

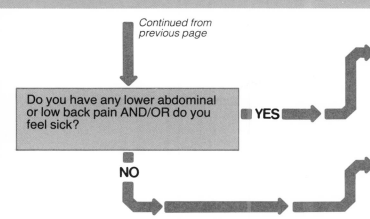

*Continued from previous page*

**Do you have any lower abdominal or low back pain AND/OR do you feel sick?**

**YES**

**NO**

**Infection of the fallopian tubes (salpingitis) and surrounding tissues** may be the cause. Consult your physician.

*Treatment:* Your physician will probably do a *vaginal examination* (opposite) and take a sample of discharge for analysis. He or she is likely to prescribe aspirin or an aspirin substitute for the pain and *antibiotics* to treat infection. In severe cases, hospital admission may be necessary.

**Trichomonal vaginitis,** or a similar vaginal infection that may be transmitted sexually, is a possibility. Consult your physician.

*Treatment:* Your physician will probably take a sample of the discharge from the vagina (see *Vaginal examination,* opposite). If the diagnosis is confirmed, **antibacterial** drugs will be prescribed. Your sexual partner(s) should receive treatment even if no symptoms are apparent. Otherwise, it is likely that you will be reinfected. See also *Sexually transmitted diseases (STDs),* below.

---

## SEXUALLY TRANSMITTED DISEASES (STDS)

Infections passed from one person to another during sexual contact (including sexual intercourse, anal and oral sex) are known as sexually transmitted (or venereal) diseases. If you think you have caught a sexually transmitted disease and/or if your sexual partner has, consult your physician or go to a clinic that specializes in such diseases (STD clinic), where you will be treated in the strictest confidence. It is important to seek medical advice promptly because of the risk of serious damage to your reproductive organs from many such diseases even when symptoms are not severe. Also, you may unknowingly pass on the infection to someone else. If you are found to have a sexually transmitted disease, you will be asked to inform any recent sexual partners so that they too may seek treatment if necessary. You should avoid sex until your physician confirms that treatment has completely cleared your symptoms.

| Disease | Incubation period* | Symptoms | Treatment |
|---|---|---|---|
| Nonspecific genital infection (*Chlamydia*) | 14 to 21 days | Often causes few or no symptoms. There may be a slightly abnormal vaginal discharge. If untreated, *Chlamydia* infection may lead to infertility. Suspect the disease if you have a sexual partner who has nonspecific urethritis (a disease usually caused by the *Chlamydia* microbe). | Your physician may take a swab from your vagina for culture (see *Vaginal examination,* opposite). Treatment is usually with *antibiotics.* |
| Trichomonal vaginitis | Variable | An infected-looking (greenish-yellow) vaginal discharge, usually causing irritation around the vagina. Pain on intercourse. | The diagnosis is confirmed by analysis of a sample of discharge taken from the vagina (see *Vaginal examination,* opposite). The usual treatment is a course of *antibiotics.* |
| Gonorrhea | 2 to 10 days | May be symptomless in women. It may sometimes cause abnormal vaginal or urethral discharge and/or painful urination. Persistent untreated infection may spread to the uterus and fallopian tubes, causing lower abdominal pain. | The disease is diagnosed by a urethral/vaginal swab (see *Vaginal examination,* opposite). Treatment consists of a course of *antibiotics.* |
| Herpes genitalis | 7 days or less | There is usually an itching feeling in the genital area followed by the appearance of a crop of small, painful blisters. Sometimes these also appear on the thighs and buttocks. The blisters burst after 24 hours, leaving small, red, moist, painful ulcers that sometimes crust over. The glands in the groin may become enlarged and painful. This may be accompanied by a feeling of being sick and a raised temperature. Outbreaks of blisters are likely to recur. | There is no complete cure for this disorder. Your physician may prescribe an *antiviral* drug or ointment to make the ulcers less sore and to speed healing. You will be advised to avoid close sexual contact while you have blisters or sores so that you do not transmit the infection to your partner. If you are pregnant and an attack occurs at the time of delivery, the baby will need to be delivered by cesarean section (p.139). |
| Syphilis | 9 to 90 days | In the first stage, a highly infectious, painless sore called a chancre develops, usually in the genital area (or in some cases in the anus). This disappears after a few weeks. In the second stage a rash that does not itch appears all over the body, including the palms and soles. There may also be painless swelling of the lymph glands and infectious wartlike lumps around the anus and/or mouth. | The disease is diagnosed by blood tests and samples taken from any sores. The usual treatment is a course of *antibiotic* injections. You will need to have periodic blood tests for 1 to 2 years after treatment to check that the disease has not reappeared. |
| Pubic lice | 0 to 17 days | Usually there is intense itching in the pubic region, particularly at night. You may be able to see the lice; they are brown and 1/16 in. (1 to 2 mm) long. | Your physician will give you a lotion or ointment that kills lice and their eggs. He or she will also check that you do not have any other sexually transmitted disease. Often, other family members may be treated. Bedding and clothing should be thoroughly laundered at the time of treatment. |

*Time between contact with the disease and the appearance of symptoms.

# 69 Genital irritation

Consult this chart if you have been suffering from itching and/or soreness in the vagina or around the vulva (external genital area). This symptom is known medically as pruritus vulvae. Such irritation may also be associated with urination and discomfort during intercourse. It may be brought on by infection in the vagina or urinary tract, or by local irritation from soaps, deodorants and douches.

**Consult this diagnostic chart only after reading chart 8, Itching.**

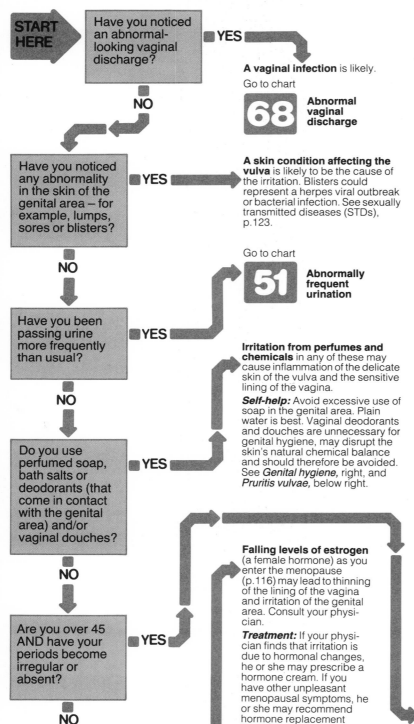

**START HERE**

**Have you noticed an abnormal-looking vaginal discharge?**

**YES** → **A vaginal infection** is likely.
Go to chart
**68 Abnormal vaginal discharge**

**NO**

**Have you noticed any abnormality in the skin of the genital area – for example, lumps, sores or blisters?**

**YES** → **A skin condition affecting the vulva** is likely to be the cause of the irritation. Blisters could represent a herpes viral outbreak or bacterial infection. See sexually transmitted diseases (STDs), p.123.

**NO**

**Have you been passing urine more frequently than usual?**

**YES** → Go to chart
**51 Abnormally frequent urination**

**NO**

**Do you use perfumed soap, bath salts or deodorants (that come in contact with the genital area) and/or vaginal douches?**

**YES** → **Irritation from perfumes and chemicals** in any of these may cause inflammation of the delicate skin of the vulva and the sensitive lining of the vagina.

*Self-help:* Avoid excessive use of soap in the genital area. Plain water is best. Vaginal deodorants and douches are unnecessary for genital hygiene, may disrupt the skin's natural chemical balance and should therefore be avoided. See *Genital hygiene,* right, and *Pruritis vulvae,* below right.

**NO**

**Are you over 45 AND have your periods become irregular or absent?**

**YES** → **Falling levels of estrogen** (a female hormone) as you enter the menopause (p.116) may lead to thinning of the lining of the vagina and irritation of the genital area. Consult your physician.

*Treatment:* If your physician finds that irritation is due to hormonal changes, he or she may prescribe a hormone cream. If you have other unpleasant menopausal symptoms, he or she may recommend hormone replacement therapy (see *The menopause,* p. 116). If irritation causes discomfort during sexual intercourse, a lubricating jelly may be helpful.

**NO**

## GENITAL HYGIENE

### Everyday care
Cleansing the genital area should be part of your normal daily washing routine. However, the skin in this area is delicate and needs to be treated gently so that it does not become inflamed and irritated. Use only plain water – bath salts and soaps, even mild ones, may be irritating. It should be necessary to wash only the external skin of the vulva. The internal lining of the vagina is kept clean by its natural secretions, which also help to protect against infection. Vaginal douches and deodorants are unnecessary and may cause irritation. They may also disrupt the chemical balance inside the vagina, increasing the likelihood of bacterial and fungal infections. If you feel strongly about douching, an *occasional* plain warm water or very diluted vinegar douche is the least irritating; douching equipment must be meticulously clean.

### Menstrual hygiene
Your choice of method of sanitary protection during menstrual periods is largely a matter of personal preference. Sanitary pads may be more suitable for women who have heavy periods because they usually provide greater absorbency. Young girls may also find pads easier to use in the first years of menstruation. Tampons have the advantage of being unnoticeable even under close-fitting clothes, and do not interfere with participation in sports such as swimming. Whichever method you choose, you will need to change your pad or tampon regularly every 3 to 6 hours depending on the heaviness of the menstrual flow.

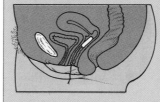

Choose the method that feels best for you – the easy-to-insert tampon or the absorbent pad.

### Toxic shock syndrome
Some women were discouraged from using tampons by reports of serious illness as a result of their use. This occurred when women experienced abnormal bacterial growth in the vagina while using certain high-absorbency tampons. Toxins (poisons) produced by the bacteria were absorbed into the bloodstream leading to life-threatening blood poisoning (toxic shock). The chance of toxic shock syndrome occurring is very slim with presently available tampons. A forgotten tampon of normal absorbency may cause an offensive discharge, but is unlikely to be a serious risk to health. Symptoms of toxic shock syndrome include fatigue, fever and skin rash. Your physician should be consulted immediately if you have these symptoms.

**Pruritus vulvae** without obvious cause is a common problem.

*Self-help:* Try to resist the urge to scratch, which will only increase the irritation. Wash the genital area carefully once a day using plain water. Do not use talcum powders, soaps, bath salts or vaginal deodorants. Choose underpants made of cotton, wear stockings rather than pantyhose, and avoid tight pants. If irritation persists for more than 2 weeks, consult your physician.

# 2 Sex and fertility symptoms

# 70 Painful intercourse

A woman may feel pain or discomfort in or around the vagina at the time of penetration, or during or following sexual intercourse. This symptom is known medically as dyspareunia. It is a relatively common problem among women of all ages, and may occur for a variety of physical (muscle spasms or problems with the vaginal lining) or emotional reasons. Whatever cause you suspect, it is worthwhile seeking medical help if this symptom persists because, if intercourse is repeatedly painful for you, there is a risk that it will affect your desire for sex and so damage your relationship with your partner.

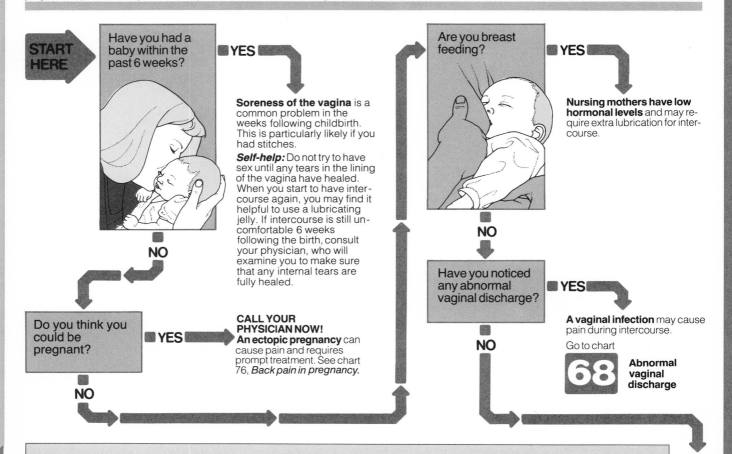

**START HERE**

**Have you had a baby within the past 6 weeks?**

**YES**

**Soreness of the vagina** is a common problem in the weeks following childbirth. This is particularly likely if you had stitches.

**Self-help:** Do not try to have sex until any tears in the lining of the vagina have healed. When you start to have intercourse again, you may find it helpful to use a lubricating jelly. If intercourse is still uncomfortable 6 weeks following the birth, consult your physician, who will examine you to make sure that any internal tears are fully healed.

**NO**

**Do you think you could be pregnant?**

**YES**

**CALL YOUR PHYSICIAN NOW!**
**An ectopic pregnancy** can cause pain and requires prompt treatment. See chart 76, *Back pain in pregnancy.*

**NO**

**Are you breast feeding?**

**YES**

**Nursing mothers have low hormonal levels** and may require extra lubrication for intercourse.

**NO**

**Have you noticed any abnormal vaginal discharge?**

**YES**

**A vaginal infection** may cause pain during intercourse.

Go to chart

**68** **Abnormal vaginal discharge**

**NO**

---

## REDUCING SEXUAL ANXIETY

Many sexual difficulties arise out of anxiety in one or both partners, and most forms of sex counseling involve advice on reducing such anxiety as a basis for improving sexual enjoyment. The following technique, called sensate focus, is often successful in heightening sexual responsiveness without provoking anxiety about performance, and may help you to overcome inhibitions and tensions that can mar sexual relationships. Usually the first step in reducing anxiety is for both partners to agree to abstain from sexual intercourse for, say, 3 weeks.

### Sensate focus
Set aside at least 3 evenings (or a period at another time of day) when you can be alone with your partner without fear of interruption for at least 2 hours. Try to create an atmosphere in which you both feel relaxed – playing some favorite music may help. During the time when you are trying this therapy you and your partner must stick to your agreement to refrain from full sexual intercourse.

### Stage 1
On the first evening, each partner should take turns gently massaging and caressing the other for a period of about 20 minutes. This is best carried out when you are both naked, and you can use a body lotion or oil if you like. The massage should involve gentle exploration of all parts of the body except the genital and breast areas. The partner being caressed should concentrate on finding pleasure from being touched, and the partner giving the caresses should concentrate on his or her own pleasure from contact with the partner's body. Once you have got over any awkwardness and are finding enjoyment from the sensations you experience during this activity – this may take several sessions – go on to stage 2.

### Stage 2
Stage 2 is similar to stage 1, but this time body massage may include genital and breast areas. Remember, however, to continue to include other parts of the body in your caresses, so that direct sexual stimulation can be felt in context with other body sensations.

### Stage 3
Most couples find that soon after reaching stage 2 they are ready to resume sexual intercourse, and in most cases find that they are more relaxed and are more able to enjoy a full range of physical and emotional sexual feelings. Couples who still are experiencing difficulties may want to consult a marital counselor or sex therapist.

*Go to next page*

*Continued from previous page*

**Does your vagina feel dry and tight so that penetration is difficult and painful?**

**YES** ▶

**Are you over 45?**

**YES** ▶

**NO** ▼

**NO** ▼

**Hormonal changes** around the time of the *menopause* (p. 116) can cause the lining of the vagina to become thinner and less well lubricated, and this often makes intercourse uncomfortable. Consult your physician.

**Treatment:** Your physician will examine you and, depending on whether you are suffering from additional menopausal symptoms and on the state of your general health, may prescribe hormone replacement therapy (see *The Menopause,* p. 116) and/or recommend that you use a lubricating jelly. He or she may also advise you and your partner on sexual techniques to assist arousal and prevent discomfort. See also *Sex in later life,* below.

**Sexual anxiety and/or lack of arousal** can lead to tension during lovemaking that prevents normal lubrication of the vagina and relaxation of the surrounding muscles and tissues. Anxiety can arise out of a specific difficulty experienced by you or your partner, or may be the result of generalized stress within the relationship.

**Self-help:** Discuss the problem with your partner. You may find that talking openly about the difficulty is in itself enough to reduce tension and help overcome the problem. Use of a lubricating jelly during intercourse may be helpful. You could also try the advice given opposite on reducing sexual anxiety. If the problem persists, consult your physician. He or she will examine you to rule out the possibility of a physical cause for your difficulty and may, if necessary, arrange for you and your partner to receive *sex counseling* (p. 128). See also chart 71, *Loss of interest in sex.*

**Do you feel pain during intercourse only occasionally or only in certain positions?**

 **YES** ▶

**NO** ▼

**Endometriosis,** a disorder in which uterine lining tissue forms outside the uterus, is a possible, although rare, cause of increased pain during periods and pain during intercourse. Consult your physician.

**Treatment:** Your physician will probably do a *vaginal examination* (p. 122) and may arrange for you to have a *laparoscopy* (p. 132). If you are found to have endometriosis, you may be given long-term hormone treatment.

**A cyst** (fluid-filled sac) of an ovary can sometimes cause pain if touched during intercourse. Such cysts may also cause abdominal swelling. Alternatively, such pain may be due to inflammation (erosion) of the cervix. Consult your physician.

**Treatment:** Your physician will examine your abdomen and probably do a *vaginal examination* (p. 122). He or she may do a cervical smear (Pap) test (see *Cervical screening,* p.121) and may arrange for you to have tests such as an *ultrasound scan* (p. 136) and possibly a *laparoscopy* (p. 132). If you are found to have an ovarian cyst, you may need to have an operation to remove it. This can sometimes be done without damaging the ovary, but in other cases it is necessary to remove the ovary and perhaps the fallopian tube as well. However, if the remaining ovary is healthy, you will still be able to have children. If you have a cervical erosion, it may be treated by laser, freezing or a minor operation.

**Pressure on an ovary or on another tender spot** during deep penetration may be the cause of such pain. If you have always noticed such pain when you have intercourse in a certain position, this is unlikely to be a cause for concern and simply trying alternative positions may overcome the problem. However, it is wise to mention the symptom to your physician, who may examine you to rule out the possibility of an underlying disorder.

**Have you just started your first or a new sexual relationship?**

 **YES** ▶

**NO** ▼

**Bruising and soreness of the genital area** commonly follows unaccustomed or unusually enthusiastic sex. This is no cause for concern and the discomfort will soon pass. If soreness is severe, abstaining from sex for a day or so may help.

**Consult your physician** if you are unable to make a diagnosis from this chart.

---

**SEX IN LATER LIFE**

Most women who have enjoyed an active and happy sex life in the first part of their lives continue to do so during middle and old age. Provided your relationship with your partner is sound, there is no physical reason why your capacity for enjoying the full range of physical and emotional sexual feelings should be diminished. In a loving relationship there is no reason why the physical changes associated with aging should reduce the attraction you and your partner feel for each other. Many women find their sex lives improve with greater experience and more leisure to enjoy their partner's company, and without the fear of pregnancy.

**Possible problems**
Although many women have no sex difficulties as they grow older, problems may arise. A common complaint of women past the menopause is discomfort during intercourse as a result of reduced vaginal lubrication. In the short term, this can sometimes be helped by hormone replacement therapy (see *The Menopause,* p.116). In the longer term, use of a lubricating jelly and adapting new and different lovemaking techniques are usually the best solutions.

Obviously, if either partner has a disabling disease, this can inhibit sexual relations. In such cases experimenting with different positions and a variety of forms of sexual contact — for example, mutual caresses and oral sex — can be helpful. You should not be embarrassed to seek your physician's advice.

Some women who have experienced sexual difficulties in the past use their advancing years as an excuse for avoiding sex altogether in later life. (Men commonly find it may take longer to achieve an erection and to ejaculate. This is normal and need not be cause for alarm.) This is no cause for concern if both partners are happy not to have sex, but if a reduction in sexual activity causes unhappiness in either partner, it is never too late to seek *sex counseling* (p. 128) for this or any other sex problem.

# 71 Loss of interest in sex

The frequency with which a woman feels the need for sex is determined by a range of inborn psychological and physiological factors, as well as being affected by experiences in early life. Some women feel the need for sex every day, others only once or twice a week or less. Both ends of the spectrum are normal. Once a normal pattern exists, changes may be questioned. A sudden falling off in the frequency of your normal level of sexual desire may be a sign of a number of problems. There may be a physical cause – for example, sickness or an infection that makes intercourse painful. Or the cause may be emotional – for example, overwork, depression, anxiety about a specific sexual difficulty or discord within the relationship. Consult this chart if you are aware of a reduction in the frequency with which you want sex and/or if you notice that you are not as easily aroused as you used to be, leading to discomfort during intercourse.

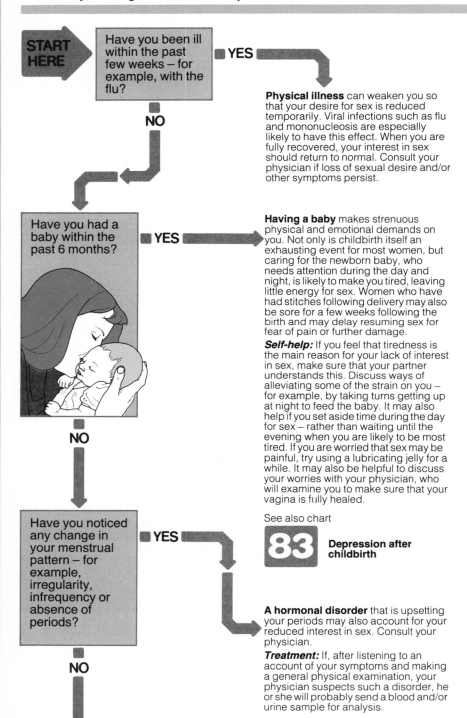

**START HERE**

**Have you been ill within the past few weeks – for example, with the flu?**

**YES**

**NO**

**Physical illness** can weaken you so that your desire for sex is reduced temporarily. Viral infections such as flu and mononucleosis are especially likely to have this effect. When you are fully recovered, your interest in sex should return to normal. Consult your physician if loss of sexual desire and/or other symptoms persist.

**Have you had a baby within the past 6 months?**

**YES**

**NO**

**Having a baby** makes strenuous physical and emotional demands on you. Not only is childbirth itself an exhausting event for most women, but caring for the newborn baby, who needs attention during the day and night, is likely to make you tired, leaving little energy for sex. Women who have had stitches following delivery may also be sore for a few weeks following the birth and may delay resuming sex for fear of pain or further damage.

**Self-help:** If you feel that tiredness is the main reason for your lack of interest in sex, make sure that your partner understands this. Discuss ways of alleviating some of the strain on you – for example, by taking turns getting up at night to feed the baby. It may also help if you set aside time during the day for sex – rather than waiting until the evening when you are likely to be most tired. If you are worried that sex may be painful, try using a lubricating jelly for a while. It may also be helpful to discuss your worries with your physician, who will examine you to make sure that your vagina is fully healed.

See also chart

**83** **Depression after childbirth**

**Have you noticed any change in your menstrual pattern – for example, irregularity, infrequency or absence of periods?**

**YES**

**NO**

**A hormonal disorder** that is upsetting your periods may also account for your reduced interest in sex. Consult your physician.

**Treatment:** If, after listening to an account of your symptoms and making a general physical examination, your physician suspects such a disorder, he or she will probably send a blood and/or urine sample for analysis.

*Go to next page*

## SEX COUNSELING

Sex counseling can take many different forms. Some family physicians have experience in dealing with the more common types of sexual difficulty and, if you are suffering from a problem in your sexual relationships, you should first consult your own physician for advice. Depending on the nature of the problem and his or her experience in this field, your physician may suggest treatment or may refer you to a specialist sex counselor or another physician who specializes in this field. Some large medical practices have sex counselors associated with them. In other cases you may be referred to a clinic, hospital outpatient department or private office.

**Treatments for sexual difficulties**
Treatments for all types of sexual difficulty have a greater chance of success if both partners attend counseling sessions. Usually, a course of counseling starts with a discussion with the counselor about the nature of the problem. In many cases this provides a couple with their first experience of talking together frankly about their sexual feelings, and this is often in itself of great help in clearing up misunderstandings and reducing anxiety. The counselor may later suggest techniques for overcoming specific difficulties or he or she may give more generalized advice on sexual technique. The counselor will also, if necessary, guide you through a prolonged therapy program to be carried out at home, such as the sensate focus technique described under *Reducing sexual anxiety* (p.126).

The success rate is high for couples who overcome their embarrassment sufficiently to seek sex counseling. So, even if you feel that your problem is unsolvable, it is worthwhile to seek your physician's advice.

**Partners take part in sex counseling together**

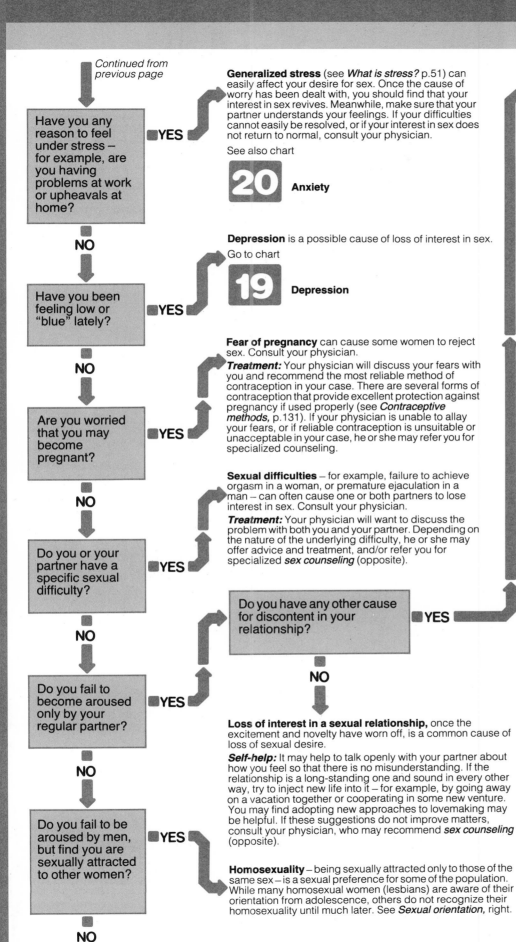

*Continued from previous page*

**Have you any reason to feel under stress – for example, are you having problems at work or upheavals at home?**

YES ▶ **Generalized stress** (see *What is stress?* p.51) can easily affect your desire for sex. Once the cause of worry has been dealt with, you should find that your interest in sex revives. Meanwhile, make sure that your partner understands your feelings. If your difficulties cannot easily be resolved, or if your interest in sex does not return to normal, consult your physician.

See also chart

**20** Anxiety

NO ▼

**Have you been feeling low or "blue" lately?**

YES ▶ **Depression** is a possible cause of loss of interest in sex.

Go to chart

**19** Depression

NO ▼

**Are you worried that you may become pregnant?**

YES ▶ **Fear of pregnancy** can cause some women to reject sex. Consult your physician.

**Treatment:** Your physician will discuss your fears with you and recommend the most reliable method of contraception in your case. There are several forms of contraception that provide excellent protection against pregnancy if used properly (see *Contraceptive methods,* p.131). If your physician is unable to allay your fears, or if reliable contraception is unsuitable or unacceptable in your case, he or she may refer you for specialized counseling.

NO ▼

**Do you or your partner have a specific sexual difficulty?**

YES ▶ **Sexual difficulties** – for example, failure to achieve orgasm in a woman, or premature ejaculation in a man – can often cause one or both partners to lose interest in sex. Consult your physician.

**Treatment:** Your physician will want to discuss the problem with both you and your partner. Depending on the nature of the underlying difficulty, he or she may offer advice and treatment, and/or refer you for specialized *sex counseling* (opposite).

NO ▼

**Do you fail to become aroused only by your regular partner?**

YES ▶

**Do you have any other cause for discontent in your relationship?**

YES ▶ **Generalized antagonism** or specific disagreements can lead to tension in a relationship that also affects your sexual feelings for each other.

**Self-help:** Talk to each other and explain how the problems with your relationship are affecting your feelings. If you find that things do not improve after a full and frank discussion, consult your physician. He or she will probably examine you to rule out any underlying physical problem, and may suggest that you and your partner seek counseling about your general difficulties, and possibly *sex counseling* (opposite) for any specific sex problems you may have.

NO ▼

**Loss of interest in a sexual relationship,** once the excitement and novelty have worn off, is a common cause of loss of sexual desire.

**Self-help:** It may help to talk openly with your partner about how you feel so that there is no misunderstanding. If the relationship is a long-standing one and sound in every other way, try to inject new life into it – for example, by going away on a vacation together or cooperating in some new venture. You may find adopting new approaches to lovemaking may be helpful. If these suggestions do not improve matters, consult your physician, who may recommend *sex counseling* (opposite).

NO ▼

**Do you fail to be aroused by men, but find you are sexually attracted to other women?**

YES ▶ **Homosexuality** – being sexually attracted only to those of the same sex – is a sexual preference for some of the population. While many homosexual women (lesbians) are aware of their orientation from adolescence, others do not recognize their homosexuality until much later. See *Sexual orientation,* right.

NO ▼

**Consult your physician** if you are unable to make a diagnosis from this chart.

---

**SEXUAL ORIENTATION**

Sexual orientation – that is, whether you are heterosexual (attracted to people of the opposite sex), homosexual (attracted to people of the same sex) or bisexual (attracted to people of both sexes) – is probably determined by a combination of in-born personality traits, upbringing and family relationships. Some researchers have suggested that there may be hormonal factors that contribute to homosexuality, but these findings have not been generally accepted. Few people are wholly heterosexual or homosexual. In particular, it is common for adolescents to go through a phase of experiencing homosexual feelings before becoming attracted to people of the opposite sex. Some, however, remain homosexual in their sexual preferences. This variation from the mainly heterosexual orientation of the majority is no cause for medical concern among most physicians as long as the individual woman is happy with her homosexuality. Treatment to change sexual orientation is unlikely to be effective and is seldom recommended. However, society's attitude toward homosexuality frequently causes homosexuals to feel guilty and abnormal, and therefore leads them to repress their sexual feelings. This can be psychologically damaging. If you think that you are homosexual and are experiencing such problems, consult your physician, who may be able to offer helpful advice and/or refer you for counseling or to one of the organizations that specializes in advising homosexuals.

# 72 Choosing a contraceptive method

Although no method of preventing pregnancy is problem-free, most couples can find a method that suits them. In most relationships it is the woman who takes responsibility for contraception. This is probably because a woman who wants to be sure of avoiding pregnancy is likely to be more confident with a method that she controls herself, and because there are more contraceptive choices available to women. However, some methods of contraception carry slight risks, so a couple in a stable relationship may wish to consider the male options that are available. In evaluating the risks of birth control, it is important to realize that pregnancy itself has substantial medical risks. This self-diagnosis chart is intended as a broad guide to help you decide which methods may be most suitable in your case, but the right contraceptive decision can only be reached through careful discussion with your physician and your partner, taking into account the possible side effects and risks of each method and your attitude toward an unplanned pregnancy.

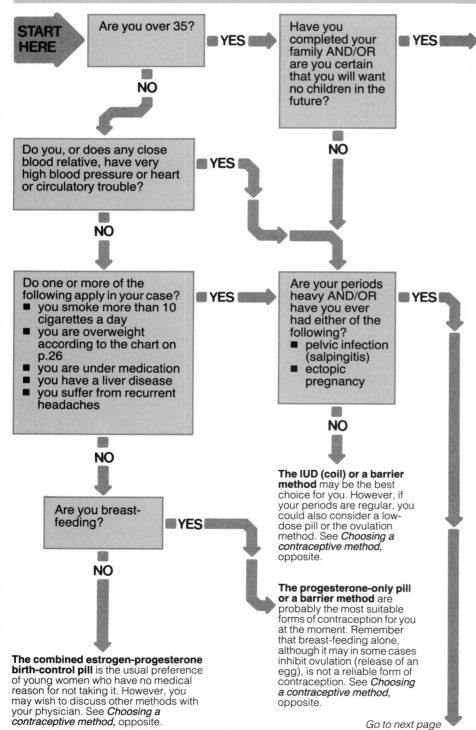

**START HERE**

**Are you over 35?**

YES → **Have you completed your family AND/OR are you certain that you will want no children in the future?**

YES → **Sterilization,** either for you or your partner, may be worth considering (see *Sterilization,* below). If this option is not acceptable to you, answer "No" to the previous question and follow the pathway.

NO ↓

**Do you, or does any close blood relative, have very high blood pressure or heart or circulatory trouble?**

YES →

NO ↓

NO →

**Do one or more of the following apply in your case?**
■ you smoke more than 10 cigarettes a day
■ you are overweight according to the chart on p.26
■ you are under medication
■ you have a liver disease
■ you suffer from recurrent headaches

YES → **Are your periods heavy AND/OR have you ever had either of the following?**
■ pelvic infection (salpingitis)
■ ectopic pregnancy

YES →

NO ↓

NO ↓

**Are you breast-feeding?**

YES → **The progesterone-only pill or a barrier method** are probably the most suitable forms of contraception for you at the moment. Remember that breast-feeding alone, although it may in some cases inhibit ovulation (release of an egg), is not a reliable form of contraception. See *Choosing a contraceptive method,* opposite.

NO ↓

**The IUD (coil) or a barrier method** may be the best choice for you. However, if your periods are regular, you could also consider a low-dose pill or the ovulation method. See *Choosing a contraceptive method,* opposite.

**The combined estrogen-progesterone birth-control pill** is the usual preference of young women who have no medical reason for not taking it. However, you may wish to discuss other methods with your physician. See *Choosing a contraceptive method,* opposite.

*Go to next page*

## STERILIZATION

Sterilization is almost always a permanent form of contraception. For this reason it is not a contraceptive option that should be chosen without careful consideration. Usually, couples thinking about sterilization are offered counseling before reaching a final decision. You will need to consider not only your present situation, but also the possibility that your life-style might change (for example, through divorce or death of a partner). Those under 35 are generally discouraged from undertaking such a final step. Sterilization may, however, be a good solution for an older couple who have completed their family or for a couple for whom pregnancy presents a serious risk.

**Female sterilization**
The usual method of sterilization for women is tubal ligation. This procedure is usually done under general anesthesia and is carried out using a laparoscope (see *Laparoscopy,* p.132). Each fallopian tube is clipped, tied and sealed off, preventing eggs from traveling down the tubes. Recovery usually takes only a few days and there are no lasting side effects. Sterilization has no documented effect on the production of female sex hormones, sexual desire or performance, or menstrual periods, although some women have claimed it has changed their menstrual cycle. You may find that it may take a little while to adjust psychologically to your loss of fertility.

**Male sterilization**
Male sterilization is achieved through a vasectomy. It is a simpler operation than that required for female sterilization and, because it does not require an abdominal incision, carries fewer risks. Usually, 2 small incisions are made in the scrotum and each vas deferens is cut and sealed so that sperm produced in the testis can no longer pass out of the body. Because sperm may remain in the male reproductive system for several months, you will need to take additional contraceptive precautions until test results confirm that the seminal fluid is free of sperm. A vasectomy has no effect on sexual performance or ejaculation.

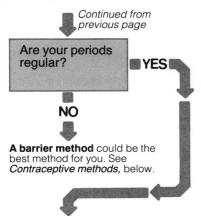

*Continued from previous page*

**Are your periods regular?** → **YES**

**NO**

↓

**A barrier method** could be the best method for you. See *Contraceptive methods,* below.

**A barrier method** or the ovulation method may be suitable options in your case. If you are a nonsmoker and are free of other medical problems, a low-dose pill also may be suitable. See *Choosing a contraceptive method,* below.

## MULTIPLE SEX PARTNERS

There are certain medical risks associated with having sex with a number of partners. The chief risk is that of contracting a sexually transmitted disease (STD, p.123). There is also evidence that women who have many sex partners have a greater-than-average risk of developing cancer of the cervix, especially if they started having sex in their teens. This is because the viruses that are now thought to cause cervical cancer may be sexually transmitted. There are precautions you can take to reduce the risk of infection and cervical abnormalities.

- Encourage your partner to wear a condom, whether or not you are using other precautions. This may help to prevent the transmission of infection and may protect the cervix. Use of a diaphragm may reduce the likelihood of cervical abnormalities.
- Make sure you have regular Pap smears (p.121).
- Report any suspicious symptoms to your physician at once. If one of your partners mentions that he has had an infection, consult your physician.
- Avoid IUDs, as they seem to increase the risk of pelvic infection. Birth-control pills and barrier methods may offer some protection against some STDs (p.123).

## ELECTIVE ABORTION

If you discover that you are pregnant and you do not want to be, you should discuss this with your physician immediately. Planned Parenthood or a local family planning clinic may be able to offer advice also.

**Methods of elective abortion**
Elective abortion is best carried out before the 14th week of pregnancy when the usual procedure is similar to a *D and C* (p.118). After 14 weeks you may undergo a similar procedure or be given prostaglandin by vaginal suppository, which stimulates the uterus to contract (as if in labor) and expel the fetus. Other riskier methods exist for more advanced pregnancies.

## CHOOSING A CONTRACEPTIVE METHOD

### Combined estrogen-progesterone pills

**How do they act?**
There are many different types of combined pills containing various dosages of estrogen and progesterone. They all act primarily by increasing the level of estrogen and progesterone in the body, which prevents the release of an egg (ovulation).

**For whom are they recommended?**
The combined pills are usually recommended for young women. They are particularly useful for those who suffer from painful or heavy periods. They are not usually advised for women over 35, who smoke, are overweight, who suffer from migraines, or who have a history of circulatory disorders (e.g., phlebitis), high blood pressure, or heart or liver disease.

**Medical supervision**
The combined pills are available only on prescription from your physician or family planning clinic. You will need to have regular medical checkups (usually every 6 months).

**Possible side effects and risks**
Possible side effects include headaches, an increase in blood pressure, depression, loss of sex drive, weight gain, breast fullness, stroke, gallstones and benign liver tumors. The combined pills may cause "spotting" between periods (breakthrough bleeding). If this is a nuisance, you may need to change your prescription. Occasionally it may take several months for ovulation to restart after stopping these pills. The main medical risk associated with prolonged use of these pills is that of circulatory problems. In particular, there seems to be an increase in the frequency of blood clots (thromboembolisms) in regular pill-takers.

### Progesterone-only pill

**How does it act?**
The progesterone-only pill is used infrequently. It increases the level of progesterone in the body, and this may prevent eggs from ripening and being released. Its important contraceptive effect is that it causes thickening of the mucus at the entrance to the cervix, thus preventing penetration by sperm.

**For whom is it recommended?**
The progesterone-only pill is usually recommended for women who want to use an oral contraceptive but for whom an estrogen-containing pill is unsuitable for any reason. In particular, it is useful for breast-feeding mothers because it does not reduce milk production. Because this type of pill needs to be taken at precisely the same time each day to be effective, it may not be suitable for those who have an irregular life-style or who tend to be forgetful.

**Medical supervision**
Same as for the combined estrogen-progesterone birth-control pills.

**Possible side effects and risks**
There is a likelihood of irregular periods and "spotting" between periods (breakthrough bleeding).

### Postcoital ("morning-after") pill

**How does it act?**
The postcoital pill contains estrogen or combined estrogen-progestin which, taken (usually in 2 separate doses) following intercourse without contraception, provokes a shedding of the uterine lining. This expels the egg and so prevents a pregnancy from developing. This should not be used as a major form of contraception.

**For whom is it recommended?**
The postcoital pill is usually used only in unusual circumstances (for rape victims or when couples have a single, unprotected episode, e.g., a damaged condom). Since the hormones are potentially hazardous and will fail to interrupt a preexisting pregnancy, "morning-after" contraception is an emergency measure and should not be used as your regular method of contraception.

**Medical supervision**
The postcoital pill needs to be prescribed by a physician.

**Possible side effects and risks**
Some women experience nausea for a day or so after taking this type of pill.

### Intrauterine contraceptive device (IUD)

**How does it act?**
The IUD (usually made of plastic and sometimes covered with copper wire) is inserted in the uterus. It prevents a fertilized egg from becoming implanted in the uterus.

**For whom is it recommended?**
The IUD is usually recommended for women in stable relationships who need effective and convenient contraception, but cannot or do not wish to use the combined pill or a barrier device. It may not be suitable for the very young, those who have had an ectopic pregnancy or those who have had pelvic infections. Many physicians feel that women who have never had children should not use the IUD.

**Medical supervision**
An IUD is prescribed and fitted by a physician. It can be inserted during a normal visit. You will be taught to see that it remains in position and will need to have yearly checkups. Depending on type, an IUD needs to be replaced every 2 to 10 years. The new copper IUDs should be replaced every 3 years.

**Possible side effects and risks**
Many women notice a slight increase in bleeding and sometimes pain during periods. There is also a slightly increased risk of pelvic infections and of ectopic pregnancy. Occasionally, an IUD may be displaced or expelled from the uterus.

### Barrier methods

A barrier method is any device that prevents sperm from entering the uterus and so fertilizing an egg. Barrier methods used by women include the sponge, diaphragm and cervical cap. Both these devices are placed over the entrance to the cervix. Used with spermicidal foam, cream or jelly, they provide an effective barrier to sperm. The condom used by men is also a barrier method. The sponge is a disc-shaped disposable, spermicide-containing barrier that a women places in her vagina. Foam and contraceptive suppositories used alone offer some protection against pregnancy, but are less effective than the diaphragm, sponge or condom.

**For whom are they recommended?**
Barrier methods are suitable for almost all women, and may be the best methods for women who cannot or do not want to use the pill or IUD. Because a diaphragm, sponge or cap needs to be inserted each time you have intercourse, such methods may not be the best for the very young or those for whom sex is usually unplanned.

**Medical supervision**
A diaphragm or cap needs to be fitted by a physician or nurse, who will also teach you how to use it properly with spermicides. Yearly checkups are needed. You will also need to have your size checked again if you gain or lose a significant amount of weight or if you have a baby. Condoms, sponges, contraceptive foam and suppositories can be bought over-the-counter.

**Possible side effects**
There are few adverse side effects, although some women find them inconvenient. A few women are allergic to rubber or to chemicals in spermicides and may need to switch brands. Beneficial side effects of using a barrier method include the possible protection they may provide to the cervix. Barriers, particularly condoms, may offer some protection against sexually transmitted diseases.

### Ovulation (rhythm) methods

**How do they work?**
There are various ovulation methods of birth control, all of which are based on the principle of a woman predicting when ovulation (release of an egg) will occur, allowing her to abstain from sex on fertile days. Ovulation can be predicted by monitoring changes in body temperature and observation of the appearance and consistency of the mucus produced by the cervix (see *The Menstrual cycle,* p.117).

**For whom are they recommended?**
Women who are reluctant to use internal or barrier methods for personal or religious reasons may find these methods attractive. However, ovulation methods may be unreliable for women whose periods are irregular, and they may be unacceptable to couples who do not wish to abstain from sex for at least 7 days each month.

**Medical supervision**
Women using ovulation methods of birth control need to be carefully taught (by a physician or other specialist trained in these methods) how to monitor and record the changes that indicate ovulation.

**Possible side effects and risks**
There are no physical side effects, but ovulation methods can lead to frustration for both partners during the fertile period.

# 73 Failure to conceive

Consult this chart if you and your partner have been having regular sexual intercourse for more than 12 months without contraception and without your having become pregnant. Failure to conceive may be the result of a problem affecting the woman or man (or both); this chart deals only with possible problems affecting the woman. Female infertility is usually the result of a failure to produce eggs, or of a blockage in the fallopian tubes. More rarely, an allergy to your partner's semen may be a factor. Failure to conceive usually requires extensive tests on both partners, usually by a specialist, to find the underlying reason for the problem.

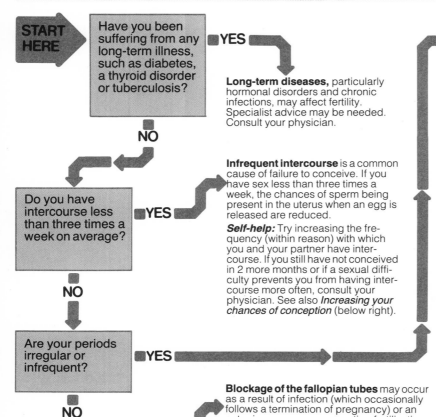

**START HERE**

**Have you been suffering from any long-term illness, such as diabetes, a thyroid disorder or tuberculosis?** → **YES**

**Long-term diseases,** particularly hormonal disorders and chronic infections, may affect fertility. Specialist advice may be needed. Consult your physician.

**NO**

**Do you have intercourse less than three times a week on average?** → **YES**

**Infrequent intercourse** is a common cause of failure to conceive. If you have sex less than three times a week, the chances of sperm being present in the uterus when an egg is released are reduced.

**Self-help:** Try increasing the frequency (within reason) with which you and your partner have intercourse. If you still have not conceived in 2 more months or if a sexual difficulty prevents you from having intercourse more often, consult your physician. See also *Increasing your chances of conception* (below right).

**NO**

**Are your periods irregular or infrequent?** → **YES**

**NO**

**Have you ever had a pelvic infection (salpingitis) or used an IUD?** → **YES**

**Blockage of the fallopian tubes** may occur as a result of infection (which occasionally follows a termination of pregnancy) or an ectopic pregnancy, preventing fertilization of the egg. Consult your physician.

**Treatment:** If your physician suspects that this may be the cause of your difficulty conceiving, he or she will probably arrange for you to see a specialist, who may arrange for you to have tests such as a *laparoscopy* (above right) or a *hysterosalpingogram* (X ray of the tubes), during which carbon dioxide may be passed up the tubes to check for blockages – a procedure known as insufflation. Sometimes this also clears minor obstructions. Otherwise surgery may be attempted to clear the tubes. If these treatments are unsuccessful, you may be offered in vitro (test tube) fertilization. This technique, which is not yet widely practiced, involves the removal from the ovaries of one or more eggs, which are then fertilized by your partner's sperm in a test tube. The developing embryo is then replaced in your uterus, where the pregnancy continues as normal. Repeated embryo implantations may be required.

**NO**

**Have you ever had a pregnancy terminated (an abortion) and/or an ectopic pregnancy (pregnancy outside the uterus)?** → **YES**

**NO**

**Consult your physician** if you are unable to make a diagnosis from this chart. The problem may be that you are not ovulating, even though your periods seem normal, or that your vaginal secretions are not compatible with your partner's sperm. Alternatively, the cause of the problem may lie with your partner. In all cases, further tests are needed.

**A hormone imbalance** that either prevents ovulation (release of an egg) or reduces the frequency with which you ovulate may explain your failure to conceive. Consult your physician.

**Treatment:** Your physician may refer you to a specialist for tests and treatment. If the tests, which may include *blood analysis* (p.22), urine analysis, a *D and C* (p.118) and *laparoscopy* (below), show a hormone imbalance, you may be prescribed hormone supplements (fertility drugs).

## LAPAROSCOPY

Laparoscopy is an endoscopic technique (see *Endoscopy,* p.77) for investigating abdominal disorders. In women it is commonly used to discover the cause of gynecological problems such as infertility or to assist in surgical procedures such as *sterilization* (p.130). Laparoscopy may also be used when other tests such as *barium X rays* (p.83) and *ultrasound scan* (p.136) fail to show the cause of symptoms such as recurrent abdominal pain.

The procedure is usually carried out under general anesthetic. Two small slits are made in the abdomen, and carbon dioxide is passed through a hollow needle inserted into one slit to distend the abdomen. An endoscope is inserted into the second slit, enabling the surgeon to see inside and find the cause of the trouble.

## PREVIOUS PREGNANCY

If you have been pregnant before by the same or by a different partner, the chances of your present failure to conceive being a result of a problem affecting you are reduced. It is nevertheless possible for any one of the disorders discussed in this chart to develop after a previous pregnancy and therefore complete testing of both partners is still required.

## INCREASING YOUR CHANCES OF CONCEPTION

Although prolonged delay in achieving conception requires professional tests and treatment, you may be able to increase your chances of becoming pregnant by following the self-help advice given below:

- Have intercourse about 3 times a week; less frequent intercourse may mean that you miss your fertile days, more frequent intercourse may reduce your partner's sperm count.
- Time intercourse to coincide with your most fertile days (see *The Menstrual cycle,* p.117).
- Following intercourse, remain lying down for 10 to 15 minutes to allow the maximum number of sperm to enter your uterus.
- Discourage your partner from wearing tight-fitting or nylon briefs or undershorts, which may in some cases damage the sperm by increasing the temperature within the scrotum.

# 3 Pregnancy and childbirth symptoms

# 74 Nausea and vomiting in pregnancy

Most women experience some nausea during the first three months of pregnancy and may actually vomit. Usually these symptoms fade after the 12th week, but they may persist. "Morning sickness" is probably the result of the dramatic increase in hormones (estrogen, progesterone and human chorionic gonadotropin [HCG]) during the early part of pregnancy. Although it commonly occurs in the morning, sickness can come at any time of day, especially when you are tired or hungry. Most women learn to control their nausea, but a few need medical treatment.

**Consult this diagnostic chart only after reading chart 41, Vomiting.**

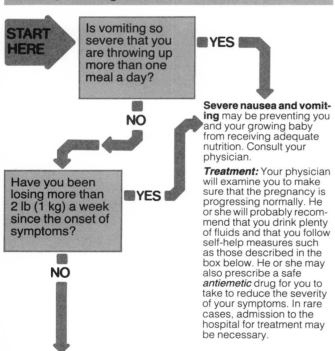

**START HERE** → Is vomiting so severe that you are throwing up more than one meal a day? → **YES**

NO

Have you been losing more than 2 lb (1 kg) a week since the onset of symptoms? → **YES**

NO

**Severe nausea and vomiting** may be preventing you and your growing baby from receiving adequate nutrition. Consult your physician.

*Treatment:* Your physician will examine you to make sure that the pregnancy is progressing normally. He or she will probably recommend that you drink plenty of fluids and that you follow self-help measures such as those described in the box below. He or she may also prescribe a safe *antiemetic* drug for you to take to reduce the severity of your symptoms. In rare cases, admission to the hospital for treatment may be necessary.

**Mild to moderate nausea,** although distressing while it lasts, is unlikely to present a risk to your general health or to that of your baby.

**Self-help:** Try the self-help measures suggested in the box below. If these do not help, and especially if you find that nausea is preventing you from eating so that you are losing weight, consult your physician.

---

### COPING WITH NAUSEA AND VOMITING

The following self-help suggestions may help to reduce the severity of nausea and vomiting during pregnancy:

- Have a light snack—for example, crackers or toast—before you get out of bed in the morning.
- Eat small, frequent meals of foods that seem to agree with you.
- Try to avoid sweet or fatty foods.
- Give up smoking and drinking alcohol.
- Get as much rest as possible.
- Take regular, light exercise in the fresh air.
- Do not take any drugs or over-the-counter medicines without first consulting your physician.

Consult your physician if nausea and vomiting are so severe that you are unable to eat a proper diet or if you are losing weight.

---

# 75 Skin changes in pregnancy

The hormonal changes of pregnancy may have a variety of effects on your skin, including changes in color. Some women find that their skin becomes more oily, others find that it becomes drier. Skin conditions (such as eczema) you have suffered from before pregnancy may either improve or get worse. The way in which your skin is affected depends on the balance of hormones and on your basic skin type.

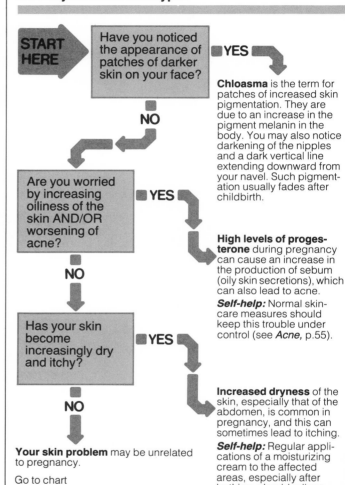

**START HERE** → Have you noticed the appearance of patches of darker skin on your face? → **YES**

NO

Are you worried by increasing oiliness of the skin AND/OR worsening of acne? → **YES**

NO

Has your skin become increasingly dry and itchy? → **YES**

NO

**Your skin problem** may be unrelated to pregnancy.

Go to chart

## 23 General skin problems

**Chloasma** is the term for patches of increased skin pigmentation. They are due to an increase in the pigment melanin in the body. You may also notice darkening of the nipples and a dark vertical line extending downward from your navel. Such pigmentation usually fades after childbirth.

**High levels of progesterone** during pregnancy can cause an increase in the production of sebum (oily skin secretions), which can also lead to acne.
*Self-help:* Normal skin-care measures should keep this trouble under control (see *Acne,* p.55).

**Increased dryness** of the skin, especially that of the abdomen, is common in pregnancy, and this can sometimes lead to itching.
*Self-help:* Regular applications of a moisturizing cream to the affected areas, especially after bathing, should relieve dryness. Alternatively, you can add some baby oil to your bath water.

---

### STRETCH MARKS

Stretch marks are red marks on the skin that later fade, leaving silvery, scarlike lines. They occur when the skin is stretched beyond its normal range of elasticity when weight is gained rapidly. In pregnancy, stretch marks commonly occur on the breasts and on the abdomen. If too much weight is gained, they may also appear on the thighs, buttocks and upper arms.

#### Avoiding stretch marks
The best way to reduce your chances of developing stretch marks is to avoid putting on too much weight. However, even those who manage to limit their weight gain to a healthy 20 to 28 lb (9 to 13 kg) may develop some marks. The regular application of any type of cream or oil does not prevent or heal stretch marks, although it may alleviate dryness of the skin.

# 76 Back pain in pregnancy

Backache is one of the most common symptoms of pregnancy. It usually occurs as a dull pain and stiffness in the middle and lower back and may make it difficult to get up from a sitting or lying position. It is likely to become more troublesome as pregnancy progresses. Most such backaches do not signify any troublesome condition. Occasionally, however, the sudden onset of pain in the back, especially if accompanied by additional symptoms such as vaginal bleeding, may be a sign of an impending miscarriage. Toward the end of a pregnancy, back pain may herald the onset of labor. If you are concerned about a backache, consult your physician.

**Consult this diagnostic chart only after reading chart 56, Back pain.**

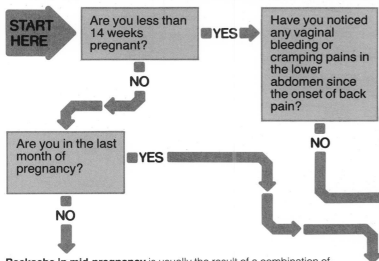

**START HERE**

Are you less than 14 weeks pregnant?

→ **YES** → Have you noticed any vaginal bleeding or cramping pains in the lower abdomen since the onset of back pain?

→ **YES** →

**NO** ↓

Are you in the last month of pregnancy? → **YES**

**NO** ↓

**CALL YOUR PHYSICIAN NOW!**
**A serious complication,** such as an impending miscarriage or ectopic pregnancy (pregnancy outside the uterus), is a possibility.
***Treatment:*** If your physician suspects either of these possibilities, you will probably be admitted to the hospital for rest and tests. If you have an ectopic pregnancy, an operation to end the pregnancy will be carried out. See also *Miscarriage,* p.136.

**NO** ↓

**Relaxation of the ligaments** supporting the spine, as a result of hormonal changes, can lead to backache even in early pregnancy. Pressure on the back from the enlarging uterus can also cause pain.
***Self-help:*** Pay attention to the advice given under *Preventing backache* (p.103). You may also find it helpful to try some gentle yoga-style exercises. Consult your physician if pain becomes severe enough to restrict your day-to-day activities.

**Backache in mid-pregnancy** is usually the result of a combination of relaxation of ligaments supporting the spine (see above right) and changes in posture to accommodate the increasing weight of the baby. Sometimes the enlarging uterus puts pressure on a nerve and you may experience a pain that shoots down the back of a leg (sciatica).
***Self-help:*** Read the suggestions for preventing backache on p.103. Be careful how you lift heavy objects, such as young children. At this stage in your pregnancy, good posture is especially important. You may find prenatal and gentle yoga-style exercises helpful. Consult your physician if pain becomes severe enough to restrict your day-to-day activities.

**The start of labor** is sometimes marked by the onset of persistent back pain, especially if the pain is different from any backache you have experienced before.

Go to chart

**81** Am I in labor?

---

# 77 Heartburn in pregnancy

Heartburn, a burning pain in the center of the chest or upper abdomen, is usually caused by the slight back-flow of acid juices from the stomach into the esophagus. It is common throughout pregnancy, but may be more severe in the later months when the growing baby and expanding uterus take up more space. Although heartburn may be uncomfortable, it is not a danger to the general health of you or your baby.

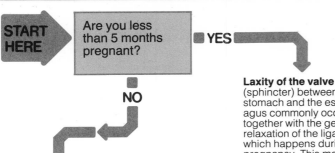

**START HERE**

Are you less than 5 months pregnant?

→ **YES** →

**NO** ↓

**Laxity of the valve** (sphincter) between the stomach and the esophagus commonly occurs together with the general relaxation of the ligaments, which happens during pregnancy. This means that the stomach contents can more easily flow back up into the esophagus, which becomes inflamed, leading to pain (heartburn).
***Self-help:*** See *Self-help for heartburn,* right.

**Pressure inside the abdomen** from the growing baby during the later stages of pregnancy can cause leakage of the stomach contents back into the esophagus. Laxity of the sphincter between the stomach and esophagus (right) also contributes to this problem, and there may be some degree of hiatal hernia (see p.89).
***Self-help:*** See *Self-help for heartburn,* right.

**SELF-HELP FOR HEARTBURN**

If you are suffering from heartburn, whatever the stage of your pregnancy, the following self-help measures should help to prevent and relieve the discomfort:

- Avoid eating large meals, especially of fried or highly spiced foods.
- Give up smoking and alcohol.
- Do not wear tight maternity girdles.
- If heartburn is troublesome at night, drink a glass of milk before going to bed and sleep propped up with pillows.
- Do not lie down after meals.

If such self-help measures do not help to alleviate the problem, consult your physician, who may prescribe a safe antacid medicine for you to take.

# 78 Vaginal bleeding in pregnancy

Consult this chart if you notice any vaginal bleeding while you are pregnant, whether it consists of only slight spotting or more profuse blood loss. This is a serious symptom that should always be reported to your physician promptly, although in a large proportion of cases there is no danger to the pregnancy. If you notice vaginal bleeding, go to bed and rest until you have received medical attention.

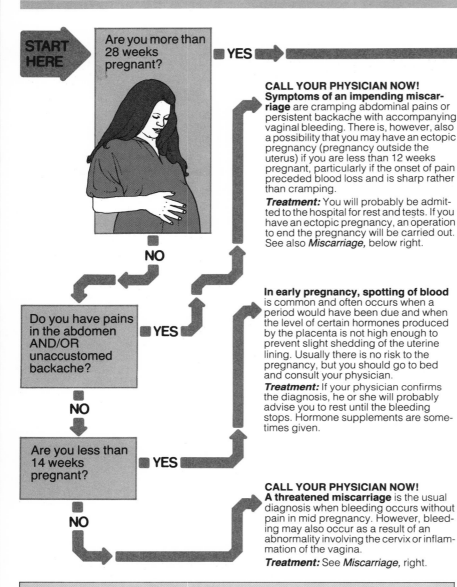

**START HERE**

**Are you more than 28 weeks pregnant?**

**YES** →

**Do you have pains in the abdomen AND/OR unaccustomed backache?**

**NO**

**YES**

**NO**

**Are you less than 14 weeks pregnant?**

**YES**

**NO**

**CALL YOUR PHYSICIAN NOW!**
**Symptoms of an impending miscarriage** are cramping abdominal pains or persistent backache with accompanying vaginal bleeding. There is, however, also a possibility that you may have an ectopic pregnancy (pregnancy outside the uterus) if you are less than 12 weeks pregnant, particularly if the onset of pain preceded blood loss and is sharp rather than cramping.
*Treatment:* You will probably be admitted to the hospital for rest and tests. If you have an ectopic pregnancy, an operation to end the pregnancy will be carried out. See also *Miscarriage,* below right.

**In early pregnancy, spotting of blood** is common and often occurs when a period would have been due and when the level of certain hormones produced by the placenta is not high enough to prevent slight shedding of the uterine lining. Usually there is no risk to the pregnancy, but you should go to bed and consult your physician.
*Treatment:* If your physician confirms the diagnosis, he or she will probably advise you to rest until the bleeding stops. Hormone supplements are sometimes given.

**CALL YOUR PHYSICIAN NOW!**
**A threatened miscarriage** is the usual diagnosis when bleeding occurs without pain in mid pregnancy. However, bleeding may also occur as a result of an abnormality involving the cervix or inflammation of the vagina.
*Treatment:* See *Miscarriage,* right.

**CALL YOUR PHYSICIAN NOW!**
**Antepartum hemorrhage** is the term used to describe any vaginal bleeding in the later stages of pregnancy. It may be due to partial separation of the placenta from the wall of the uterus, especially if the placenta is low-lying, to bleeding from a vein in the vagina or to abnormalities of the cervix. Sometimes the discharge of a blood-stained plug of mucus is the first sign of impending labor (see chart 81, *Am I in labor?*). Spotting in late pregnancy can be due to simple stretching of the cervix and may not be serious. However, your physician should be consulted.
*Treatment:* Your physician is likely to recommend a careful examination and tests, which may include an ultrasound scan (below left). Often no treatment other than bed rest is needed but, if bleeding is severe or continues, you may need to be delivered early by induction or cesarean section (see p.139).

## MISCARRIAGE

Miscarriage (spontaneous abortion) is the expulsion of the fetus from the uterus before the 28th week of pregnancy. It occurs in a high proportion of pregnancies, often before a woman knows that she is pregnant.

### Causes
The cause of a miscarriage is not always easy to discover. It may sometimes be due to an abnormality of the fetus, or to a hormonal imbalance. Occasionally, miscarriages in mid pregnancy are due to failure of the cervix to hold the fetus inside the uterus (incompetent cervix).

### Symptoms
The first sign of a threatened miscarriage is usually vaginal bleeding. Often this bleeding stops and the pregnancy continues as normal. However, bleeding may sometimes be followed by cramping pains in the abdomen or, in some cases, backache.

### Treatment
A threatened miscarriage is usually treated by complete bed rest. If there is reason to suspect a hormone deficiency, you may be given hormone supplements. Sometimes hospital admission is advised. If bleeding stops, you may need to have an ultrasound scan (left) to confirm that the pregnancy is continuing normally. If your physician thinks that a miscarriage is inevitable or if you have already lost the baby but some matter remains in the uterus, you will probably be admitted to the hospital, where the contents of the uterus may be removed (see also *D and C,* p.118). Most women who have had a miscarriage are able to conceive again without difficulty and subsequently go through a normal pregnancy.

## ULTRASOUND SCAN

Ultrasound provides a safe, painless way of examining internal organs and is often used during pregnancy to examine the uterus, placenta and fetus. The technique involves sending a beam of very high-pitched sound (ultrasound) through the tissues of the body. These sound waves are deflected off the internal organs and converted by computer into a picture that can be seen on a screen or printed on paper. Ultrasound may reveal cysts, tumors or other swellings, and in pregnancy helps to determine the position of the placenta, the size of the fetus and the stage of the pregnancy. Ultrasound scanning can reveal the presence of twins.

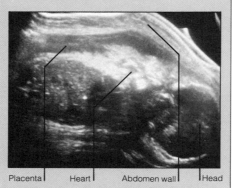

Placenta | Heart | Abdomen wall | Head

**Ultrasound picture of fetus at 35 weeks.**

# 79 Shortness of breath in pregnancy

Shortness of breath on exertion is noticed by many women after the 28th week of pregnancy. It is usually caused by restriction of the normal movement of the diaphragm and by restriction of the lungs as a result of the enlarged uterus pushing the abdominal organs up into the chest cavity. Breathlessness is often eased in the last month of pregnancy when the baby's head descends into the pelvis.

**Consult this diagnostic chart only after reading chart 37, Difficulty breathing.**

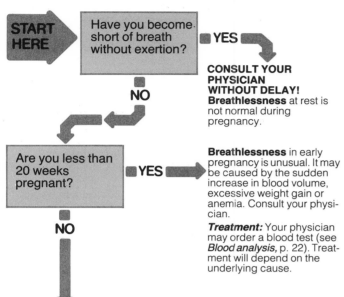

**START HERE**

**Have you become short of breath without exertion?** — **YES** →

**CONSULT YOUR PHYSICIAN WITHOUT DELAY!** Breathlessness at rest is not normal during pregnancy.

**NO**

**Are you less than 20 weeks pregnant?** — **YES** →

**Breathlessness** in early pregnancy is unusual. It may be caused by the sudden increase in blood volume, excessive weight gain or anemia. Consult your physician.

***Treatment:*** Your physician may order a blood test (see *Blood analysis,* p. 22). Treatment will depend on the underlying cause.

**NO**

**Shortness of breath** after only moderate exertion is normal after the 28th week of pregnancy, and may occasionally occur earlier, especially if you are physically unfit, if you have gained too much weight or if you smoke.

***Self-help:*** You can take steps to minimize breathlessness in late pregnancy. Try to control wieght gain, give up smoking and avoid tight clothes and girdles that constrict the abdomen. Consult your physician if breathlessness is severe enough to restrict your daily activities or if you are also feeling unusually tired or sick.

### PRENATAL CHECKUPS

If you are pregnant, go to your physician for regular checkups, where progress will be carefully monitored. In addition to a physical examination to assess the size of the uterus and the position of the baby, the following tests are carried out:

■ **Weight gain** Regular weighing enables you and your physician to ensure that you are putting on enough, but not too much, weight. Most women can expect to gain 20 to 28 lb (9 to 13 kg) during pregnancy. Usually, during the first weeks of pregnancy, little weight is gained and some may be lost (see *Weight loss in pregnancy,* p. 24). After the 12th week, weight is usually gained at the rate of about 1 lb (0.5 kg) a week.

■ **Urine** Urine is tested regularly for the presence of protein, which may be a sign of preeclampsia (below) and for the presence of sugar, which may indicate diabetes.

■ **Blood pressure** This is tested at every prenatal visit. A sudden rise may be a sign of preeclampsia.

■ **Blood tests** At the beginning of pregnancy your blood may be tested to determine whether you have syphilis, are diabetic or have had German measles and whether you may be susceptible to anemia. Black couples may be screened for sickle cell trait. Couples of Jewish extraction may be screened for Tay-Sachs disease. At 16 to 18 weeks, a blood test for malformation of the spinal column in the baby may also be carried out.

■ **Ultrasound** Many women will undergo ultrasound screening (see *Ultrasound scan,* opposite).

■ **Amniocentesis** In this test a sample of the amniotic fluid surrounding the baby is drawn off by syringe. Analysis of the fluid reveals if the baby is affected by certain abnormalities. This test is normally carried out only when there is a higher-than-average risk of disorders (e.g., if there is a family history of genetic disorder or if the mother is over 35 years old), because it may provoke a miscarriage.

# 80 Ankle-swelling in pregnancy

During pregnancy the body tends to retain more water than usual. Ankle-swelling is likely to become more marked toward the end of pregnancy. Slight ankle-swelling at the end of the day is usually no cause for concern, but it may occasionally be a sign of excessive fluid retention and high blood pressure.

**Consult this chart only after consulting chart 61, Painful or swollen joints.**

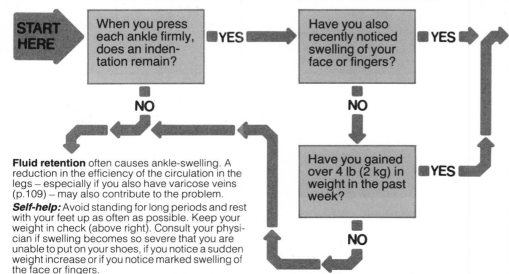

**START HERE**

**When you press each ankle firmly, does an indentation remain?** — **YES** → **Have you also recently noticed swelling of your face or fingers?** — **YES** →

**NO** ... **NO**

**Have you gained over 4 lb (2 kg) in weight in the past week?** — **YES** →

**NO**

**Fluid retention** often causes ankle-swelling. A reduction in the efficiency of the circulation in the legs — especially if you also have varicose veins (p.109) — may also contribute to the problem.

***Self-help:*** Avoid standing for long periods and rest with your feet up as often as possible. Keep your weight in check (above right). Consult your physician if swelling becomes so severe that you are unable to put on your shoes, if you notice a sudden weight increase or if you notice marked swelling of the face or fingers.

**CONSULT YOUR PHYSICIAN WITHOUT DELAY!**

**Preeclampsia** is a condition in which blood pressure rises, excessive fluid is retained and protein leaks into the urine. It may cause ankle-swelling, especially if accompanied by swelling elsewhere or sudden weight gain. Preeclampsia needs prompt treatment because it may develop into eclampsia (toxemia), in which blood pressure reaches such high levels that the health of mother and baby is threatened.

***Treatment:*** Your physician will take your blood pressure and also a urine sample. If your physician diagnoses preeclampsia, you may be advised to rest and may be given diuretics and/or medication to reduce blood pressure. You also may be advised to limit your salt intake. If your symptoms are severe, hospital admission may be necessary and your baby may need to be delivered early by *induction* (p.138) or *cesarean section* (p.139).

# 81 Am I in labor?

The average duration of pregnancy is 40 weeks, but it is quite normal for a baby to be born as early as 36 weeks or as late as 42 weeks. The onset of labor – the series of events leading to the expulsion of the baby from the uterus – is heralded by a number of different signs, including abdominal or back pains, rupture of the amniotic sac (the "bag of waters") and the passage of a plug of thick, perhaps blood-stained, mucus. The symptoms of labor experienced by each woman and the order in which they appear may vary. The diagnostic chart is designed to help you decide whether or not the symptoms you are experiencing indicate that labor has started and how urgently you should notify your physician or hospital.

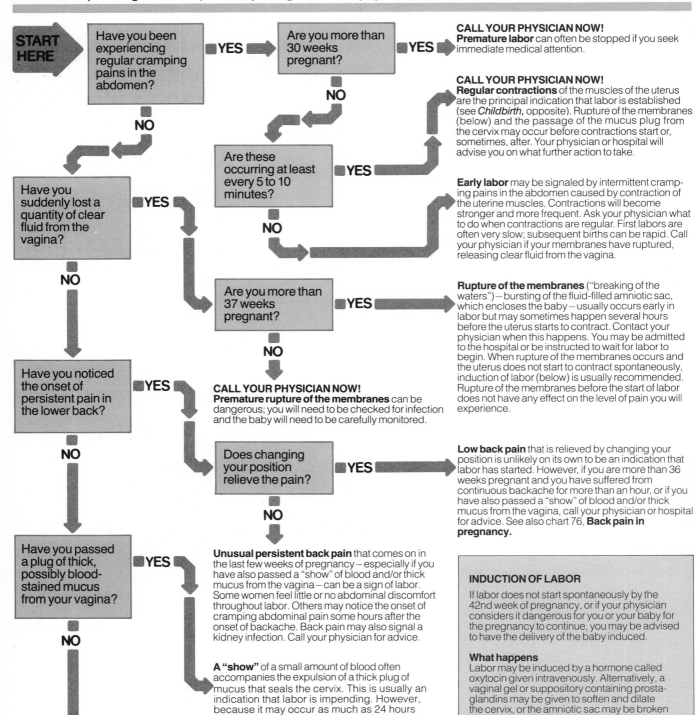

**START HERE**

**Have you been experiencing regular cramping pains in the abdomen?** — YES → **Are you more than 30 weeks pregnant?** — YES →

**CALL YOUR PHYSICIAN NOW!**
**Premature labor** can often be stopped if you seek immediate medical attention.

**Are you more than 30 weeks pregnant?** — NO →

**Are these occurring at least every 5 to 10 minutes?** — YES →

**CALL YOUR PHYSICIAN NOW!**
**Regular contractions** of the muscles of the uterus are the principal indication that labor is established (see *Childbirth*, opposite). Rupture of the membranes (below) and the passage of the mucus plug from the cervix may occur before contractions start or, sometimes, after. Your physician or hospital will advise you on what further action to take.

**Are these occurring at least every 5 to 10 minutes?** — NO →

**Early labor** may be signaled by intermittent cramping pains in the abdomen caused by contraction of the uterine muscles. Contractions will become stronger and more frequent. Ask your physician what to do when contractions are regular. First labors are often very slow; subsequent births can be rapid. Call your physician if your membranes have ruptured, releasing clear fluid from the vagina.

**Have you suddenly lost a quantity of clear fluid from the vagina?** — YES →

**Are you more than 37 weeks pregnant?** — YES →

**Rupture of the membranes** ("breaking of the waters") – bursting of the fluid-filled amniotic sac, which encloses the baby – usually occurs early in labor but may sometimes happen several hours before the uterus starts to contract. Contact your physician when this happens. You may be admitted to the hospital or be instructed to wait for labor to begin. When rupture of the membranes occurs and the uterus does not start to contract spontaneously, induction of labor (below) is usually recommended. Rupture of the membranes before the start of labor does not have any effect on the level of pain you will experience.

**Are you more than 37 weeks pregnant?** — NO →

**CALL YOUR PHYSICIAN NOW!**
**Premature rupture of the membranes** can be dangerous; you will need to be checked for infection and the baby will need to be carefully monitored.

**Have you noticed the onset of persistent pain in the lower back?** — YES →

**Does changing your position relieve the pain?** — YES →

**Low back pain** that is relieved by changing your position is unlikely on its own to be an indication that labor has started. However, if you are more than 36 weeks pregnant and you have suffered from continuous backache for more than an hour, or if you have also passed a "show" of blood and/or thick mucus from the vagina, call your physician or hospital for advice. See also chart 76, **Back pain in pregnancy.**

**Does changing your position relieve the pain?** — NO →

**Unusual persistent back pain** that comes on in the last few weeks of pregnancy – especially if you have also passed a "show" of blood and/or thick mucus from the vagina – can be a sign of labor. Some women feel little or no abdominal discomfort throughout labor. Others may notice the onset of cramping abdominal pain some hours after the onset of backache. Back pain may also signal a kidney infection. Call your physician for advice.

**Have you passed a plug of thick, possibly blood-stained mucus from your vagina?** — YES →

**A "show"** of a small amount of blood often accompanies the expulsion of a thick plug of mucus that seals the cervix. This is usually an indication that labor is impending. However, because it may occur as much as 24 hours before labor starts, it is not necessary to notify your physician immediately if you have no other symptoms. Seek medical advice as soon as you experience regular abdominal pains, persistent back pains or if your water breaks (see *Rupture of the membranes,* above right).

**None of the main indications of labor** are present in your case. Consult your physician if you have any symptom that worries you.

---

**INDUCTION OF LABOR**

If labor does not start spontaneously by the 42nd week of pregnancy, or if your physician considers it dangerous for you or your baby for the pregnancy to continue, you may be advised to have the delivery of the baby induced.

**What happens**
Labor may be induced by a hormone called oxytocin given intravenously. Alternatively, a vaginal gel or suppository containing prostaglandins may be given to soften and dilate the cervix, or the amniotic sac may be broken (artificial rupture of the membranes). Occasionally, if these procedures fail to bring about delivery or if your or the baby's medical condition requires very rapid delivery, a cesarean section will be performed.

## CHILDBIRTH

### What happens during labor
Labor is divided into three stages. In the first stage, the uterus contracts and the cervix (neck of the uterus) opens. In the second stage, the uterus continues to contract to push the baby out of the body through the vagina. In the third stage, the placenta (afterbirth) detaches itself from the wall of the uterus and is expelled from the body.

### First stage
The contractions of the uterus pull the cervix up around the baby's head until the opening is fully dilated – about 4 in. (10 cm) in diameter. This takes an average of 6 to 10 hours.

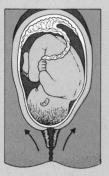
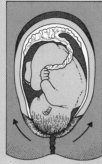

**Second stage**
When the cervix is fully dilated, further contractions of the uterus push the baby into the vagina and out of the body. This takes an average of 1 to 2 hours.

**Third stage**
After the baby has been born, contractions continue and the placenta separates from the wall of the uterus and is expelled. This takes an average of 10 to 15 minutes.

## EPISIOTOMY

During labor it is often thought advisable to make a cut to enlarge the vaginal opening, a procedure known as an episiotomy. This is commonly carried out for first babies and for forceps-assisted deliveries. The incision is normally made in the skin and muscle at the lower end of the vagina. An injection of a local anesthetic is usually given first. Following the birth, the cut is sewn up. You are likely to feel sore, especially when sitting down, for a few days following the birth, but the cut should be fully healed within 6 weeks.

**Episiotomy**
When the vagina needs to be widened, one of two types of incisions (right) is made. It is usually sewn up with catgut, which gradually dissolves away.

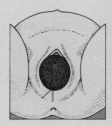

## PAIN RELIEF IN LABOR

Although a small proportion of women experience little discomfort during labor, most women can expect to suffer some pain during the first and second stages (see *Childbirth,* left). There are a variety of methods of controlling pain in labor, including self-help measures you can practice yourself and drugs or other measures administered by the physician.

### Position
Many women find that adopting a variety of upright positions during labor helps them to control the discomfort of contractions. Slowly walking up and down, perhaps supported by your partner or, for example, kneeling on all fours or squatting is often more comfortable than lying on your back. Experiment to find the positions that suit you best.

### Breathing
Most prenatal classes teach you how to breathe slowly and rhythmically to relieve discomfort and help you relax. In general, slow, deep breaths during which you concentrate on breathing out are most relaxing. Your prenatal teacher will give you detailed advice.

### Drugs
Narcotics are commonly used for the relief of pain during labor. They are administered by injection, usually in the upper thigh and/or through an intravenous line. Narcotics produce a relaxing effect, but may make you feel slightly drunk or nauseated. They are not normally given in the last part of labor, because they may make the baby sleepy and unable to breathe after delivery.

## CESAREAN SECTION

When it is not possible to deliver a baby through the vagina in the normal way, it is necessary to remove the baby from the uterus through the abdomen by an operation known as a cesarean section. A cesarean section may be carried out in any of the following circumstances:

- If the mother has an unusually small pelvic opening.
- If the baby is lying in an awkward position inside the uterus.
- If pregnancy or labor is so prolonged that mother's or baby's health is threatened.
- If induction of labor (opposite) has failed.
- If the mother has an infection such as herpes genitalis (see *Sexually transmitted diseases,* p. 123) that could be passed on to the baby.
- If the placenta is abnormally low in the uterus (placenta previa).

### What happens
A cesarean section may be performed under general, spinal or epidural anesthetic, depending on the medical situation and the mother's preference. The incision may be made horizontally or vertically in the lower abdomen. The operation takes about half an hour, and most hospitals will bring the baby to your partner while the surgeon completes the operation. Some hospitals allow the father of the baby to be in the room. Following a cesarean, you will need to stay in the hospital for a few days, but most women are well enough to be out of bed within 24 hours and are able to feed and care for their baby in almost the same way as mothers who have had a vaginal delivery. The baby is unaffected by the operation.

### General anesthesia
Occasionally, during a difficult birth – for example, when the baby is lying in an awkward position or when a painful forceps-assisted delivery is anticipated – a general anesthetic may be advised. Cesarean sections (below left) may be carried out under general anesthetic. A general anesthetic may also be needed if the placenta has to be removed by the physician.

### Local anesthesia
If you need to have a forceps-assisted delivery (below), an episiotomy (below left), or if you need stitches, a local anesthetic will be given to numb the vaginal area.

### Nitrous oxide and oxygen
Some hospitals will provide an apparatus through which you can breathe a mixture of nitrous oxide and oxygen at the start of particularly painful contractions.

### Epidural anesthesia
A hollow needle is inserted between the bones in the lower part of the spine and an anesthetic drug is fed through a fine tube into the fluid-filled space surrounding the spinal cord. This numbs from the waist down and in most cases provides total pain relief. Some hospitals will provide an epidural on request at the start of labor, or it can be given during labor when other pain-relieving measures are ineffective. The effect of the epidural is allowed to wear off during the second stage so that you can push your baby out more effectively. A forceps-assisted birth (below) may be necessary. In some hospitals, epidural anesthetics can be used for cesarean section.

## FORCEPS-ASSISTED DELIVERY

Obstetrical forceps, a pincer-like instrument with large flat blades, are sometimes used to assist delivery during the second stage of labor. The use of forceps may be necessary if the contractions of the uterus are not strong enough to push the baby out or if it is necessary to turn the baby into a more favorable position for delivery.

### What happens
For a forceps-assisted delivery you will probably need to have an episiotomy (left) to enlarge the vaginal opening. The physician carefully clasps the blades of the forceps on either side of the baby's head and, by exerting gentle pressure, helps the baby out of the vagina. Slight bruises or indentation on the baby's head left by the forceps disappear within a few days.

### Vacuum extractor
Occasionally, as an alternative to the use of forceps, a vacuum device is used to assist delivery. A suction cup is placed over the baby's head and this grips the head as it is gently pulled out of the vagina.

**Forceps**

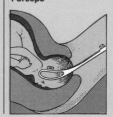

**Vacuum Extraction**

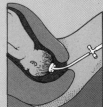

# 82 Breast-feeding problems

Medical authorities agree that breast milk is the best form of nutrition for newborn babies. It contains all the essential nutrients in their ideal proportions and in the most easily assimilated form for your baby. Breast-fed babies develop fewer allergies than babies fed on formula and are less subject to gastroenteritis. Antibodies (substances that fight infection) are present in breast milk and provide some natural protection for your baby against germs in the newborn period. It is rare for a mother to be medically unable to breast-feed, and any problems can be overcome with perseverance on your part and support and encouragement from your physician and family. Consult this chart if you have had a baby in the past few months and have any problems related to breast-feeding, including pain in the breasts or nipples, engorged breasts or inadequate milk supply.

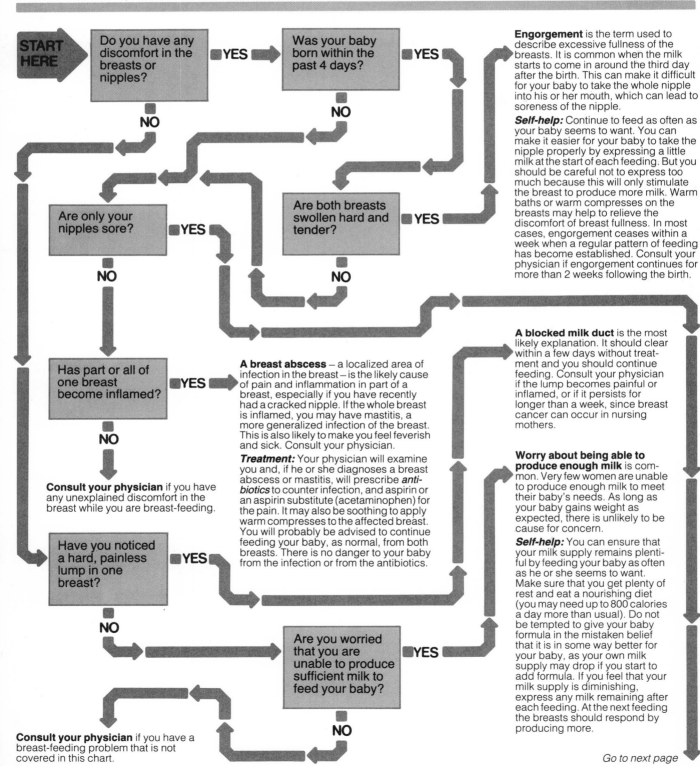

START HERE

**Do you have any discomfort in the breasts or nipples?**  → YES →  **Was your baby born within the past 4 days?**  → YES →

NO ↓   NO

**Are only your nipples sore?**  → YES →  **Are both breasts swollen hard and tender?**  → YES →

NO ↓   NO

**Has part or all of one breast become inflamed?**  → YES →

NO ↓

**Consult your physician** if you have any unexplained discomfort in the breast while you are breast-feeding.

**Have you noticed a hard, painless lump in one breast?**  → YES →

NO ↓

**Consult your physician** if you have a breast-feeding problem that is not covered in this chart.

**Are you worried that you are unable to produce sufficient milk to feed your baby?**  → YES →

NO

**Engorgement** is the term used to describe excessive fullness of the breasts. It is common when the milk starts to come in around the third day after the birth. This can make it difficult for your baby to take the whole nipple into his or her mouth, which can lead to soreness of the nipple.

*Self-help:* Continue to feed as often as your baby seems to want. You can make it easier for your baby to take the nipple properly by expressing a little milk at the start of each feeding. But you should be careful not to express too much because this will only stimulate the breast to produce more milk. Warm baths or warm compresses on the breasts may help to relieve the discomfort of breast fullness. In most cases, engorgement ceases within a week when a regular pattern of feeding has become established. Consult your physician if engorgement continues for more than 2 weeks following the birth.

**A breast abscess** – a localized area of infection in the breast – is the likely cause of pain and inflammation in part of a breast, especially if you have recently had a cracked nipple. If the whole breast is inflamed, you may have mastitis, a more generalized infection of the breast. This is also likely to make you feel feverish and sick. Consult your physician.

*Treatment:* Your physician will examine you and, if he or she diagnoses a breast abscess or mastitis, will prescribe *antibiotics* to counter infection, and aspirin or an aspirin substitute (acetaminophen) for the pain. It may also be soothing to apply warm compresses to the affected breast. You will probably be advised to continue feeding your baby, as normal, from both breasts. There is no danger to your baby from the infection or from the antibiotics.

**A blocked milk duct** is the most likely explanation. It should clear within a few days without treatment and you should continue feeding. Consult your physician if the lump becomes painful or inflamed, or if it persists for longer than a week, since breast cancer can occur in nursing mothers.

**Worry about being able to produce enough milk** is common. Very few women are unable to produce enough milk to meet their baby's needs. As long as your baby gains weight as expected, there is unlikely to be cause for concern.

*Self-help:* You can ensure that your milk supply remains plentiful by feeding your baby as often as he or she seems to want. Make sure that you get plenty of rest and eat a nourishing diet (you may need up to 800 calories a day more than usual). Do not be tempted to give your baby formula in the mistaken belief that it is in some way better for your baby, as your own milk supply may drop if you start to add formula. If you feel that your milk supply is diminishing, express any milk remaining after each feeding. At the next feeding the breasts should respond by producing more.

*Go to next page*

*Continued from previous page*

**Do you have a sharp pain at the beginning of a feeding, and does pain continue throughout the feeding?**

**YES** →

**NO**

**Soreness of the nipples** is common, especially in the first 2 weeks following the birth. Discomfort is normally felt at the start of a feeding as the baby latches on, and it wears off as the feeding continues.

*Self-help:* At first do not allow your baby to feed for more than 10 minutes on each breast at each feeding. Try to keep your breasts as dry as possible between feedings by using breast pads inside your bra and changing them frequently. Expose your breasts to the air as often as possible. Regular applications of lanolin ointment may be helpful. Consult your physician if soreness persists.

**A crack** around the base of the nipple is possible. This is usually caused by the baby failing to take the whole of the colored area of the nipple into the mouth when he or she is feeding. This may also cause bleeding.

*Self-help:* Do not allow the baby to feed from the affected breast for at least 24 hours because of the danger of infection entering the breast through the crack. Instead, express milk from the affected breast and feed it to your baby by bottle. It may help if you apply a lanolin ointment to the nipple. Once the crack has healed you can return to normal feeding, but try to prevent the problem from recurring by ensuring that your baby is latching on to the whole nipple when he or she sucks. Consult your physician if you notice pain or redness in the breast itself, or if the crack has not healed within 3 days.

# 83 Depression after childbirth

Childbirth is a traumatic event for a woman, both physically and emotionally. Not only is labor an exhausting physical experience, but it initiates a dramatic alteration in the body's hormone balance as you begin to readjust to no longer being pregnant. Your emotions are also likely to be in turmoil following this event as you start to come to terms with the reality of motherhood and the demands that a new baby will make on you and your family. It is therefore natural that childbirth should be followed by a period of emotional instability. In the first day or so following the birth, the most common feeling is that of elation, but, in the subsequent days and sometimes weeks, many women become sad, withdrawn and apathetic. They may also suffer from guilt for not responding with more enthusiasm to the arrival of the baby. Consult this chart if you suffer from such feelings of depression in the 6 months following the birth of your baby.

**START HERE** →

**Is it less than a week since your baby was born?**

**YES** →

**NO**

**Do you feel fine most of the time, but occasionally have days when you feel depressed and irritable?**

**YES** →

**NO**

**The "third-day blues"** is the common name for the feeling of tearfulness and depression that affects many women in the 7 days following the birth. It often coincides with the time when your milk comes in and when you may be suffering from engorgement and other breast-feeding problems (see opposite). The cause of such feelings is probably mainly hormonal and most women feel much better within a day or so.

*Self-help:* Try to keep the week following the birth as quiet as possible – especially around the third and fourth days. If you are in the hospital, it helps to restrict the number of visitors you have on those days. If you are at home, try to ensure you have a friend or relative to help you in the house during this first week with your baby. Discuss with your physician any feeding difficulties or other problems related to your baby's progress. Consult your physician if your depression lasts longer than 3 days.

**Periods of depression and irritability** are common in the months following childbirth, just as after any traumatic event. As well as being affected by hormonal changes and possible feelings of anticlimax, you may also be overtired as a result of frequent night feedings and may be worried about your competence as a mother or about your baby's general development. In addition, if you are used to working outside the home, it may be difficult for you to adjust to being at home all day with your baby. Consult your physician.

*Treatment:* Your physician will discuss your feelings with you and may carry out a physical examination to rule out any underlying disorder. In some cases, no medical treatment is necessary and you may simply be advised to take care not to become overtired – for example, you could have your partner get up at night to feed the baby – and to make sure that you go out on your own regularly. In other cases, *antidepressants* may be prescribed. You may also find it reassuring to join a local self-help support group for new mothers.

**Postnatal depression** is a condition that often affects new mothers in the 6 months following childbirth. You may find it difficult to respond lovingly to your baby and to cope with day-to-day chores. You may also experience problems in your relationship with your partner. Consult your physician.

*Treatment:* Your physician will examine you to assess your general health and will talk to you about your feelings. Depending on the severity of your depression, *antidepressant* drugs and/or hormones may be prescribed. You may be referred to a specialist for treatment (see also *Psychotherapy,* p.49). If you are found to be severely depressed you may be admitted to the hospital, where drug treatment and other forms of therapy can be carefully monitored. When you are over the worst of your depression, you may find it helpful to join a self-help support group for women who have suffered from postnatal depression. Postnatal depression will not necessarily recur following a future pregnancy.

# Index

Each of the symptom charts in this book is designed to help you discover the possible reason for your complaint. The book contains thousands of physiological references, and this index must of necessity be selective. For a full guide to the basic symptoms analyzed in the 83 charts and how to find the chart you need, see pp. 16-20. References within the following index are to page numbers of topics from the entire book, not just from the charts. Titles of information boxes within the charts and significant subtopics discussed in these boxes are italicized to emphasize their importance. Titles of the charts themselves and information contained within the introductory section preceding the charts are in **bold** typeface.

# INDEX